AUBURN
ENTERTAINS

Compiled by

Helen Baggett   Jeanne Blackwell
Lucy Littleton

Rutledge Hill Press
Nashville, Tennessee

All recipes appearing within have been generously contributed by members of
the Auburn community and by friends of Auburn University.

The original artwork in this edition is by William Baggett (the watercolor view of
Samford Tower which appears on the cover) and by Ray Dugas (pen and ink
drawings, throughout, of familiar Auburn structures), both of whom are faculty in
the Department of Art, Auburn University.

All quotations are selections from the plays and poems of William Shakespeare.

Published in Nashville, Tennessee, by Rutledge Hill Press, Inc., P.O. Box 140483,
Nashville, Tennessee 37214.

First Rutledge Hill Press Printing, May 1986.
Second Rutledge Hill Press Printing, September 1991.

Library of Congress Cataloging-in-Publication Data

Auburn entertains.

   Includes index.
   1. Cookery.   I. Baggett, Helen, 1948–
II. Blackwell, Jeanne, 1942–   III. Littleton,
Lucy, 1930–
TX715.A917   1986   641′.5   86-6557
ISBN 0-934395-20-9

Printed in the United States of America.
2 3 4 5 6 7 8 9 10 — 92 91

ENTERTAINING IN AUBURN

Auburn is a place unlike most others. It is, for one thing, a setting now largely absent in the American landscape—since large public universities are now rarely contained entirely within a small town atmosphere. Eighteen thousand students and eight thousand of the rest of us: diversity and complexity in a long familiar place, where the movements of life are conditioned by the annual ebb and flow of the young.

Whatever the reasons may be, generations of students and alumni have developed a remarkable feeling of identity with Auburn. And for over 125 years the interwoven relationships between "the college" and the town have created an extraordinary sense of community.

The style and character of entertaining guests are in many ways fashioned by the pattern of the academic year. Here the renewal of life comes not in the spring but in the fall. For it is then that the students return, together with the faculty from their brief Indian-summer holiday. Socializing then quickly moves to an intensity unmatched during the rest of the year because whether one is a fan or not, the football season is irresistible. Home games bring alumni by the thousands and scores of pre-game brunches, luncheons and post-game parties proceed apace.

But the recipes in this book speak, in a sense, to other times as well: Christmas; garden-parties in the spring; those by the water at Lake Martin; or those informal faculty gatherings when the quarterly exams have been graded and put away, when the town suddenly is strangely empty of students, when the sounds of life are softer.

Any collection of instructions on how to prepare this or that dish, however, ultimately suggests the continuing reenactment of one of our oldest and most civilized of rituals—friends coming together to dine. The shared values and quietly understood things which deepen and sustain friendships find their most natural expression at such times. And thus, just as entertainment in Auburn is marked by the rhythms and conditions of life in a small university town, so it is characterized also in hundreds of homes each year by those less visible social occasions which, in their own mysterious way, help bind a community together.

Perhaps this book of recipes, enclosed by the familiar sights of the University, will add a touch of Auburn to your own festive times, saying as you hear the first faint sounds of cars stopping in the drive, of conversation on the walk:

See: your guests approach.
Address yourself to entertain them sprightly,
And let's be red with mirth.
The Winter's Tale (IV-iv-52/54)

T. L.
March, 1983

TABLE OF CONTENTS

BEVERAGES 1

HORS D'OEUVRES 11

SOUPS, SANDWICHES, AND SALADS 49

EGGS, CHEESE, GRITS, PASTA 95

BREADS 109

FRUITS, VEGETABLES, AND PICKLES . . . 129

ENTREES 163

DESSERTS 233

THE GATES

BEVERAGES

Ay . . . we did sleep day out of countenance, and
made the night light with drinking.
Antony and Cleopatra (II-ii-188)

THE GATES

Located across from Toomer's Corner, they frame the most familiar entrance to the Auburn campus. They were donated by the Class of 1917, with the stone eagles atop each column secured by devoted alumnus, W. C. (Red) Sugg ('31).

BEVERAGES

TOOMER'S CORNER LEMONADE

Make 1 gallon of simple syrup as follows:

Put 5 pounds sugar in a gallon jug and fill the jug with water. Stir or shake until sugar dissolves and solution is clear. (Hot water makes the sugar dissolve more quickly.)

To make one gallon of lemonade, pour 1 pint of lemon juice and 2 pints of simple syrup in a gallon container. Finish filling the container with water and ice. Stir.

To make one large lemonade (16 ounces), squeeze the juice of one lemon into a 16-ounce cup, add 4 ounces simple syrup and finish filling with water and ice. Stir.

Mac Lipscomb

This lemonade is an Auburn tradition, second only to the gatherings to celebrate Auburn's victories on Toomer's Corner.

LIPSCOMB'S DRUG STORE FRUIT PUNCH

Make 1 gallon of simple syrup as follows:

Put 5 pounds sugar in a gallon jug and fill the jug with water. Stir or shake until sugar dissolves and solution is clear. (Hot water makes the sugar dissolve more quickly.)

To make one gallon of punch put the following in a 1-gallon container:

1 ounce (2 tablespoons) citric acid	32 ounces simple syrup
Juice of 2 lemons	8 ounces orange juice (canned is fine)
4 ounces grapefruit juice	16 ounces pineapple juice

Finish filling the container with ginger ale (sugar-free is fine) or with water. Best served with crushed ice.

May add a few drops of green food coloring if desired.

Lan Lipscomb

FAUX WINE PUNCH

3 quarts apple juice	3 12-ounce cans frozen orange juice,
3 quarts gingerale	undiluted

Combine these ingredients over ice ring in a punch bowl. Makes 1½ gallons.

A delicious nonalcoholic beverage with an alcoholic taste.

GRAPE JUICE PUNCH

1 bottle Welch's White Grape Juice   1 bottle gingerale

Pour chilled juice and gingerale over ice ring.

Gaynelle Parks (Mrs. Paul)

(This is nice to serve at wedding brunches for those who don't want champagne.)

ORANGE JULIUS

1 6-ounce can frozen orange juice   ½ cup sugar
½ cup milk   1 teaspoon vanilla
½ cup water   About 6 ice cubes

Put in blender. Blend until icy, then serve.

Joanne Patton (Mrs. Ed)

TIGER TINGLE PUNCH

2 quarts cranberry juice   ½ cup maraschino cherry juice
1 can (6 ounces) frozen lemonade   6 bottles (10 ounces) Sprite, chilled
    concentrate, thawed

Combine all ingredients. Serve over ice. Garnish with lemon slices, orange slices and cherries. Makes 40 4-ounce servings.
    Great for birthday parties, Cub Scouts or Brownies.

SUNSHINE PUNCH
(it's not just for breakfast)

1 quart orange sherbet   6 bottles Sprite (10 ounces, well
2 quarts orange juice   chilled)
1 cup lime juice

Beat orange sherbet until creamy. Stir in remaining ingredients. Add Sprite just before serving. Serve over ice in punch bowl. Garnish with orange and lemon slices. Makes 50 4-ounce servings.

THE BELL RINGER PUNCH

2 cans (46 ounces each) unsweetened   2 cans (6 ounces each) frozen orange
    pineapple juice   juice concentrate, thawed
6 bottles Sprite, chilled (10 ounces each)

Combine all ingredients. Add Sprite just before serving. Serve over ice. Garnish with orange slices and cherries. For an alcoholic punch, add a bottle of Vodka. Makes 50 4-ounce servings.

PUNCH

4 parts cider
2 parts gingerale

1 part frozen orange juice

(For an alcoholic punch, add some bourbon whiskey and use soda water in place of gingerale.)

Marjorie Tyre Sykes (Mrs. Maltby)

This punch is used by the Auburn Music Club at receptions following the Young Musicians' Concerts.

MINT TEA

7 tea bags
12 sprigs mint
Rind of 3 lemons
Juice of 7 lemons

8 cups boiling water
2 cups sugar
8 cups cold water

Steep tea, mint, and lemon rind in boiling water for 12 minutes. Remove from water. Add juice and sugar, strain, and add water. Makes 1 gallon.

PARTY TEA

2 quarts boiling water
1 cup sugar
1 sprig mint

2 family size Lipton tea bags
Juice of 2 lemons

Pour boiling water over sugar in plastic pitcher and stir. Add mint and tea bags and remove after 10 minutes. When warm or cool, add lemon juice. Serve over ice and garnish with mint leaf. Serves 10-12.

Dell Chester (Mrs. Rollie)

SPARKLING ICED TEA

3 quarts tea (2 family size tea bags in 3
    quarts water)
½ cup sugar

1 12-ounce can frozen lemon or
    limeade concentrate
1 quart gingerale

Combine tea, sugar and frozen concentrate. Pour in gingerale just before serving. Serve in iced tea glasses over ice. Makes 10 servings.

This is great to make ahead (up to mixing gingerale) for buffet luncheons, since it saves passing lemon and sugar.

INSTANT SPICED TEA MIX

2 cups Tang
½ cup sugar
½ cup instant tea

1 teaspoon cinnamon
½ teaspoon powdered cloves
1 small package lemonade mix

Blend together and store in airtight jars. To serve—use 1½ to 2 teaspoons in cup and fill with boiling water.

The Ampersand Gift Shop likes to fix this in a percolator to serve customers on cold winter days.

HOT COCOA MIX

1 8-quart box Carnation Instant Non-fat
   Powdered Milk
1 1-pound box Nestles Quik

6 tablespoons cocoa
1 1-pound box powdered sugar

Mix well. Store in airtight tin. To make 1 cup, use ⅓ cup mix plus hot water.

Jackie Norman (Mrs. Dan)

HOT CIDER

1 quart apple cider
3 cinnamon sticks
4 tablespoons lemon juice

1 teaspoon nutmeg
1 teaspoon cloves

Simmer cider, cinnamon sticks and lemon juice for 15 minutes. Add nutmeg and cloves tied in cheesecloth bag and leave as long as desired to taste.

HOT BUTTERED RUM

Cream:
  1 lb. butter
  1 box dark brown sugar
  1 box powdered sugar

Add:
  1 quart vanilla ice cream
  1 teaspoon nutmeg
  2 teaspoons cinnamon

Place 2 tablespoons (or more) of mixture in a mug. Add boiling water and *then* 1 jigger (or more) of rum. (Can substitute brandy or bourbon for the rum.)

Terry Steckler (Mrs. Joseph)

HOT PERCOLATOR PUNCH

2 quarts unsweetened pineapple juice
2 quarts cranberry juice cocktail
1 quart cold water
⅔ cup firmly packed dark brown sugar
1 tablespoon whole allspice

1 tablespoon whole cloves
4 2-inch pieces stick cinnamon, broken
   in small pieces
2 large lemons, washed and sliced

Pour juices and water in bottom part of 30-cup percolator. Place sugar and spices and lemon in basket at top. Allow mixture to percolate for 30 minutes. Serve hot. Makes 30 punch-cup servings.

HOT SPICED PERCOLATOR PUNCH

3 cups pineapple juice
2 cups water
3 cups cranberry juice
1 tablespoon whole cloves

1 tablespoon whole allspice
4 sticks cinnamon (broken)
½ cup brown sugar

Pour liquids in the bottom part of an electric percolator. Place the rest of the ingredients in the basket and perk for at least 15 minutes. Serve hot. Makes 10-12 5-ounce servings.

(Especially nice for a morning coffee in the winter.)

Terry Steckler (Mrs. Joseph)

Terry has used this punch at gatherings of the military wives in Distaff Club.

WILLIAMSBURG WASSAIL

1 cup sugar
3 or 4 sticks of cinnamon
Lemon slices
2¼ cups pineapple juice

2 cups orange juice
6 cups claret
½ cup lemon juice
1¼ cups dry sherry

Boil sugar, cinnamon sticks, and 3 lemon slices in ½ cup water for five minutes and strain. Heat, but do not boil, the remaining ingredients. Combine with syrup, garnish with lemon slices, and serve hot. Serves 20.

Wassailing is an old English tradition. The Saxon phrase Wass hail, "be whole," or "be well" was repeated by the Master of the English household. The bowl was passed and each in turn repeated the phrase.

WASSAIL BOWL

4 cups apple cider
½ cup brown sugar, firmly packed
½ cup dark rum
½ teaspoon each cinnamon, ground cloves
⅛ teaspoon ground allspice

¼ cup brandy
1 tablespoon orange-flavored liqueur
½ orange, thinly sliced
Salt
½ lemon, thinly sliced

In a large saucepan, bring apple cider to a boil over moderate heat. Add brown sugar; cook the mixture, stirring until the sugar is dissolved. Remove the pan from heat and add dark rum, brandy, orange-flavored liqueur, cinnamon, cloves, allspice, salt to taste, lemon and orange. Heat the mixture over moderate heat, stirring for 2 minutes. Serve in sparkling crystal wine glasses with a dollop of whipped cream and a sprinkling of freshly grated nutmeg. Serves 6.

CHRISTMAS AROMA PUNCH

1 fresh ginger root split
3 pieces stick cinnamon
16 whole cloves

1 teaspoon ground allspice
1-2 teaspoons pickling spice

Add 1 quart water and simmer for a wonderful spicy odor. *Do not drink*—just smell!

WA-A-AR EAGLE!

3 bottles sauterne
1 bottle dry sherry
1 bottle brandy

⅓ bottle rum
3 bottles chilled sparkling water

The day before serving, combine first four ingredients. Chill. Add sparkling water just before serving after ice ring is in punch. Do not stir.

BRANDYWINE PUNCH

1 bottle sauterne, chilled
1 cup brandy

½ to 1 bottle sparkling water, chilled

Mix in punch bowl over ice ring.

WHISKEY SOUR PUNCH

2 6-ounce cans orange juice concentrate
2 6-ounce cans lemonade concentrate
2 tablespoons bitters
4 tablespoons sugar

2 large jars red cherries
3 bottles (12 ounces each) club soda
1 fifth bourbon
Lemons and oranges sliced

Mix ahead lemonade, orange juice, bitters, sugar and juice from cherries. Chill. Chill soda. Before serving, add a fifth of bourbon to the mix. Add cherries to the mix. Stir well. Add chilled soda. Put in large punch bowl. Freeze ice blocks ahead in large jello molds with sliced oranges and lemons in it for color, or slice them for floating in the punch. Makes 33 punch cups.

Gwen Ferris-Reid

WHISKEY PUNCH

Juice of 6 lemons (6 ounces)
Juice of 8 oranges (24 ounces)
1 small can of pineapple juice (18 ounces)

1½ fifths bourbon
2 bottles gingerale
Sugar to taste—but not really necessary

Pour over ice. Decorate with lemon and orange slices. Serves 20 people.

Marleah Hobbs (Mrs. Ed)

This is a punch served by the Hobbs down through the years. It is a fruity, full-bodied punch that is easier than having all the bar set-ups on hand—cheaper also.

STRAWBERRY DAIQUIRI

Place in blender and blend until smooth:
½ small can or 3 ounces frozen limeade
10 ounces frozen strawberries (in syrup)
 (sliced into 4 parts)

10 ounces light rum
Add cracked or crushed ice to fill line

Dell Chester (Mrs. Rollie)

DAIQUIRI SLUSH

3 6-ounce cans frozen lemonade
1 6-ounce can frozen limeade

8 cups water
1 fifth light rum or vodka

Mix ingredients. Pour into plastic containers and freeze. The alcohol makes it only partially freeze, so it is ready to serve.

DEEPFREEZE DAIQUIRI

2 6-ounce cans frozen lemonade
1 6-ounce can frozen limeade
1 fifth light rum

Juice of 2 lemons
6 lemonade cans of water

Mix all ingredients. Store in jug in freezer 8-12 hours before serving. Take container out of freezer about 30 minutes before serving. This never freezes solid and makes about 2 quarts.

MAY BOWLE

Sprinkle 2 cups sliced strawberries, fresh peaches or fresh pineapple with 2 tablespoons sugar. Add 2 quarts Taylor Sauterne or Rhine Wine and allow to steep overnight or at least four hours. Strain out fruit. At serving time, pour over ice ring in punch bowl and pour over 1 bottle chilled champagne. For stronger punch, add 1-2 cups brandy to wine mixture—before adding champagne. Serve in chilled wineglasses. Makes 15 4-ounce servings.

Serve from a punch bowl surrounded by spring flowers or strawberries and leaves on May day. This is nice at spring luncheons and cocktail parties.

CHAMPAGNE PUNCH

1 bottle dry champagne
1 bottle gingerale

1 bottle sauterne

Chill all ingredients and pour over an ice ring.

PINK CHAMPAGNE PUNCH

1 magnum pink champagne
1 fifth rosé wine

1 pint vodka
1 28-ounce bottle soda water

Make ice rings. Place in bottom of punch bowl. Pour chilled wines, vodka and soda over top.

This is a nice punch for New Year's Eve.

BLOND SANGRIA

1 fifth white wine
1 cup pineapple juice
⅓ cup orange juice
3 tablespoons lemon juice

1 tablespoon lime juice
¼ cup sugar
1 7-ounce bottle club soda

Combine first six ingredients and chill. Just before serving, add club soda and garnish with lemon, lime or orange slices and sprigs of fresh mint. Serves 8.

Jean Bullock (Mrs. Bill)

SHERRY PUNCH

2 fifths dry sherry, chilled
1 16-ounce bottle whiskey sour mix

Maraschino cherries
Mint sprigs

Combine sherry and whiskey sour mix in punch bowl over ice ring. Garnish with mint and cherries.

MAKE AHEAD BLOODY MARY

2 quarts tomato juice
20-24 ounces vodka
Juice of 6 lemons

1 tablespoon salt
½ tablespoon cracked pepper
2½ ounces Worcestershire

Combine all ingredients and let stand 12 hours. This will keep in refrigerator several weeks. Makes 14 drinks.

HOME-MADE ORANGE BRANDY

Skins of 2 medium oranges
2 sticks cinnamon
1 tablespoon whole cloves

a little nutmeg
1 pint brandy

Place orange skins and spices in a glass jar. Pour in the brandy. Close the jar tightly and keep in moderate temperature for about 15 days.

After 15 days, strain the brandy and add 1½ cups syrup.

Syrup
1¼ cups sugar

1 cup water

Bring sugar and water to a boil, cool, and add to brandy.

Terry Steckler (Mrs. Joseph)

HARGIS HALL

HORS D'OEUVRES

Like as to make our appetites more keen,
With eager compounds we our palate urge . . .
Sonnet 118

HARGIS HALL

With Langdon and Samford, Hargis constitutes the historic row of nineteenth century buildings on the front campus. Constructed in 1888 and used over the years for instruction in such diverse areas as chemistry, pharmacy, music, and art, the building was formally named in 1977 for Estes H. Hargis ('17), prominent Birmingham physician whose family contributed funds toward its restoration and renovation.

HORS D'OEUVRES
Also See Sandwiches

CAMEMBERT MELT

1 4½-ounce can camembert cheese
¼ cup chopped pecans

1 teaspoon butter

Slice top off cheese. Melt butter and toss pecans to coat, then spread on top of cheese. Bake at 375° about 7-8 minutes, or until cheese melts. Serve warm with crackers.

BRIE IN PUFF PASTRY

1 4½-ounce package brie cheese

1 Pepperidge Farm patty shell

Thaw patty shell without removing top. Roll out with rolling pin until it is large enough to cover cheese. Cover cheese with patty shell, tucking edges under bottom of cheese. Bake on cookie sheet in 450° oven until brown, about 15 minutes. Serve with crackers.

This also is wonderful with slices of apple and pear.

FRITTO DI MOZZARELLA
(Fried Mozzarella)

1 pound mozzarella cheese
2 tablespoons flour
2 eggs, slightly beaten
About ¾ cup dry bread crumbs
1 can (8 ounces) tomato sauce (optional)

¼ cup sliced pitted black olives
 (optional)
½ teaspoon basil (optional)
Oil

Cut cheese in ½-inch slices, then in fingers or wedges. Coat with flour; dip in eggs, then in bread crumbs. Place on plate lined with waxed paper and chill at least 1 hour. In small saucepan heat tomato sauce, olives and basil; keep warm. Fry cheese in 2 inches hot oil (380°) until pale golden. Drain on paper towels. Serve at once with tomato-olive sauce. Makes about 20 fingers—about 10 appetizer or 4 luncheon servings.

CHEESE STRAWS

1 pound sharp or extra sharp cheese,
 grated
2 cups flour
1 stick butter

1 teaspoon baking powder
½ to 1 teaspoon salt
¼ to ½ teaspoon red pepper or
 Tabasco

Put all ingredients in food processor with dough blade and blend. If doing by hand, work butter and cheese together; add remaining ingredients and work this mixture until it forms a ball. Put dough in cookie press and press through. Bake at 325° for 20 to 25 minutes. For an added way to serve cheese straws, wrap a piece of dough around an olive.

These are delicious for cocktail parties.

CHEESE CHRISTMAS TREES

½ pound grated cheese
½ pound butter or oleo
1 teaspoon salt

½ teaspoon lemon juice
2 cups flour, sifted
Heavy pinch cayenne pepper

Cream together cheese, butter, salt and pepper. Add flour and lemon juice. Put through cookie press with tree disc. Bake 300° for 15 minutes. Sprinkle with paprika. May also make into rolls, chill, slice thin and bake.

CHEESE BALLS

Mix:
2 sticks oleo
Add:
¼ teaspoon salt
⅛ teaspoon cayenne pepper

2 cups sharp cheddar cheese, grated

2 cups flour

Mix well. Add 2 cups rice krispies, folding in by hand. Form into small balls, place on ungreased baking sheet. Bake at 325° for 15 minutes or more, until firm.

Mary Fortenberry (Mrs. Nolan)

CHEESE PUFFS

Combine thoroughly:
½ pound sharp cheese, grated

¼ pound oleo

Work in:
1¼ cups (or a little more) flour
1 teaspoon baking powder

Shake of pepper and salt

Roll into balls. Keep in refrigerator 3 or 4 days. Take out 30 minutes before baking. Bake at 350° for 10-15 minutes. Yields 4 dozen.

CHEESE CHILIES

2 4-ounce cans green chilies
1 package (10-ounce) Cracker Barrel
   Sharp Cheddar, grated

6 eggs, beaten

Arrange chilies on the bottom of a 13x9 Pyrex pan. Place grated cheese on top of the chilies. Pour eggs on top, fairly evenly. Bake in 275°F oven for 45 minutes. Cut into squares, or diamonds, and serve hot or cold as an hors d'oeurve.

Terry Steckler (Mrs. Joseph)

PUFFY TOASTED SALTINES

Melted butter
Ice water

Saltine crackers

Preheat oven to 400°. Brush baking sheet with melted butter. Fill large bowl or shallow pan with ice water. Add crackers and let float to absorb as much water as possible, about 30 seconds. Remove crackers from water using slotted spatula, allowing excess water to drain off. Transfer crackers to prepared baking sheet. Carefully brush or drizzle top of each with melted butter, covering completely (be careful not to flatten cracker). Bake 15 minutes. Reduce oven temperature to 300° and continue baking until golden brown, about 25 minutes. Let cool on wire rack. Store crackers in airtight container. These crackers are a crispy base for spreads.

HOMEMADE BOURSIN CHEESE

8 ounces cream cheese, softened
1 clove garlic, crushed
2 teaspoons freshly minced parsley
½ teaspoon basil leaves

2 tablespoons chopped chives
1 tablespoon dry white vermouth
Pinch of pepper

Blend cream cheese with garlic. Add remaining ingredients. Chill. To make a dip for crudites, add ½ cup sour cream. Best made a day ahead—keeps up to 10 days.

Donna C. Burchfield (Mrs. Ron)

RED CHRISTMAS CHEESE BALL

½ pound natural cheddar cheese, finely
   grated
1 3-ounce package cream cheese,
   softened
¼ cup coarsely chopped ripe olives

3 tablespoons sherry
½ teaspoon Worcestershire sauce
Dash onion, garlic and celery salt
½ cup dried beef, snipped coarsely

Beat all ingredients except dried beef until thoroughly combined. Shape into ball, wrap in foil and refrigerate. About 30 minutes before serving, remove foil and roll ball in dried beef until completely covered.

GREEN CHRISTMAS CHEESE BALL

¼ pound Danish blue cheese
1 tablespoon finely-chopped celery
(can use food processor)
2 green onions, finely chopped, tops and
all

2 tablespoons sour cream
3 5-ounce jars blue cheese spread
1 cup coarsely snipped parsley or
dried parsley

Beat with electric mixer at medium speed blue cheese, celery, onion, sour cream and cheese spread until fluffy. Refrigerate overnight. Shape into ball. Refrigerate until needed. Just before serving, roll in parsley.

These balls served together add a festive red and green touch to Christmas gatherings.

CHEESE PINE CONE

3 8-ounce packages cream cheese,
softened
1 cup drained preserved ginger, coarsely
snipped

1 package toasted almonds

With electric mixer at medium speed beat cream cheese with ginger until thoroughly combined. Shape into cone. Wrap in foil and refrigerate. About 30 minutes before serving, press almonds, starting at top, into cone, overlapping rows to resemble pine cone.

This is pretty and seasonal at Christmas parties.

PINEAPPLE-PEPPER-NUT CHEESE BALL

2 8-ounce packages cream cheese,
seasoned to taste with salt, garlic salt
or celery salt, and a dash of pepper
⅓ cup chopped bell pepper

½ cup chopped pecans
3 tablespoons crushed pineapple,
drained

Mix all ingredients. Add pineapple last. Shape, chill, roll in parsley flakes or chopped nuts. Serve with crackers.

Joanne McLaughlin (Mrs. Wayne)

PHILLY CHEESE RING
(especially pretty at Christmas)

2 8-ounce packages cream cheese,
softened
½ cup mayonnaise or salad dressing
⅓ cup Parmesan cheese
¼ cup green onions, sliced

10 slices crisp cooked bacon,
crumbled
Pimento (optional)
Parsley (optional)

Cream cream cheese and mayonnaise until well blended. Add remaining ingredients. Chill. Drop by tablespoonfuls around a glass to form a ring. Smooth with a knife. Serve with Triscuit crackers.

At Christmas, just before serving, put fresh parsley around top of ring and put a pimento bow at top. It looks like a wreath.

Patti Tremaine (Mrs. Chuck)

VINEYARD SPREAD

1 4½-ounce round camembert cheese
4 ounces cream cheese, softened
1 tablespoon sherry

2 tablespoons slivered almonds or pecans, toasted
2 tablespoons grapes, seeded and sliced

Cut cheese in half horizontally. Blend cream cheese with sherry and fold in grapes and almonds. Spread half of filling on bottom layer of cheese. Place top layer on this and finish with remaining cream cheese mixture. Serve with crackers.

This was served at a tailgate cocktail party after the Auburn/Alabama (23-22) game. It is a winner, too!

ANN'S CHEESE BALL

1 large package cream cheese
2 glass jars Kraft Olde English cheese

1 teaspoon garlic powder
1 teaspoon onion salt

Crush nuts and mix with dried parsley flakes. Roll above ingredients in 1 large ball or 2 small balls, in nuts and parsley. Sometimes I use only parsley flakes.

Ann Henry (Mrs. John)

ROQUEFORT-CAVIAR CHEESE BALL

16 ounces cream cheese
8 ounces roquefort cheese
½ cup mayonnaise
4 teaspoons lemon juice
1 garlic bud, pressed

1 small onion, grated
¼ teaspoon Tabasco
Caviar (to be placed in hollow in center)

Mix cheeses at room temperature. Add mayonnaise. Add remaining ingredients and blend well. Form a deep hollow on top and put caviar in center. Serve with plain or melba toast.

This was served at a party honoring Eudora Welty during her Auburn visit for the Franklin Lecture Symposium on Southern Literature.

CHEESE BALL

1 pound mild cheddar cheese (grated)
1 cup mayonnaise
Pepper and cayenne

1 onion (grated)
1 cup nuts (pecans—chopped)

Combine all ingredients and roll or shape into ball (cover with pecans). Put strawberry *preserves* on top. Serve with crackers.

Betty Buford (Mrs. Jim)

Betty has used this at her annual victory party after football games.

GERMAN BEER CHEESE

1 pound sharp cheddar cheese
2 8-ounce packages cream cheese,
  softened
Few drops hot sauce

¾ cup beer, room temperature
2 teaspoons Worcestershire sauce
2 cloves garlic, minced
Salt and pepper to taste

Grate cheddar cheese; bring cream cheese to room temperature. Combine cheeses, add remaining ingredients. Beat with electric beater until mixed. Eat at room temperature. Serve with crackers or rye bread. Can be made at least a week ahead and refrigerated.

Devon Luther (Mrs. William A.)

This was served at the University Club's Fasching Party.

HOLIDAY APPETIZER PIE

1 8-ounce cream cheese, softened
2 tablespoons milk
1 package dried beef, finely snipped
  (about ¾ cup)
2 tablespoons instant minced onion

2 tablespoons finely chopped green
  pepper
⅛ teaspoon pepper
½ cup sour cream
¼ cup coarsely chopped walnuts

Blend cream cheese and milk. Stir in beef, onion, green pepper and pepper. Mix well. Stir in sour cream. Spoon into 8-inch pie plate or small shallow dish. Sprinkle walnuts on top. Bake in moderate oven (350°) for 15 minutes. Serve with assorted crackers.

Marjorie Tyre Sykes (Mrs. Maltby)

Marjorie Tyre, distinguished harpist and one of the founders of the Auburn Chamber Music Society, serves this at receptions honoring visiting chamber music groups.

CHUTNEY PIE

1 8-ounce package cream cheese,
  softened
1 8-ounce package sharp cheddar
  cheese, softened

1 teaspoon curry powder
2 tablespoons sherry
⅔ small jar chutney
Green onions, thinly sliced

Mix cheeses, curry and sherry. Grease and fill pie tin with mixture. Chill until 1 hour before serving. Turn out on serving dish. Top with chutney and green onions. Serve at room temperature with wheat crackers.

Joanne McLaughlin (Mrs. Wayne)

SMOKEY SALMON BALL

1 15½-ounce can red Alaskan salmon, drained, boned and skinned
1 8-ounce package cream cheese, softened
¼ teaspoon liquid smoke
1 tablespoon lemon juice
2 teaspoons grated onion
1 teaspoon horseradish

Blend first 6 ingredients and form into log. Chill in plastic wrap several hours or overnight. Before serving coat with chopped parsley and finely chopped pecans. Garnish with ripe olives. Serves 24. Leftovers may be frozen.

SMOKED OYSTER ROLL

2 8-ounce packages cream cheese
1 can smoked oysters, drained and chopped
1 large clove garlic, pressed
2 tablespoons plus 2 teaspoons Worcestershire sauce
2-3 tablespoons mayonnaise
½ small onion, grated
¼ teaspoon salt (or to taste)

Combine all ingredients except smoked oysters. Blend with fork or beater until smooth. Spread into a rectangle about ½-inch thick on waxed paper. Sprinkle chopped oysters over top of cheese and roll like a jelly roll, starting off cheese with a spatula edge. Chill 24 hours. Serve with melba rounds.

This recipe can be halved for small parties, but still use whole can of smoked oysters.

TUNA PATÉ

1 10-ounce can tuna, drained
1 cup butter, softened and cut into pieces
2 drops lemon juice
2 drops Tabasco sauce
Salt
Pepper
3 tablespoons pimentos, chopped
2 tablespoons capers, drained
Toast rounds
Parsley
Stuffed green olives, sliced

Place tuna, butter, juice, Tabasco, salt, pepper in food processor; process until thoroughly mixed; add pimentos and capers. Process until combined. Spoon into an oiled 3-cup pan or several small ones and chill 24 hours. Unmold and garnish with parsley and olives. Serve with buttered toast rounds. Can be frozen, then thawed for several hours in the refrigerator before serving.

Julie Donnan
Pots 'n' Pans, Etc.

PATÉ

8 ounces chicken liver
1 small onion, finely chopped
1 clove garlic, crushed

4 tablespoons real butter
Salt, pepper, pinch of thyme
1 tablespoon brandy

Melt 1 tablespoon butter. Cook onion and garlic until soft. Add livers. Increase heat and sauté briskly 5 minutes. Cool mixture. Blend in blender or food processor. Cream remaining butter and beat well into livers. Season well and add brandy and herbs. Serve with brown bread and butter or melba toast.

SAUTÉED SCALLOP HORS D'OEUVRE

1 pound scallops, washed
¼ stick butter or margarine
Juice of ½ large lemon or 1 whole small
   lemon

Salt and pepper
½ cup sherry
1 teaspoon sugar

Sauté everything except sherry and sugar until all the liquid evaporates. Then add sherry and sugar—pour over scallops and cook until most of the sherry has cooked away. Serves 4 for hors d'oeuvres.

HOT ARTICHOKE DIP I

1 cup chopped artichoke hearts
1 cup grated Parmesan cheese
1 cup mayonnaise (Hellmann's)
½ cup chopped green onions

½ teaspoon garlic salt
½ teaspoon chopped parsley
½ teaspoon white pepper
Paprika

Preheat oven to 350°. Combine all ingredients except paprika and mix gently. Spread into 1½-quart baking dish. Sprinkle with paprika and bake 350° for 20-25 minutes. Serve as a dip with corn chips or raw vegetables.

Dotty Cavender (Mrs. Ray)

HOT ARTICHOKE DIP II

1 heaping cup of Parmesan cheese
1 8½-ounce can artichoke hearts

1 cup Hellmann's mayonnaise

Puree and bake at 400° for 15 minutes. Serve with crackers.

Betty Buford (Mrs. Jim)

ARTICHOKE DIP

1 8-ounce can of artichoke hearts,
   chopped finely
¾ cup mayonnaise

1 package of Hidden Valley Ranch
   Original Ranch Salad Dressing Mix

Mix all ingredients and refrigerate for 2 hours. Serve with crackers, nachos, or chips.

Dr. Harry Philpott

JENKS KNIGHT'S SPINACH DIP

1 package frozen spinach, cooked and drained well
1 square or little triangle of Roquefort cheese

1 carton sour cream (1 cup)
Juice of ½ lemon
Few drops of Tabasco
Little garlic powder or salt

Mix and serve hot or cold.

DIANE'S SPINACH DIP

1 10-ounce package frozen chopped spinach
1 cup mayonnaise
1 cup sour cream
1 medium onion, chopped

1 8-ounce can water chestnuts, chopped
1 package dry vegetable soup mix (Knorr)

Thaw spinach; place on paper towels, and press until barely moist. Combine all ingredients, and cover and chill for several hours. Serve with crackers or raw vegetables.

Diane Hebert (Mrs. Bob)

Diane served this at a "Book Publication" party honoring Dr. Bob Ekelund.

DIFFERENT AND DELICIOUS EGGPLANT SPREAD

1 medium eggplant
¼ cup chopped onion
½ cup milk
1 tablespoon oil
2 tablespoons lemon juice

1 tablespoon oleo
1 tablespoon flour
3 ounces Parmesan cheese
Salt, pepper and nutmeg

Prick eggplant with a fork, rub with oil and bake uncovered in 400° oven about 1 hour until pulp is soft. Scoop out pulp into saucepan, add the lemon juice and cook over medium heat until liquid has evaporated. Melt butter, sauté onion and blend in flour. Add milk and cook until smooth white sauce. Fold white sauce into eggplant and add other ingredients. Thin with milk if necessary. Store overnight before serving at room temperature with crackers. Freezes well.

GUACAMOLE DIP

4 large avocados
1 cup mayonnaise
1 lemon
Tabasco sauce to taste

Garlic salt
1 small can tomatoes and green chilies
1 medium onion grated or a bunch of green onions, chopped

Mix everything together in a blender or processor. Add salt and pepper to taste. Serve with taco chips.

Merrilyn Henry (Mrs. Robert)

GUACAMOLE PASTE

2 ripe avocados, peeled and mashed
1 medium onion, chopped fine
Juice of 2 lemons

1 teaspoon salt
1 clove of garlic
Pinch of whole cumin seed

Grind salt, garlic and cumin with pestle. Blend the above ingredients. Serve on warm toasted whole wheat bread squares.

Mary Fortenberry (Mrs. Nolan)

AVOCADO COCKTAIL DIP

1 large ripe avocado
1 8-ounce package Philadelphia cream
   cheese

Seasoning salt
Worcestershire sauce

Peel and cut avocado into small pieces. Mash to smooth consistency with fork or in blender. Mix thoroughly with cream cheese that has been left to soften at room temperature. Add seasoning salt and Worcestershire sauce to taste. Blend well.

Marietta Kettunen

DONNA'S FAVORITE GUACAMOLE

2 medium ripe avocados
1 teaspoon onion juice
1 tablespoon lemon juice
½ teaspoon salt
Dash Worcestershire sauce
¼ teaspoon fresh ground pepper
Mayonnaise to blend

3 drops Tabasco sauce
1 clove garlic, pressed
2 tablespoons finely chopped green
   chilies
1 small tomato, peeled and chopped
4 slices bacon, fried crisp, drained and
   crumbled

Mash avocados well. Blend in rest of ingredients. This is delicious as a dip with Fritos, or to stuff in hollowed out cherry tomatoes.

Nancy Beardsworth (Mrs. Jim)

HOT CHEESE DIP

2 pounds of Velveeta
1 quart jar of mayonnaise
1 large onion, chopped

1 jar Torrido chili peppers (Trappley's
   brand)
Dash salt and garlic salt

Grate cheese in a food processor or with a grater. Remove seeds from peppers and save the liquid. Chop onion and peppers in food processor or blender. Combine cheese, pepper, onion, mayonnaise and salts. Stir well. Pour ⅓ of the liquid from the peppers into the processor and add ⅓ of the cheese mixture. Process until smooth. Continue adding the liquid and the cheese mixture until all is processed.

This makes about 2 quarts. It will keep up to six months in the refrigerator. Serve with crackers or Fritos.

This tastes better after it has been made awhile.

Jan Taylor (Mrs. Mark)

TACO DIP

1 pound ground beef, brown and drain

Add 1 box (8 ounces) Velveeta cheese and 1 can Mexican tomatoes and peppers. Heat slowly until cheese melts. Serve slightly warm with taco chips.

Betty Buford (Mrs. Jim)

CURRY ALMOND SPREAD

1 8-ounce package of cream cheese
¼ cup chopped Major Grey's chutney
1 teaspoon curry powder
¼ teaspoon dry mustard
¼ cup chopped almonds

Let cream cheese reach room temperature. Mix all ingredients. This is good on rye crackers, but any cracker will do.

CHEESE-OLIVE SPREAD

1½ cups grated cheddar cheese
1 can chopped ripe olives
½ cup mayonnaise
1 teaspoon curry powder
1 teaspoon salt

Spread English muffins with soft butter and then cheese-olive mixture. Bake at 350° for 15 minutes until mixture has melted. Cut into fourths or halves, as you prefer. Serve hot.

Frances Steagall (Mrs. Henry)

The Steagalls have entertained their fellow trustees and Auburn friends at wonderful house parties in Panama City. One of the highlights is cocktails on the porch of their condominium at Bay Point.

JEZEBEL SAUCE

16-ounce jar apple jelly
16-ounce jar pineapple preserves
1 small can dry mustard
1 jar horseradish
2 teaspoons cracked black pepper

Mix together above ingredients. Spread cream cheese on Ritz crackers and top with sauce.

Carol Savage (Mrs. Morris)

Men love this.

CURRY DIP

1¾ cups mayonnaise
2 tablespoons catsup
2 tablespoons honey
2 tablespoons dry minced onion

1 tablespoon lemon juice
7 drops Tabasco
1 teaspoon curry powder

Combine and refrigerate until ready to serve. Wonderful with fresh vegetables.

SAUCES OR DIPS FOR RAW VEGETABLES, I

1 cup mayonnaise
1 cup dairy sour cream
2 tablespoons minced onion
1 large or 2 small cloves garlic, minced
1 teaspoon salt

½ teaspoon freshly ground black
  pepper
½ cup chopped parsley
1 tablespoon or more, to taste,
  prepared mustard, preferably Dijon-
  style

Blend all ingredients well and allow to stand, covered, in refrigerator 2-3 hours before serving in a bowl to accompany raw vegetables. Makes 2¼ cups.

DIP FOR RAW VEGETABLES, II

1 tablespoon vegetable oil
1 tablespoon butter
2 teaspoons curry powder
1 teaspoon paprika
¼ cup chutney

¼ cup finely chopped toasted almonds
  or peanuts
Juice of ½ lemon
1½ cups mayonnaise
Salt to taste

Heat oil and butter in very small saucepan or skillet, add curry powder and paprika and stir over medium heat 3 to 4 minutes. Combine with chutney, nuts and lemon and fold into mayonnaise. Taste for seasoning. Allow to stand 2 hours before serving. Makes about 2 cups.

If you have lots of fresh cut-up vegetables left after a big cocktail party, put them in a pot with beef or chicken broth, ½ cup wine—a bouquet garni—and a can of condensed tomato soup. Simmer and have vegetable soup for supper. Also—try steaming carrot sticks, broccoli and cauliflower together for a vegetable medley that is delicious.

VIDALIA ONION DIP

1 cup sugar
2 cups water
¼ cup vinegar

1 teaspoon celery seed
Hellmann's mayonnaise

Slice Vidalia (sweet) onions.

In a saucepan, bring sugar, water, vinegar, and celery seed to a boil. Place sliced onions in and cover. Remove from heat and let set 15-20 minutes.

Drain—Mix with mayonnaise. Serve with Towne House crackers.

Betsy Perry (Mrs. Kermit)

DILL DIP IN BREAD BOWL

1 round muffalata loaf or other round
   loaf

Pull out center and break into bite-size pieces, leaving about 1 inch along bottom and sides to form bread bowl.

Dip:
1¼ cups good mayonnaise
1 pint sour cream
4 tablespoons parsley
2 teaspoons dill weed

2 tablespoons green onion with tops,
   chopped finely
2 teaspoons seasoned salt

Combine and refrigerate at least 8 hours before serving. To serve, place bread bowl on large glass plate. Fill cavity with dill dip and surround bowl with bite-size bread pieces for dipping. This dip is also good with vegetables, and a bowl of vegetables may be put next to the bread bowl for dieting dippers.

PROTEIN DIP

1 cup sour cream
2 cups mayonnaise
1 teaspoon Accent
1 tablespoon parsley
1 teaspoon Sweet 'n Low

2 tablespoons Parmesan cheese
1 teaspoon garlic salt
1 teaspoon seasoned pepper
1 teaspoon dry onions
1 pound shredded mozzarella cheese

Combine all ingredients and chill. Serve with raw vegetables, corn chips or tortilla chips.

Jean Bullock (Mrs. Bill)

DIP FOR FRESH FRUIT

⅓ cup sugar
4 tablespoons cornstarch
¼ teaspoon salt
1 cup unsweetened pineapple juice

¼ cup orange juice
2 eggs, beaten
2-3-ounce package cream cheese

Combine dry ingredients in saucepan. Blend in fruit juices. Cook, stirring constantly, until thick and bubbly (5-8 minutes). Slowly stir some of this hot mixture into the eggs. Return to saucepan and cook over low heat, stirring constantly, 3-5 minutes, or until mixture thickens slightly. Cool slightly. Beat cream cheese into cooled mixture. Chill. Makes 2 cups.

This is nice on a buffet table. Serve in a cut glass compote, surrounded by apple wedges, green and purple grapes, and strawberries.

ORANGE FRUIT DIP

1 6-ounce can orange juice concentrate,
   thawed
1 3¾-ounce package vanilla instant
   pudding

¼ cup sour cream
1¼ cups cold milk

Mix orange juice and milk. Beat in pudding mix on low speed and beat 2 minutes. Stir in sour cream. Chill. Cut a fresh pineapple in half and scoop out pineapple. Cut into chunks.

Put dip in ½ of the pineapple and assorted fresh fruits in the other half (bananas, pineapple chunks and strawberries are especially good).

Patti Tremaine (Mrs. Chuck)

CHEESE AND APPLE SPREAD

8 ounce package Philadelphia Brand
   cream cheese
½ cup Miracle Whip salad dressing
½ cup (2 ounces) shredded Kraft Natural
   sharp cheddar cheese

½ cup finely chopped apple (red or
   golden delicious)
Apple wedges
Crackers
Party rye bread slices

Combine softened cream cheese and salad dressing, mixing until well blended. Add cheese and apples; mix well. Chill. Serve with apple wedges, crackers and bread. Makes 1½ cups.

Page Adams (Mrs. Murray)

HOT CHIPPED BEEF-PECAN DIP

½ cup coarsely chopped pecans
1 tablespoon butter
½ teaspoon salt
12 ounces cream cheese
2 tablespoons milk

1 2½-ounce jar dried beef, cut into
   pieces
¼ cup chopped green pepper
1 small onion, grated
1 cup sour cream

Mix cream cheese, milk, beef, green pepper and onion. Fold in sour cream and half the nuts. Put in baking dish and sprinkle nuts on top. Bake at 350° for 20 minutes. Serve hot with melba rounds or crackers.

CRAB DIP

12 ounces cream cheese, at room
    temperature
1 small onion, chopped fine

2 tablespoons Worcestershire sauce
1 teaspoon garlic salt

Mix well; spread in shallow 10x10 serving dish. Pour ½ bottle of chili sauce over the cheese mixture and spread evenly. Sprinkle over the chili sauce 1 can of crab meat, drained, and top with chopped parsley. Serve with Ritz crackers and provide a butter spreader.

Mary Fortenberry (Mrs. Nolan)

CRAB MEAT DIP

½ cup catsup
¼ cup horseradish
¼ cup green peppers (optional)
2 tablespoons lemon juice
2 cans Atlantic white crab meat (6½
    ounces) (Do not use chunk meat, only
    shredded.)

½ teaspoon sugar
½ teaspoon curry powder
1 tablespoon prepared mustard

Mix all ingredients except crab meat. Right before using, rinse crab meat, check for shells, and add to mixture.

Ann Henry (Mrs. John F.)

An attractive way to serve seafood dips is to place the dip in a small ocean clam or bear claw shell and use a large shell for the crackers. This is also nice for boiled shrimp and sauce using the large shell for the shrimp and the small shell for the cocktail sauce. The shells may be placed on a silver or bamboo tray, depending on whether your party is formal or informal.

SMOKED MULLET PATÉ

2 cups smoked mullet, flaked
2 8-ounce packages cream cheese,
    softened
2 dashes Worcestershire sauce
1 egg-sized onion, grated

½ teaspoon Accent
¼ teaspoon liquid smoke
2 dashes Tabasco
Chopped pecans

Combine all ingredients except pecans. Roll into 2 logs and roll in chopped pecans.

Smoked catfish substituted for the mullet tastes even better in this recipe. Professor John Plumb, Department of Fisheries, is Auburn's premier catfish smoker!

SHRIMP SPREAD

1 can shrimp   3 tablespoons horseradish
4 tablespoons mayonnaise

Rinse shrimp in colander and mash. Stir in mayonnaise and horseradish. Mix well. Serve on Triscuits or rye crackers.

Dotty Cavender (Mrs. Ray)

This is a quick hors d'oeuvre for unexpected guests.

SHRIMP DIP I

1 large package cream cheese (8 ounces)   1 to 3 teaspoons horseradish
1 small can shrimp, rinsed and drained   3 drops Tabasco sauce
¼ to ½ cup catsup   Salt and pepper to taste
1 tablespoon Worcestershire sauce   Lemon juice to sprinkle on shrimp

Mix all ingredients except shrimp. Crumble shrimp. Add to mixture and mix in mixer until smooth.

Barbara Wilson (Mrs. Stan)

SHRIMP DIP II

1 can drained shrimp (or fresh)   ⅓ cup mayonnaise
1 large package cream cheese   Dash Worcestershire sauce
1 small grated onion   ¼ teaspoon lemon juice
3 tablespoons catsup

Mash shrimp with fork; add to cream cheese. Add other ingredients. Mix with mixer on low speed. Chill. Good with vegetables or chips.

Betty Buford (Mrs. Jim)

HOT CRAB MEAT DIP I

3 large packages cream cheese (8   ⅔ cup dry white wine
   ounces)   2 teaspoons confectioner's sugar
3 cans crab meat   1 teaspoon onion juice
½ cup mayonnaise   Dash Lawry's seasoned salt
2 teaspoons prepared mustard   Dash garlic salt

Cream cheese, mayonnaise, and wine. Add all seasonings. Fold in crab meat by hand. Heat and serve hot in chafing dish. May be frozen.

Barbara Wilson (Mrs. Stan)

This dip is popular for the Wilson's after-game parties when an Auburn victory has whetted appetites.

HOT CRAB DIP II
(Microwave)

1 package (8 ounces) cream cheese
½ cup mayonnaise
2 green onions, sliced
1 tablespoon dried parsley flakes
1 can (6 ounces) crab meat, drained and
flaked

½ cup slivered almonds
2 tablespoons dry white wine
1 tablespoon horseradish
¼ teaspoon Worcestershire sauce

Place cream cheese in medium glass mixing bowl. Microwave about 2-2½ minutes on medium high until softened. Add remaining ingredients and microwave 4 to 6 minutes on medium high, or until hot.

Carolyn Mathews (Mrs. Jim)

ROAST BEEF SPREAD

1 8-ounce package cream cheese
½ cup butter

¼ cup mayonnaise
¼ cup horseradish

Blend together well softened cream cheese and butter. Blend in mayonnaise and horseradish. This is an excellent spread to use for rolls, party rounds or breads for roast beef sandwiches at cocktail buffets.

ALWAYS PERFECT EYE OF ROUND, RIB EYE OR BOTTOM ROUND

Rub roast with pepper. Put it into preheated 500° oven. Close the door and bake 5 minutes a pound. Turn heat off, and leave in oven with door closed until 2 hours from starting time. This roast is always pink in the middle and delicious for slicing thin for sandwiches at cocktail suppers.

BARBECUED SPARE RIBS

2½ pounds spare ribs (Have the butcher
cut them in half and then cut each rib
apart. Should be about 2-inch
sections.)
Marinade:
¼ cup cocktail sherry (or 1 teaspoon
sherry flavoring)
½ cup pineapple juice

1 cup soy sauce
2 tablespoons dark brown sugar (or
brown sugar substitute)
1 clove garlic, crushed

Place the ribs in a plastic bag or bowl and cover with the marinade mixture. Marinate for at least one day, turning frequently if the marinade does not cover all of the ribs. Remove ribs from the marinade and put in a broiler pan (not on a rack) and broil for 7 minutes on one side and then turn and broil on the other side for 5 minutes.

CHICKEN WINGS

Remove the end of the chicken wing at the first joint. Then divide the rest of the wing at the joint, coat each piece of the wing with 1 tablespoon honey, 1 teaspoon lemon juice, 2 tablespoons cocktail sherry, and 1 teaspoon ginger root, that has been put through a garlic press and allow to marinate for 15 minutes. Repeat coating and broil for 5 minutes on each side, or bake at 300° for 1½ hours.

MARINATED BARBECUED CHICKEN WINGS

Disjoint and discard tips of 35-50 chicken wings. Place in flat pan and pour marinade over wings and let stand 1 hour or overnight. Heat together:

1 stick margarine	2 teaspoons dry mustard
1 cup brown sugar	Garlic salt and pepper, to taste
½ cup soy sauce or Worcestershire	¼ cup fresh lemon juice
½ cup red wine	

Put thoroughly marinated wings in 350° oven. Reduce heat immediately to 250° and bake 4-5 hours, turning wings 2-3 times. If all sauce has not been absorbed, pour off excess and dry wings out a bit before serving. These can also be used as a main course and will serve 8-10. Serves 35-50 for hors d'oeuvres.

BARBECUED SAUSAGE BALLS

1 pound pork sausage	½ cup catsup
1 egg, slightly beaten	2 tablespoons brown sugar
⅓ cup fine dry bread crumbs	1 tablespoon vinegar
½ teaspoon sage	1 tablespoon soy sauce

Mix sausage, egg, bread crumbs, and sage. Shape into small balls. Cook in 350°F oven on a cookie sheet until lightly browned—about 15 minutes.
Combine remaining ingredients and pour over meatballs in ungreased skillet. Cover and simmer 30 minutes, stirring occasionally. Serve hot.

Terry Steckler (Mrs. Joseph)

STUFFED MUSHROOMS

1 box mushrooms	½ stick butter
Herb stuffing mix	¼ cup Parmesan cheese
½ small onion	

Wash mushrooms and break out stems. Put ½ onion in food processor and chop fine. Next chop mushroom stems. Melt butter and sauté onion and mushroom stems. Stir in enough herb stuffing to make mixture consistency of chicken dressing. Shake in Parmesan cheese to taste. Fill mushroom caps and bake 10-12 minutes at 350°.

STUFFED MUSHROOM CAPS

12 large fresh whole mushrooms
1 small onion, finely chopped
¼ pound ground beef, chuck
2 slices ham, coarsely chopped
¼ cup seasoned dry bread crumbs
¼ cup grated Parmesan cheese

2 tablespoons vegetable oil
1 teaspoon garlic powder
½ teaspoon pepper
⅓ cup dry sherry
1 teaspoon salt

Gently remove stems from mushrooms. Chop stems fine; put aside. Place mushroom caps on a cookie sheet. Heat oil in a large skillet over moderate heat; cook onion and beef until lightly browned, stirring frequently. Add the chopped stems, ham and sherry to onion-beef mixture and cook 5 minutes. Add bread crumbs, garlic powder, salt and pepper and mix well. Stuff mixture into mushroom caps with a spoon. Sprinkle with cheese. Broil mushrooms in a preheated broiler 3 inches from source of heat for 2-5 minutes. Serve hot. May be reheated in a 350° oven for 5 minutes.

Betsy Judkins (Mrs. Joe)
Betsy's on Ross

STUFFED CHERRY TOMATOES

36 cherry tomatoes

Slice top; reserve. Scoop out pulp; sprinkle with salt. Invert on rack; drain 15 minutes. Mash 1 avocado, 1 medium grated onion, 2 tablespoons lemon juice, ½ teaspoon curry powder, ½ teaspoon chili powder. Beat well. Fill. Replace tops. Or can stuff with ¾ cup cottage cheese, ½ cup blue cheese, ½ teaspoon grated onion, chives, salt and pepper.

MOLDS

COEUR A LA CREME WITH CAVIAR

8 ounces cream cheese
8 ounces cottage cheese
¾ cup whipping cream

1 teaspoon lemon juice
¾ teaspoon onion, grated
1 jar caviar

Put cottage cheese and cream cheese through sieve. Beat whipping cream into cheeses gradually. Add onion and lemon juice, beating until mixed. Line coeur a la creme mold with cheesecloth and fill with cheese mixture. Place mold on plate and let stand overnight in the refrigerator to drain and set. Unmold and top with caviar. Serve with melba toast. Serves 24.

Great treat for a Valentine's day cocktail party.

SPINACH MOLD

1 package frozen spinach, cooked and
    drained
1 teaspoon salt
1 tablespoon finely chopped onion

1 cup mayonnaise
½ envelope unflavored gelatin in ½
    cup warm water

Mix ingredients and pour into mold. Let stand overnight in refrigerator. Unmold. Frost with sour cream (½ pint) and cover with grated boiled eggs (3).

Jenny Jenkins (Mrs. Jimmy)

VEGETABLE MOLD

1 package gelatin
¼ cup cold water
¼ cup boiling water
1 3-ounce package cream cheese
1 pint Durkee's mayonnaise
1 tablespoon white vinegar
Salt and pepper

1 small onion, chopped, or 2 spring
    onions, tops and all
2 tomatoes, finely chopped and
    drained
1 green pepper, chopped
1 cup celery, chopped finely
1 cucumber, peeled and chopped

Soften gelatin in cold water, add boiling water and stir to dissolve. Add cream cheese and blend well. Cool. Add other ingredients and blend well. Put in mold and refrigerate.

Keeps well in the refrigerator. Use as spread for crackers, sandwich filling, or cherry tomato stuffer.

TUNA (TASTES LIKE SHRIMP) MOLD

2 cans tuna
1 can tomato soup
1½ packages unflavored gelatin
1 package cream cheese (8 ounces)

½ cup each finely chopped celery,
    onion and green pepper
1 cup Durkee's dressing
1 small bottle stuffed olives

Heat soup and melt cream cheese in it. Smooth with whisk or hand mixer. Dissolve gelatin in soup and cool. Chop olives and flake tuna and add it to soup mixture along with other ingredients. Mix well. Pour into well-greased fish mold and chill. Spread on crackers. This is pretty served on a fish platter—use an olive slice for the eye of the fish and put parsley around the mold.

SALMON OR TUNA MOUSSE

1 16-ounce can red salmon, or 2 6½-
   ounce cans tuna
11 ounces cream cheese
1 cup mayonnaise
1 cucumber, peeled
4 ribs celery
1 small onion

3 tablespoons gelatin
Juice of 1 lemon
1 tablespoon fresh basil
1 tablespoon fresh chives
1 tablespoon parsley
1 10-ounce can tomato soup
Salt and pepper to taste

Drain, skin, flake and bone salmon. Put cucumber, celery, onion in food processor. Drain thoroughly. Combine liquid from vegetables with lemon juice and gelatin and set aside to soften. Heat tomato soup. Add finely chopped herbs and softened gelatin to soup. Stir until gelatin dissolves. Combine salmon with cheese, mayonnaise, vegetables, and soup. Season and pour into oiled ring mold. Refrigerate at least 3 hours before serving.

SHRIMP MOLD

1½ pounds shrimp, cooked and cooled
½ cup (or less) grated onion
½ cup finely chopped celery
2 envelopes Knox gelatin (dissolved in ½
   cup cold water)

1 3-ounce package cream cheese
1 cup mayonnaise
1 can condensed tomato soup

Heat soup as is, add pinch salt. Melt cheese in this and beat until smooth. Add gelatin. When cool, add other ingredients, adding shrimp last. Pour into mold. Refrigerate. Garnish either with parsley or stuffed olives. Use as spread or salad.

Jenny Jenkins (Mrs. Jimmy)

SHRIMP MOUSSE

12 ounces canned shrimp
2 envelopes Knox gelatin
8 ounces cream cheese
1 can celery soup
2 tablespoons chopped onion

1 teaspoon salt
2 teaspoons lime juice
1 green bell pepper
⅓ cup mayonnaise
Water

Drain shrimp. To the liquid drained from shrimp, add enough water to make 1 cup of liquid. Refrigerate. Add pepper, onion, cheese, salt, mayonnaise to soup and heat. Mash shrimp and add to mixture. Add gelatin to water. Stir to dissolve. Add to soup mixture. Pour into mold, oiled with Wesson oil or olive oil. Refrigerate. Serve with crackers.

Dotty Cavender (Mrs. Ray)

BLUE CHEESE MOLD WITH APPLES

1 envelope unflavored gelatin
⅓ cup white wine
1 6-ounce package blue cheese,
   crumbled
1 tablespoon lemon juice
½ cup mayonnaise

6 apples
2 tablespoons chopped parsley
½ teaspoon paprika
1 to 1½ tablespoons finely chopped
   green onion
1 cup whipping cream

Soften gelatin in wine. Set over hot water and heat until gelatin is completely dissolved. Mix cheese with lemon juice. Blend in mayonnaise, mixing until smooth. Stir in gelatin. Blend well. Add parsley, paprika and onion. Beat cream to soft peaks. Fold into mixture. Turn into 1-quart mold. Chill overnight. Unmold. Serve with apples dipped in 4 cups water and juice and rind of 2 lemons. Drain and sprinkle with confectioner's sugar. Serves 20.

SHERRY PARTY MOLD

12 ounces Philadelphia cream cheese
1 stick butter
½ cup sour cream
½ cup sugar
1 envelope plain gelatin

¼ cup cold water
½ cup white raisins
1 cup slivered almonds, toasted
Grated rind of 2 lemons
Saltines

Let cream cheese, butter and sour cream come to room temperature. Cream well, add sugar. Soften envelope of gelatin in ¼ cup water. Dissolve over hot water. Add to cream cheese mixture. Then add raisins, etc. Put in 1-quart mold. Refrigerate. Unmold. Serve with saltines only. Will freeze. Serves 35.

MOLLY'S EGG SALAD AND CAVIAR MOLD

12 hard-boiled eggs
2 packages gelatin
¼ cup cold water
¾ cup hot water
1 cup Hellmann's mayonnaise

Juice of 1 lemon
1 teaspoon grated onion
1½ teaspoons salt
Tabasco to taste

Grate eggs finely. Pour gelatin in cool water, soften, add hot water and stir until dissolved. Add salt, pepper, lemon juice and onion. Cool until the consistency of cream. Mix with mayonnaise and eggs. Pour into mold. Chill until firm. Unmold on plate—spread caviar over top—garnish with parsley and serve with Triscuits.

Molly Duncan (Mrs. Billy)

CHAFING DISH

CHAFING DISH OYSTERS

1 pound butter
1 jar creamed horseradish
1 can cream of mushroom soup

Salt and pepper
Dash of Worcestershire sauce
1 gallon oysters, drained

Put all ingredients except oysters in saucepan and heat, blending well. Put in oysters, but don't cook. Serve in chafing dish over low flame with melba rounds.

PARTY SEAFOOD DIP

2 cans cream of mushroom soup
1 can cream of celery soup
1 8-ounce package cream cheese
1 pound small shrimp, peeled and
   deveined (or 3 cans small shrimp,
   drained and rinsed)
2 small cans water chestnuts, chopped
1 pound lump crab meat
2 8-ounce cans mushrooms, chopped

⅓ cup green onions, chopped
⅓ cup parsley, chopped
2 small jars pimento, chopped
1 teaspoon Tabasco
2 teaspoons dry mustard
2 teaspoons curry powder
2 teaspoons paprika
4 tablespoons Worcestershire sauce
Salt and cayenne pepper to taste

Heat soups; stir in cheese until melted. Add remaining ingredients. Serve hot in a chafing dish with your favorite crackers. Serves 60-70.

Dr. Bob Hebert

HOT SEAFOOD DIP

1 large can crab meat
Scallops or shrimp, optional (chopped)
1 pound fresh mushrooms (stems, too)
Bunch of green onions
4 tablespoons flour
2 tablespoons milk

1 large cream cheese
2 cups sour cream
Salt and pepper
Paprika
Dash hot sauce
Wheat toasts

Sauté mushrooms, onions, scallops, crab meat in butter. Sprinkle with flour. Add milk and half of sour cream. Continue to cook until mushrooms are tender. Add seasonings, remaining sour cream, and 1 large cream cheese. Serve hot. Serves large crowd.

Merrilyn Henry (Mrs. Robert)

MUSHROOM EAGLE'S NEST

1 pound butter
2 cups flour
12 large cans mushrooms, sliced, or
   stems and pieces
6 cans beef bouillon

4 cans mushroom juice
12 lemons, juice and rind
2 cups chopped parsley
Black pepper
Kitchen Bouquet

Make a medium roux of butter and flour. Drain mushrooms and reserve juice. Add mushrooms to roux, beef bouillon, mushroom juice and lemon juice to taste. Add parsley, pepper, and Kitchen Bouquet for color. It may be thickened with cornstarch if necessary. Serve hot in chafing dish with melba rounds or toast cups. Leftovers freeze well.

TOAST CUPS FOR CHAFING DISH

Sandwich bread   Melted butter

Trim crusts off bread and cut each slice into 4 squares. Spread with melted butter and press into miniature muffin tins. Toast in 350° oven until light brown. These may be made ahead and frozen or kept 2-3 days in an airtight tin.

QUICK HOT MUSHROOM DIP

1 pound fresh mushrooms, or 2 large
   cans, sliced
4 tablespoons butter
1 tablespoon grated onion
1 tablespoon Dijon mustard
½ teaspoon salt

⅛ teaspoon ground nutmeg
⅛ teaspoon garlic powder
2 tablespoons dried parsley
¼ teaspoon Tabasco
1 cup commercial sour cream

Wash, dry and slice lengthwise the mushrooms (or drain the canned). Melt butter in frying pan, add remaining ingredients except sour cream and cook over medium heat for 7-10 minutes until mushrooms are tender. Fold in sour cream, correct seasoning and serve hot from chafing dish on melba rounds. Makes 72 servings.

This was served at a Department of History party honoring C. Vann Woodward while he was in Auburn to deliver the annual Draughon Lecture in Southern History.

JENKS KNIGHT'S HOT BROCCOLI DIP

3 ribs celery, chopped medium fine
1 large onion, chopped
1 4-ounce can sliced mushrooms,
   chopped
(I add some hot stuff—Worcestershire—and little lemon juice.)

1 package frozen chopped broccoli
1 can cream of mushroom soup
1 roll garlic cheese

Sauté celery, onion and mushrooms in little butter or oleo. Add mushroom soup and cheese to above mixture and stir until cheese melts. Cook broccoli and drain. Combine this to above mixture. Serve in chafing dish. Freezes beautifully. Serve with Fritos or Doritos. Serves 12.

HOT SPINACH DIP

8 boxes frozen chopped spinach
1 cup oleo
½ cup flour
½ cup chopped onion
2 cups evaporated milk
2 cups juice (reserved from cooked
spinach)

2 teaspoons pepper
3 teaspoons celery salt
2 teaspoons garlic salt
Salt to taste
4-6 ounces rolls of Jalapeño cheese
4 teaspoons Worcestershire sauce

Cook spinach. Drain and reserve liquid. Melt oleo, add flour and stir until blended. Add onion and cook until onions have softened. Add liquid slowly, stirring constantly. Cook until smooth and thick. Continue stirring and add seasonings and cheese. Stir until cheese melts. Combine with drained spinach. May be frozen. Serve hot in chafing dish with Fritos. Serves 100.

Freda White (Mrs. Herb)

This recipe was shared by a friend in North Alabama and has been used for many years during football season. A favorite with men!

HOT SPINACH DIP

1 package cream cheese (8 ounces)
½ cup mayonnaise
2 sliced green onions
1 package frozen chopped spinach
(defrosted and thoroughly drained)

6 slices of crisply cooked bacon
⅓ cup Parmesan cheese
2 teaspoons lemon juice

Soften cream cheese and blend all remaining ingredients. Heat at a low temperature and serve in a chafing dish with crackers. Can be doubled.

Carol Pittard (Mrs. Joel)

PORK IN CURRY SAUCE

2½ pounds pork stew meat
⅓ cup all-purpose flour
4 teaspoons curry powder
2½ teaspoons salt

¼ teaspoon pepper
⅓ cup salad oil
1 13¾-ounce can chicken broth
½ teaspoon ginger

About 2 hours before serving:
Cut pork into bite-size chunks. On waxed paper, combine flour, curry powder, salt and pepper; use to coat pork well. In 12-inch skillet over medium-high heat, in hot salad oil, brown pork well. Reduce heat to medium-low; add chicken broth and ginger; cover and simmer 1 hour and 15 minutes or until pork is fork-tender, stirring occasionally. Serve in chafing dish to keep hot. Provide cocktail picks. Makes 12 appetizer servings.

CHICKEN DIP

1 can mushroom soup
8 ounces cream cheese
5-ounce can chicken
2¾ ounces slivered almonds

2-ounce can mushrooms
½ teaspoon Worcestershire sauce
½ teaspoon garlic powder
⅛ teaspoon pepper

Heat mushroom soup and cream cheese. Add remaining ingredients. Place in chafing dish and serve with crackers.

Patti Tremaine (Mrs. Chuck)

SWEET AND SOUR MEATBALLS

1 pound hamburger
¾ cup catsup
½ cup water
3 bay leaves
2 teaspoons Worcestershire sauce

4 tablespoons vinegar
Juice of ½ lemon
4 tablespoons brown sugar
Pinch of dry mustard
2 small ginger snaps

Roll ground meat into small balls and drop into boiling water to which a teaspoon of salt has been added. Boil gently 20 minutes. Drain, mix together rest of ingredients in saucepan. Add meatballs and simmer for 1 hour. Serve in chafing dish and have toothpicks handy. Makes 40-50 small balls.

Freda White (Mrs. Herb)

CRUNCHY COCKTAIL MEATBALLS

¼ cup water
1 egg
½ cup bread crumbs
2 tablespoons horseradish

1 cup finely chopped water chestnuts, drained first
1 pound hamburger meat

Sauce:
4 tablespoons sugar
1 tablespoon cornstarch
¼ cup vinegar

¼ cup soy sauce
½ cup water
1 small onion, finely chopped

Mix first 6 ingredients and shape into balls. Place on jelly roll pan and bake 12-15 minutes at 350°. Mix sauce ingredients and simmer 10 minutes. Pour over meatballs and serve from chafing dish. Makes 3 dozen balls. This recipe is easily doubled, and can be made ahead and refrigerated.

EASY CHAFING DISH HOT DOGS

2 packages hot dogs
2 12-ounce jars red currant jelly

6-ounce jar Dijon mustard

Cut hot dogs into bite-sized pieces. Melt jelly over low heat; add and blend mustard, then add sliced hot dogs. Simmer 15 minutes. Serve in chafing dish with toothpicks alongside.

HELEN NANOS' GREEK ARTICHOKE HEARTS

Juice of 2 lemons
1 or 2 large onions, sliced
1 or 2 cloves of garlic, chopped or crushed
½ cup white wine

¼ cup olive oil
1 teaspoon salt
Pepper to taste

Combine all ingredients and boil for 5 minutes. Pour over 1 can drained artichoke hearts. Refrigerate overnight.

Ruth L. Brittin (Mrs. Norman)

ANTIPASTO

Cut into large bite-sized pieces:
½ head cauliflower
1 green pepper
3 carrots

2 stalks celery
Mushrooms
Jar of stuffed olives

Place in large skillet. Add ¼ cup water, ¾ cup wine vinegar, ½ cup olive oil, 2 tablespoons sugar, 1 teaspoon salt, ½ to 1 teaspoon oregano, ¼ teaspoon black pepper. Bring to a boil. Simmer for 5 minutes, stirring occasionally. Refrigerate for 24 hours. Drain before serving.

Carla Candler (Mrs. Bill)

MARINATED MUSHROOMS

1 pound fresh mushrooms, washed and dried or canned button mushrooms
1 bottle Italian dressing

1 garlic clove, split
¼ cup olive oil
Black pepper

Lightly sauté mushrooms in oil. Place in dish with cover and pour dressing with garlic clove over this. Marinate overnight and drain. Serve with cocktail picks.
If you use canned mushrooms, don't sauté.

RAMAKI

2 pounds chicken livers
2 packages thin bacon, cut in half
2 5-ounce cans water chestnuts

1 large bottle soy sauce
½ cup brown sugar

Half livers and cut a slice of bacon in half. Wrap each slice around a piece of raw liver and a water chestnut. Put toothpick in to secure. Arrange in a large rectangular pan. Pour soy sauce mixed with brown sugar over and marinate overnight or freeze. Thaw, drain and broil 3-4 minutes on each side or until bacon is crisp.

Merrilyn Henry (Mrs. Robert)

MARY WOODY'S TOASTED PECANS

4 cups pecan halves
¼ cup butter

3 teaspoons salt

Place pecans in single layer on baking sheet. Bake in 325° oven 10 minutes. Add butter and stir until pecans are covered. Sprinkle salt over all, lower heat to 250° and bake 20-25 minutes longer, checking to see when they are crunchy and brown. Cool in pan and store in glass jar.

Mary Woody

Dean Woody serves these at the Deans' brown bag luncheons.

PARMESAN POTATO STICKS

Canned potato sticks (use best brand)   Parmesan cheese

Spread potato sticks on cookie sheet and sprinkle generously with cheese. Bake at 300° for 10 minutes.

Molly Duncan (Mrs. Billy)

ARTICHOKE SQUARES

14-ounce can artichoke hearts, drained
½ pound sharp cheese, grated
1 green onion, chopped
4 eggs

6 saltine crackers, crushed
Few dashes Tabasco
Salt and pepper to taste

Chop artichoke hearts into small pieces. Sauté chopped onion in small amount of oil. Beat eggs. Put onion with other ingredients in bowl and mix. Pour mixture into greased 9-inch square pan and bake at 350° for 20-30 minutes until firm. Cut into tiny pieces and serve hot or cold. This can also be used as a vegetable cut into serving size squares.
    Cook in Pyrex, Corning or glass pan.

HOT SPINACH BALLS

2 10-ounce boxes frozen chopped
   spinach, cooked and drained well
2 cups herb bread stuffing mix
1 onion, finely chopped
6 eggs, beaten

¾ cup oleo, melted
½ cup grated Parmesan cheese
1 tablespoon garlic salt
½ teaspoon thyme

Mix ingredients well and chill. Form into balls not quite 1-inch in diameter (about 1 teaspoon). At this point I usually put them in Tupperware boxes and layer with a sheet of waxed paper between and freeze or refrigerate until party time. Then bake in preheated 350° oven for about 20 minutes. Makes 5 dozen. These can be frozen after baking but they're not as good. They are great to keep in the freezer for unexpected guests.

These were served at a party for Robert Penn Warren whose recent visit to Auburn reunited him with former friends from LSU and Vanderbilt.

COCKTAIL SPINACH SQUARES

2 10-ounce packages frozen chopped
   spinach
3 tablespoons butter
1 medium onion, chopped
¼ pound mushrooms, sliced
4 eggs, beaten

¼ cup fine bread crumbs
1 can cream of mushroom soup
¼ cup grated Parmesan cheese
⅛ teaspoon pepper
⅛ teaspoon oregano
⅛ teaspoon basil

Thaw spinach and press out water. Melt butter in frying pan and sauté onion and mushrooms. Combine eggs, bread crumbs, mushroom soup, 2 tablespoons cheese, seasonings and spinach. Blend with onion mixture. Turn into greased 9-inch square pan and sprinkle with remaining cheese. Bake uncovered at 325° for 35 minutes. Cool slightly and refrigerate. Cut into 1-inch squares and serve. This makes 80 squares. It can be reheated in 325° oven for hot hors d'oeuvres.

This is good for a vegetable at cocktail suppers.

CHILE-CHEESE APPETIZER

2 cups Bisquick
½ cup cold water
½ pound "hot" bulk sausage
½ pound ground beef

Small can green chilies
½ cup onion, minced
2 cups (8 ounces) Monterey Jack
   cheese, grated

Heat oven to 350°. Grease 13x9x2-inch pan. Mix Bisquick and water into soft dough. Press into bottom of pan. Cook and stir ground beef and sausage until brown; drain off excess fat. Cut chilies into strips and arrange on dough in pan. Top with meat, onion, then cheese. Cover loosely with foil and bake 20 minutes; remove foil and bake 5-10 minutes until cheese is bubbly. Let stand 15 minutes before cutting into 1 to 1½-inch squares or triangles.

Martha W. Edwards (Mrs. Jim)

INSTANT PARMESAN APPETIZER

1 cup grated Parmesan cheese
1 cup mayonnaise

Grated onion to taste

Mix above ingredients. Spread on party rye or Pepperidge Farm very thin bread cut into desired shape. Bake in 300° oven till puffy (about 5-8 minutes).

SHRIMP-MUENSTER ROLL

1½ cups shredded Muenster or other semisoft cheese (6 ounces)
1 cup cooked shrimp, chopped, or 1 can (6½ or 7 ounces) tuna, drained and flaked
¼ cup thinly sliced green onions with tops (about 3)
2 eggs

¼ to ½ teaspoon salt
⅛ teaspoon pepper
1 package (8 ounces) refrigerated crescent rolls
1 tablespoon butter or margarine, melted
1 egg yolk beaten with 1 tablespoon water (optional)

In large bowl stir together cheese, shrimp, onions, eggs, salt and pepper; set aside. Unroll crescent-roll dough onto lightly floured surface. Pinch together perforations on both sides of dough. Fold in half crosswise and, with lightly floured rolling pin, roll out to 14x9 inch rectangle. Brush with butter. Spread cheese-shrimp mixture in 2-inch strip along one long edge of dough; roll up as for jelly roll. Firmly pinch seam and ends together, then moisten slightly with water and smooth lightly with dull edge of knife to seal dough well. Carefully lift roll onto ungreased cookie sheet. Brush with egg-yolk mixture. Bake in preheated 400° oven for 25 minutes or until golden brown. Cool on rack 20 minutes. With sharp knife, cut in ½-inch slices. Makes 28 appetizer servings.

PEPPER JELLY TARTS

1 3-ounce package softened cream cheese
1 stick butter

1 cup flour, sifted
Pinch salt
Pepper jelly

Cream cream cheese and butter. Add flour and salt gradually until well blended. Make into dough ball and refrigerate until well chilled. Roll out dough and cut into circles with wine glass. Put 1 teaspoon pepper jelly on each circle and fold in half. Seal edges and bake at 400° 10 minutes. To use as dessert, fill with jam and dust with powdered sugar after baking.

PEPPER JELLY

12 medium sweet green peppers
1 medium hot green pepper
7 cups granulated sugar
1 teaspoon turmeric

1½ cups cider vinegar
6-ounce bottle liquid fruit pectin
10 drops green food coloring

Cut peppers in half, remove stem and seeds and put peppers through food processor or blender. Chop fine. Drain well and measure 2 cups green pepper into large saucepan. Add sugar, vinegar, turmeric. Mix well. Place over high heat, bring to a full rolling boil and let it boil hard for 1 minute, stirring constantly. Remove from heat and stir in pectin immediately. Stir and skim off foam for 5 minutes. Add the food coloring and mix well. Ladle quickly into hot, sterilized glasses. Pour melted paraffin over top to seal. Makes about ten 6-ounce glasses.

Shirley Bartels (Mrs. Jan)

This is good served with the turkey, venison or as an appetizer served over cream cheese and on crackers.

PEPPER JELLY

½ cup ground hot pepper (¼ if you prefer mild rather than too hot)
½ cup bell pepper (ground)
1 onion (ground)

6½ cups sugar
1½ cups apple cider vinegar
1 bottle Certo or 1 box (both packages)

Mix and bring to medium boil. Boil 1 minute. Remove from heat, add Certo and stir about 5 minutes. Fill containers and seal with wax or tops.

Josephine Teague (Mrs. Wayne)

FROZEN CHEESE SQUARES

2 jars Olde English cheese
1 stick butter or oleo

¼ teaspoon garlic powder
About ½ loaf of white bread

Melt first three ingredients in top of double boiler. Beat well. Cut off crust of bread. Spread cheese between two slices of bread and cut in four or six pieces. Spread cheese mixture on sides and top. Put on cookie sheet and freeze. Take from freezer to oven and bake 350° for 12-15 minutes.

Jonnie Dee Little (Mrs. Ted)

Great to keep on hand for unexpected company.

CHEESE BOXES

½ pound sharp cheese, grated
½ pint mayonnaise
1 teaspoon Dijon mustard
1 tablespoon Worcestershire sauce

Onion or garlic juice to taste
Salt and pepper
Sandwich bread

Blend cheese, mayonnaise, sauces and seasonings. Trim crust from bread. Spread 2 slices with cheese mixture and place one on top of the other. Cut into 4 squares, repeat until number of boxes are made. Ice sides of boxes with cheese mixture. Toast at 400° immediately before serving. This makes enough spread for 2 loaves of bread.

This is especially nice to serve at morning coffees or brunches.

EASY CHEESE CUBES

1 loaf unsliced white bread
1 3-ounce cream cheese
4 ounces sharp cheddar, broken

1 stick butter or margarine
2 egg whites, beaten
Dash of dry mustard, cayenne

Cut bread in 1-inch cubes. Melt cheese and butter in double boiler, fold in egg whites and seasonings. Dip bread into cheese mixture. Put on cookie sheet and brown under broiler. Makes 60-80 puffs. You may freeze on cookie sheets before broiling. Store in plastic bag. Thaw to cook.

ANCHOVY OR SMOKED OYSTER PUFFS

½ pound oleo or butter
½ pound cream cheese

2 cups all-purpose flour (or use 1 package pie crust mix prepared per directions)

Mix crust ingredients and chill slightly. Roll thin, and cut with small biscuit cutter. Place piece of smoked oyster, or else spread anchovy paste, in middle of dough. Fold in half, press edges of dough together and bake at 450° for 10 minutes. (These are different and delicious served piping hot.)

SAUSAGE SWIRLS

2 8-ounce cans crescent dinner rolls
3 tablespoons hot mustard (Dijon preferably)

1 pound hot pork sausage, uncooked

Separate rolls into 8 rectangles and pinch together serrated edge in the middle of each rectangle. Spread with mustard and then with a thin layer of sausage. Roll by beginning with long edge. Pinch remaining edge into roll. Wrap in waxed paper and chill at least 2 hours. Thinly slice each roll (10 swirls to a roll) and place on ungreased pan. Bake at 400° for 18-20 minutes. Serve hot. Yields 80 swirls.

Caroline Lipscomb (Mrs. Lan)

TINY PARTY PIZZAS

Cook and drain:
1 pound regular sausage

1 pound hot sausage

Add to meat and stir until cheese melts:
2 pound package Velveeta cheese
1 green pepper, chopped

1 onion, chopped

Keep mixture warm while spreading on party rye bread, open face. Top each with slice of pepperoni sausage if desired. This makes enough for 3 loaves of party rye bread. May be frozen in layers with waxed paper between. Run in oven and heat until cheese bubbles.

Helen Funderburk (Mrs. Hanly)

ONION CANAPÉS

Combine an 8-ounce package cream cheese, 1 cup Hellmann's mayonnaise, ½ cup finely chopped onions and ¼ cup Parmesan cheese. Spread on bread rounds or party rye. Bake at 350° until puffy.

CHEESE TRIANGLES
(Tiropetes—Greek Name)

4 eggs, well beaten
1 8-ounce package cream cheese
1¼ pounds feta cheese

1 pound filo
3 sticks butter or margarine

Beat eggs with electric mixer until fluffy. Add cream cheese, continue beating until well blended. Remove bowl from mixer. Crumble feta cheese with fork and combine with egg mixture. Cut package of filo into 5 strips while still rolled. Unroll one strip at a time; each sheet will be 1 triangle. Brush each strip with butter and fold in half. Place a heaping teaspoon cheese mixture at one end of strip, folding strip diagonally until triangles are formed. Brush tops with melted butter. Repeat for each triangle. Place unbaked buttered triangles in plastic containers, separating layers with waxed paper and place in freezer. When ready to serve, place frozen triangles on ungreased pan and bake. (May be frozen up to 2 months.) Bake in oven at 375° for 20 minutes or until golden. Serves 100.

Joanne Patton (Mrs. Ed)

AMERICAN CHEESE APPETIZER

1 pound American cheese
½ pound breakfast bacon
1 egg-sized onion

½ teaspoon Worcestershire sauce
½ teaspoon mustard

Put cheese, bacon and onion through meat grinder or food processor. Add Worcestershire sauce and mustard. Spread on whole wheat rounds and run under broiler for 10 minutes. Serve hot with soups or fruit salad, or use as hors d'oeuvre.

SWISS-CRAB APPETIZERS

4 ounces Swiss cheese, shredded
3 green onions, chopped
1 can crab meat or ½ pound fresh crab meat
½ cup mayonnaise

1 teaspoon lemon juice
½ or ¼ teaspoon curry powder (¼ is better)
1 package flaky refrigerator rolls
1 can water chestnuts, sliced

Combine all ingredients except rolls and water chestnuts. Separate rolls (each one) into 3 layers. Place on an ungreased baking sheet and spoon on crab mixture. Top each with a few slices of water chestnuts. Bake at 400° for 10-12 minutes or until golden brown. Serves 36.

CRAB CANAPES

1 can snow crab, drained
1 jar Olde English cheese
1 stick butter

1½ teaspoons garlic salt
1-2 tablespoons mayonnaise
1 package English muffins, halved

Mix first 5 ingredients and spread on English muffins. Freeze. When ready to serve, slice in wedge shapes and broil 10-15 minutes until brown and bubbly.

Stephanie Bond (Mrs. Gordon)

COCKTAIL QUICHE

Pastry:
½ cup butter
1 package cream cheese (3 ounces)

1 cup flour

Filling:
1 cup grated Swiss cheese
1 large egg
½ cup milk

¼ teaspoon salt
Paprika

Cream softened butter and cream cheese. With fingers, work in flour. Roll into a ball and chill. Divide into 24 small balls and press into a lightly greased miniature muffin pan, forming pastry shell. For filling, beat eggs, milk and salt. Pour this over the cheese, which has been placed in each shell. You may add bits of bacon, ham, Canadian bacon or other favorite quiche ingredients.

GAZEBO I'S PETITE QUICHE

Pastry:
2 sticks butter, softened
6 ounces cream cheese, softened

2 cups flour

Mix all ingredients together with your hand and press into small tartlet shells. Put aside.

Filling:
1 package cream of onion soup (or leek)
  dry mix
2 cups milk
1 cup cream
4 eggs

½ pound Swiss cheese, grated
1 teaspoon dry mustard
1 teaspoon salt
¼ teaspoon black pepper

Bring soup and milk to boil, cool slightly. Stir in cream—cool. Beat eggs with remaining ingredients and add to soup. Fill pastry cups about ¾ full. Bake at 375° until brown. May be frozen. If so, reheat in foil. Makes about 4 dozen.

This is delicious! It is served at tea time at Gazebo I. Try it: add whatever you have left over into your next quiche. Any bits of meat, potatoes or other vegetables add interest and save money at the same time.

CHEESE TARTLETS
(a traditional Swiss appetizer or snack)

Pie dough for 16 tartlet pans, or store-bought tart shells
2 cups grated Swiss cheese (½ pound)
1 scant cup heavy cream

2 eggs
¼ teaspoon salt
¼ teaspoon dry mustard
⅛ teaspoon cayenne pepper

Line 2-inch tartlet pans with pie dough. Blend eggs and heavy cream. Mix in all other ingredients and spoon mixture into lined tartlet pans, each about ½ full. Bake in preheated oven (400°) for 15 minutes or until golden brown. Can be made in advance and reheated.

CRABMEAT QUICHE

2 cans (7½ ounces) crabmeat (2 cups)
2 cups coarsely grated Swiss cheese (½ pound)
1 package (10 ounces) pie crust mix
6 eggs

3 cups light cream
½ cup dry sherry
1 tablespoon salt
1 teaspoon nutmeg
½ teaspoon pepper

Drain crabmeat from 2 cans, discarding any cartilage. Flake crabmeat and toss lightly with 2 cups coarsely grated Swiss cheese. Set aside. Prepare 1 package pie crust mix and roll out on a lightly-floured surface to an 18x12-inch rectangle. Fit into a 15½x10½x1-inch jelly roll pan. Spoon combined crabmeat and cheese into crust. Combine eggs, light cream, sherry, salt, nutmeg and pepper. Beat well. Pour over crabmeat in pie crust and bake 15 minutes at 425°. Reduce heat to 325° and bake 20 to 30 minutes more or until knife inserted in center of custard comes out clean. Serve warm, cut in 1x2-inch rectangles. Makes 150 pieces.

This may be prepared in advance in two steps. First, the crabmeat and cheese may be spooned into the pie crust, then well-covered and refrigerated. Second, the custard mixture may be prepared, covered, and refrigerated. Remove both from refrigerator about 30 minutes before baking. Beat custard mixture well, pour over crabmeat and bake as above. If any quiche is left over, reheat, covered with foil, 10 to 15 minutes at 325°. You may use 2 cups cooked, fresh crabmeat or 2 cups frozen crabmeat, defrosted, instead of the canned.

LANGDON HALL

SOUPS, SANDWICHES, AND SALADS

. . . the sweet-marjoram of the salad, or rather the herb of grace.
All's Well that Ends Well (IV-v-19)

LANGDON HALL

The oldest building on the Auburn campus was originally constructed in 1846 at what is now the site of the Auburn National Bank (Magnolia and Gay Streets), and was moved to its present location in 1883; named for Charles Carter Langdon who served as Trustee during a formative period in the university's history (1872-89).

SOUPS

AVOCADO SOUP

2 cups milk
2 cups half and half
1 cup chicken broth
¼ teaspoon salt
¼ teaspoon pepper

2 ounces flour
½ stick butter
2-3 small avocados
2 tablespoons chopped chives

Heat milk and half and half, broth, salt, and pepper until surface steams but do not boil. Add 1 tablespoon chives. Melt butter, stir in the flour, and let cook for 2-3 minutes, stirring constantly. Slowly add the cream mixture and stir to thicken. Cool. Mash the avocado meat with a fork and place in a blender. Add the cooled cream mixture and blend until smooth. Taste for seasoning. Chill. Pour into soup bowls and garnish with remaining chives. Serves 6.

BROCCOLI SOUP

3 tablespoons butter
1 onion, chopped
1 bunch broccoli, cut into florets
2 potatoes, peeled and diced

6 cups chicken broth
Salt and pepper
2 tablespoons parsley flakes
1 cup half and half

Melt butter in saucepan. Sauté onions until transparent. Add broccoli, potatoes and broth to onions, and bring to a boil. Season to taste with salt and pepper. Lower heat and simmer covered (about 20 minutes) until broccoli is tender. Cool. Drain liquid from vegetables and reserve. Puree vegetables and return to broth. Add half and half and parsley flakes. Stir well to blend. Refrigerate until needed. This soup is good hot or cold.

BROCCOLI-CHEESE SOUP

2 10-ounce packages chopped broccoli
  (prepare according to directions)
¾ cups chopped onions
6 chicken bouillon cubes
1 teaspoon salt
Pepper to taste
1 pound pasteurized processed American
  cheese (cut in big cubes)

6 cups water
8 ounces fine egg noodles (can use
  medium)
6 cups milk
⅛ teaspoon garlic powder

Heat butter and sauté onions. Add water and bouillon cubes. Boil and *gradually* add noodles and salt. Cook uncovered 3 minutes and add cooked, drained broccoli and garlic powder. Cook for 3 minutes and add milk, cheese and pepper. Stir *constantly* until cheese melts.

Freezes well for a month. Reheat in double boiler. Makes 4 quarts.

Elizabeth Glynn

CHEDDAR CHEESE SOUP

4 tablespoons butter
2 stalks celery, chopped
1 onion, chopped
1 carrot, chopped
4 tablespoons flour
2 cups chicken stock

1 cup beer
1 cup cream
¾ cup grated cheddar cheese
1 tablespoon parsley flakes
Salt and pepper to taste

Melt butter, and sauté vegetables until they are soft. Stir flour and parsley flakes into the vegetable mixture. Take off stove and slowly stir in the flour. Then stir in the chicken stock, adding it gradually, until it is all well blended. Bring to a boil, add beer, and simmer until the vegetables are tender. Add cream and cheese and stir over low heat until the cheese melts. Correct seasoning, and serve hot.

SWISS CHEESE SOUP

1 cup grated Swiss cheese
1 tablespoon butter
1 pint half and half

¾ cup milk
Salt and pepper to taste

Put all ingredients in top of double boiler and heat well but do not boil. This is good, quick and easy.

BETTE'S MYSTERY SOUP

1 10¾-ounce can condensed cheddar
cheese soup
1 10¾-ounce can condensed golden
mushroom soup
3 tablespoons chili sauce
½ teaspoon curry powder

⅛ teaspoon salt
Milk
½ cup finely shredded carrot
¼ cup paper thin slivered green
pepper

Into a medium saucepan, turn the undiluted soups, chili sauce, curry powder and salt. Fill cheese-soup can with milk and mushroom-soup can with water; whisk in milk and water a little at a time. Add carrot and green pepper, stirring often because soup tends to stick. Slowly bring to a boil. Makes 6 servings.

Bette Oliver (Gazebo I)

AUNT MARGARET'S CHEESE SOUP

2 potatoes
2 carrots

2 ribs of celery
1 onion

Chop very fine and cover with water and cook (do not add salt). Do not drain liquid. Add 1 package frozen vegetables.

Cheese sauce:
½ cup oleo
½ cup flour

2 cups milk

Cook until thickened. Add 1 pound Velveeta cheese and melt. Add vegetables. Makes thick soup. May be thinned by adding a little milk, if desired.

Helene Alexander (Mrs. Milton)

CORN CHOWDER

2 slices bacon, diced
¼ cup chopped onion
1 medium potato, cubed (raw)
Water to cover potato (for cooking)

1 can (1 pound size) creamed corn
1 tablespoon flour
1 tablespoon butter (or margarine)
½ cup milk

Cook bacon until crisp, drain on paper towel. Cook chopped onion in bacon drippings until golden brown. Meanwhile, cook cubed potato until tender. In double boiler mix butter and flour; add water from cooked potatoes; add milk and stir constantly until thickened. Add can of corn, potatoes, bacon bits and onions. Mix gently, heat and serve hot. Makes 4 servings.

Martha Applebee (Mrs. Frank)

This is a hearty winter soup for the family.

GAZPACHO I

2 1-pound cans peeled tomatoes
½ cucumber, peeled and chopped
4 tablespoons green pepper, chopped
4 tablespoons salad oil
2 tablespoons wine vinegar

1 tablespoon onion, minced
2 cups tomato juice
1 tablespoon Worcestershire sauce
⅛ teaspoon Tabasco

Put all ingredients in blender or food processor and blend quickly. Do not over process. Season with salt and pepper to taste and chill.

GAZPACHO II

1 package tomato soup mix

4 cups cold water, stock or bouillon

(Tomato juice or V-8 juice may be substituted for the above ingredients.)

1 tablespoon minced onion flakes
¼ teaspoon salt
½ teaspoon cracked pepper
½ teaspoon crushed oregano
1 scant tablespoon sugar (may omit)
Dash of Tabasco sauce
4 medium tomatoes, chopped

1 small cucumber, chopped
¼ cup each finely chopped cucumber, celery, green pepper, carrot
1 or 2 tablespoons oil (may be omitted)
2 tablespoons wine vinegar, garlic flavored

Empty package of tomato soup mix into saucepan, gradually stir into the four cups of liquid. Add next 6 ingredients, heat until boiling, then simmer 4 minutes, stirring occasionally. Remove from heat, cool then add oil and vinegar. Taste for seasoning. Chill until serving time. Ladle into bowls and serve, accompanied by side dishes of finely chopped raw vegetables and croutons.

Croutons:
   Remove crusts from 4 slices of white bread. Stack and cut in ¼-inch cubes. Place in a lightly oiled pan and toast in slow oven, stirring occasionally until delicately browned. Watch carefully so that they do not burn. Remove from heat and sprinkle with a few dashes of garlic salt if desired.

Joanne Patton (Mrs. Ed)

BARBARA'S GAZPACHO

4 cups tomato juice (V-8 if desired)	Juice of one lemon
1 cucumber, medium, chopped fine	2 teaspoons prepared horseradish
2 tablespoons scallions, minced	1 clove garlic, minced
1 teaspoon Worcestershire sauce	Tabasco to taste
1 green pepper, chopped fine	½ teaspoon oregano

Garnish with lemon wedge, salt and parsley. Serve with celery stalk stir stick.

Joanne Patton (Mrs. Ed)

TOMATO GAZPACHO WITH AVOCADO

½ cucumber, peeled if you like	3 tablespoons olive oil or salad oil
½ mild red or white onion, peeled	2 tablespoons wine vinegar
1 avocado, peeled	4 cups canned tomato juice
½ teaspoon oregano, crumbled	2 limes, cut in wedges

Cut off a few slices of cucumber and onion; save for garnish. Chop rest of cucumber and onion in small pieces; slice or chop avocado. Put onion, cucumber, avocado, oregano, oil, and vinegar in a serving bowl. Pour in the tomato juice. Top with cucumber and onion slices; chill. Ladle into bowls, adding lime juice to taste. Serves 6. I often use more cucumber and add chopped fresh tomatoes.

Wanda Dobie (Mrs. Jim)

TOMATO BOUILLON

3 or 4 thin slices of onion	2 cups beef bouillon
1 tablespoon green pepper, chopped	2 cups tomato juice
½ carrot, sliced	Salt, pepper
2 stalks celery, diced	1 whole clove
1 teaspoon butter	

Sauté vegetables in butter until tender. Add juice, bouillon, seasonings. Simmer 5 minutes. Serve with parsley.

This is great for company and can be made ahead.

MULLIGATAWNY

In 2 tablespoons butter, sauté ½ cup chopped onion, 1 small chopped carrot, and 1 stalk chopped celery. Stir in 1½ tablespoons flour and 1 teaspoon curry powder. Cook 5 minutes. Add 4 cups chicken broth (or 2 cans Campbell's chicken broth and 1¼ cups water). Simmer for 30 minutes. Add:

½ cup apples, chopped
½ cup boiled rice
1 cup cooked chicken, chopped

¼ teaspoon black pepper
⅛ teaspoon thyme
Salt

Simmer 45 minutes. Add ½ cup cream and serve.

Carla Candler (Mrs. Bill)

GREEK LEMON SOUP

6 cups chicken broth (fresh or canned)
¼ cup long grain rice
1 teaspoon salt

3 eggs
¼ cup *fresh* lemon juice
1 lemon, sliced thin

Combine broth, rice and salt in saucepan. Bring to boil, cover and simmer until rice is tender. Remove from heat. Beat eggs in a bowl until fluffy and add lemon juice. Slowly pour and stir about 2 cups hot broth into egg and lemon mixture and whisk vigorously. Pour this mixture back into remaining broth. Whisk until slightly thickened. Serve warm or refrigerate until cold and serve. Garnish with lemon slices.

Jack Blackburn

SQUASH SOUP

48 ounces chicken broth
16 ounces cream cheese (break into small pieces)

1 large onion, sautéed in butter
3 cups cooked squash, mashed
Salt and pepper to taste

Sprinkle nutmeg on top just before serving. Serve hot or cold.

Jackie Norman (Mrs. Dan)

CHILLED SQUASH SOUP

1 pound yellow squash, thinly sliced
1 onion, chopped
1 cup chicken stock or broth
½ cup more chicken stock

½ cup sour cream
Salt and pepper to taste
Dill weed, dried

Bring to a boil the squash, onion and 1 cup chicken stock. Boil for 30 minutes. Puree in blender and transfer to a bowl. Stir in ½ cup more stock, the sour cream and seasonings. Chill well and serve with fresh dill weed.

PEANUT SOUP

2 ribs celery, chopped
1 medium onion, chopped
¼ cup butter
1 tablespoon flour

2 quarts chicken broth or stock
1 cup smooth peanut butter
2 cups light cream
Chopped peanuts

Cook celery and onion in butter until soft but not brown. Stir in flour until well blended. Add chicken broth, stirring constantly, and bring to a boil. Remove from heat and rub through a sieve. Add peanut butter and cream, stirring to blend thoroughly. Heat on low but do not boil. Garnish with peanuts. May be served hot or cold.

Polly Philpott (Mrs. Harry)

Mrs. Philpott often served this as a first course to her dinner guests in the President's home. It is elegant!

FRENCH ONION SOUP I

8 ounces onion, finely sliced
1½ ounces butter
1 tablespoon flour
2 pints stock

Salt, pepper
Bay leaf
Slices of French bread
Cheddar cheese

Heat pan and when butter is foaming, add onions. Lower heat and cook slowly for 15-20 minutes until pale brown. Stir in flour and cook a few minutes. Remove pan from heat. In saucepan, heat stock to boiling point. Pour stock over onion mixture. Add seasonings, bay leaf and simmer for 30 minutes. Have casseroles ready with sliced rolls laid on bottom. Pour in boiling soup after removing bay leaf. Scatter grated cheese thickly over top and cook at 400° for 10 minutes.

FRENCH ONION SOUP II

2 thinly sliced large onions
3 tablespoons butter or margarine
¼ teaspoon pepper
5 beef bouillon cubes

5½ cups water
1 teaspoon salt
2 tablespoons grated Parmesan cheese

Sauté onions in butter until a rich, golden brown, sprinkling them with pepper while cooking. Dissolve bouillon cubes in the water, then bring to boil. Add browned onions and salt. Continue simmering, covered, for 1 hour. Sprinkle with cheese and serve. Serves 5.

Joanne Patton (Mrs. Ed)

ONION-POTATO SOUP

¼ cup butter or margarine
3 medium onions, thinly sliced
4 medium potatoes, peeled and thinly
   sliced (about 1 quart)
1 quart hot chicken broth

6 peppercorns
6 whole allspice
1 cup finely chopped celery tops
½ cup heavy cream (optional)
Salt and pepper

Melt butter in heavy 3- to 4-quart kettle or Dutch oven. Add onions and potatoes and sauté, stirring, 5 minutes. Add next 3 ingredients. Bring to boil, cover and simmer 30 minutes, or until potatoes are very tender. Beat soup with whisk until potatoes are in small pieces. Add celery tops; add cream, if desired. Heat and season to taste with salt and pepper. Makes about 2 quarts.

   If preferred, substitute ½ cup minced celery root for celery tops and sauté with onion and potatoes.

VICHYSSOISE

4 cups potatoes, cubed
1 cup celery, sliced
1 cup onion, chopped
2 cups chicken broth
1 cup milk

1 cup heavy cream
3 tablespoons butter
2 teaspoons salt
⅛ teaspoon pepper

Cook potatoes, onion, celery and salt in broth until vegetables are tender. Put vegetables and broth mixture through blender or food processor to puree, and pour back into pot. Add remaining ingredients, heating for a few minutes until well-blended. Chill.

   This makes a nice luncheon served with hot ham biscuits and avocado/ grapefruit salad.

QUICK VICHYSSOISE

1 cup chopped cucumber
¼ cup chopped green onions
2 tablespoons oleo
1 can cream of potato soup

½ soup can each: milk, water, sour
   cream
Chopped chives

Sauté cucumber and onions in oleo till tender. Add other ingredients, heat till blended. Put in blender or food processor till blended. Chill 6 hours or more. Sprinkle each serving with a few chopped chives.

Donna C. Birchfield (Mrs. Ron)

CARROT VICHYSSOISE

2 cups potatoes, peeled and diced
1½ cups carrots, scraped and sliced
1 medium onion, sliced

3 cups chicken stock
¼ teaspoon salt
1 cup half and half

Place vegetables in saucepan and bring to boil. Reduce to simmer for about 30 minutes or until vegetables are tender. Puree in blender, season to taste and add cream. Chill well. Serve in soup bowl with grated carrot garnish.

ZUCCHINI SOUP

2 medium zucchini, scrubbed, sliced	½ cup plain yogurt
2 medium onions, chopped	Pepper
2 10-ounce cans chicken broth	Chopped chives

Combine zucchini, onion and broth in saucepan, heat to boiling. Simmer 15 minutes. Add yogurt and pepper to taste. Puree soup. Chill. Add chives.

Variation: Scrape and grate 6 carrots. Follow instructions, substituting carrots for zucchini.

CLAM-VEGETABLE SOUP

6 tablespoons butter or margarine	2 green onions, sliced
2 cups diced, peeled potatoes	1 package (10 ounces) frozen cut corn
2 cups diced carrots	2 cans (6½ ounces each) minced or
1 cup sliced celery	chopped clams
1 can (10½ ounces) clam juice	Salt and pepper
¼ teaspoon each basil and thyme leaves	Chopped parsley

Melt butter in heavy 4-quart kettle or Dutch oven. Add potatoes, carrots and celery and sauté, stirring, 5 minutes. Add 3 cups hot water, the clam juice and herbs. Bring to boil, cover and simmer 20 minutes, or until vegetables are almost tender. Add onions and corn and simmer 5 minutes longer. Add clams with liquid and heat. Season to taste with salt and pepper. Sprinkle with parsley. Makes about 2 quarts.

ITALIAN-STYLE VEGETABLE-SAUSAGE SOUP

3 medium potatoes, peeled and cut in fine strips (about 3 cups)	4 green onions, sliced
	6 cups hot beef broth
3 carrots, peeled and cut in fine strips (about 2 cups)	8 ounces link sausages
	Salt and pepper
1 parsnip, peeled and cut in fine strips (about 1 cup)	Parsley
	Grated Parmesan or Romano cheese (optional)
2 cups cauliflorets	Croutons or toast (optional)
¼ cup olive oil	
1 clove garlic	

Prepare all vegetables and set aside. Heat oil in heavy 4- to 5-quart kettle or Dutch oven. Add garlic and green onions. Sauté, stirring, about 5 minutes. Add vegetables and sauté 2 minutes. Add broth, cover and simmer 35 minutes, or until vegetables are very tender. Meanwhile, cook sausages according to package directions. Drain on absorbent paper and slice thin. Add to soup, season to taste with salt and pepper and sprinkle with parsley. Serve with cheese and croutons, if desired. Makes about 3 quarts.

ITALIAN BEAN & SAUSAGE SOUP

¼ cup olive oil
2 onions, chopped
3 leeks (white part only), sliced
2 garlic cloves, minced
4 celery stalks, chopped
2 turnips, peeled and chopped
2 carrots, chopped
2 green bell peppers, chopped
8 cups very rich chicken broth
4 cups small white beans, cooked
1 tablespoon basil
1 tablespoon rosemary
1 bay leaf
Juice of one lemon
1 pound Italian sausage, cooked and
    sliced
2 cups shredded cabbage (½ head)
1 cup shredded fresh spinach leaves
Salt and pepper to taste
¼ cup parsley, minced
Parmesan cheese (freshly grated is
    better)
Sauce Verte

Heat ¼ cup olive oil in large Dutch oven over medium heat. Add onion, leek, and garlic, cook until just soft, about 6 minutes. Add celery, turnip, carrot, bell pepper. Stir in broth, beans, basil, rosemary, bay leaf and lemon juice. Simmer about 10 minutes. (Soup can be prepared up to 2 days ahead to this point.) Heat sausage in pan and brown on all sides until cooked. Drain and cut into ½-inch slices. About 10 minutes before serving, bring soup to simmer, add cabbage and sausage, cook about 6 minutes. Add spinach and parsley, salt and pepper to taste. Serve with Parmesan cheese and Sauce Verte. Unlike most soups, this soup is best right after it is cooked. Makes 10-12 servings.

Sauce Verte:
½ cup stale French or Italian bread (fresh
    bread can be dried out in a low oven
    for 30 minutes)
1 tablespoon red wine vinegar
½ cup fresh parsley
1 hard-cooked egg
2 tiny dill pickles
1 tablespoon capers
2 anchovy fillets
1 clove garlic
2 tablespoons olive oil
1/4 teaspoon lemon juice

Place bread in processor and sprinkle with vinegar. Add rest of ingredients and blend until smooth. Sauce will be thick. Can be fixed the day before. Have guests stir a spoonful or two of this into their soup for more flavor. Makes about ⅔ cup.

This is a rich and hardy soup. Serve with French or Italian bread, followed by a light fruit dessert. Start with a mixed green salad.

Gail Collins Gilchrist (Mrs. Dick)

PORTUGUESE BEAN SOUP

1 cup dried red kidney beans
3 onions, sliced
2 cloves garlic, minced
¼ cup bacon fat
6 potatoes, peeled and diced
2 bay leaves
½ teaspoon ground allspice
1 can (6 ounces) tomato paste
Salt and pepper to taste

Put beans and 2 quarts water in kettle and bring to boil. Boil 2 minutes, then remove from heat, cover and let stand 1 hour. Bring again to boil and simmer, covered, 1½ hours, or until beans are tender. Sauté onions and garlic in the fat until golden. Add with remaining ingredients to beans. Cover and simmer 1½ hours. Makes 3 quarts.

SUNDAY NIGHT SOUP

2 cups chopped onion
6 cloves garlic, minced
6 tablespoons oil
10 cups beef stock (canned or
   homemade, not cubes)
1 pound garlic flavored smoke pork
   sausage links (cut in bite size pieces)
1 #303 can kidney beans, undrained

1 head green cabbage, cored and cut
   up
12 small new potatoes, unpeeled and
   quartered
¼ to ½ cup vinegar
1 16-ounce bottle catsup
Salt and pepper

Sauté onion and garlic in oil until transparent. Add sausage and brown lightly. Add other ingredients, bring to boil, then simmer 35-45 minutes. Even better the next day. Keeps one week in refrigerator. Makes one gallon.

BOUILLABAISSE

4 pounds red fish, red snapper or trout
2 cloves garlic
4 tomatoes
1 tablespoon parsley
3 onions

1 pinch saffron
½ cup olive oil
Salt, pepper to taste
Water

Put olive oil in saucepan, add chopped tomatoes, onions, garlic and parsley. Let all this simmer, then add pinch of saffron, season with salt and pepper. Now put in sliced fish, cover with water and bring to a boil. Cover the saucepan well and allow the fish to boil gently for 12 to 15 minutes. Sprinkle the sauce and fish with parsley. Serve on slices of French toast.

A collection of seashells can be made into a beautiful centerpiece for the dining table. Arrange large coral and other shells, and finish the arrangement with sand dollars and small shells. This centerpiece is especially attractive when serving seafood.

CREOLE COURTBOUILLON

4 to 5 pounds fish (red fish, red snapper,
   catfish—any firm fish) cut in pieces
½ cup cooking oil
2 tablespoons flour
3 cups onion, finely chopped
1 large green pepper, chopped
1 large can tomatoes
1 cup celery, chopped

3 cloves garlic, minced
4 cups water
1 teaspoon Worcestershire sauce
Salt and pepper to taste
⅓ cup parsley, minced
1 cup white wine
1 lemon, thinly sliced

Heat oil, add flour and cook to medium brown. Add onions and cook until transparent. Add tomatoes, green pepper, celery, and garlic and cook slowly for about 25 minutes. Add 1 cup of the water and allow to cook down again. Then add remainder of water, fish, Worcestershire sauce, salt, pepper, and parsley. Let simmer about 20-25 minutes. In the last 5 minutes of cooking, add the wine and sliced lemon. Serve over bowls of cooked rice.

Claire Debardeleben (Mrs. Charles)

CRABMEAT SOUP

3 tablespoons butter
3 tablespoons flour
5 cups chicken broth
½ teaspoon curry powder

1 cup heavy cream
1 pound lump crabmeat
Salt and white pepper to taste
Croutons or parsley

Melt butter in large 2½-quart saucepan. Stir in flour and cook slowly for 3 minutes, stirring constantly. Add stock and blend well with wine. Whisk. Mix curry with a little of the stock and strain into soup. Cook slowly, uncovered for ½ hour. Add cream, crabmeat, salt and pepper. Serve with croutons or cold with parsley.

CATFISH GUMBO

1 pound skinned catfish fillets or other
   fillets, fresh or frozen
½ cup celery, chopped
½ cup green pepper, chopped
1 clove garlic, finely chopped
¼ cup fat or oil, melted
2 beef bouillon cubes
2 cups boiling water
1½ cups hot cooked rice

1 can (1 pound) tomatoes
1 package (10 ounces) frozen okra,
   sliced
2 teaspoons salt
½ teaspoon pepper
¼ teaspoon thyme
1 whole bay leaf
Dash liquid hot pepper sauce
½ cup onion, chopped

Thaw frozen fillets. Cut into 1-inch pieces. Cook celery, green pepper, onion and garlic in fat until tender. Dissolve bouillon cubes in water. Add bouillon, tomatoes, okra and seasonings. Cover, simmer for 30 minutes. Add fish. Cover and simmer for 15 minutes longer or until fish flakes easily when tested with a fork. Remove bay leaf. Place ¼ cup rice in each of 6 soup bowls. Fill with gumbo. Serves 6.

Dan Gardner

SEAFOOD GUMBO

3 strips bacon
2 cloves garlic, pressed
1 teaspoon pepper
1 package frozen okra
Large can of tomatoes
Hot sauce
Cayenne to taste
2 chopped onions

4 chicken bouillon cubes
4 cups water
Filé powder
½ pound shrimp
4 bay leaves
1 tablespoon salt
4 dashes Worcestershire

Fry bacon. Sauté onions in fat. Add seasonings and remaining ingredients except seafood. Simmer 1-2 hours. Add seafood 30 minutes before serving. Add cooked rice or serve over rice. Can add crab, oysters, etc. Serves 6-8.

Carol Pittard (Mrs. Joel)

SEAFOOD GUMBO

Sprinkle 1 chicken breast with Accent and paprika. Cook in ¼ cup margarine over low heat. When done, pull meat from bone and add to: ½ cup minced onion that has been cooked with 1 strip of bacon chopped finely. Add to chicken and onion mixture:

½ teaspoon liquid garlic	1 can V-8 juice (12 ounces)
½ teaspoon thyme	12 ounces water
½ teaspoon basil	2 packages frozen chopped okra
¼ teaspoon cayenne	2 beef bouillon cubes
½ teaspoon filé potion	2 squirts soy sauce
½ teaspoon parsley flakes	

Cook 2½ hours over low heat. Add any seafood desired and cook until done.

SEAFOOD GUMBO

1 pound frozen cut okra	1 large bay leaf
3 tablespoons Wesson oil	1 tablespoon chili sauce
2 tablespoons Wesson oil	1 teaspoon garlic salt
2 tablespoons flour	2 sprigs parsley
2 large onions, chopped	6-8 cups water
½ cup celery, chopped	1½ pounds raw shrimp
1 can tomatoes	1 pound crab meat
2 cans stewed tomatoes	1 pound crab claws
10 drops Tabasco	1 cup raw rice

Cook okra in 3 tablespoons oil for about 20 minutes. Heat in another large pan for 5 minutes: 2 tablespoons oil, 2 tablespoons flour and chopped onions. Add okra, celery, tomatoes, parsley, chili sauce, garlic salt, Tabasco, bay leaf and water. Simmer about 20 minutes to 1 hour. Add shrimp, crab meat, crab claws and rice. Simmer about 20 minutes, stirring two or three times. Add salt and pepper to taste. Cover and let stand 2 hours. Heat and serve.

Dell Chester (Mrs. Rollie)

PACIFIC CHOWDER

3-5 slices bacon	½ cup chopped onion
2 tablespoons chopped green pepper	1 6½-ounce can tuna
1 can potato soup	Dash salt and pepper
2 cups milk	

Cook bacon until crisp, drain and set aside. Put 2 tablespoons bacon drippings in saucepan and sauté onion and green pepper. Add soup, milk, salt and pepper. Heat in saucepan until boiling. Drain tuna and stir into soup mixture along with crumbled bacon. Add a dash of paprika. Let soup simmer a few minutes after all ingredients are added. Serves 3. Double to serve 6.

This is fabulous and inexpensive. Serve with French bread and salad.

SEAFOOD STEW
(a delicious seafood mixture)

¾ cup salad oil
¾ cup flour
1 large onion, chopped
1 8-ounce can tomato sauce
3 stalks celery with leaves, chopped
2 cloves garlic, pressed
1 small bell pepper, chopped
1 12-ounce can V-8 vegetable juice
2 cups water
1 cup tomato juice

1½ cups burgundy wine
1 teaspoon sugar
Salt and pepper to taste
3 pounds catfish, or other firm fish, cut
   in bite-sized pieces
2 pounds shrimp
2 tablespoons chopped parsley
Bouquet garni
3 dashes hot pepper sauce

Heat oil in Dutch oven, stirring in flour to make a dark brown roux. Add tomato sauce and chopped onion and simmer until oil separates from mixture. Stir frequently to prevent sticking. Add celery, bell pepper, garlic, V-8 juice, tomato juice, sugar and bouquet garni. Cook covered for 30 minutes. Add fish and cook until tender. Remove fish and keep warm. Discard bouquet garni. Add shrimp and wine and cook 15 minutes longer. Add parsley, and hot pepper sauce. Return fish to pot and serve in soup bowls with rice or crusty French bread. This is delicious on a cold winter's day. It is also good with crab or oysters added.

TAZEWELL'S SEAFOOD GEECHEE GUMBO

In order to make the world's finest gumbo, I start with the world's finest cigar. The aroma starts sometime around 9:00 a.m. I start my roux—the roux is prepared in a large steel skillet by adding bacon drippings and a spoon of flour. Let the flour brown. Add chopped onion and celery. Always cook slowly. Time for a puff. In the largest pot you can find, boil some water and some Morton's salt. Next add tomatoes and tomato paste, next okra, then the roux. At this point, take time out for a puff. Always keep a low light under the pot and cook very slowly, very slowly. Some say keep the eye on low. 10:30 a.m.—add a touch of garlic, some filé, hot sauce, a little beer or white wine, salt to taste. If you can't find Morton's salt, just add salt. Oh! I almost forgot the bell peppers. Chop some up and drop 'em in. Some people of late are putting all the vegetables in a food processor or automatic chopper. *NOT ME!* Puff! Add a little more filé to taste of course. Stir the pot slowly. Back to when you start the big pot of boiling water, toss in a ham hock. Turn the eye down real low, stir, and take a nap. You mustn't nap too long or the gumbo will stick to the bottom of the pot and burn. 3:00

p.m.—stir, taste, stir, taste, add a touch more filé, a little wine and a bay leaf. Do not forget the bay leaf! I guess by now you have noticed that my nap was a bit too long, which has caused me to have to change pens. The pen I used above has clogged. The moment has come. 20 minutes until 9:00, add the blue claw crab and the shrimp. 9:00—serve over a bed of fluffy rice with a glass of white wine.

Tazewell Morton

FAIRBANKS CHOWDER

1½ pounds haddock, or any firm white fish
1½ cups cold water
⅜ cup salt pork or 5 strips lean bacon, chopped
3 cups thinly sliced raw potatoes
⅓ cup chopped onion
1 cup water
3 cups milk
1½ cups light cream
1½ teaspoons butter
Salt and pepper and paprika
¼ cup chopped parsley

In a saucepan, place the fish and cold water. Simmer, covered, for 10 minutes. Lift out fish and remove skin and bones. Flake and set aside. Reserve stock. In another large saucepan, place the bacon and cook slowly for 10 minutes, stirring, being sure not to brown it. Drain off the grease. To the bacon add the potatoes, onions, ½ cup water and the reserved stock. Simmer uncovered for 15 minutes. Stir for a minute to break up the potatoes. Fifteen to twenty minutes before serving, add the fish, milk, cream, salt, pepper and paprika. Heat slowly. Do not boil. Garnish to taste with parsley.

SANDWICHES

SANDWICHES

ASPARAGUS ROLLS

Soft, thin-sliced bread
Mayonnaise
Blue cheese spread

Whipped cream cheese
Asparagus spears, drained
Melted butter

Trim crusts from bread and roll flat with rolling pin. Combine mayonnaise, blue cheese spread and whipped cheese in equal amounts. Put asparagus in center, diagonally, and roll. Secure with toothpick, if necessary. At serving time, brush with melted butter and bake at 325° for about 25 minutes.

Variation: Spread bread with only mayonnaise and sprinkle with Parmesan cheese before rolling asparagus. These are delicious as hors d'oeuvres or luncheon sandwiches to serve with chicken salad.

Merrilyn Henry (Mrs. Robert)

BACON-PEPPER SANDWICH

2 cups crumbled crisp bacon
1 cup finely chopped pecans
¼ cup finely chopped bell pepper

1 teaspoon lemon juice
Mayonnaise

Mix first 4 ingredients with enough mayonnaise to bind the mixture and make it spreadable. Makes filling for 10-12 sandwiches.

CUCUMBER SANDWICHES

2 3-ounce packages cream cheese
1 medium cucumber, peeled and
 chopped
½ small onion, chopped

2 drops Tabasco
Salt
Cream
Buttered bread rounds

Chop cucumber and onion in food processor or blender. Add this to softened cream cheese, salt, Tabasco and enough cream to make spreading consistency. Spread on buttered bread rounds. These freeze well.

CUCUMBER SANDWICHES

1 8-ounce package cream cheese
1 package Good Seasons dried Italian
 dressing mix

1 large cucumber, peeled

66

Mix cream cheese with dried mix. Spread this mixture on bread and top with cucumber. Spread mayonnaise on top slice of bread and cut sandwiches in half. For party sandwiches, use cookie cutters to shape the bread into rounds. Top with cream cheese mixture. Garnish with parsley sprig.

COCKTAIL SANDWICH SPREAD

Cream 8 ounces cream cheese. Add ½ cup mayonnaise. Blend, then add ½ cup chopped, stuffed olives, ½ cup toasted chopped almonds.

MUSHROOM SANDWICHES

1 tall can mushrooms, drained	Mayonnaise
Juice from large onion	Fresh or dried parsley

Chop mushrooms. Pour onion juice on mushrooms. Add mayonnaise to bind. Set in refrigerator in A.M. to use in P.M. Chop parsley fine and mix with above. Spread mayonnaise on fresh bread. Make sandwiches. These keep well in Tupperware boxes in the refrigerator. A favorite of the distinguished American poet, Archibald MacLeish, when he visited Auburn as a Franklin Lecturer.

PEPPER-NUT SANDWICH SPREAD

1 cup pecan meats	½ cup American cheese
1 bell pepper, cleaned and coarsely chopped	Mayonnaise to moisten

Put first 3 ingredients through fine blade of food grinder (or shred cheese and chop nuts in Cuisinart). Add just enough mayonnaise to bind ingredients together. Unusual and great for tea or cocktail sandwiches. These can be spread the day before and stored in Tupperware containers unless you are using it for open-faced sandwiches.

PEANUT-CARROT SANDWICH

1 small can salted peanuts	Salt and pepper to taste
3 large carrots	1 teaspoon dry mustard
2 tablespoons India relish	

Grind peanuts and finely grate carrots. Mix together remaining ingredients. Spread on bread rounds.
A colorful sandwich for fall parties.

RADISH SANDWICH

8 radishes, grated	1 teaspoon freeze-dried chives
2 3-ounce packages cream cheese	Lemon juice
2 tablespoons butter	Salt and pepper
1 tablespoon fresh parsley, chopped or dried	Thinly-sliced Pepperidge Farm whole wheat bread, cut into rounds

Drain grated radishes in colander and press out all liquid. Cream cheese and butter until fluffy; add grated radishes, parsley flakes, chives, lemon juice, salt and pepper. Spread mayonnaise on bread rounds, then spread radish-cream cheese filling. Top with 2nd bread round. Chill in Tupperware sandwich boxes until serving time. Garnish serving plate with parsley and radish roses.

To make radish roses:

Thinly slice stem end off radish. Make 6 thin slices to form petals almost down to root end. Put in ice water until petals open.

WATERCRESS SANDWICHES

Spread thin slices of de-crusted sandwich bread (white) with a soft mixture of mayonnaise and cream cheese (about half and half). Lay drained watercress sprigs on mixture. Add touch of salt, if needed. Very simple to do.

Marleah Hobbs (Mrs. Edward)

Marleah serves these at her punch parties for the Arts and Sciences faculty. They are delicious!

VEGETABLE SANDWICHES

2 medium cucumbers (not peeled)   1 green pepper
2 scallions or very small onions

Cut into blender. Blend to puree. Drain off juice.

2 carrots, grated, add to puree
1 package gelatin, dissolved in 2 tablespoons vegetable juice.

Heat in double boiler. Add to vegetable puree and carrots. Add 1 cup mayonnaise to vegetables. Salt and pepper to taste. Refrigerate overnight. Can be used as sandwich spread or dip for raw vegetables or crackers. Can be stored in refrigerator for long length of time.

Joanne Patton (Mrs. Ed)

WHIPPED CREAM TEA SANDWICHES

½ pint whipping cream   ½ cup finely chopped pecans
½ cup white raisins   ¼ cup preserved ginger

Whip cream and mix all ingredients together. Spread on white bread to make finger sandwiches.

DEVILED HAM CORNUCOPIAS

20 slices thin white bread, cut with round
   cookie cutter (2½ inches)

Flatten with rolling pin. Spread both sides of bread circles with salad dressing or mayonnaise. Roll into cornucopia shape, fasten with toothpick, taking care cornucopia does not collapse. Bake on ungreased cookie sheet, 350°, 12-15 minutes.

Filling:

3 tablespoons salad dressing, or mayonnaise
1 4½-ounce can deviled ham

2 hard-cooked eggs, chopped finely
1 tablespoon prepared mustard

Combine filling ingredients. Chill. Fill each cornucopia with 1 generous teaspoon of filling. Sprinkle with parsley or paprika.

Martha Applebee (Mrs. Frank)

(Martha serves these with cocktails and they are popular!)

LIBBA'S TOMATO SANDWICH

Cut rounds of thinly sliced bread with a cookie cutter. Cut small cherry tomatoes in slices in horizontal manner. Put round of tomato on top of the bread which has been mayonnaised. Put tiny piece of parsley in middle of tomato. (The bread bottom should be larger than the tomato slice so the white bread will show under it.)

Libba Lipscomb
Gazebo I

APPLE SANDWICH

Cut apples horizontally into thin slices. Add brown sugar, cinnamon (very little), and a dash of allspice to softened cream cheese to taste. Spread mixture between two slices of the apple.

Gazebo I

CREAM CHEESE 'N BACON APPETIZERS

4 ounces cream cheese, softened
1 tablespoon mayonnaise
⅓ cup crumbled crisp bacon

4 teaspoons finely chopped green onion
1 loaf sliced party rye bread
Paprika

Mix thoroughly the cream cheese, mayonnaise, bacon, and onion. Spread mixture on rye bread slices. Sprinkle tops lightly with paprika. Makes about 3 dozen open-face sandwiches.

LUNCHEON OR SUPPER SANDWICHES

SALMON LOAF

1 loaf French bread
2 small bunches parsley
8 ounces whipped butter

Grated onion to taste
7½-ounce can red or pink salmon
8 ounces whipped cream cheese

Cut bread in half lengthwise. Scoop out bread, leaving about a 1-inch thick shell. Put bread that is scooped out through food processor, or crumble to make crumbs and reserve. Remove stems from parsley and chop finely. Mix parsley, onion, butter and half the bread crumbs together and put in half of bread boat, slightly mounding in center. Mix salmon, cream cheese and other half of bread crumbs and put in other half of bread boat. Put loaf back together and press firmly so sides go back together. Wrap tightly in French bread bag or foil and refrigerate overnight. Slice thinly with electric knife and arrange in rows on serving plate. Decorate with parsley, carrot sticks, black olives and cherry tomatoes.

This sandwich was served at a fall luncheon of Holy Trinity Episcopal Churchwomen from a basket garnished as above. It really was wonderful looking and tasty too.

CAMEL-RIDER SANDWICHES

Slice round steak across the grain so that slices are 1½ inches long and ⅛ inch or less thick. Put 1 teaspoon margarine in skillet. Heat until butter melts. Over high heat, cook beef stirring constantly. Add 1 tablespoon soy sauce before meat is done. Stir until there is no liquid left in pan. Remove from heat. Split pieta bread in half. Open and layer with shredded lettuce, diced tomatoes, and meat. Pour low-calorie Italian dressing over sandwich and serve.

HOT CHICKEN SANDWICH

Cooked chicken, cut up
3 cups milk
8 thin slices English type cheddar cheese

1 teaspoon salt
16 slices bread (crust trimmed off)
Butter as needed

Butter all bread on both sides and put half into buttered baking dish. Place chicken pieces over 8 slices bread and cover each with a slice of cheese. Top with rest of bread. Mix other ingredients and pour over sandwiches. Cover baking dish and refrigerate *overnight*. Remove and allow to set at room temperature for about an hour. Bake, *uncovered,* at 250°, for 1½ hours. This has a delightful, different taste and can be made ahead of time.

Chris Danner (Mrs. Dan)

INSTRUCTOR'S SALARY SANDWICH

2 tablespoons butter or margarine
2 tablespoons all-purpose flour
¼ teaspoon salt
Dash freshly ground pepper
1 cup milk
1 slightly beaten egg
¾ cup (3 ounces) shredded natural cheddar cheese

1 tablespoon lemon juice
1 10-ounce package frozen broccoli, cooked and drained
6 slices white bread, toasted
6 slices bacon, crisp-cooked, drained, and crumbled

In saucepan, melt butter or margarine; blend in flour, salt, and pepper. Add milk all at once. Cook and stir till mixture thickens and bubbles. Stir a moderate amount of hot mixture into egg. Return all to saucepan and continue cooking till thickened. Remove from heat. Stir in cheese and lemon juice, stirring to melt cheese. Arrange cooked broccoli on split English muffins or toast, spoon lemon-cheese sauce over. Garnish with bacon. Makes 6 sandwiches.

This is a great luncheon dish served with fruit salad.

HAM AND CHEESE SANDWICHES, FRENCH TOASTED

1 egg
¼ cup milk
8 slices whole-wheat bread

4 slices Edam or Gouda cheese
4 slices ham
Butter or margarine

Beat egg and milk together in shallow dish or pie plate. Make 4 sandwiches with ham, cheese and bread; dip both sides in egg and milk mixture. Grill in hot well-buttered skillet or griddle over medium heat until golden brown on both sides. Serve at once.

SUPER HAM SANDWICH

½ cup margarine
½ cup flour
3 cups milk
2 egg yolks
1 pound thinly sliced ham
6 English muffins, toasted

½ cup cheddar cheese, grated
6 slices tomato
6 tablespoons butter
2 tablespoons brown sugar
6 slices bacon, cooked
½ cup mushrooms, sautéed

Make white sauce and season to taste. Gradually add a small amount to egg yolks, beating slowly. Then add this back to cream sauce. Stir over low heat until thickened. Put ham on muffins. Add some sauce. Put some grated cheese on top of this followed by a slice of tomato. Dot with margarine and sprinkle a little brown sugar over the tomato. Broil until cheese melts. Garnish with a strip of bacon and some mushrooms.

A great Sunday night supper.

PIZZA-WICHES

1 pound hamburger
2-3 onions
1 can tomato soup
½ cup salad oil

½ teaspoon oregano
1 teaspoon garlic salt
1 pound grated cheddar cheese
1 small can black olives, cut up

Brown meat with onions. Drain. Add rest of ingredients. Mix well. Spoon on slices of French bread and put under broiler until cheese melts. Freezes well.

CAROLYN LIPSCOMB'S HOT SHRIMP SANDWICHES

Boiled shrimp (finely chopped) (can use
   drained canned shrimp)

Cheddar cheese, grated
Mayonnaise

Mix equal parts finely chopped shrimp and grated cheese. Stir in mayonnaise to make spreading consistency. Spread on English muffins or halves of hamburger buns. Broil till bubbly and golden brown.

STUFFED HAM BUNS

Open finger rolls. Scoop out insides and spread with mixture of butter and French's mustard, creamed together. Blend ham and hard boiled egg together (use 1 or 2). Add India relish (to taste). Soften with mayonnaise if necessary. Stuff buns full. Place in hot oven and turn off heat. Let the buns stay long enough to get nice and hot.

Grace Jones (Mrs. Allen)

SALADS

SALADS

My salad days,
when I was green in judgment.

Cleopatra, in *Antony and Cleopatra* (I-v-19)

ASPARAGUS SALAD

½ cup liquid (drained from asparagus)
¼ cup white vinegar
½ cup sugar
¼ teaspoon salt
1 envelope gelatin

½ cup celery, chopped
½ cup pimento, chopped
½ cup pecans or almonds, chopped
1 cup green asparagus, cut up

Put liquid, vinegar, sugar and salt in saucepan and bring to boil. Soften gelatin in ¼ cup cold water. Add to boiling liquid. Remove from heat. Stir until completely dissolved. Let partially cool. Add remaining ingredients. Mold and refrigerate several hours or overnight.

AVOCADO MOLD

1½ envelopes plain gelatin
½ cup cold water
¾ cup boiling water
2 tablespoons lemon juice
1 teaspoon onion, grated

1¼ teaspoons salt
2 dashes Tabasco
2½ cups avocado, sieved
1 cup sour cream
1 cup mayonnaise

Soften gelatin in cold water for 4-5 minutes. Dissolve in boiling water. Add lemon juice, onion, salt, and Tabasco. Cool to room temperature and stir in avocado, sour cream, and mayonnaise. Pour into 6 cup ring mold. Chill until firm.

This is very nice filled with grapefruit or cherry tomatoes or chicken or shrimp salad.

AVOCADO-TOMATO ASPIC

Column A
3 cups V-8 juice
2 slices lemon
2 slices onion
Handful of celery tops
1 bay leaf

Column B
2 envelopes unflavored gelatin
½ teaspoon salt
Dash of pepper
1 teaspoon horseradish
1 or 2 avocados
1 cup chopped celery
12 large ripe olives

Combine items in Column A and simmer for ½ hour. Strain and add 2 envelopes of gelatin that has been softened in ½ cup of water for 5 minutes. Stir until dissolved. Season with salt, pepper and horseradish. Chill until syrupy. Peel and

74

dice avocado; add to syrup along with chopped celery and chopped ripe olives. Pour into large ring mold if served at buffet meal or in 8 individual molds if served at seated dinner. Chill overnight.

Marietta Kettunen

MILDRED PITTS' BUTTERMILK ASPIC

Soften 2 envelopes of Knox gelatin in ½ cup cold water at least 5 minutes. Add ½ cup boiling water and stir until gelatin is thoroughly dissolved. Cool. Mix 2 cups buttermilk, 2 teaspoons salt, 1 tablespoon lemon juice, 2 teaspoons sugar, ½ teaspoon Worcestershire sauce, 1 cup Heinz ketchup and 1 tablespoon grated onion. Add gelatin mixture and stir until well blended. Chill until syrup consistency. Fold in 1 cup of finely chopped celery. Chill in 1½-quart ring mold. Fill center of ring mold with cottage cheese and chives. Can be made days ahead. Serves 8.

MOLDED GAZPACHO

3 envelopes gelatin
3 cups V-8 juice
¼ cup tarragon vinegar
1 clove garlic, crushed
2 teaspoons salt
¼ teaspoon pepper

Dash of Tabasco
2 large tomatoes, chopped and drained
1 medium onion, finely chopped
¼ cup pimento chopped
1 large cucumber, chopped and drained

Dressing:
½ cup sour cream
½ teaspoon salt

⅓ cup mayonnaise
2 teaspoons horseradish

Heat 1 cup V-8 juice with the gelatin until completely dissolved. Add remaining juice, vinegar, garlic, 2 teaspoons salt, pepper and Tabasco. Cool mixture, then add tomatoes, onion, green pepper, cucumber, pimento and pour into a 6-cup mold that has been sprayed with Pam. Chill until set. Unmold on salad greens and top with dressing, or serve dressing on the side. Serves 8.

BEET SALAD (CONGEALED)

1 3-ounce package lemon jello   1 cup hot water

Dissolve the above ingredients. Chill until partially set. Add:

¾ cup beet liquid
2 tablespoons wine vinegar
¼ teaspoon salt
1½ cups canned beets, drained and diced
½ cup celery, chopped and also bell pepper, if preferred

1 teaspoon horseradish
1 teaspoon Worcestershire sauce
1 teaspoon onion, grated
4 drops Tabasco

Chill until firm

Caroline M. Draughon (Mrs. Ralph)

Very good in winter with pork chops and string beans or field peas.

MYSTERY SALAD

3 3-ounce packages raspberry gelatin
1¼ cups hot water
6 drops Tabasco

3 cans (1 pound each) stewed
tomatoes with onions and peppers

Dressing:
1 pint sour cream
1 tablespoon creamed horseradish

½ teaspoon salt
½ teaspoon sugar

Dissolve gelatin in water. Stir in tomatoes, breaking with spoon. Add Tabasco. Pour into lightly oiled 12-cup mold. Chill until firm. Put a spoon of dressing on top of each serving.

ASPARAGUS VINAIGRETTE

1 jar asparagus
½ cup salad oil
3 tablespoons vinegar
1 tablespoon onion, minced

1 tablespoon chopped sour pickle
1 teaspoon salt
¼ teaspoon pepper

Pour liquid off of asparagus and refill jar with other ingredients. Chill for several hours.

Joanne Patton (Mrs. Ed)

AVOCADO BACON SALAD

Juice of 2 limes
¼ cup vegetable oil
½ cup sour cream
¼ cup mayonnaise
Salt and pepper

2 cloves garlic, pressed
8 strips bacon, fried and crumbled
1 head lettuce, washed and torn into
bite-sized pieces
2 small avocados, cubed

Combine first 6 ingredients for dressing. Cook bacon, drain and crumble. Combine at serving time the lettuce, avocado and bacon. Toss gently with dressing. Tomato wedges are a nice addition or garnish to this salad.

CAULIFLOWER SALAD

1 medium head cauliflower
1 cup radishes, sliced
1 bunch green onions, sliced
4 stalks celery, sliced

1 cup sour cream
1 cup mayonnaise
1 tablespoon caraway seeds
1 package ranch dressing (dry)

Wash cauliflower and break into flowerets. Combine cauliflower, radishes, green onions and celery. Stir together the remaining ingredients and pour over the vegetables. Chill and serve.

SOUR CREAM CUCUMBERS

½ teaspoon salt
1 tablespoon sugar
2 tablespoons cider vinegar
1 cup sour cream

2 tablespoons chives, chopped
2 tablespoons fresh dill, chopped
1 teaspoon celery seed
2 firm cucumbers, unpeeled

Dissolve salt and sugar in vinegar; add sour cream and stir until smooth. Add chives, dill, and celery seed. Slice cucumbers paper thin and combine with dressing. Chill 1 hour or more. Makes 4-6 servings.

HERBED TOMATO SLICES

6 large tomatoes, peeled and thickly
   sliced
1 teaspoon salt
¼ teaspoon pepper
½ teaspoon dried thyme or marjoram

¼ cup snipped chives
¼ cup snipped parsley
⅔ cup salad oil
¼ cup tarragon vinegar

Put tomatoes in deep bowl. Sprinkle each layer of tomatoes with combined dry ingredients. Combine oil and vinegar, whisking vigorously to thicken. Pour over tomatoes, tilting bowl so all tomatoes are coated. Cover and chill 1 hour or more, occasionally spooning dressing over tomatoes. These also are good layered with purple onion rings.

VEGETABLE MEDLEY SALAD

2 yellow squash, sliced thinly
1 zucchini, sliced thinly
2 cups cauliflower buds
1 green pepper, cut in strips
2 cups whole green beans

1 head lettuce, pulled into chunks
¼ cup green onions, chopped
4 mushrooms, sliced
2 tomatoes, cut in wedges

Cook first 5 ingredients in saucepan until tender crisp, about 10 minutes. Place shredded lettuce in bottom of salad bowl. Arrange chilled cooked vegetables on top of lettuce, then onions, mushrooms and tomato wedges. Serve with blue cheese dressing. Serves 6. This can double as salad and vegetable.

COLD VEGETABLE SALAD I

1 can shoe peg corn (Green Giant)
1 can LeSeur peas
1 can French-style green beans
1 medium jar pimento, chopped
2 bell peppers, chopped
4 stalks celery, chopped

1 purple onion, chopped
¾ cup vinegar
¾ cup sugar
1 teaspoon black pepper
⅓ cup salad oil

Bring to boil last four ingredients. Cool. Pour over vegetables that have been thoroughly drained. Refrigerate.

COLD VEGETABLE SALAD II

1 package frozen broccoli
1 package frozen French-style beans
2 packages frozen cut asparagus, or 1 can

2 packages artichokes (I use only one can)
1 green pepper, sliced
1 cucumber, sliced thin

Cook frozen vegetables ½ time as on package or if using fresh vegetables, just steam ½ the time. Drain and chill. Add cucumber and green pepper.

Dressing:
¼ cup onion, finely chopped
3 teaspoons anchovy paste (I do not use this)
½ cup half and half cream
3 tablespoons lemon juice

2 tablespoons garlic vinegar (cut up garlic and let stand in vinegar)
1 cup mayonnaise
Salt and pepper to taste
Sprinkle with paprika

Pour dressing over vegetables and let stand overnight. Serves 8.

Joanne Patton (Mrs. Ed)

Try this. It is wonderful!

SALAD MERRILYN

The secret to a good salad is crisp greens, a good dressing, and using lots of different vegetables for an adventure in tastes and textures, and coating each piece with dressing by tossing well.

1 head lettuce   1 head romain

Clean, break into bite-sized pieces and drain. Put into pillowcase in refrigerator at least 1 hour ahead. Mix dressing. My favorite is Good Seasons Garlic or Italian. Some of the ingredients I like to use are: tomatoes, cucumber, raw zucchini, squash, green onions, purple onions, avocado slices, artichoke hearts, mushrooms, green pepper. I prepare some of these ahead so that all I have to do is toss with the lettuce and dressing at the last minute and sprinkle with salad crispins and Parmesan cheese, black pepper, and serve. If combining lettuce and vegetables ahead, put in the refrigerator and sprinkle the salad with lemon juice to keep it fresh. Don't put the dressing on until last minute.

Merrilyn Henry (Mrs. Robert)

LAYERED POTATO SALAD

8 medium red potatoes, scrubbed and
  boiled
1½ cups mayonnaise
1 cup sour cream
2½ teaspoons horseradish
½ teaspoon salt

½ cup chopped parsley (fresh)
½ cup celery, diced
½ cup green onions, chopped
1 pound bacon, fried, drained, and
  crumbled

Peel cooled potatoes and cut into thin slices into a bowl. In second bowl mix
chopped vegetables. In third bowl mix mayonnaise, sour cream, salt and horseradish. Into serving bowl (a straight-sided salad bowl is pretty), layer potatoes,
vegetable mixture, spread with dressing, then top with crumbled bacon. Continue layering until finished, sealing sides of bowl with dressing. Cover tightly and
refrigerate overnight. Just before serving, put parsley sprigs thickly around edge
of bowl and garnish with whole or quartered cherry tomatoes.

SOUR CREAM POTATO SALAD

6 medium potatoes, boiled in skins
1½ cups mayonnaise
1 cup sour cream
1½ teaspoons celery seed
1½ teaspoons horseradish

1 teaspoon salt
1 cup fresh parsley, chopped, or ½
  cup dried parsley flakes
1 cup spring onions, chopped

Peel cooled potatoes and cut in small pieces. Combine mayonnaise, sour cream,
celery seed, horseradish and salt. Mix parsley and onions. Layer potatoes,
onions, parsley and dressing. Refrigerate overnight. Mix before serving. Put on
lettuce leaves and garnish with tomato wedges and black olives, or with hard-
boiled egg quarters.

POTATO SALAD

No set amounts on this recipe. It is all according to taste and desired consistency.
Boil potatoes—cool and peel. Chop or cube potatoes. Add chopped dill pickle
and chopped onion that has been marinating in vinegar. Over all this pour a few
teaspoons of celery seed, ½ bottle (or more) of Good Season's salad dressing
mix that has been made with your own vinegar and oil, enough mayonnaise to
thoroughly moisten potatoes. Add salt, pepper, paprika, but keep tasting. Garnish can be hard-boiled egg slices and parsley sprigs.

Marleah Hobbs (Mrs. Ed)

POTATO SALAD

6 medium potatoes, peeled, boiled and
  cubed
1 medium onion, chopped

2 hard-boiled eggs, chopped
2 stalks celery, chopped

Blend dry ingredients together:

Sauce:
⅓ cup mayonnaise
1 teaspoon mustard
1 teaspoon celery salt

½ teaspoon white pepper
1 teaspoon salt

Blend with dry ingredients, refrigerate before serving. Serves 8.

Keith McPheeters

MARINATED POTATO SALAD

6 medium potatoes, cooked and diced
1 bottle Italian dressing
1 onion, finely chopped
1 cup mayonnaise
2 teaspoons Dijon mustard

2 hard-boiled eggs, chopped
1 teaspoon celery seed
½ cup celery, chopped
Salt and pepper

Marinate potatoes overnight in Italian dressing. Drain. Combine with other ingredients and chill until serving time. Serves 6-8.

RICE SALAD

¾ cup sour cream
⅓ cup Italian salad dressing
½ teaspoon each salt and pepper
⅓ cup onion, finely chopped
1 can cut green beans, drained

3 cups rice, cooked
⅓ cup cooked bacon, crumbled
3 small tomatoes, quartered, or box
  cherry tomatoes

Blend together sour cream, salad dressing and seasonings. Pour over onion, green beans, rice and bacon. Toss lightly. Chill. Spoon into salad bowl and garnish with cherry tomatoes. This is a good luncheon dish to serve with ham and biscuits.

TABBULI

1 cup cracked wheat
2 cups boiling water
2 cups peeled, diced tomatoes
1 cup finely chopped scallions
2 tablespoons chopped fresh mint, or 1
  teaspoon dry mint flakes, crumbled
1 cup finely chopped parsley

½ cup olive oil
½ cup lemon juice
2½ teaspoons salt
¼ teaspoon pepper
2 cucumbers, chopped
1 green pepper, chopped

Place cracked wheat into large bowl and pour boiling water over it, and allow to sit for at least 1 hour to soak. Drain excess water after an hour and add remaining ingredients. Chill and eat as salad.

MARINATED SLAW

1 head cabbage
1 large red onion, sliced into rings

1 large bell pepper, sliced into rings
1 cup sugar

Marinade:
1 tablespoon sugar
1 tablespoon salt
1 teaspoon celery seed
1 teaspoon dry mustard

½ cup white vinegar
½ cup water
¾ cup Wesson oil

Shred cabbage. In a large bowl put half of shredded cabbage. Put a layer of onion and pepper rings. Fill bowl with cabbage. Top with onion and pepper rings. Pour 1 cup of sugar over the top. (Don't stir.) In a small saucepan bring marinade to a boil. Pour liquid over cabbage. Don't stir. Cover tightly and cool to room temperature. Refrigerate at least six hours, or as long as needed. Stir well before serving.

Betsy Perry (Mrs. Kermit)

SWEDISH SLAW

1 head cabbage
1 small onion
1 cup vinegar
½ teaspoon tumeric
1 teaspoon salt

1 bell pepper
1 cup celery
1 cup sugar
½ teaspoon mustard seed

Boil sugar, vinegar, tumeric, mustard seed and salt. Let come to a boil. Pour over slaw while hot. Chill.

Donna Beardsworth (Mrs. Jimmy)

APPLE-CABBAGE SLAW

4 cups green cabbage, shredded
½ cup mayonnaise
4½ teaspoons sugar
4½ teaspoons fresh lemon juice
1 tablespoon milk

1 teaspoon celery seed
¾ teaspoon salt
⅛ teaspoon pepper
2 red apples, cored and chopped
   (sprinkle with lemon juice to prevent
   darkening)

To prepare cabbage, remove tough outer leaves and discard. Cut into quarters, cut out core and cut into thin shreds with a knife or shred on a coarse grater. In large bowl, blend mayonnaise with sugar, lemon juice, milk, celery seed, salt and pepper. Add cabbage and mix well. Chill several hours. Add apple just before serving. Make eight servings.

SPINACH SALAD

8 strips of bacon, cooked and crumbled
1 medium purple onion, sliced very thin

2 bunches spinach, washed and
  broken into pieces

Dressing:
½ cup salad oil
⅓ cup catsup
¼ cup vinegar

Dash of salt
⅓ cup sugar
1 can water chestnuts, sliced

Heat oil enough to melt sugar. Add all other ingredients and pour over spinach and toss. Serve cold.

Angie Dollar (Mrs. Mason)

SPINACH SALAD

Tear fresh spinach into bite-size pieces. Add sliced fresh mushrooms, bacon (crisply fried and crumbled), thinly sliced onion and sliced boiled eggs. Toss with dressing below and serve.

Dressing:
½ cup vegetable oil
¼ cup red wine vinegar

3 tablespoons lemon juice
1 teaspoon sugar

Betty Jean Pearce (Mrs. Duke, Jr.)

APRICOT RING MOLD

2 envelopes unflavored gelatin
½ cup sugar
⅛ teaspoon salt
2 cups apricot nectar

¾ cup water
1 cup white wine
1 cup sour cream

Combine first five ingredients in saucepan and stir over low heat until gelatin dissolves. Stir in wine and remove from heat. Stir sour cream until smooth then fold in gelatin mixture. Pour into 5-cup crown mold. Chill until set. Unmold onto salad greens and ring with cantaloupe and honeydew balls, mixed with canned chilled and drained pineapple chunks.

BLUEBERRY SALAD

2 packages grape jello
1 can crushed pineapple, large

1 can blueberry pie filling

Add 2 packages grape jello to 2 cups hot water and dissolve. Add 1 can crushed pineapple, *not* drained, and 1 can blueberry pie filling. Mix well and let congeal in a 9 x 13 pan or dish. Top with:

8-ounce package soft cream cheese   ½ cup sugar
½ pint sour cream

Blend well and add ½ cup chopped nuts, 1 teaspoon vanilla. Spread over gelatin and return to refrigerator. This makes a lot of servings and is so rich it could be served as a dessert.

Chris Danner (Mrs. Dan)

CRANBERRY MOLD
(made in the blender or food processor)

¼ cup cold water
1 envelope unflavored gelatin
1 3-ounce package cherry gelatin
1 cup boiling water

1 orange, seeded and peeled (white
   membrane removed)
Rind of 1 orange
1 1-pound can whole cranberry sauce

Put cold water into blender container. Add gelatins and boiling water. Cover and process on *stir* until dissolved. Push *grind* button, remove feeder cap and add orange and rind. Process until finely chopped. Remove feeder cap and add cranberry sauce. Process only until blended. Pour into 1-quart mold. Chill until firm. Unmold on bed of greens. Serves 6.

CRANBERRY SALAD

1 6-ounce package cherry jello
2 cups boiling water
1 can whole cranberry sauce

½ cup chopped pecans
1 cup sour cream

Dissolve gelatin in boiling water. Cool slightly. Add mashed cranberry sauce and mix well. Cool a little longer and add nuts and sour cream. Blend, leaving sour cream slightly streaked. Pour into mold and congeal in refrigerator.
    Quick, easy and delicious!

PORTWINE CRANBERRY MOLD

3-ounce package raspberry gelatin
¼ cup boiling water
1 large can crushed pineapple, undrained
1 large can whole berry cranberry sauce

¾ cup port wine
¾ cup chopped pecans
1 8-ounce package cream cheese
1 cup sour cream

Dissolve gelatin in boiling water, and stir in cranberry sauce which has been mashed with back of spoon, pineapple and wine. Chill until mixture is slightly thickened, fold in nuts and pour into 2-quart rectangular pyrex dish. Chill until firm. Soften cream cheese. Blend cream cheese and sour cream together until smooth and spread it over gelatin. Chill until serving time, cut into squares and serve on lettuce leaf.

Variation: Reserve pecans, parch them, and sprinkle them over the cream cheese just before serving.

FROZEN CRANBERRY SALAD

1 16-ounce can whole berry cranberry
  sauce
1 8¼-ounce can crushed unsweetened
  pineapple, drained

1 8-ounce carton sour cream
¼ cup confectioner's sugar, sifted

Mix all ingredients together and freeze in 8x8 pan. To serve, let stand 15 minutes and cut into squares. Serve on bed of lettuce.

Patti Tremaine (Mrs. Chuck)

CRANBERRY WINE SALAD

1 6-ounce package raspberry jello
1 16-ounce can cranberry sauce with
  whole berries
1 8½-ounce can crushed pineapple,
  undrained

½ cup burgundy or rosé wine
½ cup chopped pecans
1 3-ounce package cream cheese

Dissolve jello in 2 cups boiling water. Stir in mashed cranberry sauce, pineapple, and wine. Chill until partially set. Fold in nuts. Pour into oiled mold and congeal. Meanwhile freeze cream cheese. When salad is unmolded, grate frozen cream cheese over top as garnish. Serves 10-12.

FROSTY MELON MOLD

1 medium-sized honeydew or cantaloupe
3-ounce package raspberry jello
1 cup hot water

10-ounce package frozen raspberries
8-ounce package cream cheese
2 tablespoons milk

Peel the melon, cut a slice from one end, remove seeds and drain. Dissolve jello in hot water. Chill until it begins to congeal. Fold fruit into jello mixture and fill the melon. Chill until jello is firm. Blend milk with softened cream cheese until it is smooth, and frost the melon. Slice to serve. The jello and fruit may be varied to suit your taste. Mint leaves make a nice garnish.

Thelma Thomas says to be sure to choose very firm melons or the gelatin will separate from the melon.

GRAPEFRUIT-AVOCADO MOLD

2 envelopes unflavored gelatin
1 cup cold water
¾ teaspoon salt
¼ cup sugar
2 tablespoons lime juice

1 pint (2 cups) sour cream
1 tablespoon dried chives
2 cups grapefruit sections, with juice
1 large avocado, peeled

Sprinkle gelatin over cold water in saucepan. Place over low heat; stir constantly, until gelatin is dissolved. Add salt, sugar, lime juice, sour cream and chives. Beat with wire whisk or rotary beater until mixture is smooth. Pour small amount of gelatin mixture in bottom of 6-cup ring mold; place about 3 grapefruit sections and 3 avocado sections in mold; chill until almost firm. Cut up the remaining grapefruit sections and dice the avocado. Add grapefruit with juice and avocado to gelatin mixture. Chill until slightly thickened. Carefully spoon gelatin-fruit mixture over the fruit in ring mold. Chill several hours or overnight. Serve with additional grapefruit sections.

PEACH PICKLE SALAD MOLD

2 packages orange or lemon-flavored
  gelatin
2 large jars or cans spiced peaches
2 cans white seedless grapes, drained

1 #2 can pineapple tidbits, well
  drained
1 cup chopped almonds

Bring to boil, 2½ cups pickle juice and stir in the fruit-flavored gelatin. Set aside to cool. Cut peaches into bite-sized bits; add these with grapes and pineapple to above mixture. At room temperature, stir in almonds, and ladle into 1 large and 1 small mold.

TEA ROOM SALAD

1 large can crushed pineapple
1 large box peach jello

9 ounces cool whip
2 cups buttermilk

Bring pineapple to a boil. Remove from heat and stir in gelatin. Let cool. Stir in cool whip and buttermilk. Chill in small ring or 9-inch square pan. Refrigerate until set.

EASTER EGG SALAD

Several weeks before Easter, start saving your egg shells and egg cartons from the grocery store. To get eggs out, punch a hole larger than the ones you have to do when you are blowing eggs, but don't make the holes too large. When the eggs are out of the shell, wash out the shell and put it back into the carton.

A couple of days before Easter, make up a batch of any flavor gelatin. Pour enough gelatin into each egg to cover about the bottom fourth of the egg. After you think this gelatin is set enough for you to pour another kind in, do that. Repeat with different colors as much as you like or you can stick with one color and the effect will be almost as good. Serve on Easter Sunday on a bed of shredded lettuce. Even the big kids will love these colorful Easter eggs when served on a lettuce "nest."

You can get fancy if you want to and fill a decorator tube with a colored cream cheese and decorate the eggs even more.

Gazebo I

MARY TIMBERLAKE'S FRUIT IN MELON BASKETS

Watermelon
Cantaloupe
Honey dew melon

Canned pineapple chunks, drained
1 can lemonade concentrate,
  undiluted, thawed

Cut watermelon into basket and scoop out red part of melon. With melon baller, cut melons into balls and put into large bowl. Add drained pineapple chunks. Stir in lemonade concentrate and refrigerate until serving time. Pile melon balls into basket and garnish with mint. This is also nice to use as an hors d'oeuvre with picks to spear the balls.

Variation: Serve the salad in scooped out pineapple halves. Substitute the fresh pineapple for the canned.

CANDIED APPLE SALAD

6 cooking apples
1 cup sugar

½ cup water
1 package red hots

Filling:
3 ounces cream cheese
½ cup pecans, finely chopped
½ cup white raisins, finely chopped

¼ teaspoon lemon juice
¼ teaspoon zest of lemon
Milk

In saucepan boil sugar, water and candy until candy melts. Meanwhile, peel and core apples. Boil 2 or 3 apples at a time on medium heat until apples are tender. Place in flat pyrex dish and pour over remaining syrup to glaze apples. Cool. Beat cream cheese with milk until fluffy. Add lemon juice, lemon zest, nuts, and raisins and stir until well mixed. Stuff apples and refrigerate until serving time.

SHERRY PEACH SALAD

¼ cup fresh lemon juice
3 or 4 tablespoons sugar
¼ cup dry sherry
3 medium peaches, peeled and sliced

2 bananas, sliced
1 cup seedless grapes
½ cup blueberries

Combine lemon juice, sugar and sherry and stir until sugar is dissolved. Add fruit, toss gently. Cover, refrigerate until served. A refreshing summer salad which may also be used as a dessert.

Dean Hays (Mrs. Kirby)

Dean has served this at a luncheon with chicken salad pie.

PASTEL PARADISE

3 lettuce leaves
1 scoop fruit flavored frozen yogurt
2 tablespoons sliced orange
2 tablespoons sliced strawberries
2 tablespoons sliced grapefruit

2 tablespoons sliced apples
2 tablespoons sliced grapes
2 tablespoons sliced bananas
1 tablespoon coconut
1 tablespoon chopped pecans

Arrange lettuce on luncheon plate. Place frozen yogurt in center. Top with fruit. Sprinkle with coconut and nuts. Serve immediately. Increase recipe as needed. Serves 1.

Donna C. Burchfield (Mrs. Ron)

TWENTY-FOUR HOUR SALAD WITH FRUIT

Cook in a double boiler until thick, stirring constantly:

2 eggs	¼ cup lemon juice
½ cup heavy cream	One pinch salt
¼ cup sugar	

Cool, then add:

2 cans pineapple chunks, drained	1 package mini marshmallows (white only)
2 cans mandarin orange segments, drained	1 12-ounce carton cool whip

Mix well and refrigerate for 24 hours. May be used as either salad or dessert. Serves 16-20.

Pat Jemian (Mrs. Wartan)

The Jemians serve this at their homecoming barbecue for former students.

FROZEN FRUIT SALAD

1 tablespoon gelatin	*2 bananas, diced
¼ cup cold water	3 tablespoons lemon juice
*1 cup pineapple, diced	½ cup sugar
*1 cup apricots, diced	1 cup mayonnaise
*1 cup peaches, diced	1 cup whipped cream
*or your choice of fruit	

Soak gelatin in water for 5 minutes. Dissolve over hot water. Combine fruit, lemon juice and sugar. Stir in dissolved gelatin and chill. As mixture begins to congeal, fold in whipped cream and mayonnaise. Freeze in refrigerator tray or individual molds. Cut into squares or unmold individual molds and serve on lettuce leaf. Serves 8.

PAELLA SALAD

1½ cups saffron rice, uncooked	1½ teaspoons salt
4 whole chicken breasts, skinned and boned	1 pound shrimp, peeled and deveined
6 tablespoons olive or vegetable oil	1 small onion, grated
¼ cup white wine	1 garlic clove, crushed
	1 cup pitted ripe olives

Sauce:

¾ cup mayonnaise	1 teaspoon lemon juice (or more to taste)
1 tablespoon brandy (or more to taste)	

Cook rice, cool. In skillet, cook chicken in 3 tablespoons oil for about 5 minutes, coating each piece well. Add wine. Sprinkle chicken with salt. Simmer 15 minutes. Turn chicken and add shrimp. Simmer uncovered 10 more minutes until shrimp turns pink. Remove and set aside. In same skillet sauté onion and garlic in remaining oil until tender. Add onion and garlic to rice. Cut chicken into bite-sized pieces. Add shrimp, chicken, and olives to rice. Chill. Garnish with tomato wedges and serve with sauce. Serves 6-8.

FISH SALAD

2 cups of cooked, deboned fish (tilapia, carp suitable)
2 tablespoons lemon juice

2 cooked potatoes
¼ cup of mayonnaise or salad dressing
1 small onion or chives

1. Mix the lemon juice with the mayonnaise.
2. Cut the potatoes into small pieces and add to the fish.
3. Add chopped onion or chives and mayonnaise to fish. Season with salt to taste. Mix gently.
4. Decorate a plate with lettuce and place the mixture in a mound. Tomato slices, parsley, olives and boiled egg slices make a nice garnish.
Serve chilled.
This recipe is often served at Fisheries Department gatherings.

MACARONI-CRABMEAT SALAD

1 8-ounce package shell macaroni
1 6½-ounce can crab, drained (I like 2 cans better)
½ cup celery
1 small onion
2 hard-cooked eggs, chopped
3 slices bacon, crumbled

½ cup mayonnaise
1 tablespoon sweet relish
1½ teaspoons lemon juice
½ teaspoon salt
¼ teaspoon parsley
¼ teaspoon pepper

Cook macaroni, drain, cool. Add remaining ingredients. Chill at least 2 hours. Makes 8-10 generous servings.

Bobbie Umbach (Mrs. Arnold)

LAN'S FAVORITE CARROT-SHRIMP SALAD

2 cups boiled shrimp, cut in bite-sized pieces
3 cups carrots, grated
4 hard-boiled eggs, chopped
1 tablespoon onion, grated

1 cup mayonnaise
Salt and pepper to taste
1 teaspoon mustard
⅓ cup lemon juice (bottled or fresh)

Combine all ingredients and serve on a bed of lettuce. Garnish with wedges of tomatoes and hard-boiled eggs. Serves 8.

Carolyn Ellis Lipscomb (Mrs. Lan)

CURRIED SHRIMP SALAD

2 packages (1 pound) frozen, peeled and deveined shrimp
2 teaspoons salt
Juice of half a lemon
1 bay leaf
2 to 3 whole peppercorns or dash of freshly ground black pepper

1 cup mayonnaise
2 teaspoons curry powder
2 teaspoons soy sauce
3 tablespoons green onion, minced
½ cup celery, minced
Cherry tomatoes
Whole black olives

Cook shrimp according to package directions, adding salt, lemon juice, bay leaf and peppercorns. Drain and cool; then chill. Mix together mayonnaise, curry powder and soy sauce. Chill. When ready to serve, combine chilled shrimp, green onion and celery. Add mayonnaise mixture and toss lightly. Garnish with tomatoes and whole black olives.

CRABMEAT SALAD OR HORS D'OEUVRE RING

1 envelope plain gelatin
¼ cup cold water
3 ounces cream cheese
1 can mushroom soup
1 small onion, grated
1 tablespoon lemon juice

1 tablespoon Worcestershire sauce
½ teaspoon salt
1 cup mayonnaise
1 cup celery, finely cut
1 10-ounce can fresh crabmeat, or 2 cans canned

Soften gelatin in water. Heat next 5 ingredients until softened and blend well. Remove from heat and stir in gelatin until dissolved. Cool. Check crabmeat for shells and add to soup mixture with remaining ingredients. Pour into 1½-quart mold or individual molds.

As hors d'oeuvre: fill center of ring with cherry tomatoes and surround with parsley. Serve with crackers.

As salad: serve on lettuce leaf on slice of cranberry sauce.

CHINESE CHICKEN SALAD

1 3-pound chicken
Gently simmer in water and cover until tender.

3 green onions
2 teaspoons salt

Cool in broth. Then remove skin and bones and return them to one pot and gently boil down stock to 6 cups. Strain and then either use for soup or freeze for later use. Shred meat and refrigerate.

½ pound fresh bean sprouts

4 green onions, finely shredded

Remove yellow sprout ends, if you have the patience. I use canned bean sprouts, drained. When ready to serve, mix chicken, onion, sprouts and toss with sauce.

Sauce:
8 teaspoons soy sauce
2 teaspoons sesame seed oil
2 tablespoons hot pepper oil

2 teaspoons white vinegar
1 clove garlic, minced

Serve immediately on bed of finely shredded lettuce; garnished with more shredded green onion tops.

Sesame seed oil and hot chili pepper oil can be bought in a Chinese grocery store. There is one in Columbus, GA and in Atlanta.

Ursula Higgins

GREENHOUSE CHICKEN SALAD

12 whole chicken breasts

Simmer, covered, in water to cover with 2 tablespoons salt and 1 onion, quartered, until tender, about 30-40 minutes. Cool in stock. Remove skin and bones and chop or shred.

1 cup oil
⅓ cup tarragon vinegar

3 green onions, diced
2 teaspoons salt

Mix and marinate chicken overnight in refrigerator.

6 cups thinly sliced chicken
1½ cups Hellman's mayonnaise
1 teaspoon white pepper

1 cup sour cream
1 tablespoon salt

Add the next day. On leaf lettuce-lined luncheon plate, place 4 slices of cantaloupe with chicken salad in center. Surround with wedges of watermelon, fresh pineapple, grapes and strawberries. Makes 25 servings.

This is the Greenhouse summer specialty.

CHICKEN SALAD PIE

1 9-inch pie shell, baked and cooled
2 cups cooked chicken, chopped
¾ cup American cheese, shredded
½ cup celery, diced
½ cup crushed pineapple, drained
½ cup pecans, chopped

½ teaspoon paprika
½ teaspoon salt
¾ cup mayonnaise
½ cup whipping cream
Carrots, shredded

Combine first 7 ingredients and ½ cup mayonaise. Put into pie shell. Whip cream carefully by hand. Fold in remaining ¼ cup mayonnaise. Spread on pie. Garnish with carrots. Chill for 3 hours or overnight. Serves 6.

Jean Cox (Mrs. Grady)

Jean has served this on many different occasions, including luncheons for brides, new faculty wives and department heads' wives in the School of Engineering and most recently at a luncheon for the Deans' wives at Auburn University.

MUSHROOM LOVERS' CHICKEN SALAD

1 chicken, cooked with a few stalks of celery and an onion

½ pound mushrooms sautéed in 3 tablespoons butter

Debone chicken and cut into cubes. Add mushrooms and butter. Add enough salad dressing to make the salad creamy. Add mustard. Refrigerate.

CHICKEN CARROT SALAD

1 tablespoon lemon juice
1 cup mayonnaise
2 cups diced cooked chicken
1 cup carrot, shredded
¾ cup celery, diced

½ cup slivered blanched almonds
1 tablespoon onion, grated
Salt
Lettuce

Stir lemon juice into mayonnaise. Toss with chicken, carrot, celery, almonds, onion and salt. Chill. Serve in lettuce cups. Makes 4 servings.

BRAZILIAN SALAD

1 large bunch spinach or red tipped lettuce
2 cans (small) tuna, drained
1¼ cups celery, thinly sliced
1¼ cups juliene cut green pepper
6 green onions, thinly sliced
¼ cup parsley, finely chopped
¾ cup oil (olive preferred)
¼ cup fresh lime juice

1 teaspoon lime rind, grated
1 teaspoon sugar
¾ teaspoon ground cumin
⅛ teaspoon cayenne pepper
Salt to taste
3 bananas
¼ cup salted peanuts, chopped
¼ cup fresh coconut, shredded

Clean greens and break into pieces. Combine tuna, celery, green pepper, onions, and parsley. In another bowl, mix oil, lime juice and rind, cumin, cayenne pepper and salt. Pour over tuna mixture. Toss. Chill 1 hour or overnight Line 6 plates with greens. Mound with tuna mixture. Surround each plate with ½ sliced banana, thinly sliced. Sprinkle with peanuts and coconut. Makes an unusual luncheon dish. Serves 6.

Donna C. Burchfield (Mrs. Ron)

TUNA SALAD

1 6½-ounce can white chunk tuna in spring water (stir thoroughly until uniform)

2 green onions, including stems, chopped fine

1 stalk celery, chopped fine

6 small pimento stuffed olives, chopped fine

2 tablespoons mayonnaise

Blend all ingredients. Serves 2 as tomato filling or for sandwiches.

Keith McPheeters' original receipe

FISHERMAN'S WHARF AVOCADO SALAD

1 package chicken flavored Rice-a-Roni
2 tablespoons wine vinegar
2 tablepsoon lemon juice
1 tablespoon sugar
½ teaspoon garlic salt

1 cup tomato, diced
½ cup celery, diced
¼ cup green onion, sliced
1 7-ounce can white albacore tuna, drained
3 ripe avocados

Prepare rice accoridng to package directions. Combine vinegar, lemon, garlic and sugar. Toss this mixture with rice and all remaining ingredients, and chill. Peel avocados and fill each half with rice/tuna mixture. Serve on bed of lettuce. Serves 6.

Jean Bullock (Mrs. Bill)

SPANISH SEAFOOD SALAD

½ cup olive oil
¼ cup wine vinegar
1 clove garlic, minced
½ teaspoon salt
⅛ teaspoon pepper
1 pound raw shrimp in the shell, cooked, shelled and cleaned or ¾ pound packaged frozen shrimp, cooked

½ pound scallops, cooked
1 can (7 ounces) tuna, drained and separated into chunks
1 can (7¾ ounces) crabmeat, drained (optional)
2 ripe tomatoes, cut in wedges
2 onions, sliced and separated into rings

"THE BEST" TOMATO MARINADE

4 to 5 tomatoes
½ cup salad oil
3 tablespoon vinegar
1 teaspoon Worcestershire sauce
¾ teaspoon salt

1 tablespoon sugar
⅛ teaspoon pepper
½ clove garlic, minced
1 teaspoon sweet basil
2 tablespoons green onions, chopped

Peel and wedge or slice tomatoes. Combine all ingredients and pour over tomatoes. Sprinkle chopped parsley over and refrigerate for at least 1 hour.

Mary Christiansen (Mrs. Dan)

TOMATO DRESSING

3 whole green onions, minced
3 sprigs parsley, chopped
2 large tomatoes, diced

¼ cup Parmesan cheese
1 tablespoon vinegar
1 cup sour cream

Combine all ingredients and refrigerate at least 1 hour before using. Great with fresh, raw summer vegetables.

POTATO SALAD DRESSING

¼ cup vinegar
¼ cup sugar

Heat to boiling point.

1 tablespoon mustard
Salt and pepper

¼ cup water
2 eggs, well beaten

Add to eggs a little of above mixture first. Stir, then add balance of above mixture. Return to heat and cook until thickened. Add 4 to 5 tablespoons salad dressing (Miracle Whip) and stir well. Yield: ½ gallon potato salad.

Frances Steagall (Mrs. Henry)

BLUE CHEESE OR ROQUEFORT DRESSING

1 cup blue cheese or roquefort
1 cup mayonnaise
¼ cup vinegar

2 tablespoons sugar
½ cup sour cream
1 clove garlic, minced

Beat until fluffy.

POPPY SEED DRESSING

¾ cup sugar
1 teaspoon dry mustard
1 teaspoon salt
⅓ cup cider vinegar

1 tablespoon onion juice
1 cup salad oil
1½ tablespoons poppy seed

In a medium bowl combine sugar, mustard, salt, vinegar and onion juice. Use electric mixer and gradualy beat in oil until mixture is thick and smooth. Stir in poppy seed. Store, covered in refrigerator. This dressing is good with any fruit salad.

Merrilyn Henry (Mrs. Robert)

UNIVERSITY CHAPEL

EGGS, CHEESE, PASTA

They are up already, and call for eggs and butter.
1-*Henry IV* (II-i-59/60)

UNIVERSITY CHAPEL

Built in 1850-51 as a Presbyterian Church, it served during the 19th century also as Civil War Hospital, and as a college classroom building after the "Old Main" burned in 1887. For a few years after WWI it became the "Y Hut" or community YMCA; and, after coming into possession of the college, became the "Little Theater," serving as home for the drama department for some 40 years. Under a restoration design by Professor Nicholas Davis, the building was returned to its original religious purpose in 1974 when it was designated as the University Chapel.

EGGS, CHEESE & PASTA

ASPARAGUS DEVILED EGGS

8 hard-cooked eggs
3 tablespoons mayonnaise
3 teaspoons grated lemon rind
½ teaspoon curry powder

¼ teaspoon dry mustard
16 asparagus tips
Salt to taste

Hard cook eggs. Cut lengthwise, scoop out and mash yolks. Add mayonnaise, lemon rind, salt, curry powder, and mustard. Correct seasoning and fill egg whites with mixture. Garnish with asparagus tips. Serves 8.

DEVILED HAM AND EGGS FOR BRUNCH

3 cans green asparagus pieces, drained
12 hard-boiled eggs
3 2¼-ounce cans deviled ham
1 teaspoon dry mustard
½ teaspoon red pepper
2 teaspoons grated onion

6 tablespoons butter
6 tablespoons flour
3 cups half and half
2 cups grated medium sharp cheddar
1 teaspoon Worcestershire sauce
1 cup buttered bread crumbs

Drain asparagus and place in buttered casserole dish. Slice eggs in half lengthwise and remove yolks. Mash yolks with onion, dry mustard, red pepper and deviled ham. Stuff egg whites with this mixture and arrange on top of asparagus. Make a white sauce with butter, flour and half and half. Add cheese to white sauce, stir until melted. Pour over eggs and asparagus. Cover with bread crumbs and bake at 400° for 20 minutes. May be made the night before and heated just before serving.

This recipe has been a lifesaver for brunches, overnight company, and lake weekends.

EGG PUFF

10 eggs, separated
1 cup sour cream
1 teaspoon salt

4 tablespoons butter or margarine
Grated cheddar cheese

Beat yolks until thick. Beat in salt and sour cream. Beat whites until just thick. Fold whites into yolks, melt butter in soufflé dish in 325° oven, then pour mixture into dish. Sprinkle grated cheese over top. Bake 20 minutes. Serves 8.

97

EGGS PORTUGAL

1½ pounds skinless sausages, cut in thirds
8 slices crustless white bread, cubed
¾ pound grated cheddar cheese

4 eggs
2½ cups milk
Dash salt
¾ tablespoon mustard

1 can mushroom soup
¼ cup vermouth

1 small can mushroom pieces

Cut sausage and brown. Put bread cubes in 9x13 casserole. Put cheese over bread and then add sausage over cheese. Beat eggs, milk, salt and mustard. Pour over ingredients in casserole. Cover and refrigerate overnight. Mix mushrooms, mushroom soup and vermouth. Pour over casserole. Cook at 350° for 1 hour. Serve with Danish, fruit and champagne.

Joanne McLaughlin (Mrs. Wayne)

MUSHROOM FRITTATA

3 tablespoons vegetable oil
1 small onion, thinly sliced
½ pound fresh firm mushrooms, thinly sliced
6 eggs

2 tablespoons fresh parsley, chopped
½ cup Swiss cheese, grated
½ teaspoon salt
¼ teaspoon white pepper

Heat oil in frying pan. Add onion and sauté until soft. Add mushrooms and sauté 4 more minutes. Beat eggs with parsley, cheese, salt and pepper. Pour mixture over mushrooms and onions and cook while stirring until the mixture begins to set. Remove pan from heat and place a plate upside down over frittata. Turn frittata onto plate and slip frittata, cooked side up from plate into frying pan and cook 3 more minutes. Serves 4.

SAUSAGE AND EGG CASSEROLE

6 slices bread—butter generously and cube
5-6 ounces medium cheddar cheese, grated

12-16 ounces sausage, browned and drained

In 9x13 pan layer bread, sausage and cheese. Pour this over:
1 teaspoon salt, ½ teaspoon dry mustard, 2 cups half and half, and 5 beaten eggs. (Beat all these ingredients.) Refrigerate overnight. Bake 45-60 minutes at 350°, uncovered.

Edie Irwin (Mrs. Dave)

SCRAMBLED EGG CASSEROLE

First make cheese sauce as directed below:

2 tablespoons butter or margarine	1/8 teaspoon pepper
2 1/2 tablespons all-purpose flour	1 cup shredded processed American
2 cups milk	cheese or we use cheddar most of
1/2 teaspoon salt	the time

Melt butter in heavy saucepan on low heat. Blend in flour; cook one minute. Gradually, add milk. Cook over medium heat. (Stir constantly.) Add salt, pepper, and cheese, stirring until the cheese melts and mixture is smooth. Keep warm. This is added to the recipe below:

1 cup cubed ham (or bacon or sausage)	1/4 cup melted butter
1/4 cup chopped green onions	2 1/4 cups soft bread crumbs
3 tablespoons melted butter	1/8 teaspoon paprika
1 can sliced mushrooms, drained	1 dozen eggs, beaten

Sauté meat and green onion in 3 tablespoons butter in big skillet until onion is tender. Add eggs, and cook over medium high heat, stirring so big, soft curds will form as when you are scrambling eggs. When eggs are set, stir in mushrooms and cheese sauce. Spoon egg mixture into a greased 9x13x2 baking pan. Combine 1/4 cup melted butter and crumbs; mix well. Spread on top of the egg mixture. Sprinkle with paprika. Cover. Chill overnight if desired. Uncover and bake at 350° for about 30 minutes or until heated thoroughly. 12-15 servings.

This is served at bridal brunches at the Gazebo.

PEPPERED EGGS AND SALMON

1 1-pound can salmon, drained	1/2 teaspoon salt
3 strips bacon, cooked, drained and	1/4 teaspoon cayenne pepper
crumbled	6 eggs, lightly beaten
2 tablespoons butter	1/4 cup light cream
1/2 cup green onions with tops, chopped	1 teaspoon Worcestershire sauce
1 green pepper, diced	

Flake salmon. Melt butter in chafing dish. Add onions and green pepper; sauté until onions are transparent. Add seasonings and salmon. Combine eggs, cream and Worcestershire sauce. Add to salmon mixture; cook over moderate heat, stirring constantly until eggs are just set but still creamy. Sprinkle with bacon.

Devon Luther (Mrs. William A.)

(The Luthers serve this dish at large brunches before football games.)

BASIC FRENCH (PLAIN) OMELET
(1 serving)

Multiply the recipe for as many servings as you need and use 1/2 cup of the egg mixture for each 2-egg omelet. For a sweet dessert omelet, substitute a pinch of sugar for the salt and pepper.

2 eggs
2 tablespoons water
⅛ to ¼ teaspoon salt

Dash pepper
1 tablespoon butter

Mix eggs, water, salt and pepper until blended. Heat butter in a 7- to 10-inch omelet pan or skillet over medium-high heat until just hot enough to sizzle a drop of water. Pour in egg mixture. (Mixture should immediately set at edges.) With an inverted pancake turner, carefully push cooked portion at edges toward center, so uncooked portion can flow to hot pan surface. Tilt skillet as it is necessary to hasten flow of uncooked eggs. While top is still moist and creamy looking, fill if desired. With pancake turner, fold omelet in half or roll, and invert onto plate with a quick flip of the wrist or slide from pan to plate.

Filling: We use one, a combination, or all of the following fillings for our omelet supper: grated cheddar cheese, bell pepper, ham, mushrooms (well-drained, if canned), and freeze-dried chopped chives.

For dessert:

PEACHES AND CREAM OMELET
(1 serving)

1 French or plain omelet
1 1-pound can sliced peaches, well-
  drained
¼ cup sour cream

1½ teaspoons confectioner's sugar,
  optional
2 tablespoons brandy, 70 proof,
  optional

To serve, spread half of sour cream on omelet. Place peach slices on omelet. Fold in half. Spread remaining sour cream on top. Garnish with a few peach slices.

To flambé: Dust with confectioner's sugar; pour brandy over omelet. With long-stemmed fireplace match, carefully light, tilting pan so brandy will burn out. Serve immediately from pan.

Jane Brewer (Mrs. Robert)

(Jane and Robert Brewer entertain the Poultry Science students at an annual omelet supper at their home. Jane spends hours and hours ahead of time chopping the ingredients for the fillings of the omelets. A typical assortment includes: onion, mushrooms, cheeses, ham, turkey, olives, tomatoes, bell peppers, shrimp, bacon, sausage, sour cream, bean sprouts. For dessert omelets, the fillings may include: jellies, jams, sweetened berries and fruits, sour cream, whipped cream, shaved chocolate, nuts, coconut. Jane makes pitchers of egg mixture and has it waiting in the refrigerator. As students arrive, they are taught to make their own omelets, adding the ingredients they prefer for the filling. When each finishes a masterpiece, he serves himself to tossed salad, cheese grits casserole, and toasty muffins and finds a place in the Brewer's large home to eat. Later, he returns to try a different combination of stuffings, or to prepare a sweet dessert omelet. The omelets are made on small, portable gas burners with omelet pans placed on the kitchen counter or on the round kitchen table.)

GARLIC CHEESE GRITS

1 cup grits, cooked in 4 cups salted water   3 eggs
1 roll garlic cheese   1 stick margarine, melted

Cook grits. Add garlic cheese. Allow to cool. Beat eggs and add to cooled grits. Mix well, adding melted margarine. Save a little margarine to pour on top. Place in casserole and bake 45 minutes at 350° until firm but not dry. Can be made a day ahead but do not cook until ready to serve. Serves 6-8.

CHEESE GRITS

Quaker Quick Grits (doubled recipe on
   box serves 18-20)

Follow directions, doubled for 6 servings. After grits are ready, drop in 1 egg and stir until mixed. Add:

1 stick butter   1 10-ounce medium cheddar cheese

Stir until melted.

Edie Irwin (Mrs. Dave)

(This was served at a brunch honoring new members of the Electrical Engineering faculty.)

CHEESE CREPES FOR BRUNCH

1 stick butter or margarine
½ to ¾ cup flour (all-purpose)
2 cups milk
1/3 to 1/2 cup cheese (Swiss or Gruyère)
Prepared crepes
Pinch of salt, pepper and cayenne
3 egg yolks
1 whole egg plus 1 tablespoon water, beaten
Seasoned bread crumbs

Stir flour and butter together for 5 minutes as you would in making a white sauce. Gradually add milk and stir with a whisk until thick and smooth. Add cheese and continue stirring over low heat until cheese is melted. Add seasonings. Remove from heat and beat in egg yolks. Pour this mixture into an oiled dish and allow to cool in refrigerator. When ready, cut mixture into rectangles about 3 inches by 1 inch. Fold each crepe around a cheese rectangle and dip cheese crepes into beaten egg and roll in bread crumbs. Fry in deep fat until golden brown.

CHEESE STRATA

6 slices buttered stale bread (take crust
   off and cube in ½-inch cubes)
1 pound New York cheese (grated)
6 eggs slightly beaten
2½ cups milk
1 teaspoon sugar
¼ teaspoon paprika
½ teaspoon oregano
½ teaspoon salt
½ teaspoon dry mustard
1 teaspoon minced onion flakes
1 teaspoon Lea and Perrins
Cracked pepper to taste

Grate cheese. In a large buttered casserole put bread and cheese in alternate layers. Add seasoning to milk and eggs and pour over bread and cheese. Refrigerate for 24 hours. Bake in a pan of water at 325° about 45 minutes or until "set." Don't overcook. Serve as soon as possible. Serves 12-16. (CAUTION: Fill casserole only ⅔ full to prevent disaster!)

Jonnie Dee Little (Mrs. Ted)

Peace, peace; this piece of toasted cheese will do't.

King Lear (IV-vi-89)

CHEESE SOUFFLÉ

3 tablespoons oleo
3 tablespoons flour
½ teaspoon salt
1 cup milk

½ cup grated cheese
3 eggs
Few grains cayenne pepper

Melt oleo and add flour, making a smooth paste. Scald milk and add salt and cayenne pepper. Add this to first mixture and cook until thick and smooth. Add cheese and remove from fire. Add well-beaten egg yolks. Cool mixture and fold in egg whites beaten until stiff. Pour into buttered baking dish and bake 20 minutes in moderate oven.

Ethel Carrington (Mrs. Jack)

(Very, very good. Ethel's whole family agrees.)

PIMENTO-CHEESE SOUFFLÉ

6 tablespoons butter or margarine
6 tablespoons flour
1 teaspoon salt
⅛ teaspoon dry mustard
Dash of cayenne
1½ cups milk

1½ cups shredded cheddar or colby
  cheese (6 ounces)
1 jar (4 to 6 ounces) pimentos,
  drained and chopped
6 eggs, separated

In medium saucepan melt butter. Blend in flour, salt, mustard and cayenne. Gradually stir in milk; stir over medium heat until mixture thickens and begins to boil. Stir in cheese and pimentos until cheese melts; set aside. In large bowl of mixer beat egg whites until stiff but not dry; set aside. In small bowl beat yolks until thick and lemon-colored. Stir cheese mixture into yolks and blend thoroughly. Pour slowly over egg whites; fold in quickly and lightly. Pour into 2-quart soufflé dish. Bake in preheated 350° oven 45 minutes or until puffed and golden and knife inserted in center comes out clean. Serve at once. Makes 6 servings.

APPLE AND SAUSAGE QUICHE

½ pound bulk sausage
½ cup chopped fresh onion
¼ teaspoon dried leaf thyme
2 apples, pared, cored and cut into ½-inch cubes (1½ cups)
1 tablespoon fresh lemon juice

1 tablespoon sugar
½ cup (2 ounces) shredded cheddar cheese
4 eggs, beaten
2 cups light cream
Pastry for single-crust 9-inch pie

In large skillet cook sausage, onion and thyme until sausage is browned and onion is tender, about 10 minutes. Remove from heat; drain off excess fat. In bowl, toss apples with lemon juice and sugar. Add prepared sausage mixture, cheddar cheese, eggs and cream; mix well. Line a 9-inch quiche dish or pie plate with pastry. Turn apple mixture into dish. Bake in 350° oven 40 to 45 minutes, or until custard is set. Let stand 10 minutes before cutting to serve. Makes 6 servings.

AVOCADO CRABMEAT QUICHE

Custard:
4 eggs
1½ cups cream
¼ cup dry white wine
Salt, pepper
Pinch of nutmeg

Filling:
1 avocado
2 teaspoons lemon juice
6½-ounce can crabmeat
Hot pepper sauce
¼ teaspoon salt

Beat first 6 ingredients until well blended with whisk or fork. Into partially baked and cooled pie shell slice one avocado and arrange in the bottom of pie shell. Sprinkle with lemon juice and salt. Wash, drain and pick over crabmeat for shells. Toss with dash of hot pepper sauce and spread evenly over avocado. Pour custard over this and bake for 40-45 minutes in 350° oven. Cool 5 minutes before serving.

SWISS QUICHE WITH CRABMEAT SAUCE

1 unbaked 9-inch pie shell
4 slightly beaten egg yolks
1½ cups light cream
½ teaspoon salt

⅛ teaspoon ground nutmeg
4 egg whites
1½ cups shredded Swiss cheese

Bake pastry shell in 450° oven for 7 minutes. Remove. Reduce heat to 350°. Combine egg yolks, cream, salt and nutmeg. Beat egg whites until stiff. Fold into yolk mixture. Fold in cheese. Pour into shell. Bake 350° for 40-45 minutes or until knife inserted just off-center comes out clean. Let stand 5 minutes. Serve with crabmeat sauce: Heat 1 6- to 7-ounce package frozen, drained crabmeat in 2 tablespoons margarine. Blend in 2-4 teaspoons flour and ⅛ teaspoon salt. Add 1 cup light cream; cook and stir until thick. Serves 6-8.

SWISS CHEESE, LEEK AND HAM PIE

1 1⁷/₈-ounce package dry cream of leek
   soup mix
2 cups milk
1 cup light cream
4 eggs
2½ cups grated Swiss cheese (½ pound)
1 teaspoon dry mustard

1 teaspoon salt
¼ teaspoon pepper
2 4½-ounce cans deviled ham
3 tablespoons dry bread crumbs
   (packaged)
10-inch pie shell

With wooden spoon, blend soup mix with milk in medium saucepan. Bring to boil over medium heat, stirring constantly. Remove from heat, cool slightly, stir in cream. Refrigerate until cold, about 20 minutes. Preheat oven 375°. With rotary beater beat eggs with soup mixture. Mix in cheese, salt, pepper and mustard. Mix crumbs and deviled ham. Spread ham mixture evenly over bottom of pie shell. Pour in filling. Bake 50 minutes until set. Cool slightly. Serves 8. This also makes very good tiny tarts for cocktail parties, if you stir the ham-crumb mixture into the soup mixture and spoon into miniature tart pans. Reduce cooking time according to tart size.

GREEK SPINACH PIE

Pastry for 2-crust 9-inch pie
3 eggs
1 large onion, chopped
3 tablespoons butter or margarine
1 cup cottage cheese

8 ounces feta cheese, crumbled
1 10-ounce package frozen chopped
   spinach, thawed & well-drained
½ teaspoon salt
¼ teaspoon pepper

Use pastry for one pie and brush egg white on pie shell after separating one egg. Add remaining egg white, yolk and 2 eggs into a large bowl, set aside. Sauté onion until tender in butter. Beat eggs and stir in cheese, spinach, salt, pepper and onion; turn into pie shell. Place carefully the remaining pie shell over the pie and crimp edges. Bake in preheated 425° oven for 30 minutes, or until crust is golden. Cool on rack 10 minutes. Serves 6 to 8.

TOMATO-CHEESE TART

½ package pie crust mix
4 ounces cheddar cheese, shredded
   (1 cup)
2 packages (6 ounces each) process
   Gruyère cheese, shredded
3 ripe medium-size tomatoes
1 teaspoon salt

1 teaspoon leaf basil
1 teaspoon leaf oregano, crumbled
⅛ teaspoon pepper
½ cup chopped green onions
2 tablespoons butter or margarine
2 tablespoons soft bread crumbs

Prepare piecrust mix, following label directions, adding ½ cup of the cheddar cheese. Roll out to a 12-inch round on a lightly floured pastry board; fit into a 9-inch pie plate. Trim overhang to ½ inch; turn under; flute to make a standup edge. Prick well with fork. Bake in hot oven (425°) 10 to 15 minutes, or until golden; cool. Spoon remaining cheddar cheese and Gruyère into piecrust. Slice tomatoes in half lengthwise and then into thin wedges. Arrange, slightly overlapping, in an attractive circular pattern over the cheese. Sprinkle with salt, pepper, basil and oregano. Sauté green onions in butter or margarine until tender in a small skillet. Spoon in the center of pie; sprinkle with bread crumbs. Bake in moderate oven (325°) 20 minutes, or until tomatoes are tender.

VIDALIA ONION QUICHE

3 tablespoons butter
½ pound Vidalia onions, sliced thin
¼ teaspoon salt

Freshly ground black pepper
½ cup Swiss cheese, grated

Custard mixture:
4 eggs
1½ cups heavy cream
¼ cup dry white wine

Pinch of salt
Freshly ground black pepper
Freshly grated nutmeg

Roll out and line a 9-inch pie plate with pastry; partially bake. Heat butter, add onions and sauté for 5 minutes until soft; add salt and pepper. Spread onions in pie shell and sprinkle with cheese. Beat custard ingredients together and pour over onions and cheese. Bake for 40 minutes at 375°. Serves 6.

Julie Donnan
Pots 'n' Pans, Etc.

ZUCCHINI QUICHE

1 9½- to 10-inch unbaked pastry shell
2 tablespoons Dijon or Gulden's mustard
3 cups grated zucchini
Salt
8 large mushrooms, sliced
2 tablespoons butter or margarine
2 cups grated Monterey Jack cheese

1 cup cream cheese
½ cup whipping cream (I use undiluted canned milk)
½ teaspoon oregano leaves
2 whole eggs
Salt and pepper

Preheat oven to 450°. Spread bottom of pastry with mustard and bake 10 minutes. Cool. Reduce heat to 350°. Place zucchini in colander, sprinkle with salt and drain about 5 minutes. While the zucchini is draining, sauté mushrooms in butter. Sprinkle 1 cup grated cheese into bottom of the pastry shell. Spoon mushrooms on top. Squeeze zucchini to remove the last bit of moisture and put into pastry shell, separating and fluffing with fingers. Beat together cream cheese, cream, oregano, eggs. Season with salt and pepper. Set pastry dish on baking sheet and carefully pour in cream-egg mixture. Sprinkle remaining cheese on top. Bake 35 minutes until top is puffed and golden and knife comes out clean. Let set 5 minutes before cutting. Serves 8.

Lamar Sargent (Mrs. G.T., Jr.)

FETTUCINI ALFREDO

1 package noodles (fettucine)
1 stick butter
1 clove garlic

1 cup Parmesan cheese
1 carton whipping cream
½ cup parsley (optional)

Boil water for noodles. In a small saucepan melt butter and add clove crushed garlic. Keep warm. In another small pan heat until warm a container of whipping cream. At the last 10 minutes cook noodles until tender, drain and toss quickly with butter, cream, Parmesan cheese and parsley. Pepper and serve right away as a first course or with meat dish.

Merrilyn Henry (Mrs. Robert)

PASTA PRIMAVERA

1 cup zucchini, sliced
1½ cups broccoli, broken into flowerets
1½ cups snow peas
1 cup baby peas
6 stalks asparagus, sliced
1 pound spaghetti
12 cherry tomatoes, cut in half
3 tablespoons olive oil
2 teaspoons garlic, minced

Salt, freshly ground black pepper
¼ cup Italian parsley, chopped
10 large mushrooms, sliced
⅓ cup butter
½ cup Parmesan cheese, freshly grated
1 cup heavy cream
⅓ cup fresh basil, chopped
⅓ cup chicken consommé (optional)

Blanch zucchini, broccoli, snow peas, baby peas, and asparagus in boiling salted water for 1-2 minutes each until just crisp tender. Drain and refresh under cold water. Set aside. This can be done ahead of time. Cook pasta in lots of boiling salted water until al dente, about 8-11 minutes. Drain. While pasta is cooking, sauté tomatoes in 1 tablespoon oil with 1 teaspoon garlic, salt, pepper, and parsley. Set aside. Add remaining garlic and all vegetables. Simmer a few minutes until hot. In a pan large enough to hold pasta and vegetables, melt butter. Add cheese, cream and basil. Stir to blend and melt cheese. Add pasta and toss to coat with sauce. If sauce gets too thick, thin with a little chicken consommé. Add about ⅓ of the vegetables, toss again. Divide pasta among 6 broad soup plates and top with remaining vegetables. Top with cherry tomatoes. Season to taste with salt, pepper and more grated Parmesan, if desired. Serves 6.

ZUCCHINI LASAGNE

12 lasagna noodles
Enough sliced zucchini to completely cover 1 layer of noodles
2 tablespoons oil
1 medium onion, chopped
2 garlic cloves, minced
1 8-ounce can tomato sauce
1 6-ounce can tomato paste

1 cup water
¾ teaspoon dried basil
¾ teaspoon dried oregano
Salt and pepper
2 cups ricotta or cottage cheese
1 cup grated mozzarella cheese
1 cup freshly grated Parmesan cheese

Cook noodles until tender, drain and set aside. Heat oil in skillet, sauté onion and then garlic. Into onion and garlic, stir in tomato sauce and paste, water, basil, oregano, salt and pepper. Simmer about 20 minutes. Lay 6 noodles on bottom of 9x13-inch dish or pan. Place sliced zucchini evenly on top of noodles. Spread ricotta or cottage cheese on top of squash and then ½ of tomato mixture. Put remaining noodles over sauce and then put remaining ½ sauce on top of second layer of noodles. Top with grated Parmesan cheese. Cover with foil and bake until bubbly in 350° oven.

Jack Blackburn

COMER HALL

BREADS

. . . the kneading, the making of the cake, the heating the oven, and the baking; nay, you must stay the cooking too, or you may chance burn your lips.

Troilus and Cressida (I-i-25-8)

COMER HALL

The dominant structure on "Ag Hill," the building dates from 1910 but was rebuilt in 1922; named for Braxton Bragg Comer, prominent Alabama industrialist and progressive Governor who showed especial interest in Auburn during his administration (1907-1911).

BREADS

Margie Kemp, whose husband was Head of Architecture, taught a bread class in Auburn. She was nice enough to share some of her recipes and basics of bread making with us.

BASICS

Ingredients:

Yeast—a living plant which makes batters and doughs rise.

Flour—All purpose wheat flour is most often used for bread making. Other flours such as whole wheat, rye, oat, and other cereals may be used, but *must be combined* with all-purpose flour to have desired results. Flour is the ingredient which forms the gluten and furnishes a place for the yeast to take action.

Sugar—furnishes food for the yeast, adds flavor, and helps crust to brown.

Salt—brings out flavor. It also controls the action of the yeast.

Liquids—Milk, water, and water in which potatoes have been cooked are the liquids usually used for yeast breads. Milk is usually scalded then cooled. *Never* use cold liquid—it will kill the yeast. *Water* makes crusty breads with good wheaty flavor. *Milk* makes bread with a softer crust.

Fat—butter, margarine, shortening, or lard are used to help make bread tender and keep the baked item soft. Butter or margarine also adds flavor.

Eggs—add food value, color, rich flavor. They also help make the crumb fine and the crust tender.

Other ingredients—spices, herbs, raisins, candied fruits, nuts, grated orange or lemon rind.

Utensils:

1. A large bowl—at least 2 quart size. Glass or crockery bowl is especially good. When warmed, it holds the dough at an even temperature. It also protects the dough from sudden temperature changes or chilling.
2. A set of measuring cups for dry ingredients.
3. A set of measuring cups for liquid measure—one which has a pouring lip.
4. Standard measuring spoons.
5. A small saucepan for scalding liquids and melting shortening.
6. A large wooden spoon for mixing.
7. A bread board or broad clean counter. Wood is better because it isn't so cool.

111

8. A bowl scraper.
9. A large sharp knife or kitchen scissors.
10. A medium-size spatula or small knife.
11. Baking pans or cookie sheets.

In addition, I find the following tools helpful:

Wire racks
Rolling pin (wooden for bread)
Whisk or eggbeater
Pastry brush
Electric mixer

Terms:

Dissolving yeast—this means adding yeast to water which is 110° to 115° F.

Mixing—the combining of liquid and dry ingredients. Beat vigorously after first half of flour has been stirred in.

Kneading—Turn dough out on a lightly floured surface. If the dough seems too sticky, sprinkle a *little* bit of flour on it and flour your hands. Press the dough into a flat thick pancake with the palms of your hand. Fold the dough in half toward you; then, with the heels of your hands push down and away. Turn the dough one quarter turn and repeat the action. Continue kneading and turning the dough until it is smooth and elastic. It will have the appearance of satin.

Rising—Cover your kneaded dough with a cloth while you wash your mixing bowl with hot water and dry it. Grease the inside of the bowl. Press the top of the dough into the bottom of the bowl and turn it to grease on all sides. Cover and place in a *draft free* place (80°-85°F) until it doubles in bulk. *TIP:* It can be placed, bowl and all, inside a plastic bag to assure no draft.

Double in bulk—After the time allowance given in the recipe for rising double check your dough. Take 2 fingers and press them into the dough about ½ inch. If the dents remain, the dough is ready to punch down. If the dents disappear or spring back—let the dough rise a little longer and test again.

Punching down—When the dough has risen, plunge your fist into the center and turn the dough completely over.

BASIC BREAD

¾ cup milk
2 tablespoons sugar
1 teaspoon salt
2 tablespoons shortening

½ cup warm water
1 egg
2½ to 3 cups flour

In small pan scald milk, sugar, salt, and shortening. Let cool. Dissolve yeast in warm water. Mix together milk and yeast. Add egg and beat well. Gradually add flour until you get a thick dough. Cover and let rise one hour. Flour board. Use ½ dough, roll out until about ¼ inch thick. Brush with melted butter. Sprinkle with garlic powder and minced onions (freeze dried). Roll dough as jelly roll. Twist into figure 8. Brush top with melted butter. Put in cold oven to rise for 30 minutes. Bake at 400° for 12-15 minutes.

Joanne Patton (Mrs. Ed)

WHITE BREAD (Standard Method)

½ cup milk
3 tablespoons sugar
2 teaspoons salt
3 tablespoons margarine

1½ cups warm water (105°-115°F)
1 package or cake yeast, active dry or
  compressed
5½ cups unsifted flour (about)

Scald milk; stir in sugar, salt and margarine. Cool to lukewarm. Measure warm water into large warm bowl. Sprinkle or crumble in yeast; stir until dissolved. Add lukewarm milk mixture and 3 cups of flour; beat until smooth. Add enough additional flour to make a soft dough. Turn out onto lightly floured board. Knead until smooth and elastic, about 8-10 minutes. Form into smooth ball. Place in greased bowl, turning to grease top. Cover; let rise in warm place; free from draft, until doubled in bulk, about 1 hour. Punch down. Let rest for 15 minutes. Divide dough in half. Shape each half into a loaf. Place each loaf in a greased 9x5x3 inch bread pan. Cover; let rise in warm place, free from draft, until doubled in bulk, about 1 hour. Bake in hot oven (400°F) about 30 minutes. Remove from pans and cool. Makes 2 loaves.

Margie Kemp (Mrs. Ed)

. . . friend, you must eat no white bread.

The Two Noble Kinsmen (III-v-80)

WHOLE WHEAT BREAD

¾ cup milk
3 tablespoons sugar
4 teaspoons salt
⅓ cup margarine
⅓ cup molasses

1½ cups warm water (105°-115°F)
2 packages or cakes yeast, active dry
  or compressed
4½ cups unsifted whole wheat flour
2¾ cups unsifted white flour (about)

Scald milk; stir in sugar, salt, margarine and molasses. Cool to lukewarm. Measure warm water into large warm bowl. Sprinkle or crumble in yeast; stir until dissolved. Stir in lukewarm milk mixture, 2 cups whole wheat flour and 2 cups white flour. Beat until smooth. Add enough of the remaining flours to make a soft dough. Turn out on lightly floured board and knead until smooth and elastic, about 8-10 minutes. Place in greased bowl, turning to grease top. Cover; let rise in warm place, free from draft, until doubled in bulk, about 1 hour. Punch down. Divide in half. Shape into loaves. Place in two greased 9x5x3 inch bread pans. Cover; let rise in warm place, free from draft, until doubled in bulk, about one hour. Bake in hot oven (400°F) about 25-30 minutes. Remove from pans and cool. Makes 2 loaves.

Margie Kemp (Mrs. Ed)

Margie and Ed Kemp often entertained at informal sandwich suppers. She made different kinds of breads and guests served themselves off a great big old tailor's ironing board.

QUICK & EASY FRENCH BREAD
(for the food processor)

1 package active dry yeast
1 teaspoon sugar (for quick rising)
1 cup warm water (120°)
2 tablespoons oil

¼ cup butter, melted
2 cups flour (bread or other gluten
  flour)
1 teaspoon salt
Flour to form dough ball

Dissolve yeast and sugar in warm water. If yeast is alive, gray foam will form on surface within 2 to 5 minutes. With steel knife in work bowl, sift 2 cups high gluten flour and salt with 2 or 3 quick on/offs. Add dissolved yeast. Process with 5 or 6 on/offs. If dough ball starts to form, process 10 to 20 seconds to knead. Add more flour if dough is soupy and will not form a ball. The dough should be sticky; a wet dough will produce tighter bread. For 2 rises, place dough in warm oiled bowl, turning dough to coat well with oil. Permit to rise in warm place until double in bulk (30 to 45 minutes), punch down. Shape in oil as desired. Brush with melted butter and let rise in pan again in warm place until almost doubled (20-40 minutes). Brush carefully with melted butter again. Bake in preheated 425° oven 15-20 minutes (depending on pan size). Larger loaves will require 20 to 30 minutes.

Good with brie as an appetizer or with a meal. Is an almost foolproof recipe.

Stephanie Bond (Mrs. Gordon)

FRENCH BREAD

Scald ½ cup milk. Add to it:
1 cup boiling water

1½ tablespoons melted margarine

While this liquid cools, dissolve 1 package yeast in ¼ cup warm water with 1 tablespoon sugar added to it. Let rest 10 minutes and add to milk/water mixture. Measure into large bowl:

4 cups all-purpose flour
2 teaspoons salt

2 teaspoons sugar

Make a well in the center of the dry ingredients; pour in liquid mixture. Stir to mix thoroughly, cover with damp cloth and set in warm place to rise for 2 hours. Place on lightly floured board and shape into 2 oblong loaves. Then place on a greased baking sheet. Cut diagonal ¼-inch slits across the tops with kitchen scissors. Set in warm place to rise 1 hour longer. Preheat over to 400°. Bake bread for 15 minutes. Reduce heat to 350° and bake 30 minutes longer. Five minutes before they are finished, brush the loaves with a glaze of 1 beaten egg white and 1 tablespoon cold water. Sprinkle with sesame or poppy seeds.

Libby Brown (Mrs. Jerry)

BATTER ROLLS

¾ cup milk
¼ cup sugar
1 teaspoon salt
¼ cup (½ stick) margarine
½ cup warm water (105°-115°F)

2 packages or cakes yeast, active dry
   or compressed
1 egg
3½ cups unsifted flour (about)

Scald milk; stir in sugar, salt and margarine; cool to lukewarm. Measure warm water into large warm bowl. Sprinkle or crumble in yeast; stir until dissolved. Add lukewarm milk mixture, egg and 2 cups flour; beat until smooth. Stir in enough remaining flour to make a soft dough. Cover; let rise in warm place, free from draft, until doubled in bulk, about 30 minutes. Punch down and shape into 2 dozen rolls. Place on greased baking sheet, cake pans or in muffin cups. Cover; let rise in warm place, free from draft, until doubled in bulk, about 30 minutes. Bake in hot oven (400°F) about 15 minutes. Makes 2 dozen rolls.

Margie Kemp (Mrs. Ed)

YUMMY BISCUITS

2 cups self-rising flour
1 (8-ounce) carton of sour cream

1 stick of margarine

Melt margarine, stir in sour cream, next add your flour and mix thoroughly. Drop from a mixing spoon into *hot* buttered muffin tins. Bake at 375° until puffy and lightly brown.

Angie Dollar (Mrs. Mason)

BUTTER CRESCENTS

2 packages yeast
1 cup warm water
½ cup sugar
3 eggs, well beaten

1 teaspoon salt
6 cups flour
1 cup melted butter

Place 1 cup water in large *warm* bowl, add yeast and dissolve. Add sugar, salt, and 1½ cups flour; stir well. Let this mixture rise for 25 minutes. Then add melted butter, eggs, and remaining flour. Roll out into circle and cut into wedge-shaped pieces. Roll wedges, beginning, at large end first.

Roll in melted butter and place on pan with rolled tip on the underside. Let rise again for 30 minutes. Bake at 450°F 15-20 minutes. Makes 48 medium size rolls.

Margie Kemp (Mrs. Ed)

REFRIGERATOR ROLLS

1¾ cups warm water (105°-115°F)
2 packages active dry yeast
½ cup sugar or honey
1 tablespoon salt
1 egg, unbeaten

6 cups, sifted all-purpose flour (I use
   stone ground whole wheat flour)
¼ cup soft butter or oleo
1 tablespoon butter or oleo, melted

Pour warm water into a large bowl (first rinsed well in hot water). If possible, check temperature with thermometer. The water should be warm, not hot on underpart of wrist. Sprinkle yeast over water, add sugar and salt; stir to dissolve completely. Add egg, soft butter and 3 cups flour. With wooden spoon or mixer at medium speed, beat very hard for 2 minutes or until smooth. Gradually add 1 cup flour, beating hard after each addition. Using hands, work remaining 2 cups flour into dough. Continue working dough, with hands until smooth and elastic. Brush top of dough with melted butter; cover with a double thickness of saran or damp towel. Let rise in refrigerator at least 2 hours, or until doubled in size. Punch down dough and refrigerate 1-3 days, punching it down once a day. Shape and bake as below.

Margie Kemp (Mrs. Ed)

BOWKNOTS

Remove dough from refrigerator. On lightly floured surface, with palm of hands, roll dough into a 12-inch cake. Divide to 12 pieces. Roll each piece into an 8-inch strip. Pull slightly. Tie each length loosely into a knot. Place 2 inches apart on greased cookie sheet; press ends on cookie sheet. Cover with towel. Let rise in warm place (85°), free from draft, until doubled in size—1 hour. Meanwhile preheat oven to 400°. Brush rolls lightly with melted butter. Bake 12 to 15 minutes or until golden brown. Serve hot.

Margie Kemp (Mrs. Ed)

RICH DINNER ROLLS

1 cup milk, scalded
¼ cup sugar
1 teaspoon salt
¼ cup (½ stick) margarine

½ cup warm water
2 packages yeast
2 eggs, beaten
5¼ cups *unsifted* flour

Scald milk and add to it margarine, sugar and salt. Set aside to cool. Dissolve yeast in warm water—stir until dissolved. Add lukewarm milk mixture, eggs, and 2 cups flour and beat until smooth. Stir in enough of the remaining flour to make a soft dough. Turn out on a lightly floured board and knead until smooth and elastic (8-10 minutes). Place in greased bowl; turn to grease both sides. Cover and let rise until double (about 30 minutes). Punch down. Turn out on floured board and shape as desired. Bake at 375°.

Margie Kemp (Mrs. Ed)

GREAT DINNER ROLLS

1 cup hot water	1 cake yeast
¼ cup shortening	1 teaspoon sugar
½ cup sugar	4 cups flour
1 egg	1 teaspoon salt

Put hot water, shortening and sugar in large bowl. Add egg, and beat well. Put ¼ cup warm water in a cup and add yeast and teaspoon sugar, let set a few minutes. Add this to first mixture and mix well. Add 2 cups flour and salt, mix well. Add 2 more cups flour, mix well and let stand in warm place until double in size. Roll out and cut into any size or shape you desire. Let rise again. Bake in 400° oven for 10 minutes.

Donna Beardsworth (Mrs. Jim)

PARKER HOUSE ROLLS

1 cup scalded milk	1 package yeast
1 teaspoon salt	3 tablespoons lukewarm water
¼ cup sugar	1 egg (room temperature)
5 to 6 tablespoons shortening	4 to 5 cups flour

Combine milk, salt, sugar and shortening in large bowl. Stir until shortening melts. Dissolve yeast in water. Add to mixture. Beat egg slightly and add, stirring in about half of flour. Continue adding flour until dough can be handled. Knead well, cover and let rise. Roll dough about ½" thickness. Cut in circles and fold with a dab of butter. Place in greased pan and let rise again. Bake 425° about 15 minutes. Will make about 36 rolls. These freeze well, too. I use the same recipe for cinnamon rolls dough.

Chris Danner (Mrs. Dan)

Make a holly wreath out of bakers clay for an unusual kitchen table centerpiece at Christmas. On cookie sheet, roll a "snake" the length of the circumference you want your wreath to be. Shape into a circle, and pinch the ends together. Flatten slightly. Roll out the remaining bakers clay and cut holly leaves out with a cookie cutter or a sharp knife. Slightly overlap on top of ring, covering ring fully. Make tiny balls for berries and press on top of leaves. Bake until dry and lightly browned. Varnish when cool. Fill center with red votive candles and surround wreath with real holly. You'll enjoy it! Animal cutters, Santas and trees, or gingerbread men are attractive used in this manner, too.

PARMESAN CASSEROLE BREAD

1 package yeast	½ teaspoon salt
¼ cup warm water	⅓ cup butter or margarine
¼ cup scalded milk	1 beaten egg
1½ cups sifted all-purpose flour	½ cup grated Parmesan cheese
1 tablespoon sugar	2 tablespoons chopped parsley

Dissolve yeast in warm water. Scald milk and cool to lukewarm. Sift dry ingredients into mixing bowl (flour, sugar, salt). With a *pastry blender* cut butter into dry mixture until it resembles coarse meal. Add egg, yeast mixture, and milk and beat well. Stir in cheese and parsley. Turn into 8x1½-inch round pan, cover with *damp* cloth and let rise till double, about 40 minutes. Bake at 375° for 20-25 minutes. Cut in pie-shaped wedges and serve.

RICH BASIC SWEET DOUGH

½ cup milk
½ cup sugar
1½ teaspoon salt
¼ cup (½ stick) margarine
½ cup warm water (105°-115°F)

2 packages or cake yeast, active dry or compressed
2 eggs, beaten
4½ cups unsifted flour (about)

Scald milk; stir in sugar, salt and margarine; cool to lukewarm. Measure warm water into large warm bowl. Sprinkle or crumble in yeast, stir until dissolved. Stir in lukewarm milk mixture, beaten eggs and half the flour; beat until smooth. Stir in remaining flour to make a slightly stiff dough. Turn dough out on lightly floured board. Knead until smooth and elastic, about 8 minutes. Place dough in greased bowl, turning to grease top. Cover; let rise in warm place, free from draft, until doubled in bulk, about 1 hour. Punch down; turn out on lightly floured board and shape as desired.

An easy-to-handle kneaded dough for sweet rolls and coffee cake.

Margie Kemp (Mrs. Ed)

PECAN STICKY BUNS

1 recipe Basic Sweet Dough or Rich Sweet Dough
1 cup (2 sticks) margarine

2½ cups brown sugar
1½ cups chopped pecans

Prepare dough. Before time to shape, melt margarine. Stir in 1½ cups brown sugar and 1 cup chopped pecans. Spoon into greased muffin pans. Combine remaining 1 cup brown sugar and ½ cup chopped pecans. Divide dough in half. Roll out each half to a 12-inch square. Sprinkle each half with the brown sugar-pecan mixture. Roll up lengthwise as for a jelly roll. Cut into 1-inch slices and place in prepared pans. Cover; let rise in warm place, free from draft, until doubled in bulk, about 1 hour. Bake in moderate oven (350°F) about 25 minutes. Makes 2 dozen.

Margie Kemp (Mrs. Ed)

PUMPKIN BREAD

3⅓ cups flour
2 teaspoons soda
3 cups sugar
1 teaspoon salt
1 teaspoon cinnamon
1 teaspoon nutmeg
¾ teaspoon ginger

1 cup chopped nuts
1 cup oil
⅔ cup water
4 eggs
2 cups pumpkin, or 1 can
1 tablespoon vanilla

Sift dry ingredients, make a well in middle. Beat eggs, add water and pumpkin. Mix oil and vanilla and add to egg mixture. Pour into well in dry ingredients and beat until smooth. Add nuts. Divide equally into 3 loaf pans that are well greased and floured. Bake 1½ hours at 325°.

Claudia Highfill (Mrs. Bill)

Claudia gives this delicious bread for Christmas gifts to her friends. It is delicious toasted for breakfast.

MARY'S PUMPKIN BREAD

3 cups sugar
2 cups salad oil
5 eggs
3 cups all-purpose flour
2 teaspoons soda

1 teaspoon salt
1 teaspoon cinnamon
1 cup nuts, chopped
2 cups canned pumpkin
2 packages coconut cream instant pie filling, or toasted coconut cream instant pie filling

Mix oil, sugar, eggs, and pumpkin. Sift dry ingredients. Add nuts and pie filling to dry ingredients. Then add slowly to pumpkin, etc. Divide into 3 loaves. Bake at 350° for 1 hour.

Nancy Gardner (Mrs. Dan)

DILL BREAD

1 package dry yeast (dissolved in ¼ cup lukewarm water for 10 minutes)
1 cup large curd cottage cheese (heated)
1 egg, lightly beaten
2 tablespoons grated onion

1 tablespoon melted butter
1 tablespoon sugar
1 tablespoon dill seed
1 teaspoon salt
¼ teaspoon baking soda

Sauté onion in butter till tender. Soften yeast in water. In a large warm bowl place cottage cheese, sugar, onion, dill seed, salt, soda, egg, and yeast, and mix well. Add enough flour to make a stiff dough. Beat well. Cover and let rise until double—about 1½ hours. Stir down. Divide dough with sharp knife and place in 1 large or 2 small well greased loaf pans. Let rise again (30 to 40 minutes). Bake at 350°F for 50 to 55 minutes. Makes 1 large or 2 small loaves.
Large loaf = 9½" x 5" x 2"
Small loaf = 7½" x 3½" x 2"

Carla Candler (Mrs. Bill)

OLIVE CHEESE BREAD

2⅓ cups biscuit mix
½ cup grated cheddar cheese (about 2 ounces)
¼ teaspoon dry mustard
⅛ teaspoon onion powder

⅓ cup coarsely chopped or sliced pimento-stuffed olives
1 tablespoon butter or margarine, melted
¾ cup milk

Combine biscuit mix, cheese, dry mustard and onion powder in medium bowl. Add olives, butter and milk. Stir just until ingredients are blended. Turn into greased loaf pan. Bake at 375° for 45 minutes. Serve warm or cold with butter or cream cheese.

CHEESE PEPPER BREAD

1 package active dry yeast
¼ cup hottest tap water
2⅓ cups flour
2 tablespoons sugar
1 teaspoon salt

1 cup shredded cheddar cheese
½ teaspoon pepper
¼ teaspoon soda
1 cup sour cream
1 egg

Grease two 1-pound coffee cans. In large mixer bowl dissolve yeast in hot water. Add 1½ cups of the flour, salt, soda, sour cream and egg. Blend 3 minutes; then stir remaining flour, cheese and pepper. Divide batter between the two cans. Let rise in a warm place 50 minutes. Bake 40 minutes or until golden brown at 350°. Immediately remove from cans. Cool slightly before slicing.

ZUCCHINI TEA BREAD

3 eggs
1 cup oil
2 cups sugar
2 cups grated zucchini
1 tablespoon vanilla
3 cups flour

1 tablespoon cinnamon
1 teaspoon salt
1 teaspoon baking soda
1¼ teaspoons baking powder
¾ cup nuts, chopped

Beat eggs, add oil, sugar, zucchini, and vanilla. Mix all dry ingredients and add to the egg mixture. Stir in nuts. Pour in greased and floured loaf pan and bake for one hour at 350°. If you use smaller pans, cook slightly less.

This is a great breakfast bread or serve with cream cheese for a delicious snack.

LUCY BURWELL'S ORANGE NUT BREAD

Juice and grated rind of 1 large or 2
   small oranges
1 cup white raisins
1 cup sugar
2 cups flour
1 cup chopped pecans

2 tablespoons shortening
1 egg beaten
1 teaspoon baking powder
1 teaspoon soda
1 teaspoon vanilla
1 teaspoon salt

Squeeze juice into measuring cup, and fill cup with boiling water. Grate yellow part of orange rind. Put rind and raisins in large bowl and add orange juice, and boiling water. Stir in soda, then sugar, shortening and vanilla. Add beaten egg, then flour which has been sifted with baking powder and salt. Beat thoroughly and stir in chopped nuts.

Place in greased pan and bake in 350° oven about 50 minutes. Cool in pan before slicing. These also can be made in small loaf pans, but baking time must be adjusted.

BREAD STICKS

8 hotdog buns   1 stick oleo

Cut buns in 4 pieces lengthwise. Melt oleo. Dip one side of each stick in oleo. Place on cookie sheet and bake 250° or 275° for 2 hours. Delicious with soup or just as snack food. If you like, garlic salt can be sprinkled on with oleo.

Josephine Teague (Mrs. Wayne)

BREAD STICKS

1 loaf French bread   ½ teaspoon onion salt
1 cup butter, softened   1 teaspoon chervil
½ teaspoon garlic powder or salt   1 teaspoon basil leaves

Cut bread in half lengthwise. Then cut half into 1 inch sticks. In small bowl combine remaining ingredients; spread butter on cut bread wedges. Bake on ungreased sheet at 425° for 7-10 minutes or until brown. Serve warm.

These sticks are good served with venison, and especially good with spaghetti.

Shirley Bartels (Mrs. Jan)

PARMESAN BREAD STICKS

Remove crusts from bread and cut into 1 inch square or strips. Roll in melted garlic butter and sprinkle with Parmesan cheese, Accent, and sesame seeds. Bake at 300° 20 minutes or until crisp. Delicious!

NEVER-FAIL BISCUITS

1 cup self-rising flour   ⅓ cup milk
3 tablespoons Crisco

Mix flour and Crisco until mixture resembles cornmeal. Add milk and stir only to moisten. Roll on smooth surface using only enough self-rising flour to prevent sticking. Bake at 400° for 8-10 minutes. Makes about 10 biscuits, but can easily be doubled.

These can be used with ham for a delectable appetizer. Use smallest can mushrooms come in as a cutter. Use same can to cut thinly sliced ham to fit biscuits.

REFRIGERATOR BRAN MUFFINS

1 cup boiling water
3 cups All Bran cereal (divided)
½ cup (rounded) shortening
1½ cups sugar
2 eggs

2 cups buttermilk
2½ cups plain flour
2½ teaspoons soda
½ teaspoon salt
1 cup raisins

Pour boiling water over 1 cup of the All Bran. Set aside. Cream shortening and sugar in a very large bowl. Add eggs one at a time and beat well. Add buttermilk and scalded All Bran and mix well. Sift flour, soda, salt together and add with the other 2 cups of All Bran to the liquid mixture. Beat until just blended. Add raisins. Bake in greased or Pam-sprayed muffin tins for 15-20 minutes at 400°. The batter will keep in a tightly covered container in the refrigerator for a month or more to be cooked whenever desired. Yields 2¼ quarts batter or 3½ dozen muffins.

Gay Ellis Smyer (Mrs. Robert F.)

FIESTA CORN MUFFINS

1 15-ounce package corn bread mix
1¼ cups milk
½ cup oil (bacon grease is even better)
3 eggs
1 large onion, chopped
4 slices bacon, cooked and crumbled

1 12-ounce can whole kernel corn, drained
¼ pound shredded cheddar cheese
1 teaspoon salt
¼ cup chopped pimento
¼ cup chopped Jalapeño pepper (optional)

Beat eggs, add oil and milk. Stir in corn bread mix. Add all other ingredients and mix well. Bake 20-25 minutes at 325°. Makes 36 muffins.
    Use paper muffin liners.

Jean Bullock (Mrs. Bill)

HUSH PUPPIES

2 cups water-ground cornmeal
1 tablespoon flour
½ teaspoon soda
1 teaspoon baking powder

1 teaspoon salt
1 whole egg
3 tablespoons chopped onion
1 cup buttermilk

Mix all dry ingredients together. Add onion, then milk and last the beaten egg. Drop by the spoonful into the pan or kettle in which fish is being fried. Fry to a golden brown. Drain on paper, the same as fried fish. If a deep kettle is being used the hush puppy bread will float when done.

LACE-EDGED CORN CAKES

2 cups cornmeal
1 teaspoon soda
1 teaspoon salt

1 egg
3 cups buttermilk

Break egg into bowl into which have been sifted together meal, soda and salt. Add buttermilk, stirring to blend. Batter should be thin. Bake in small cakes on hot, greased griddle. Each cake should have a crisp, lacy edge.

SOUR CREAM CORN BREAD I

1 package corn muffin mix
3 eggs
½ cup Wesson oil

1 small can creamed corn
½ pint sour cream

Beat 3 eggs and ½ cup Wesson oil. Add 1 package corn muffin mix (envelope), 1 small can creamed corn and ½ pint sour cream. Pour into oiled 13x9 pan. Bake at 350° 35-40 minutes.

This is great to serve with soup or chili. Leftovers are good reheated.

SOUR CREAM CORNBREAD II

1 cup self-rising meal
2 eggs
1 8³/₄-ounce can yellow cream-stye corn

1 cup sour cream
½ cup Wesson oil

Combine all ingredients, mixing well. Bake in greased 9-inch square pan 400° 20-30 minutes. Makes 9 servings. If desired, add 2 tablespoons Jalapeño peppers.

Johnnie McGraw (Mrs. Leon)

COFFEE CAKE

2 loaves frozen white bread (Rich's bread)
1 small package regular vanilla pudding
5 tablespoons butter

1 cup pecans (chipped)
1 tablespoon milk
¾ cup brown sugar
1 tablespoon cinnamon

Grease bundt pan. Cut up bread while still partially frozen in 1½ to 2-inch squares. Mix butter, milk, sugar and cinnamon and heat to syrup consistency. Throw in a few pecans. Add about ½ of bread chunks, a layer of pecans, ½ pudding and ½ syrup. Add remaining bread, pecans, pudding and syrup. Cover with Saran Wrap and refrigerate overnight. (This will rise in refrigerator.) Bake 350° for 30 minutes.

Edie Irwin (Mrs. Dave)

ONE-STEP TROPICAL COFFEE CAKE

1½ cups all-purpose flour
1 cup sugar
2 teaspoons baking powder
½ teaspoon salt

8-ounce carton (1 cup) plain or fruit-
flavored yogurt or dairy sour cream
½ cup cooking oil
2 eggs

Using solid shortening, grease 8 or 9-inch square pan. Lightly spoon flour into measuring cup, level off. Combine all ingredients in large bowl. Stir 70 to 80 strokes until well blended. Pour into greased pan. Set batter aside. Combine in small bowl:

1 cup coconut or chopped nuts
⅓ cup sugar

1 teaspoon cinnamon

Sprinkle over batter. Bake at 350° for 35 to 45 minutes or until toothpick inserted in center comes out clean.

NUTMEG COFFEE CAKE

2¼ cups light brown sugar, firmly packed
3 cups sifted all-purpose flour
¾ cup butter or oleo
1 cup dairy sour cream

1½ teaspoons baking soda
2 eggs
1 teaspoon ground nutmeg
¾ cup chopped walnuts

Heat oven to 350°. Grease and flour 9x13x1½-inch baking pan. Blend brown sugar, flour, and butter or oleo into crumbs with pastry blender or 2 knives. Reserve ¾ cup of mixture. Mix sour cream and baking soda. Stir eggs, nutmeg and sour cream mixture into remaining crumbs. Pour into prepared pan and sprinkle with nuts and remaining crumb mixture. Bake 40 minutes or until cake tests done. Cut into squares. Makes 12 servings.

Helene Alexander (Mrs. Milton)

HAWAIIAN BANANA NUT BREAD
(makes 2 regular or 5 baby loaves)

3 cups flour
2 cups sugar
1 cup chopped pecans
1 teaspoon baking soda
1 teaspoon salt
1 teaspoon cinnamon

Mix all together in a large bowl. Set aside.

3 eggs, beaten
2 cups ripe banana, mashed
1½ cups vegetable oil
1 cup crushed pineapple, drained
2 teaspoons vanilla

Combine in medium bowl. Add to flour mixture and stir by hand until flour is just moistened.

Pam-spray loaf pans and turn batter into pans. Bake at 350° for 1 hour or until toothpick inserted in center comes out clean. Cool in pan for 10 minutes before removing and cooling on rack.

SAUSAGE-COFFEE CAKE

1 pound sausage	1½ teaspoon salt
½ cup chopped onion	2 tablespoons chopped parsley
¼ cup grated Parmesan cheese (fresh)	2 cups Bisquick
½ cup Swiss cheese	¾ cup milk
1 egg, beaten	¼ cup mayonnaise
¼ teaspoon Tabasco	1 egg yolk in 1 tablespoon water

Brown sausage and onion. (Cook until onion is clear.) Drain on paper towel. Add next 6 ingredients. Make batter of Bisquick and mayonnaise. Grease square 9x9 cake pan. Put ½ of batter in pan (this will be thin. Take fingers and press into pan.) Put sausage mixture in pan. Top with rest of batter. (Spread with spatula.) Whip egg yolk and water. Brush over top. Bake 400° for 25-30 minutes until cake leaves edges. Cool 5 minutes before cutting. Cut in 3 inch squares.

Can be frozen after baking. Let cool. Wrap in aluminum foil. Pull back foil when reheating.

Rose Ann Denson (Mrs. John V.)

This was used at a welcome brunch for new coaches' wives.

BLUEBERRY MUFFINS

4 tablespoons oleo (½ stick)	1 cup sugar

Cream the above 2 ingredients. Add 1 egg. Then add:

2 cups flour, mixed with 1 tablespoon baking powder	1 cup milk
	¾ to 1 cup blueberries

Grease muffin pans with Crisco, flour well, then shake out. Bake at 375° for 25 minutes.

Theo Mosley (Mrs. Kelly)

Kelly is a past president of the Auburn Alumni Association.

EASY CRESCENT DANISH ROLLS

8-ounce package cream cheese, softened	2 cans refrigerated crescent dinner rolls
½ cup sugar	4 teaspoons preserves
1 tablespoon lemon juice	

Glaze:
½ cup powdered sugar	2-3 teaspoons milk
1 teaspoon vanilla	

Blend first 3 ingredients until smooth. Separate rolls into eight rectangles; firmly press perforations to seal. Spread about 2 tablespoons cream cheese mixture on each rectangle. Starting at longer side, roll up; press edges to seal. Gently stretch each roll to about 10 inches. Coil loosely into spirals with seam on inside. Seal ends. Make deep indentation (thumb prints) in center of each roll. Fill with ½ teaspoon preserves. Bake on ungreased cookie sheets (or small muffin pans) 20 minutes until deep golden brown. Drizzle glaze over warm rolls. Serve warm.

Betty Ann Rainer (Mrs. Rex)

FRENCH PANCAKES

3 eggs, separated
1 teaspoon sugar
½ teaspoon salt

1 cup milk
½ cup all-purpose flour
1 tablespoon melted butter

Separate the eggs and beat the yolks until lemon colored. Add the sugar, salt and ½ cup of the milk; beat to mix. Sift the flour, measure and add to the egg yolk mixture. Add the remaining milk and beat with mixer until smooth. Stir in the melted butter. Fold in the stiffly beaten egg whites. Pour ½ cup batter into a heated lightly greased skillet, spread with back of spoon to fill pan. When brown on underside, turn and brown on other side. Spread with jelly or preserves and roll. Sprinkle with powdered sugar. This is really worth the trouble!

FAYE'S MAPLE SYRUP

4 cups sugar
½ cup brown sugar
2 cups water

1 teaspoon vanilla
1 teaspoon maple flavor

Combine sugars and water, stir, bring to boil. Cover, boil gently for 10 minutes. Remove from heat, add flavorings. Makes 1 quart.

KATHARINE CATER'S FAVORITE SPOON BREAD

1 cup cooked *quick* grits
1 tablespoon butter
½ cup cornmeal

2 eggs
½ teaspoon salt
1 cup milk

Add butter to hot grits, cooked 5 minutes, and stir in milk. Add cornmeal, salt and last of all well-beaten eggs. When smooth and well mixed, pour in deep, greased baking dish and bake in moderately hot oven (350°) for 50 minutes. Serves 4.

Henrietta Davis (Mrs. Neil)

Neil and Henrietta Davis, who for decades owned and published the *Auburn Bulletin*, remember many occasions over the years when they and others shared the happy results of this recipe with their friend, the late Dean Cater.

ALABAMA SPOON BREAD

1 cup cornmeal
1 cup boiling water
3 eggs
1 teaspoon salt

1½ cups milk
⅓ cup melted butter
3 teaspoons baking powder

Pour boiling water over cornmeal, stirring to prevent lumping. Beat the eggs well and put them into the milk. Also put salt and baking powder into milk. Add liquid slowly to meal mixture. Mix in melted butter last. Pour into well-buttered casserole and bake at 375° for a little more than half an hour.

PRESIDENT'S HOME

FRUITS AND VEGETABLES

Be kind and courteous to this gentleman . . .
Feed him with apricocks and dewberries,
With purple grapes, green figs and mulberries.
A Midsummer Night's Dream (III-i-178-80)

PRESIDENT'S HOME

Commanding an elevated site at the corner of Samford and College, the mansion was constructed in 1938 under the Projects Works Administration at a cost of $38,000. President L. N. Duncan was the first occupant.

FRUITS AND VEGETABLES

BAKED APRICOTS

1 4-ounce stack Ritz Crackers
5 17-ounce cans apricot halves
⅔ cup light brown sugar

1 stick melted butter
1 teaspoon cinnamon

Roll crackers into crumbs. In a casserole dish (3-quart) alternate layers of apricots, crumbs and brown sugar. Pour butter over top. Sprinkle with cinnamon. Bake at 300° for 30 to 45 minutes. Serves 12.

This is good with chicken and turkey. It serves a large crowd, and leftovers freeze beautifully.

SHERRIED FRUIT CASSEROLE

1 can pineapple chunks
1 can peach halves
1 can pear halves
1 can apricot halves
1 jar apple rings

Sauce:
1 stick butter
2 tablespoons flour
½ cup light brown sugar
1 cup sherry

Cook sauce in double boiler until thick and smooth. Layer drained fruit in 2-quart casserole. Pour hot sauce over fruit. Cover. Refrigerate overnight. Bake at 350° 30 minutes until fruit is bubbly. Serve hot.

BAKED FRUIT

1 large can each: pear halves, peach
   slices, pineapple chunks, apricot
   halves, marachino cherries

¾ cup light brown sugar
⅓ cup butter, melted
⅔ cup blanched slivered almonds

Drain all fruit. Add sugar to melted butter. Arrange fruit and nuts in layers in casserole, pour butter over all and bake at 325° for 1 hour uncovered. Refrigerate over night—reheat at 350° and serve. You may add 3 teaspoons curry powder to above. Add more fruit for larger crowds. Serves 10-12.

Edie Irwin (Mrs. Dave)

HOT FRUIT

Simmer 15 minutes:
   1 29-ounce can peach halves
Drain and place in baking dish.

1 29-ounce can apricot halves.

131

Add:
3 apples, sliced   2 cups strawberries

Mix:
½ cup cointreau   ½ cup brown sugar
½ cup honey   2 teaspoons cinnamon
1 teaspoon nutmeg

Pour over fruit. Cover for 3-4 hours. Then bake uncovered at 400° for 20 minutes. Add 2 bananas, sliced lengthwise, and bake 10 minutes more.

Carla Candler (Mrs. Bill)

ARTICHOKES AND PEAS

16 ounces frozen peas   3 tablespoons butter or margarine
14 ½ ounce canned or frozen artichoke   ¼ pound bleu cheese, crumbled
  hearts, drained   Cashews, chopped (optional)

Heat peas and artichokes through; drain well. Combine quickly in a casserole dish; add butter and cheese. Serve sprinkled with chopped cashews.

BEAN BUNDLES I

2 cans whole green beans
Sauce: ½ pound bacon cut in half
3 tablespoons butter   1 teaspoon paprika
3 tablespoons tarragon vinegar   1 teaspoon parsley dried (or fresh)
½ teaspoon salt   1 teaspoon onion juice

Drain beans and divide into bundles of about 5 beans each. Wrap with half slice bacon. Broil on rack until bacon is done. Combine sauce ingredients. Simmer until hot and pour over cooked bean bundles. Serve.

BEAN BUNDLES II

2 16-ounce cans Blue Lake whole green   1 bottle 1890 French salad dressing
  beans   Bacon strips cut in half

Drain beans and marinate overnight in French dressing. Divide beans into 10 even bundles. Wrap each bundle with half strip bacon. Place in oblong casserole and bake in preheated 350° oven 25-30 minutes until bacon is brown and crisp. Makes 10 servings.

Both these recipes are delightfully easy to serve at buffet meals.

GREEN BEANS IN RED WINE

2 pounds green beans strung and
  snapped in 1-inch pieces (or 2 cans
  green beans)
6 tablespoons butter
4 teaspoons flour
1 cup beef broth

½ cup red wine
Juice of ½ lemon
2 teaspoons chopped parsley
Salt and pepper

Cook beans in boiling salted water about 20 minutes. Drain. Melt 3 tablespoons butter and stir in flour, stirring constantly until bubbly. Remove from heat and stir in broth and wine until smooth. Cook, stirring constantly, until thickened. Add remaining butter and parsley to the beans and cook 5 more minutes, then add the sauce and heat until warm, stirring constantly. Season with lemon juice, salt and pepper. Makes 6-8 servings.

COMPANY BEANS

1 package frozen French green beans
1 package frozen baby lima beans
1 package frozen English peas
1 cup mayonnaise
1 tablespoon oil

1 tablespoon Worchestershire sauce
Dash Tabasco
1 medium onion, minced
4 hard cooked eggs, sliced
Salt and pepper to taste

Cook vegetables and drain. Mix other ingredients for a sauce and keep at room temperature. Put vegetables in casserole dish and spread sauce over top. Garnish with sliced eggs. Good hot or cold.

Jean Bullock (Mrs. Bill)

GREEN BEANS IN SOUR CREAM

1 cup sour cream
½ cup mayonnaise
1 teaspoon lemon juice
¼ teaspoon onion juice

1½ tablespoons chopped chives
½ teaspoon dry mustard
1½ tablespoons horseradish

Drain 2 number 2 cans green beans. Add 1 thinly sliced onion. Sprinkle with freshly ground pepper. Toss in 1 tablespoon oil and 1 tablespoon vinegar. Marinate 3-4 hours. Drain, combine above ingredients and pour over beans. Sprinkle with chives.

Joanne McLaughlin (Mrs. Wayne)

RUSSIAN GREEN BEANS

1 cup sour cream
2 cans French-style green beans
2 tablespoons minced onion
2 tablespoons minced pimento

2 tablespoons vinegar
½ teaspoon salt
½ teaspoon prepared mustard
⅛ teaspoon pepper

Drain liquid from beans into a medium saucepan and bring to a boil. Add beans and heat thoroughly. Remove from heat and drain. Add all other ingredients and thoroughly heat but do not boil. Serves 6.

Jean Cox (Mrs. Grady)

REFRIED BEANS

1 pound dried pinto or pink beans, cleaned
5 cups water

1 or 2 medium-sized onions, diced
½ to 1 cup hot bacon drippings, butter, or oleo

Combine beans in a pan with water and onions. Bring to a boil, cover, and remove from heat for 2 hours (or soak beans in cold water overnight). Return to heat, bring to a boil, and simmer slowly until beans are very tender, about 3 hours. Mash beans with a potato masher, and add bacon drippings, butter, or oleo. Mix well; continue cooking, stirring frequently until beans are thickened and fat is absorbed. Salt to taste. Makes 5 to 6 cups.

Wanda Dobie (Mrs. Jim)

BARBECUED BAKED BEANS

3-pound can Campbell's pork and beans
¾ cup catsup
1 package Bryan's frozen barbecue pork, thawed

1 tablespoon prepared mustard
½ cup chopped onion
½ cup brown sugar
½ cup dark Karo syrup

Combine all ingredients. Bake in greased 9x11 casserole dish at 425° for 35-40 minutes. Serves 10 to 12.

Johnnie McGraw (Mrs. E. L.)

These are very good with all barbecued meats, hamburgers and hotdogs.

TALLAHASSEE BAKED BEANS

Use earthenware beanpot. Line bottom with slices of salt pork or bacon. Then add a thin layer of cooked, salted Navy beans or canned pork and beans, then a layer of ham, bacon, thinly sliced weiners and onion slices (use 1 large onion to each beanpot). Add another layer of beans, another weiner etc. layer and so on to the top. When the pot is filled, pour in a mixture of 1 can condensed tomato soup, 2 tablespoons dark molasses, 1 tablespoon mustard, salt and pepper. Bake in 350° oven for 3½ hours. Remove cover last hour. Serve with cole slaw and brown bread.

Hazel Richards (Mrs. Harold)

BROCCOLI GRUYERE

1 bunch broccoli (1½-2 pounds), cut in
spears, or 2 packages (10 ounces
each) frozen spears, cooked and
drained (reserve ½ cup liquid)
3 tablespoons butter or margarine
2 tablespoons flour

¼ cup milk
¼ teaspoon salt, or to taste
⅛ teaspoon pepper
½ cup Gruyere cheese, shredded
(about 2 ounces)
2 tablespoons fine dry bread crumbs

Arrange broccoli in greased shallow flameproof dish; set aside and keep warm. In small saucepan melt butter, then blend in flour. Stir in reserved broccoli liquid and milk; cook and stir until thickened. Season with salt and pepper. Pour sauce over broccoli; sprinkle with cheese, then bread crumbs. Broil about 8 inches from heat 3 to 5 minutes or until golden brown. Makes 4 to 6 servings.

SOUFFLÉED BROCCOLI ROULADE

4 tablespoons (½ stick) butter or
margarine
½ cup sifted all-purpose flour
½ teaspoon salt
2 cups milk

4 eggs, separated
2 packages frozen broccoli
3 ounces Swiss cheese, shredded (¾
cup)
Swiss Cheese Sauce (recipe follows)

Grease a 15x10x1-inch jelly-roll pan; line with wax paper; grease paper; dust with flour. Melt butter or margarine in a medium-size saucepan. Off heat, blend in flour and salt; stir in milk. Cook, stirring constantly, until mixture is very thick. Beat egg whites until they form soft peaks in a medium-size bowl. Beat egg yolks slightly in a large bowl. Slowly beat hot mixture into egg yolks, until blended. Fold beaten egg whites into egg yolks until no streaks of yellow remain. Spread evenly in pan. Bake in moderate oven (325°) 45 minutes, or until golden and top springs back when touched. While omelet roll bakes, cook broccoli, following label directions; drain; cut into 1-inch pieces. Reserve ½ cup for garnish. Make Swiss Cheese Sauce. Remove omelet roll from pan this way: Loosen around edges with spatula; cover with wax paper or foil. Place a large cookie sheet or tray on top, then quickly turn upside down. Lift pan; peel paper. Arrange broccoli in a single layer on top of roll; sprinkle with cheese and drizzle ½ cup hot cheese sauce over. Starting at a 10-inch end, roll up omelet, jelly-roll fashion, lifting wax paper or foil as you roll to steady and guide it. Lift roll onto a heated large serving platter with two wide spatulas. Drizzle about ½ cup more sauce over roll and garnish with reserved broccoli. Cut roll into thick slices. Pass remaining sauce to spoon over. Makes 6 servings.

SWISS CHEESE SAUCE

⅓ cup butter or margarine
⅓ cup flour
½ teaspoon salt

⅛ teaspoon pepper
2 cups milk
3 ounces Swiss cheese, shredded

Melt butter or margarine over low heat in a medium-size saucepan. Stir in flour, salt, and pepper; cook, stirring constantly, just until mixture bubbles. Stir in milk; continue cooking and stirring until sauce thickens and bubbles 1 minute; stir in cheese until melted. Keep warm. Makes 2½ cups.

CREAMY BROCCOLI CASSEROLE

1 bunch broccoli, about 1½ pounds
½ teaspoon salt
1 can (10½ ounces) condensed cream of
  chicken soup
½ cup mayonnaise

¼ teaspoon curry powder
2 tablespoons lemon juice
½ cup soft stale-bread crumbs
2 tablespoons butter or margarine,
  melted

Peel stalks of broccoli and slice about ¼" thick. Cut tops in quarters. Cook in small amount of boiling water with the salt until tender; drain. Put in shallow 2-quart casserole. Mix soup with mayonnaise and curry powder. Sprinkle lemon juice over broccoli and pour sauce over top. Sprinkle with bread crumbs and drizzle with melted butter. Bake in preheated 350° oven for 20 minutes, or until bubbly. Makes 6 servings.

BROCCOLI AND CAULIFLOWER CASSEROLE

½ head cauliflower
½ head broccoli
¼ cup Parmesan cheese

Salt and pepper to taste
1 cup veloute sauce (recipe follows)

Cut broccoli and cauliflower into chunks and simmer in salted water until just barely tender. Drain and chop coarsely by hand or in a food processor. Mix vegetables with seasonings, half of the Parmesan cheese and the veloute sauce. Spread evenly in buttered casserole, top with remaining cheese and bake in a 350° oven for 25-30 minutes. Makes 4-6 servings.

VELOUTE SAUCE

1 tablespoon butter
1½ tablespoons flour

1 cup milk
Salt and pepper to taste

In a saucepan over low heat, melt the butter. Stir in the flour and cook slowly while stirring for two minutes. Add the milk and continue stirring while bringing liquid to a boil. Simmer, while stirring, until sauce thickens. Makes 1 cup.

MARINATED BROCCOLI

3 bunches broccoli
1 cup cider vinegar
1 tablespoon sugar
1 tablespoon dill weed

1 teaspoon salt
1 teaspoon pepper
1 teaspoon garlic salt
½ to 1½ cups vegetable oil as desired

Cut tops off broccoli and do not use heavy stems. Steam tops for a few minutes until tender-crunchy. Combine other ingredients and pour over broccoli. Refrigerate 24 hours. Drain before serving. Serves 20.

This can be used as a cold vegetable or at cocktail buffets.

BRUSSELS SPROUTS AND MUSHROOMS

1 quart (1¾ pounds) Brussels sprouts
Salt
2 tablespoons finely chopped onions
½ pound fresh mushrooms, sliced

3 tablespoons butter or margarine
Pepper
Canned pimento, cut in strips

Wash and trim sprouts. Put in saucepan with 1 cup boiling water; add salt to taste. Cook, uncovered, 5 minutes. Cover and cook 10 minutes, or just until crisp-tender; drain. Meanwhile, cook mushrooms in the butter until tender and golden brown. Add to sprouts and season with salt and pepper to taste. Put in serving dish and garnish with pimento strips. Makes 6 servings.

Two boxes (10 ounces each) frozen Brussels sprouts can be substituted for the fresh. Cook as directed on the label. Drain and proceed as directed.

BRUSSELS SPROUTS WITH TARRAGON-MUSTARD SAUCE

1 pound Brussels sprouts, washed and
trimmed
Salt
1½ tablespoons butter or margarine
1½ tablespoons flour

¾ teaspoon dry mustard
¼ teaspoon tarragon leaves, crushed
1 cup chicken broth or bouillon
1 tablespoon vinegar

Cook sprouts in small amount of lightly salted boiling water until just tender. Sauté onion in the butter until tender but not browned. Stir in flour, mustard and tarragon. Add broth and vinegar and cook, stirring, until smooth and thickened. Serve over drained sprouts. Makes 4 servings.

BRUSSELS SPROUTS IN SWEET AND SOUR SAUCE

½ pound sliced bacon, cooked and
drained
6 10-ounce packages Brussels sprouts,
thawed
1 medium onion, chopped

⅓ cup cider vinegar
3 tablespoons sugar
1½ teaspoons salt
½ teaspoon dry mustard
¼ teaspoon pepper

In bacon drippings, cook Brussels sprouts with remaining ingredients until tender-crisp, about 10 minutes, stirring occasionally. Stir in crumbled bacon. Serves 18.

DEVILED BRUSSELS SPROUTS

2 cups cooked Brussels sprouts
½ cup butter
2 tablespoons minced onion
1 tablespoon mustard

½ teaspoon salt
1 teaspoon Worcestershire sauce
Dash red pepper

Cook Brussels sprouts until crisp. Melt butter and cook onion. Blend in remaining ingredients. Drain sprouts and turn in casserole dish. Pour sauce over and serve.

Donna Beardsworth (Mrs. Jim)

SWISS STYLE GREEN BEANS

1 large package frozen green beans or 4
    cans green beans (French-style is best)

Bring to boil in 1 cup water and cook 5 minutes. (If canned, simply drain.) Put beans in slow cooker along with:

2 cans, undiluted, cream of mushroom
    soup
8 ounces Swiss cheese, shredded

1 tablespoon Worcestershire sauce

and let cook on high setting while you go to the football game (or 3-4 hours). This could also be put in a buttered casserole and baked at 350° for 45 minutes. Serves 12-16.

Pat Jemian (Mrs. Wartan)

Pat uses this at their annual homecoming barbecue supper for Materials Engineering students, alumni and friends. They send invitations only to students and new people since others know that if they have been once invited, they still are, and they are welcome to bring parents, family and dates. They say it is always great to see the alumni and other friends.

CARROT PENNIES

2 pounds carrots
1 green pepper, sliced in rings

1 medium sized onion, sliced in rings

Marinade:
½ cup salad oil
½ cup sugar
¾ cup vinegar
1 teaspoon prepared mustard

1 teaspoon Worcestershire sauce
1 can condensed tomato soup
Salt and pepper to taste

Scrape, slice and boil carrots until tender. Drain and cool. In bowl: alternate layers of carrots, green pepper rings, and onion slices. Pour marinade over vegetables. Cover and refrigerate. Keeps well for some time. Serve as salad or as separate vegetable.

Martha Applebee (Mrs. Frank)

The marinade alone makes a delicious salad dressing.

GLAZED CARROTS

1½-2 pounds carrots, scraped, cut into
  2″ pieces
1 can beef bouillon

2 tablespoons brown sugar
6 tablespoons butter or margarine

Combine all ingredients in heavy saucepan. Cover and cook 40 minutes. Check liquid level occasionally. Serve with 2 tablespoons chopped parsley.

ORANGE GLAZED CARROTS

2 pounds carrots
1 tablespoon sugar
2 teaspoons cornstarch

½ teaspoon salt
¾ cup orange juice

Wash carrots thoroughly; scrape; cut into 2″ pieces. Bring about 1 inch water to boiling in a large saucepan. Add salt and carrots. Cook, covered, 10 minutes, or until carrots are just tender. Drain. Combine sugar, cornstarch and salt in saucepan; add orange juice. Cook over medium heat, stirring constantly, until sauce thickens and bubbles. Add cooked carrots to sauce; heat 3 minutes. Makes 6 servings.

Orange juice in the sauce brings out the fresh taste in carrots.

SOUFFLE OF CAULIFLOWER

1 cauliflower
1 stick margarine
⅓ cup all-purpose flour
1½ cups milk

3-ounce package cream cheese,
  softened
4 eggs, separated
Dash of salt and pepper
Dash of thyme

Cook cauliflower after breaking into small flowerets until tender (about 10 minutes). Drain. Put into food processor until smooth. Add flour to melted margarine in a heavy pan. Stir until smooth; cook one minute, stirring constantly. Slowly add milk to make a white sauce. Beat egg yolks until thick and lemon colored. Stir 2 ounces (¼ cup) of white sauce slowly into yolks; add this mixture into remaining white sauce. Stir in cream cheese until melted. Add cauliflower and spices and stir well. Beat egg whites until stiff and gently fold into cauliflower mixture. Bake at 350° in soufflé dish for 45 to 50 minutes. Serve immediately. Serves 6 to 8.

SKILLET CABBAGE

4 cups shredded cabbage (½ head)
1 green pepper, shredded
2 cups diced celery
2 large onions, sliced

2 tomatoes, chopped
¼ cup bacon drippings
2 tablespoons sugar

Combine all ingredients in large skillet. Cover and cook over medium heat for 5-7 minutes, stirring occasionally. Season with salt and pepper to taste.

HOMINY BAKE FOR COOKOUTS

2 cans white hominy
2 4-ounce cans green chilies, chopped
Salt and pepper to taste
Sour cream

Butter
½ cup heavy cream
1 cup (or more if you like) Monterrey
   Jack cheese

Drain and rinse hominy. Butter a large casserole dish. Layer the ingredients in this order: hominy, green chilies, salt and pepper, dot with sour cream and butter. Repeat layers, ending with hominy. Dot top with butter and pour cream over all. Sprinkle with cheese. Bake at 350° for 25-30 minutes. Serve hot.
   This is a great dish to serve with meat cooked on the grill.

PATTY'S CORN CASSEROLE

1 can 16-ounce cream style corn
1 cup yellow cornmeal
2 eggs
¼ cup corn oil
1 chopped bell pepper
1 chopped white onion

1 can B&B mushrooms, bits and
   pieces, drained
½ teaspoon salt
½ teaspoon baking soda
1 cup buttermilk
1 cup grated cheddar cheese

Beat eggs and mix all together. Grease 8x8x2 casserole. Bake at 350° for 1 hour, or until slightly brown.

Page Adams (Mrs. Murray)

This is great for barbecues—especially good with ribs. The Adams use it for special holidays like Father's Day or Fourth of July.

CORN PUDDING

2 cups corn (fresh or frozen, chopped a
   little)
2 tablespoons flour
1 teaspoon salt

3 tablespoons butter (melted)
3 eggs
2 tablespoons sugar
1¾ cups milk

Blend butter, sugar, flour and salt. Add eggs, beating well. Stir in corn and milk. Pour all into buttered (or Pam sprayed) casserole and bake 45 minutes at 325°.

Stir over halfway through cooking time. When done—golden brown and knife comes out clean.

Jack Blackburn

SIMPLE CORN SOUFFLÉ OR PUDDING

1 can creamed-style yellow corn
8 eggs, beaten well
¾ cup milk

2 tablespoons flour
¼ stick butter, melted

Mix corn and flour. Mix beaten eggs and milk and melted butter. Combine corn and egg mixture. Bake in greased soufflé dish or casserole 350° until puffed and slightly browned (about 40 minutes).

Patti Tremaine (Mrs. Chuck)

EGGPLANT CAKES

1 measuring cup *full* of cooked eggplant
⅓ cup sifted flour
⅛ teaspoon baking powder

¼ teaspoon salt
2 tablespoons sugar (slightly rounded)

Pare and slice eggplant about ½ inch thick. Cook in deep boiler in plenty of water until perfectly tender. This will not take long, about 15 or 20 minutes. Drain off all water. Put in mixing bowl, add flour, salt, baking powder and sugar. Put about 1 inch of grease in skillet—don't have too hot. Drop batter as for batter cakes. These burn easily, so watch. This amount will make 8 nice size cakes. Any batter left can be kept in refrigerator to be used later.

Theo Mosley (Mrs. Kelly)

Auburn has no more loyal or generous supporters than the Kelly Mosleys. Kelly's personal gifts and corporate leadership have been directly responsible over the last 15 years in establishing programs which have enhanced the cultural life of the University, the Franklin Lectures in Science and Humanities, and the Draughon Lectures in Southern History.

MOUSSAKA

1 very large or 2 medium or small
  eggplants (you need enough for 3
  layers in casserole)
Flour (to coat eggplant)
½ cup oleo (to brown eggplant)
1 pound ground chuck or steak
2 8-ounce cans tomato sauce

½ teaspoon salt
1 envelope onion soup mix
1 pint (2 small boxes) sour cream (you
  really need 2)
2 eggs
Parmesan cheese

Pare and slice eggplant into ½- to ¼-inch slices and either half or quarter; dust with flour and brown on both sides. Drain on towels. Arrange ⅓ of eggplant in bottom of 2-quart casserole (9x13). Brown meat in skillet. Add tomato sauce and salt and simmer about 5 minutes. Use half of meat and top the eggplant. Combine: onion soup mix, sour cream and 1 tablespoon flour. Beat eggs and add to sour cream mixture. Spread half this mixture over the ground beef. Top with ⅓ of eggplant. (May be spaced fairly apart.) Add the remaining ground beef, and finally last of eggplant. Top with sour cream and sprinkle with Parmesan cheese. Serves 8 (maybe 10) generously. Bake 375° until bubbly hot and golden brown, 30-40 minutes.

STUFFED GARDEN EGGPLANT

2 large eggplants
½ cup chopped celery
¾ cup chopped onion
½ cup chopped bell pepper
2 cloves garlic, chopped

½ cup parsley, chopped
1 cup ham (ground)
¾ stick butter
2 eggs
1½ cups cracker crumbs

Sauté onions, garlic, bell pepper and celery in butter. Scoop out eggplants and boil in salted water. Drain and add to sautéed ingredients. Add cracker crumbs, beaten eggs and ground ham. Season with black pepper, pinch of sugar, Worcestershire sauce and Tabasco. Put all in skillet and cook for awhile. Then put into shells that have been scalded. Cover with crumbs, Parmesan cheese and paprika. Bake 15 minutes.

Ethel Vaughan (Mrs. Tom)

EGGPLANT CASSEROLE

1 large eggplant, peeled and sliced
3 medium tomatoes, peeled and sliced
1 large bell pepper, diced
1 large onion, sliced and separated into
  rings

Bacon strips
1½ cups bread crumbs

Cook eggplant in salt water. Drain. Layer in buttered 2½-quart casserole the eggplant, tomato slices, onion, pepper, and bread crumbs. Salt and pepper each layer. Repeat ending with bread crumbs. Place bacon strips on top. Bake at 350° for 1 hour.

STUFFED EGGPLANT

1 eggplant
1 green pepper, chopped
1 small onion, chopped
1 cup chopped ripe olives
1 cup grated cheese
1 cup Pepperidge Farm seasoned stuffing

1 teaspoon salt
½ teaspoon pepper
1 tablespoon butter
Paprika
1 teaspoon chopped parsley

Boil eggplant (cut in half lengthwise) for 20 minutes or until tender. Cool. Scoop out the pulp leaving shells intact—or just make a casserole with scooped out pulp. Mash the pulp and add remaining ingredients, reserving some cheese and crumbs for topping. Refill the shells or put in buttered casserole. Dot with butter. Top with crumbs, cheese and paprika and parsley.

DEEP-FRIED EGGPLANT

1 eggplant
6 tablespoons self-rising flour
½ teaspoon salt

2 teaspoons soy sauce
2 cups salad oil, or peanut oil

Cut eggplant into halves, then cut each half in ¼-inch thick slices. Combine flour and ½ to ¾ cup cold water. Add water gradually to make a smooth batter. Heat oil in wok until very hot. Dip eggplant slices into the batter and deep-fry until golden brown. Drain on a paper towel and serve immediately.

FRIED MUSHROOMS

Batter:
1 egg, beaten
¾ cup self-rising flour

2 tablespoons cooking oil
Salt to taste

Mix above ingredients together. (Mixture will be stiff.) Then gradually add *ice water* until batter is runny.
Dip whole mushrooms in batter and deep fry. Serve with a sauce made of:

½ cup mayonnaise
2 tablespoons lemon juice

1 tablespoon grated onion
2 tablespoons pickle relish

Lamar Ellis Sargent (Mrs. G.T., Jr.)

This batter works wonderfully for shrimp, fish, eggplant, onion rings, etc.

CEPES SAUTÉS PAYSANNE
(French Mushrooms)

6 slices bacon
2 pounds fresh, raw mushrooms, sliced
1 teaspoon lemon juice
1 small onion, finely chopped
1 clove garlic, crushed

2 tablespoons fine, dry breadcrumbs
½ teaspoon salt
Freshly ground pepper
1 tablespoon finely chopped parsley

Cook bacon until crisp. Drain and crumble. In the same pan, sauté mushrooms in bacon grease for about 3 minutes (do not overcook). Add butter if necessary. Sprinkle with lemon juice. Add onion, garlic, and bread crumbs and sauté, stirring constantly, for 3 more minutes. Add bacon, salt, pepper and parsley and mix well. Serve hot. Especially good with steaks. Serves 4 to 6.

Jean Bullock (Mrs. Bill)

CREAMED MUSHROOMS

½ pound fresh mushrooms
2 tablespoons butter or margarine
1 tablespoon oil
2 tablespoons chopped green onion

1 teaspoon flour
¾ cup whipping cream
⅛ teaspoon salt, pinch pepper
2 tablespoons Madeira or sherry

Sauté mushrooms in butter and oil for 4 to 5 minutes over medium heat. Add onions and stir for a few minutes. Add flour and cook for 2 minutes. Remove from heat and stir in cream and seasonings. Return to heat until cream thickens. Add Madeira or sherry. Stir one minute and then serve.

BROUN HALL MUSHROOMS

1 pound fresh mushrooms
4 tablespoons oleo or butter
1 tablespoon finely chopped onion
¾ teaspoon salt
¼ teaspoon ground nutmeg

⅛ teaspoon ginger
4 tablespoons all purpose flour
½ cup milk
3 dashes Tabasco
2 large eggs, well beaten

Wash, dry and coarsely chop mushrooms. Melt 4 tablespoons butter in heavy skillet and sauté onion until transparent. Add mushrooms and stir constantly for 5 minutes. Add flour and seasonings, blend, then take pan off fire and blend in milk and Tabasco. Return to heat and stir until mixture thickens. Cool. Then add well-beaten eggs. Oil 1-quart casserole or 8-cup ring mold and pour in mushroom mixture. Bake in 350° oven 30 minutes or until top lightly browns.
The mushroom ring can be filled with peas for variation.

PUREED PARSNIPS WITH MADEIRA

5 to 6 pounds parsnips
Butter
¼ cup heavy cream
1½ teaspoons salt

Few grains of nutmeg or mace
¼ cup Madeira or bourbon
Sesame seeds

Wash parsnips, put in large pot and cover with water. Boil on medium-high heat 25 minutes, or until tender and pierceable; drain. When cool enough to handle, peel and put in food processor. Whip with ¾ cup butter, softened, the cream, seasonings, and Madeira and whip well. In buttered shallow 3-quart baking dish spoon in and cover with dots of butter and sesame seeds. Bake in preheated 350° oven for 20 to 25 minutes. Serve hot. Makes 8 servings.

FRIED OKRA

2 pounds small okra pods
1 cup cornmeal

Bacon drippings
Salt and pepper

Wash okra, cut off stem and slice in 1-inch pieces. Dry on paper towels. Sprinkle with salt and pepper. Put cornmeal in paper sack and shake okra pieces in bag to coat with cornmeal. Fry in bacon drippings until light brown. To oven fry okra, prepare as above, place in a single layer on a cookie sheet and at 350° until tender and crisp.

STUFFED ONIONS

6 large sweet Spanish onions
1 package (10 ounces) frozen mixed
  vegetables, cooked and drained
1 can condensed cheddar cheese soup

½ teaspoon salt
⅛ teaspoon pepper
1 tablespoon butter, melted
¼ cup seasoned bread crumbs

Peel onions, cut slice from top of each. Cook in boiling salted water in a large saucepan just until tender, about 45 minutes. Drain. Carefully remove onion centers, leaving 3 outer rings intact. Chop enough of the centers to measure 2 cups. Wrap remaining onion centers in plastic or foil; freeze for later use in casseroles or meat loaves. Combine the chopped onion with cooked vegetables, soup, salt and pepper. Place onion shells in a shallow 6-cup baking dish; fill with vegetable mixture. Combine butter with bread crumbs; sprinkle over filled onions. Bake in moderate oven (375°) 20 minutes, or until crumbs are browned.

ONION PIE

2 pounds onions, thinly sliced
1 stick butter
3 eggs, well-beaten
1 cup sour cream

1 unbaked pastry shell
Dash Tabasco
Grated Parmesan cheese

Sauté onions in butter. Combine eggs and sour cream. Add to onion mixture. Season mixture and pour in pastry shell. Season to taste. Top with cheese. Bake at 450° for 20 minutes, then at 325° for 20 minutes more.
    A wonderful addition to any beef meal.

Will you have some more sauce to your leek?

Henry V (V-i-50)

GARDEN MEDLEY

4 small yellow squash or zucchini
4 tablespoons butter and bacon fat
  mixed
1 large onion, thinly sliced
2 green peppers, cut in strips
4 tomatoes, peeled and wedged

1½ teaspoons salt
½ teaspoon freshly ground pepper
⅛ teaspoon cayenne
1 10-ounce can corn, or if fresh, cut
  from three ears

Dice squash into ½-inch pieces. Melt butter and bacon fat and sauté squash in it until partly brown. Remove squash and add onions and green pepper. Cook until vegetables are limp. Add tomatoes. Season with salt, pepper, and cayenne. Cook, uncovered, for 30 minutes. Return squash to pan and heat thoroughly. Wonderful as a side dish with chicken.

POTATO CASSEROLE

1 8-ounce package cream cheese, softened
5 cups hot mashed potatoes
1 beaten egg

Salt and pepper to taste
2 tablespoons minced chives

Mix hot potatoes and cream cheese until well blended. Add remaining ingredients and beat thoroughly. Put into oiled 1½-quart casserole. Dot with butter and bake uncovered at 350° for about 40 minutes.

POTATO PIE

1 10-inch unbaked pastry shell
1 pound cottage cheese
2 cups mashed potatoes (mashed or instant)
½ cup sour cream

2 eggs
2 teaspoons salt
⅛ teaspoon cayenne
½ cup scallions or green onions, sliced
3 tablespoons grated Parmesan cheese

Blend cottage cheese to make it smooth and beat potatoes into cottage cheese. Beat in sour cream, eggs, salt and cayenne. Stir in scallions or onions. Spoon into pastry shell. Sprinkle with Parmesan. Bake for 50 minutes at 450°, or until golden brown.

Jack Blackburn

POTATOES AND CHEESE RISOLLE (RIS SOW LAY)

2 pounds potatoes
½ stick of butter (¼ cup)
6 egg yolks
½ teaspoon white pepper and salt
1 teaspoon red pepper

1 pound Swiss cheese, grated—use sharp
Sifted all-purpose flour
2 eggs
Soft bread crumbs

Peel potatoes, cut into eighths, and boil with 1 tablespoon salt for about 15 minutes. Drain potatoes and mash well. Place in a dry saucepan and add the butter. Cook over low heat, stirring constantly, until butter is melted and mixture is dry. Refrigerate in a bowl until cool. Beat in egg yolks, pepper and salt to taste. Add the cheese and stir until well mixed. Chill again. Shape with hands into 4-inch sausage-shaped rolls; coat each roll well with flour. Beat the eggs with ¼ cup water until mixed. Dip potato rolls into eggs, then coat well with bread crumbs. Place on a cookie sheet and chill thoroughly. Fry in deep fat until brown; do not overcook. Drain on paper towels and place on platter. Garnish with chopped parsley. Keep warm in 200° oven. This recipe may be prepared and refrigerated for 24 hours before frying. Serves 8.

FRENCH-FRY BAKE

1 16-ounce package frozen French-fried
  potatoes
1 cup diluted Pet milk
¼ cup chopped green pepper

¼ cup chopped onion
6 slices American cheese
2 tablespoons butter
Salt and pepper

Layer the above ingredients in a generously oiled 1½-quart casserole. Cover and bake for about 45 minutes in 350° oven. Garnish with parsley and bacon bits. Serves 6.

Hazel Cooper (Mrs. Ben)

Easily prepared for formal meal for 6 or patio buffet for 60.

PARTY PIMENTO POTATOES

6 cups cubed cooked potatoes
1 stick butter
¼ cup sliced green onions
½ cup chopped green pepper
¼ cup chopped pimento, undrained
2 teaspoons salt

¼ teaspoon pepper
1 tablespoon parsley flakes
1 teaspoon paprika
6 tablespoons flour
4 cups milk
½ pound shredded sharp cheese

Sauté onions, green pepper and pimentos about 1 minute. Add seasonings and flour. Blend in milk, stirring until thickened. Add potatoes and 1 cup cheese. Stir until cheese is melted. Pour into a casserole. Spread remaining cheese on top. Bake at 350° for 30 to 45 minutes. Makes 10 to 12 servings. Make ahead and refrigerate before baking. Freezes well.

POTATO CASSEROLE

2 cups instant potato flakes
2 cups boiling water
1 teaspoon salt
¼ stick butter

1 small can evaporated milk
1 clove garlic, crushed in press
Salt and pepper

Put potato flakes into boiling water and stir. Add milk, butter, garlic, salt and pepper. Put in 2-quart casserole, dot with additional butter, and bake, uncovered, in 375° oven 20 minutes. Serve hot.

This is a great dish to serve at the lake or in emergency situations at home because the ingredients can be stored on a supply shelf and don't have to be transported.

BAKED POTATOES IN CRUMB COATS

Peeled baking potatoes
1 tablespoon butter per potato, melted
Bread crumbs

Paprika
Salt and pepper

Roll washed, peeled potatoes in melted butter, then coat in bread crumbs, mixed with salt, pepper and paprika. Place in shallow, oiled casserole, pour over left-over butter, cover tightly with foil and bake for 40 minutes in 350° oven. Remove foil and bake 20 more minutes to brown potatoes.

POTATO CASSEROLE

2 pounds frozen hash browns
½ cup margarine, melted
1 teaspoon salt
½ teaspoon pepper
1 can cream of chicken soup, undiluted

2 cups grated cheddar cheese
½ onion, chopped
2 cups sour cream
2 cups cornflakes, crushed and mixed
    with ½ stick melted butter

Mix all except cornflakes. Put in 3-quart casserole. Spread cornflakes and butter on top. Bake at 350° for 45 minutes to 1 hour.

Peggy Holloway (Mrs. Clarke)

The Holloways served this at a dinner for one of their favorite students and her family when she graduated from vet school. (Her father and brother are both psychiatrists, which for some reason raised Peggy's anxiety level; however, the whole family was delightful and this dish was a big hit!)

SWEET POTATO CASSEROLE

4 or 5 boiled sweet potatoes (big)
2 tablespoons salt in water
1 small can evaporated milk
2 eggs
1 cup sugar

1 teaspoon vanilla
1 stick melted oleo
1 jigger bourbon
¼ cup orange juice
1 cup chopped nuts (pecans)

Mix together all the above with electric mixer and put in a buttered casserole.

Topping:

1 stick oleo
1 cup chopped pecans

1 cup brown sugar
1 cup flour

Mix and spread on top. Bake 45 minutes at 350°.

Carol Savage (Mrs. Morris)

VERY GOOD SWEET POTATOES

2 cups mashed sweet potatoes
½ cup melted butter
1 cup sugar
2 eggs
¼ teaspoon nutmeg

¼ teaspoon cinnamon
⅛ teaspoon cloves
1 cup evaporated milk
½ cup coconut

Blend potatoes, butter and sugar. Add eggs, beating after each. Add spices and milk. Mix thoroughly. Bake in buttered pan in moderate oven 375° for 35 minutes. Remove from oven and sprinkle with coconut. Return to oven and bake 10 minutes longer. Serve warm or cold.

Gaynell Parks (Mrs. Paul)

These are good with ham and turkey.

YUMMY YAMS

4 pounds sweet potatoes or yams,
   cooked and mashed
1 stick butter or margarine
¼ to ½ cup bourbon
⅓ cup orange juice

⅓ cup firmly packed brown sugar
1 teaspoon salt
½ teaspoon apple pie spice
½ cup chopped pecans

Combine all ingredients except pecans in large bowl. Mix well. Pour into greased 2½-quart casserole. Combine ¼ cup brown sugar and the chopped pecans and sprinkle over top of casserole. Garnish with shredded orange rind. Bake 350° for 45 minutes. Makes 8-10 servings.

Dotty Cavender (Mrs. Ray)

SWEET POTATO SPECIAL

3 cups cooked mashed sweet potatoes
1 cup sugar
2 eggs

1 teaspoon vanilla
½ stick oleo
1 can coconut

Combine all the above and add topping:

1 cup brown sugar
½ stick oleo

1 cup chopped pecans
½ cup flour

Mix this well and put on top of potato mixture. Bake 1 hour at 350° until brown.

Angie Dollar (Mrs. Mason)

STUFFED SWEET POTATOES

6 sweet potatoes
½ cup butter
1 cup drained, crushed pineapple

5 tablespoons brown sugar
½ cup orange juice
¼ cup chopped pecans (optional)

Bake potatoes and cut in half lengthwise. Scoop out potato and reserve shells. Beat potato with remaining ingredients until fluffy. Fill potato shells. Sprinkle pecans on top, if desired, and bake at 350° about 20 minutes. These freeze beautifully.

Variation: Use rum in place of the orange juice.

Sweet potatoes are very pretty put into orange halves from which the pulp has been scooped out. This is more trouble, but worth it for special occasions.

RICE ORIENTAL

3 teaspoons soy sauce   ½ cup Wesson oil

Mix these two ingredients in a heavy skillet and when hot add five chopped onions and cook for 5 minutes. Pour in 2½ cups dry regular rice and 1 small can chopped olives. Add 5 cans of consommé and garlic salt to taste. Cover and cook for one hour at low heat on top of the stove or in a 350° casserole or skillet. Remove lid and add 1 stick of butter, 3 teaspoons soy sauce and 2 or 3 pounds cooked and peeled shrimp. Let stand for about one hour. Serves 8.

WINE RICE

1 cup rice	Red wine
1 cup chopped fresh tomatoes	2 teaspoons salt, ¼ teaspoon pepper
½ cup onion	1 cup tiny peas, drained
1 pound fresh mushrooms, sliced	½ cup butter
Chicken broth	¼ to ½ cup grated Parmesan cheese

Place rice, mushrooms, onion and tomato in large skillet. Add the amount of chicken broth to equal the amount needed to cook the rice, less ½ cup. Add the ½ cup wine, salt and pepper. Mix well. Simmer 30-40 minutes, covered. Stir in peas and butter and season with cheese.

Variation: Add shrimp, cut up chicken, or ham for a main dish. Leftover rice makes a delicious salad when blue cheese dressing is stirred in. Makes 8 servings.

RICE ROMANOFF

3 cups cooked rice	1 teaspoon salt
½ cup chopped green onion	¼ teaspoon pepper
1½ cups grated sharp cheddar cheese	Paprika
1 cup sour cream	

Combine rice, green onion, ½ cup cheese and toss lightly. Turn into buttered 1½-cup casserole. Blend together remaining cheese, sour cream, salt and pepper. Spread over top of rice. Sprinkle with paprika. Bake at 350° 30 minutes. Makes 6 servings.

CURRIED RICE

6 tablespoons butter
3 tablespoons oil (to prevent butter from burning)
½ cup slivered almonds (chop whole almonds) cashews are good, too
2 large or 3 or more cloves garlic (whole cloves—peel and chop)
1 cup chopped onion (fry 1-2 minutes, medium high)

2 teaspoons curry powder
1 teaspoon coriander
1½ cups long grain rice
3¾ cups *hot* chicken broth
¼ cup dry vermouth
1 teaspoon salt
½ teaspoon white pepper
½ cup golden raisins soaked in ¼ cup dry sherry

Use heavy pan. Sauté nuts in oil and butter; brown, remove to paper towel and drain. Add garlic, onions, curry, coriander, rice (medium high heat). Add vermouth—cook down about 2-3 minutes. Add salt and pepper. Add chicken broth (hot), 1 cup at a time. Cook with top off. Stir from time to time. When liquid is absorbed, add another cup, etc., 30-35 minutes. Will be wet. Hold on low temperature—don't overcook. At end put in almonds and raisins when ready to serve. Serves 6-8.

This was served at Holy Trinity Episcopal Churchwomen's Christmas luncheon.

GEORGE'S FAVORITE SPINACH

2 10-ounce packages frozen chopped spinach
1 package frozen artichokes, or 1 can artichokes, drained

½ cup butter or oleo, melted
1 8-ounce package cream cheese, softened
1 teaspoon lemon juice

Cook spinach and artichokes according to package directions and drain well. Add softened cream cheese, butter, and lemon juice to spinach and blend together. Put artichokes on bottom of greased casserole, top with spinach mixture, then cracker or bread crumbs. Dot with butter. Bake at 350° 25 minutes.

This is just as good and less expensive without the artichokes.

Dorothy Wells Littleton (Mrs. George)

SPINACH AND ARTICHOKE CASSEROLE

5 10-ounce packages frozen chopped spinach
1 14-ounce can artichoke hearts
2 cups sour cream

1 envelope onion soup mix
Salt and pepper
Parmesan cheese and bread crumbs

Cook spinach and drain well. Slice artichokes into fourths. Combine all ingredients except Parmesan cheese and bread crumbs. Pour into oiled 2-quart casserole. Sprinkle top with bread crumbs and Parmesan cheese. Dot with butter and bake at 350° 30 minutes. Serves 12.

SPINACH WITH SOUR CREAM

1 package frozen chopped spinach	½ cup sour cream
1 tablespoon grated onion (more if you like onion)	1 cup grated Parmesan cheese
	2 tablespoons butter
2 eggs	Salt and pepper to taste

Cook spinach with onion. Drain. Beat eggs and mix all ingredients with spinach and onions. Bake in greased casserole for 25-30 minutes in 350° oven or until center is set. Do not overcook as it will separate. Serves 4.

This recipe can be doubled. Leftovers are good warmed in microwave.

HOT SPINACH SQUARES

4 eggs	½ teaspoon thyme
¼ cup melted butter	½ teaspoon nutmeg
⅔ cup milk	2 packages frozen chopped spinach, cooked and drained
½ cup minced onion	
2 tablespoons parsley	2 cups cooked rice
1 teaspoon Worcestershire sauce	2 cups shredded cheese
1½ teaspoon salt	
Garlic salt to taste	

Beat eggs. Add milk, onion, parsley, Worcestershire sauce and seasonings. Mix well. Combine remaining ingredients. Add egg mixture and mix well. Pour in shallow 2 quart baking dish. Bake 325° for 1 hour. Cut into squares.

Sarah Orgel (Mrs. Frank)

SPINACH MIMOSA

5 pounds fresh spinach

Cook 5 or 6 minutes in boiling salted water which covers by several inches. Cover kettle with rack and stand under cold water running until cool. Transfer to colander and squeeze out as much water as possible. Transfer to a cutting board and chop finely with a stainless steel knife. Cook spinach in 6 tablespoons of butter over moderate heat, stirring until moisture has evaporated. Add 1½ to 2 cups heavy cream, ½ cup at a time, stirring. Season spinach with nutmeg, salt and pepper and simmer it over low heat until it is hot and the cream is reduced to the desired consistency. Transfer to heated serving dish. Mark with spatula, sprinkle edges with sliced yolks of two hard-boiled eggs. Garnish with sautéed croutons (cut into decorator shapes if desired).

Marjorie Tyre Sykes (Mrs. Maltby)

SPINACH-STUFFED SQUASH

12 firm medium yellow squash	Seasoned salt to taste and pepper
2 packages frozen chopped spinach	1 onion, chopped
1 cup sour cream	Saltine cracker crumbs
1 tablespoon butter	Grated Parmesan cheese

Cut squash in half lengthwise and scoop out seeds and discard. Cook in salted water until barely tender. Drain. Cook spinach. Drain well, press out extra water. Combine spinach with sour cream, butter, salt, onion and pepper. Stuff squash with spinach mixture. Sprinkle with cracker crumbs and cheese. Bake at 325° for 30 minutes. Zucchini may be used instead of yellow squash. Serves 12-24.

SPINACH-STUFFED TOMATOES

2 packages frozen chopped spinach
6 strips of bacon
8 tomatoes
1 onion, chopped
1 cup sour cream

Salt and pepper to taste
Tabasco
6 ounces grated mozzarella cheese
2 slices mozzarella cheese, cut in strips

Cook spinach according to package directions. Drain well. Shell tomatoes and chop insides. Drain shells; salt inside and turn upside down on paper towels. Cook bacon until crisp, drain and crumble. Save 2 tablespoons drippings to sauté onions in. Add bacon and onion to spinach and tomatoes. Add sour cream, salt, pepper and Tabasco to taste. Add grated cheese. Fill shells with mixture. Top with strips of cheese. Heat in buttered pan until cheese is melted, about 20 minutes 350°. May be made a day ahead. Serves 8.

ABBIE'S SQUASH SOUFFLÉ

2 pounds yellow squash, sliced
1 small onion, chopped
2 eggs, beaten with fork
1 tablespoon flour

1 teaspoon baking powder
1 teaspoon sugar
Salt and pepper

Cover onion and squash with water and cook. Drain well, mash and cool. Add remaining ingredients and mix well. Put in buttered 2-quart casserole. Sprinkle bread crumbs on top, dot with butter and bake ½ hour at 350°.

MARINATED SQUASH

⅔ cup vinegar
⅓ cup sugar
¼ teaspoon celery salt
¼ teaspoon pepper

½ teaspoon onion salt
½ teaspoon oregano
1 small onion, thinly sliced
9 small squash, thinly sliced

Make marinade by mixing together first 6 ingredients and stirring until sugar is dissolved. Pour over onion and squash slices. Marinate overnight. Serves 12.

This can be used as a vegetable or as an ingredient in vegetable trays at cocktail parties.

BAKED BUTTERNUT SQUASH

½ squash per person   Margarine or butter
Brown sugar

Wash squash and cut lengthwise. Remove seeds. Rub outside with vegetable oil. Put 1 tablespoon brown sugar and ¼ cup margarine in hollow left by seeds. Bake at 325° for 1 hour, basting top of squash once or twice with mixture of margarine and brown sugar from hollowed-out place. Great with any kind of pork.

SQUASH AND VIDALIA ONIONS

Layer slices of squash and onions in greased casserole dish. Season to taste. Pour ½ cup whipping cream over vegetables. Sprinkle top with bread crumbs. Dot top with butter. Cook 25 minutes in 300° oven.

SQUASH CASSEROLE

1 pound squash, cut up   ½ cup chopped onion
½ cup chopped green pepper   Salt

Boil until tender. Drain and add:
½ cup pimento   ½ cup mayonnaise (or sour cream or
½ cup grated cheese   cream of celery soup)
½ stick oleo   1 teaspoon sugar
1 beaten egg

Cover with corn bread crumbs, or crushed potato chips or bread crumbs. Bake at 350° for 30 minutes. Serves 4-6.

NEW ENGLAND SQUASH PIE

1 can prepared squash (14½ ounces)   ½ teaspoon nutmeg
½ cup sugar   ½ teaspoon cinnamon
½ teaspoon salt   2 eggs (beaten)
1 teaspoon ginger   1½ cups milk

Mix sugar, salt and spices. Blend well into squash. Beat 2 eggs separately, add milk, stir well and blend into squash mixture. Pour into 9″ pie plate lined with crust. Preheat oven to 425°. Bake 20 minutes at 425° then bake 45 minutes at 375°.

Martha Applebee (Mrs. Frank)

This was a favorite of Frank Applebee's mother, Hattie Murray.

SQUASH POULET POTAGE

3 pounds yellow summer squash
1 small onion, chopped
1 carrot, grated
Chopped parsley
1 10¾-ounce can condensed cream of
chicken soup

1 cup sour cream
Hot pepper sauce to taste
½ stick butter
Pepperidge Farm herb seasoned
stuffing

Wash and slice squash. Cook squash, onion and salt in water in covered saucepan until tender. Drain well, and mash thoroughly with fork. Add carrot, parsley, undiluted soup, sour cream and pepper sauce to taste. Oil large flat casserole. Cover bottom of casserole with stuffing mix. Top this with squash, then sprinkle on layer of stuffing mix. Dot with butter and bake uncovered 50 minutes at 325°. Freezes well. Serves 12.

TOMATO AND SQUASH CASSEROLE

2 pounds yellow summer squash
4 ribs celery
1 large onion
2 cloves garlic, minced
½ to ¾ cup margarine

1 tablespoon oregano
1 tablespoon basil
1½ teaspoon salt
1 teaspoon freshly ground black
pepper
¼ to ½ cup grated Parmesan cheese

Clean and slice vegetables. Cook squash and celery in boiling salted water until barely tender. Put drained vegetables into lightly oiled 2-quart flat casserole. Sauté onions in margarine until tender. Put onions over other vegetables, but keep margarine in skillet. Sauté garlic and all other seasonings in margarine. Put half of this mixture over vegetables. Peel and slice tomatoes and put a layer over vegetables in casserole. Spread remaining seasonings and margarine over tomatoes. Sprinkle Parmesan cheese over all. Bake uncovered at 350° for 20 minutes or until bubbly. Casserole can be assembled early, refrigerated and baked just before serving. Serves 6-8.

Anna Louise McKown (Mrs. Delos)

TOMATO CASSEROLE

1 large can of tomatoes (1 pound)
½ cup herb bread stuffing
½ teaspoon garlic salt
¼ teaspoon oregano

2 teaspoons sugar
1 cup grated cheese
1 large onion, sliced
2 tablespoons butter or margarine

Preheat oven to 350° and grease the baking pan. In mixing bowl combine stuffing, garlic salt, oregano and sugar; mix well. Arrange half of the tomatoes and juice in pan. Top with layer of stuffing. Sprinkle with half the grated cheese. Next, add a layer of sliced onions. Repeat layers ending with cheese. Dot with butter and bake for 30 minutes.

WINTER BROILED TOMATOES

Drain canned tomatoes well—arrange in glass pie pan or pyrex baking dish. Sprinkle each with salt, pepper, sugar, garlic powder, ⅛ teaspoon dried basil and chives, 1-2 teaspoons grated Parmesan cheese. Put under broiler until heated and cheese is lightly browned, 5-10 minutes. Do not overcook or cheese will be bitter.

TOMATOES LANGDON

2 pounds tomatoes halved, peeled and
  seeded
¼ teaspoon sugar

½ stick butter or oleo
1 cup heavy cream (I use half and
  half)

In large skillet, cook tomatoes with sugar, salt and pepper over low heat for 5 minutes. Stir in cream and cook 5 minutes more. Transfer tomatoes to vegetable dish and cook sauce until it is reduced by half. Pour over tomatoes. They are delicious as is, or may be garnished with crisp crumbled bacon or chopped parsley.

This is nice for brunch served on toast with crisp bacon strips criss-crossed on top.

BROILED TOMATOES

4 large ripe tomatoes, halved
1 cup seasoned stuffing mix
½ cup Parmesan cheese, grated

4 tablespoons melted butter
Hot prepared mustard to taste

Combine mix, butter and cheese; spread mustard over tomatoes. Spoon mixture over mustard. Broil until top is browned.

Shirley Bartels (Mrs. Jan)

ITALIAN VEGETABLE STEW

1 large onion, chopped
2 cloves garlic, minced
1 large or 2 small zucchini, sliced
1 green pepper cut into thin strips
¼ cup oleo
¼ cup olive or salad oil
1 medium eggplant, pared and cut into
  strips

3 tablespoons flour
4 medium tomatoes, peeled and cut
  into wedges
¼ cup tomato catsup
1 teaspoon salt
¼ teaspoon pepper
1 teaspoon vinegar
½ teaspoon oregano

Sauté first 4 ingredients in oleo and oil until onion is transparent. Coat eggplant with flour and sauté. Add tomatoes. Combine catsup with remaining ingredients. Pour over vegetables, cover, and simmer, stirring occasionally, until vegetables are tender, about 30 minutes. Serves 8.

CHINESE VEGETABLES

1 onion, quartered
Sauté in ¼ cup butter. Add:
¼ pound fresh mushrooms

1 can bean sprouts
1 can bamboo shoots
1 can water chestnuts, sliced

Season with seasoned salt. Simmer 5 minutes.

GREEN AND GOLD CASSEROLE

1 medium onion, chopped
1 tablespoon butter or margarine
1 can (10½ ounces) cheese soup
1 roll (6 ounces) nippy cheese
½ teaspoon garlic powder

1 can (8 ounces) mushrooms (stems and pieces)
1 package (10 ounces) frozen broccoli, cooked and drained
3 cups hot cooked rice
1 can (3 ounces) French fried onions

Cook onions in butter until soft. Add soup, cheese and garlic powder. Cook over low heat, stirring until cheese melts. Add mushrooms plus their liquid, broccoli, and rice. Turn into shallow casserole, top with French fried onions. Bake at 350° for 15-20 minutes or until hot and bubbly. Makes 8 servings

This may be put in several small casseroles and frozen. Bake at 350° for 45 minutes, if frozen.

MARINATED VEGETABLE PLATTER

¼ cup wine vinegar
¼ cup salad oil
½ cup mayonnaise
1 hard cooked egg, grated
4 tablespoons chives
1 can whole green beans

1½ teaspoon prepared mustard
¼ teaspoon salt
¼ teaspoon garlic powder
1 can asparagus spears
1 can artichoke hearts
1 can carrots

Whisk together vinegar and oil. Add mayonnaise, mustard, salt, and garlic powder and continue to whisk. Fold in egg and chives. Using vegetables listed or any other vegetables desired, drain and arrange them separately in a large Pyrex baking dish—do not mix them. Pour marinade over vegetables and refrigerate.

Claire DeBardeleben (Mrs. Charles)

Claire served this at a sewing club luncheon in the spring. It looked beautiful and tasted so good.

Claire DeBardeleben makes a beautiful centerpiece of vegetables in a silver basket. She suggests cabbage, cauliflower, eggplant, peppers—whatever is in season and combines nicely. It's a nice change from fruit or flowers!

VEGETABLE BOUQUET

1 can (1 pound) cut green beans, well drained
1 can (1 pound) red kidney beans, well drained
1 can ripe olives
1 can artichoke hearts, chopped
1½ cups diagonally-sliced celery
1 medium onion, thinly sliced (I use purple)
¼ cup tarragon vinegar
½ cup salad oil

1½ teaspoons MSG
1 can (6-8 ounces) whole or sliced mushrooms
1¼ teaspoons salt
1 4-ounce jar diced pimento
2 tablespoons capers
1 tablespoon fine herbs
¼ teaspoon sugar
¼ teaspoon Tabasco
¼ cup chopped parsley

Combine drained vegetables, celery and onion. For dressing, measure vinegar into container. Add MSG, salt and sugar. Stir until dissolved. Add fine herbs, Tabasco and salad oil. Beat or shake until blended. Pour over vegetables and refrigerate several hours or overnight. Turn into serving bowl and sprinkle with chopped parsley and capers

Fran Hartsfield (Mrs. Hank)

CRISP VEGETABLE MEDLEY

2 cups fresh cauliflower
2 cups fresh broccoli

1 cup carrots, sliced lengthwise

Wash vegetables and put in steamer. Steam 4 minutes. Drain and place in warm bowl. Sprinkle with ¼ cup Parmesan cheese, ¼ cup melted margarine or butter.

MEXICAN STUFFED ZUCCHINI

6 zucchini
1 garlic clove, crushed
1⅓ cups dry breadcrumbs
1 tablespoon chopped fresh basil

1½ cup cheddar or Monterrey Jack cheese
2 eggs lightly beaten
4 tablespoons butter, melted

Scoop flesh from zucchini within ¼ inch of skin. Chop the flesh and press all liquid out. Preheat oven to 400°F. Combine the drained zucchini, garlic, breadcrumbs, basil, cheese, eggs, ½ melted butter. Salt and pepper to taste. Arrange the zucchini shells, skin side down, in a greased shallow baking dish. Stuff with breadcrumb mixture and pour over the remaining melted butter. Bake for 20 to 30 minutes or until the top is brown and bubbling.

ZUCCHINI AND TOMATOES

3 to 4 zucchini, thinly sliced
1 large can tomatoes (juice and all)
1 large onion, thinly sliced

Salt and pepper
1 tablespoon sugar

Add all ingredients and cook over medium heat until zucchini is tender (8 to 12 minutes). Be careful not to scorch. Top with grated cheese of your choice. This is very low in calories.

ZUCCHINI CUSTARD MOLDS

¼ stick butter
1 medium tomato, peeled, cored, seeded
and finely chopped
½ teaspoon dried basil, crumbled
2 egg yolks
1 egg

1 cup whipping cream
Salt and freshly ground pepper
Freshly grated nutmeg
2 cups thinly sliced zucchini, blanched
and well drained

Preheat oven to 375°. Generously butter six 4¾-ounce turban molds or custard cups and set aside. Melt butter in heavy small saucepan over medium-hight heat. Add tomato and cook, stirring frequently, 5 minutes. Remove from heat and add basil. Combine yolks and egg in small bowl and beat lightly. Gradually add cream, blending well. Add salt, pepper and nutmeg. Combine tomato and zucchini in small bowl. Divide evenly among molds, filling each cup ¾ full. Pour cream mixture over vegetables, filling to slightly below rim. Set molds in shallow baking dish. Pour in enough hot water to come halfway up sides of molds. Bake until custard is set, about 30 to 35 minutes (if custard browns too quickly, reduce heat to 350°). Remove molds from water bath and let stand at room temperature 5 minutes. Invert onto individual plates. Serve warm.

SQUASH PICKLES

1 gallon yellow squash, thinly sliced
8 small white onions, chopped
1 green pepper
1 sweet red pepper, chopped
½ cup ice cream salt
5 cups sugar

½ teaspoon turmeric and ½ teaspoon
ground cloves
2 tablespoons mustard seed
2 tablespoons celery seed
5 cups vinegar

Layer squash, onions and peppers in large pot. Cover with ice cream salt and fill with ice and water. Cover and set aside for 3 hours. Combine remaining ing.e-dients and bring to a boil. Drain ice and water from squash and place pot on stove. Pour hot vinegar mixture over squash. Bring to a boil. Stir to coat squash well. Spoon immediately into hot jars. Seal. Makes 8 pints.

MARY GEORGE LAMAR'S CARROT-CUCUMBER RELISH

3½ cups coarsely ground cucumbers	2½ cups sugar
1½ cups coarsely ground carrots	1½ cups vinegar
1 cup coarsely ground onions	1½ teaspoons celery seed
2 tablespoons salt	1½ teaspoons mustard seed

Combine ground vegetables and stir in salt. Let stand three hours and then drain well. Combine remaining ingredients and bring to boil in large container. Add vegetables and simmer, uncovered, for 20 minutes. Seal at once in hot, sterilized jars. This quantity makes 2½ pints. Chill before using.

Mary George Lamar

ICE GREEN TOMATO PICKLES

7 pounds green tomatoes, sliced	1 teaspoon cloves
3 cups lime	1 teaspoon allspice
2 gallons water	1 teaspoon celery seed
5 pounds sugar	1 teaspoon mace
3 pints vinegar	1 teaspoon cinnamon

Dissolve lime in water and pour over sliced tomatoes and let soak for 24 hours. Drain. Soak in fresh water for 4 hours, changing water every hour. Drain. Combine sugar, vinegar and spices. Bring to a boil. Pour over tomatoes and let stand overnight. Boil about 1 hour. Pack into hot sterilized jars and seal.

(I begin making these in the middle of the morning. Cucumbers may be substitued for the green tomatoes).

Mary Timberlake (Mrs. Sam)

DILLED OKRA PICKLES

3 pounds young okra, uncut	1 quart water
Celery leaves	1 pint white vinegar
Garlic cloves	½ cup salt
Large heads of dill with stems	

Scrub okra pods with stiff brush to remove dirt and fuzz. Pack okra pods into hot sterilized pint jars, putting pods in straight up and down. Put a few celery leaves, a clove of garlic, and a head of dill in each jar.

Make brine of quart of water, pint of vinegar, and salt. Heat to boiling. Pour over okra in jars so that it covers pods and reaches nearly to the top of each jar. Seal tightly. Let stand three or four weeks before using. This makes about six pints.

WATERMELON RIND PRESERVES

1 pound cut-up watermelon rind
2 quarts water
2 tablespoons lime

2½ cups sugar
1 quart water
1 lemon sliced

Cut all green and all pink from watermelon rind and cut into bite-size pieces. Soak in the mixture of water and lime for several hours. Drain and rinse well. Soak in clear water an hour. Drain. Cover with water and boil gently for an hour. Bring syrup of 2½ cups sugar and quart of water to boil, add watermelon rind (drained) and boil for an hour. During last part of cooking, add thinly-sliced lemon. When pieces of rind are clear and syrup is thick, put in hot, sterile jars and seal. Cover with syrup before sealing.

KATHARINE COOPER CATER HALL

ENTREES

. . . go to thy fellows, bid them cover the table, serve
in the meat, and we will come in to dinner.
The Merchant of Venice (III-v-56/7)

CATER HALL

Originally built in 1915 as the home for Auburn's Presidents, the house since 1938 has served as the "Social Center" and as administration building, first for women students and currently for the division of student affairs. Named for Katharine Cooper Cater, Auburn's Dean of Women for over thirty years.

BEEF

KABOBS URSULA

Marinade for beef:
1½ pounds beef—cut for kabobs—2-
    inch cubes
Juice of 2 lemons
¼ cup oil, olive or vegetable
2 tablespoons grated onion
1 tablespoon crushed chili pepper

1 tablespoon salt
2 teaspoons curry powder
1 teaspoon coriander
1 teaspoon powdered ginger
1 smashed garlic clove
1 cup chili sauce

Mix together and marinate chunks of beef for about 2 hours—or longer. Alternate on skewers with bell peppers, fresh pineapple, mushrooms, and onions. Grill over charcoal. Serve atop Chutney Rice.

Chutney Rice:
1 cup chopped onions
1 cup sliced celery
4 tablespoons chicken fat, butter, or oleo
3 cups cooked rice
½ cup flaked coconut

¼ cup chopped mango chutney
½ teaspoon ground ginger
1 teaspoon curry powder
½ teaspoon salt

In a skillet, sauté onions and celery in fat until tender crisp. Add rice, chutney, and seasonings. Toss lightly, heat thoroughly.

Ursula Higgins
Greenhouse Restaurant

SHISH KABOB
(A Meal by Itself)

1½ pounds lamb or sirloin, cut in cubes
2 #303 cans small whole potatoes
1 large green pepper cut into squares

1 large onion quartered and separated
2 tomatoes, quartered
8-10 whole mushrooms

Alternate ingredients on a skewer with more meat than other ingredients. Cook over a charcoal fire and baste with a sauce made from butter and Worcestershire sauce.

CURRIED RICE AND BEEF SHISH KABOBS

Marinade for beef:
Juice of 2 lemons
¼ cup oil, olive or vegetable
2 tablespoons grated onion
1 tablespoon crushed chili pepper
1 tablespoon salt

2 teaspoons curry powder
1 teaspoon coriander
1 teaspoon powdered ginger
1 smashed garlic clove

165

Mix together and marinate chunks of beef for about 2 hours. Use a fairly tender cut of meat, like sirloin. Grill or broil to taste. Makes enough marinade for beef for 6.

Chutney Rice:

1 cup chopped onions	½ cup flaked coconut
1 cup sliced celery	¼ cup chopped mango chutney
4 tablespoons chicken fat, butter or margarine	½ teaspoon ground ginger
	1 teaspoon curry powder
3 cups cooked rice	½ teaspoon salt

In a skillet, sauté onions and celery in fat until tender crisp. Add rice, chutney and seasonings. Toss lightly, heat thoroughly.

Stephanie Bond (Mrs. Gordon)

Stephanie likes to serve these shish kabobs at informal dinners.

BEEF TURNOVERS

Filling:

1 pound ground chuck	¼ cup chopped green pepper
1 tablespoon flour	¼ cup finely chopped onion
1 can celery soup (condensed) or mushroom	⅓ cup raisins
	1 teaspoon salt
⅓ cup milk	⅛ teaspoon pepper
¼ cup finely chopped carrot	

Brown meat and drain off drippings. Sprinkle flour over meat. Mix well. Measure ⅓ cup condensed soup. Reserve remaining soup for sauce. Mix milk with soup and add to meat. Stir in green pepper, carrot, raisins, salt and pepper. Cover tightly and cook slowly for 20 minutes. Prepare dough.

Dough:

2 cups all-purpose flour	6 tablespoons shortening
3½ teaspoons baking powder	1 cup buttermilk
¼ teaspoon soda	¾ teaspoon salt

Sift flour, baking powder, salt and soda together. Cut in shortening with pastry cutter until mixture is fine, even crumbs. Add milk and stir until well-mixed. Turn onto floured surface and knead gently 6 or 7 times. Roll out to ⅛-inch thickness circles or squares. Place a generous amount of meat mixture in the center of each. Moisten the edges. Fold over and seal with a fork. Place on baking sheet and bake in 400° oven until lightly browned.

Sauce: Add milk to remaining soup and heat.

Serve over turnovers.

Make these larger for buffet suppers and small for parties. Great for brunch, too.

Dartie Flynt (Mrs. Wayne)

Dartie served these at a brunch given for members of the History Department and other friends before a football game. They are so good!

STEAK AND KIDNEY PIE

Pie crust for top and bottom
4 pounds round steak
2 pounds veal kidneys
Salt, pepper, flour

Sauce:
2 cans beef broth
2 teaspoons Worcestershire sauce
2 teaspoons each salt and pepper
Dash cayenne
2 bay leaves

½ cup melted butter
1 onion, sliced
1 large can mushroom stems and
 pieces

1 teaspoon each thyme and basil
1 cup water
½ cup red wine
4 tablespoons cornstarch

Cut steak into bite-sized pieces and dredge in mixture of salt, pepper and flour. Skin and thinly slice kidneys. Brown steak and kidney in melted butter. Add onion and sauté until transparent. Add drained mushrooms. To make sauce, put broth in saucepan and add seasonings. Make a paste of the cornstarch and ¼ cup of the water. Combine wine with rest of the water and add to the broth mixture. On medium heat, add cornstarch paste gradually to hot broth. Cook, stirring constantly, until thick. Combine sauce with meat, mixing thoroughly. Roll out pie crusts (or use ready made). Line casserole with bottom crust, pour in meat mixture and cover with top crust. Prick top crust with fork. Put in preheated 450° oven for 10 minutes. Reduce heat and bake at 350° for 20-25 minutes. This will serve 12 or can be halved for 6.

BEEF ROULADES IN RED WINE

This recipe is based upon preparation of 6 roulades. Get thin slices of beef steak (sirloin tip or round) for each person to be served. Rub each slice with cut clove of garlic. Sprinkle steaks with little salt and pepper. Spread thin layer of bulk port sausage over meat slices. Sprinkle meat slices with a little finely chopped parsley and onion. Roll up each roulade and secure at both ends. (I tie mine with string.) Dredge roulades in flour, brown in oil in a casserole and add 1½ cups red wine for every 6 roulades. Mix 1½ tablespoons tomato paste with little red wine and stir into meat mixture. Cover the casserole and cook slowly for 1 hour, or until beef is tender. About the last 15 minutes of cooking time, add ¾ cups pitted olives. Serve from casserole with rice or noodles.

Jack Blackburn

STEAK AND OYSTER ROULADE

1 pint oysters
1 onion, grated
Bread crumbs to hold mixture
Parsley
Butter
1 round steak, pounded thin

1 cup red wine
Gravy:
1 8-ounce carton sour cream
1 box mushrooms, washed, sliced and
 sautéed

Roulade: Sauté all ingredients except steak and wine in butter. Spread over steak and roll like jelly roll. Dot with butter. Place in baking dish and pour wine over steak. Bake at 325° about 1 hour. If it seems to be drying out, cover during last half of cooking.

For gravy: Sauté mushrooms. Combine with sour cream and heat. To serve: Slice roulade and serve gravy in separate container to spoon over roulade.

LEMON VEAL AND MUSHROOMS

2 pounds veal cutlets	6 tablespoons dry white wine
Flour, salt, pepper	1 tablespoon lemon juice
2 tablespoons olive oil	1 pound sliced fresh mushrooms
2 sticks butter or margarine	Lemon slices (optional)

Cut veal into serving pieces. Pound veal. Dust veal lightly with flour, salt and pepper. Melt 2 tablespoons butter and add olive oil in fry pan. When butter and olive oil are hot, add floured veal and sauté on both sides. Remove veal from pan and keep warm. Add wine to fry pan and heat; then add remaining butter and lemon juice. Sauté mushrooms in heated mixture. Arrange veal pieces on individual plates or platter. Top veal with mushrooms and sauce. Arrange lemon slices on top. Serve immediately.

Dr. Jack Blackburn

SAUERBRATEN

5-6 pounds beef roast (rump, round or sirloin tip)	3-5 sprigs parsley
1 cup red wine vinegar	2 garlic cloves, crosscut
½ bottle burgundy	1 onion, quartered
10 peppercorns	3 strips lemon rind
1 teaspoon salt	¼ teaspoon nutmeg
1 bay leaf	3 celery stalks, chopped
6 cloves	2 carrots, chopped

Rinse roast, pat dry and place in large glass or stainless steel container. Place all other ingredients over roast and marinate in refrigerator 3-4 days. Turn twice each 24 hours. Remove roast from marinade, pat dry and brown in a small amount of cooking oil. Brown very slowly on all surfaces. This takes about an hour and is important. Add 2 cups beef broth to marinade and place in a separate saucepan over low heat. When roast is browned, add 1 to 2 cups of marinade and cover. Cook over very low heat 3½ to 4 hours. Add marinade and baste roast throughout. When done, remove roast. Press vegetables through a sieve and remove fat. Add cornstarch for thickness and serve gravy with roast.

Anna Louise McKown (Mrs. Delos)

This is not difficult; you just need to start early.

POLYNESIAN BEEF

Brown:
    1½ pounds cubed beef
    1½ teaspoons garlic

1 teaspoon paprika

Add:
    Juice from 1 can pineapple chunks
    1 cup beef broth

2 tablespoons wine vinegar

Simmer for 1½ hours. Add:
    ½ cup sliced celery
    ½ green pepper, cubed
    1 cup sliced onion

1 can drained pineapple chunks
1 basket cherry tomatoes

Blend together:
    1 tablespoon soy sauce
    3 tablespoons brown sugar
    1 tablespoon cornstarch

½ cup water
2 tablespoons vinegar

Add to meat and vegetable mixture. Simmer until sauce thickens. Serve over cooked rice.

Judy Godsil (Mrs. Ray)

ROAST MARINADE

1 teaspoon Accent
⅓ cup vinegar
¼ cup catsup
2 tablespoons oil
1¼ teaspoons garlic powder

2 tablespoons soy sauce
1 tablespoon Worcestershire sauce
1 teaspoon mustard
1 teaspoon salt
¼ teaspoon pepper

Sprinkle roast with Accent. Mix other ingredients and marinate roast several hours—turning. Cook on charcoal grill. It is best rare. Slice on the diagonal. It is good even after frozen. You may use this on sirloin tip roast, but boneless chuck is best.

Bobbie Umbach (Mrs. Arnold)

SIMPLY ELEGANT STEAK AND RICE

1½ pounds round steak
1½ teaspoons vegetable oil
2 large onions, cut into ½-inch slices and
    separated into rings
1 4-ounce can sliced mushrooms,
    drained (reserve liquid)

1 can (10¾ ounces) condensed cream
    of mushroom soup
½ cup dry sherry
1½ teaspoons garlic salt

Cut steak into thin strips. In large skillet, brown meat in oil over high heat. Add onions and sauté until tender crisp. Blend soup, sherry, mushroom liquid and garlic salt and pour over steak. Add mushrooms. Reduce heat, cover, and simmer for 1 hour or until steak is tender. Serve over rice.

This is very easy and a great budget-stretcher.

BEEF WITH MUSHROOMS

1 pound flank or other steak, cut in ¼-inch slices about 2 inches long
¼ cup soy sauce
1 tablespoon cornstarch
1 tablespoon dry sherry
1 teaspoon sugar
¼ teaspoon monosodium glutamate
4 tablespoons vegetable oil
½ teaspoon salt
6-8 ounces fresh mushrooms, sliced, or 2 cans (4 ounces each) sliced mushrooms, drained
1 slice ginger root or ¼ cup sliced onion

Mix first 6 ingredients and set aside. Put 2 tablespoons oil in hot skillet over high heat. Add salt and mushrooms. Cook, stirring, about 2 minutes. Remove from skillet. Add remaining oil to skillet and add ginger. Keeping skillet over high heat, add beef mixture and cook, stirring, less than 2 minutes. Add mushrooms and mix well. Serve at once. Makes 2 or 3 servings.

Beef with Green Peppers:
Follow above recipe, substituting 2 medium green peppers for the mushrooms. Wash peppers and dry before cutting. Discard white membrane and cut peppers in chunks. Cook in the oil less than 1 minute. Proceed as directed.

Beef with Pea Pods:
Follow basic recipe, substituting ¼ pound pea pods for the mushrooms. Cook in the oil less than 1 minute. Proceed as directed.

TURNIPS AND ROUND STEAK

1 large piece of round steak, cut in 6 servings
¼ cup olive oil
1½ cups chopped onions
6 large turnips, diced
1 teaspoon sugar

Marinate steak (if desired—this is optional) in 1 part burgundy, 1 part red wine vinegar, and 1 part water. Peel and dice turnips and boil just until slightly tender—do not overcook. Drain turnips and set aside. Salt and pepper meat and brown in oil, add onions and small amounts of water as needed and simmer until meat is tender. Add the turnips and cook slowly in a covered pot for about one hour. Serve with wild rice—or brown and wild rice mixture.

SAVORY STUFFED ROUND STEAK

2 pounds boneless round steak, ½-inch thick
2 tablespoons butter or margarine
½ cup celery, chopped
¼ cup onion, chopped
2 cups (½-inch) bread cubes
½ teaspoon salt
½ teaspoon rubbed sage
⅛ teaspoon pepper
1 tablespoon water
All-purpose flour
3 tablespoons vegetable oil
1 can cream of mushroom soup, undiluted
2 teaspoons Worcestershire sauce
1 clove garlic, minced
½ cup water
Hot cooked rice

Trim excess fat from steak; pound steak into ¼-inch thickness. Cut steak into 4 equal pieces. Melt butter in large skillet, sauté celery and onion in butter until tender. Remove from heat. Stir in bread cubes, salt, sage, pepper and 1 tablespoon water. Place ¼ of mixture on each piece of steak, spreading to within ½-inch of edge. Roll up each piece, jelly roll fashion; secure with wooden picks, and cut in half crosswise. Dredge each steak roll in flour, and brown in hot oil in large skillet. Combine soup, Worcestershire sauce, garlic, and ½ cup water. Stir well and pour over steak rolls. Cover and simmer 1 hour, stirring occasionally. Serve with rice. Yield: 8 servings.

Patti Tremaine (Mrs. Chuck)

BEEF BURGUNDY I

2 pounds boneless chuck or bottom
   round, cut into 2-inch pieces
2 tablespoons flour
1 teaspoon salt
⅛ teaspoon pepper
¼ cup butter or margarine
1 clove garlic
1 medium onion, sliced
½ pound sliced mushrooms, or 4-ounce
   can
1 cup water

1 cup dry red wine
1 10-ounce can tomatoes
Parsley
2 stalks celery with leaves, cut
   diagonally
2 carrots, cut diagonally
1 teaspoon thyme
1 bay leaf
2 tablespoons flour
3 tablespoons cold water

Coat meat with flour, salt and pepper. Melt butter in Dutch oven. Brown meat lightly on all sides. Add garlic, onion and mushrooms. Cook over low heat until onion is tender. Add water, wine, etc. Simmer gently, stirring occasionally 2-2½ hours, until meat is tender. Blend flour-water. Stir in. Bring to boil. Simmer 2 minutes. Salt. Serve in hot rice ring. Serves 4-6.

This is delicious and elegant enough for dinner parties.

BEEF BURGUNDY II

Two pounds chuck roast, cut into 1½-inch cubes. Toss in bowl with 1 tablespoon Kitchen Bouquet, 2 teaspoons salt, ⅛ teaspoon each pepper, thyme, and marjoram. Add ¼ cup cream of rice. Put in Dutch oven. Add 2 cups thinly sliced onions, 1 cup sliced celery, 4-6 carrots (cut into quarters lengthwise and in half crosswise), 1 clove garlic (crushed). Pour over 1½ cups red burgundy and 1 cup beef stock. Cook at 325° for 2½ to 3 hours. Stir occasionally and add a little water or beef stock, if necessary to keep gravy fluid. Last 30 minutes, add 2 cans B&B Whole Mushrooms (3 ounces). Serve with rice. Serves 6-8.

UKRANIAN GOULASH

¼ cup salad oil
3 pounds beef chuck, cut in 1½-inch
   cubes
4 medium onions, finely chopped
¼ cup tomato paste
1½ cups water

¼ cup chopped parsley
2 teaspoons salt
1 teaspoon dried thyme
¼ teaspoon pepper
1 small bay leaf

Heat oil in Dutch oven. Add beef and brown on all sides. Remove beef. Add onions to pan drippings and sauté until golden brown. Return meat to pan and stir in remaining ingredients. Bake covered for 2 hours at 300°. Serve in a cheese noodle ring or with plain noodles.

Mary Christiansen (Mrs. Dan)

STUFFED ZUCCHINI

6 medium zucchini
½ pound chopped uncooked lamb or
 ground beef
½ cup washed rice

2 cups tomato sauce
Salt, pepper, cinnamon to taste
2 chopped garlic cloves

Remove ¼ of zucchini lengthwise and scoop out center with melon baller from remaining ¾'s, leaving boat shape. Lightly mix meat, rice, half cup tomato sauce and seasonings until well blended. Fill cavity with meat and rice mixture making sure to press into cavity. Do not overstuff as rice will expand during cooking. Line Dutch oven with chopped zucchini trimmings and garlic cloves. Place filled zucchini on top and pour remaining tomato sauce over top. Add enough water to raise liquid to edge of zucchini, being careful not to cover. Cover Dutch oven and simmer for about 45 minutes or until rice is done. Pan residue can be poured over boats when serving. Makes 6 servings.

STUFFED PEPPERS

6 large peppers
¼ cup olive oil
½ cup chopped onions
1 clove garlic, finely chopped
¾ pound ground beef
¾ cup Parmesan cheese

2 cups cooked rice
3 tablespoons parsley
3 tablespoons red wine
Salt and pepper
¾ cup tomato juice

Cut tops from peppers and remove seeds. Place in boiling water for 3 minutes. Remove and drain. Rub outsides with oil. Brown beef in skillet with oil, onion and garlic. Pour off any grease. Mix with rest of ingredients and stuff peppers. Bake 25 minutes at 300°.

CALIFORNIA CASSEROLE

2 pounds ground beef
1 large onion, chopped
1 clove garlic, minced
2 tablespoons chili powder
3 cups tomato sauce
½ teaspoon sugar

2 teaspoons salt
1 cup sliced black olives
1 4-ounce can chopped green chilies
1 dozen corn tortillas
Cooking oil

Brown meat in large skillet with onion and garlic. Sprinkle with chili powder, mixing well. Add tomato sauce, sugar, salt, *half* the olives, and all the chilies. Simmer over very low heat 15 minutes. While sauce cooks, fry tortillas briefly in hot oil, one at a time (do not allow to brown), drain on paper towels, and cut into quarters. Beat together and set aside: 2 cups small curd cottage cheese and 2 eggs. Grate ½ pound Monterey Jack cheese. Spread ⅓ of meat sauce in bottom of a 3-quart casserole. Cover with ½ of cheese, ½ cottage cheese-egg mixture, and ½ the tortillas. Repeat 4 layers; end with the remaining meat sauce. Top with 1 cup grated cheddar cheese. Bake, uncovered, at 350° until thoroughly heated and cheese is melted, about 30-40 minutes. Serve with remaining olives and ½ cup chopped green onions, and ½ cup sour cream. Casserole can be prepared a day ahead and refrigerated. Allow to return to room temperature before baking. Serves 6-8.

Janet Rogers (Mrs. Jack)

Many members of the Math Department solve their equations quickly after eating their favorite tex-mex dishes at the departmental covered dish suppers.

CHASEN CHILI

½ pound pinto beans
5 cups canned tomatoes
1 pound chopped green pepper
1½ tablespoons salad oil
1 pound chopped onion
2 cloves garlic
½ cup parsley
½ cup butter

2½ pounds ground chuck
1 pound lean ground pork
⅓ cup chili powder
2 tablespoons salt
1½ teaspoons pepper
1½ teaspoons cumin seed
1½ teaspoons Accent

Wash beans, soak overnight in 2 inches of water above beans. Simmer covered in same water until tender. Add tomatoes and simmer 5 minutes. Sauté pepper in oil 5 minutes. Add onion and cook till tender. Add garlic and parsley. Melt butter and sauté meat 15 minutes. Add meat to onion mixture. Add chili powder. Cook 15 minutes. Add to beans, add spices. Simmer covered 1 hour. Cook uncovered 30 minutes. Skim off fat. Makes 4 quarts. Freezes well.

Bobbie Umbach (Mrs. Arnold)

Bobbie says this is the best chili recipe she's found!

FRANKLIN'S FAVORITE CHILI

4 tablespoons bacon drippings
⅔ cup chopped onion
1 clove garlic, sliced
1 pound ground beef
4 cups cooked kidney beans or 2 #303 cans
⅔ cup minced green pepper

4-5 cups cooked or canned tomatoes
2 bay leaves, crushed
4 teaspoons sugar
About 2 tablespoons chili powder
Salt and pepper

Brown onion and garlic in drippings. Add meat and cook slowly a few minutes, stirring occasionally. Add remaining ingredients. Season and simmer about an hour. Serves 8.

BEEF AND BEAN ENCHILADAS

1½ pounds ground beef
1 medium-sized onion, chopped
2-3 cups refried beans (see recipe p. 134)
1 teaspoon salt
⅛ teaspoon garlic powder
⅓ cup bottled or canned Taco sauce
1 cup quartered, pitted ripe olives
12 corn tortillas

Salad oil or shortening for frying tortillas
2 cans (10-ounces each) Enchilada sauce (I use "hot")
3 cups shredded cheddar cheese
Sliced pitted ripe olives for garnish
Sour cream
Canned green chili sauce

In a frying pan crumble ground beef and sauté with onions until meat is browned and onions are soft. Stir in beans, salt, garlic powder, Taco sauce and olives. Heat until bubbly. Dip tortillas, one at a time, in hot oil to soften. Drain quickly. Heat Enchilada sauce. Pour about half into an ungreased, shallow 3-quart baking dish. Place about ⅓ cup of ground beef filling on each tortilla, and roll to enclose filling. Place, flat side down, in the sauce in the bottom of the baking dish. Pour remaining Enchilada sauce evenly over tortillas; cover with cheese. Bake uncovered in a 350° oven for about 15 to 20 minutes, or until thoroughly heated. May be covered and refrigerated up to 1 day. If taken directly from refrigerator, increase baking time to 45 minutes. I think the refrigeration time enhances the flavors. Garnish with olive slices. Spoon sour cream and green chili sauce over each serving—or pass in separate bowls. Makes 4-6 servings.

Wanda Dobie (Mrs. Jim)

The Dobies like things Mexican so they often entertain with a Mexican Dinner Party. They begin with Margaritas and Nachos and move on to Gazpacho, followed by Bean and Beef Enchiladas. They like to try and seat everyone at a table even if it means spreading out over the entire house; so for dessert they like to serve Chocolate Peppermint Brownies, which can be passed around from table to table. The peppermint flavor goes well with dark, rich coffee after a spicy meal.

MEXICAN CASSEROLE

In deep loaf-type dish, place in layers:
6 tamales with sauce
2 cups chili with beans
Chopped onions to cover

Crushed corn chips to cover
6 ounces grated Monterey Jack cheese
Crushed corn chips for topping

Bake in moderate oven about 30 minutes. Serves 4.

CURRY BEEF IN PASTRY

3 tablespoons oil
½ cup chopped onion
1 pound ground round
2 cups chopped mushrooms

2 teaspoons salt
½ teaspoon pepper
1 tablespoon curry powder
1 cup thick cream sauce

Heat oil in skillet. Sauté onion, beef and mushrooms 10 minutes. Add sauce, pepper, curry powder, and cream sauce. Mix well and set aside to cool.

Pastry:
2 cups sifted flour
2 teaspoons baking powder
½ teaspoon salt

4 tablespoons butter
½ cup (scant) white wine
1 egg yolk, beaten

Sift flour, baking powder and salt into bowl. Cut in butter, stir in white wine gradually until ball of dough is formed. Roll out dough into a rectangle ⅓-inch thick. Spread beef mixture down center. Bring edges together on top and seal. Brush with beaten egg. Bake in 400° oven about 30 minutes or until browned. Serve with 1 cup sour cream mixed with ¼ cup chopped chutney. Serves 8.

Page Adams (Mrs. Murray)

Page served this at her dinner group as the main dish.

PORCUPINE MEATBALLS

2 cups tomato juice
1 tablespoon sugar
4 whole cloves
1 tablespoon Worcestershire sauce
½ cup uncooked rice
1 pound ground beef

1 tablespoon minced onion
1 clove garlic, minced
2 tablespoons chopped green pepper
1 teaspoon salt
½ teaspoon celery salt
½ teaspoon monosodium glutamate

Heat the tomato juice, sugar, cloves and Worcestershire sauce in a skillet while preparing meat. Mix rice, meat, onion, garlic, pepper, celery salt and mono-sodium glutamate with wet hands; form into balls 1½ inches in diameter. Remove the cloves from the tomato juice; add the meatballs; cover tightly; simmer for 45-60 minutes. Serves 6.

Judy Godsil (Mrs. Ray)

SOUR CREAM HAMBURGER BAKE

1 pound hamburger
1 clove garlic
1 teaspoon salt
Dash of pepper
1 teaspoon sugar
2 15-ounce cans tomato sauce

1 3-ounce package cream cheese
1 cup sour cream
6 green onions, chopped
8 ounces egg noodles
1 cup grated cheese

Fry hamburger and garlic together, breaking into small bits. Add salt, pepper, sugar and tomato sauce. Simmer 15-20 minutes. Mix cream cheese, sour cream and chopped green onions together. Cook noodles and drain. In greased casserole, place alternate layers of third of noodles, sour cream mixture, and tomato sauce. Repeat twice. Put grated cheese on top. Bake 350° until bubbly, 45 minutes to 1 hour. Yield: 8-10 servings.

Patti Tremaine (Mrs. Chuck)

GROUND BEEF CASSEROLE

2 pounds ground chuck

Brown and drain well. Add:
½ cup chopped celery
½ cup chopped onion
¼ cup chopped green pepper
Salt and pepper

1 can tomatoes
1 can cream of chicken soup
1 can cream of celery soup
1 small can mushrooms

Simmer until vegetables are done (about 30 minutes). Add:
Cooked noodles (8 ounces raw)

1 package frozen green peas (or 1 small can)

Cook until peas are done or heated through. (You may add a carton of sour cream at this time if you like.) Pour in a casserole dish and cover with grated cheese and heat until cheese melts in a 325-350° oven.

Laucita Swinson (Mrs. Frank)

This can be used to feed a small gathering or increased to feed a large group. It was used to feed a group of engineers here for the Southeastern Seminar in Photo Mechanics in the spring of 1981.

HEARTY SUPPER CASSEROLE

1 pound ground steak
Onions
white potatoes

1 can bean sprouts
1 can tomato soup
Salt and pepper to season layers

Pan fry hamburger steak. Peel and slice potatoes and onions. Spread ½ hamburger in casserole, then thinly sliced onions, bean sprouts (½ can), thinly sliced potatoes in this order. Make a second layer of hamburger, onions, bean sprouts, potatoes. Pour 1 can tomato soup over top. Bake 1 hour at 300-350°.

Thelma Thomas (Mrs. B.F., Jr.)

SOUR CREAM ENCHILADAS

2 cups sour cream
1 cup chopped green onions, including some of tops
½ teaspoon cumin

3 to 4 cups shredded cheddar cheese
12 corn tortillas
Oil for frying tortillas
1 can enchilada sauce

Blend sour cream, onion, cumin and 1 cup cheese. Set aside. Dip tortillas, one at a time, in hot oil to soften; drain quickly. Dip tortillas into enchilada sauce. Fill each tortilla with about ⅓ cup sour cream mixture. Fold over and place in ungreased pan. Top with shredded cheese. Bake uncovered in a 375° oven for 20 minutes.

Ruth L. Brittin (Mrs. Norman)

This is a good dish to carry to a covered dish affair.

RICAGNE

1 cup Uncle Ben's Converted brand rice
1 egg, slightly beaten
¼ cup plus 2 tablespoons grated
  Parmesan cheese
1 pound ground beef
1 medium onion, chopped
1 can (16 ounces) tomatoes
1 can (6 ounces) tomato paste

2 teaspoons oregano
1 teaspoon parsley (dried)
1 teaspoon basil
1 teaspoon salt
⅛ teaspoon pepper
2 cups mozzarella cheese, shredded
1 cup Swiss cheese, shredded
¼ cup cottage cheese

Cook rice according to package directions. Cool. Stir in egg and ½ cup of the Parmesan cheese. Brown beef in 10-inch skillet. Add onion and cook until onion is tender but not brown. Add tomatoes, tomato paste, oregano, parsley, basil, salt and pepper. Cover and simmer ½ hour. Combine cheeses, mixing well. Spoon half of the rice mixture onto bottom of 13x9x2 baking dish. Cover with half the cheese mixture. Spoon half the meat mixture over the cheese mixture. Repeat layers. Sprinkle top with remaining 2 tablespoons Parmesan cheese. Bake 375° until hot, about 20 minutes. Yield: 6-8 servings.

Patti Tremaine (Mrs. Chuck)

MEXICAN MANICOTTI
(for microwave)

½ pound lean ground beef
1 cup refried beans
1 teaspoon oregano, crushed
½ teaspoon ground cumin
8-10 manicotti shells
1¼ cups water

1 8-ounce can picante sauce or taco
  sauce
1 8-ounce carton sour cream
¼ cup finely chopped green onions
¼ cup sliced pitted ripe (black) olives
½ cup shredded Monterey Jack cheese

Combine ground beef, refried beans, oregano and cumin. Mix well. Fill *uncooked* manicotti shells with meat mixture. Arrange in 10x6x2-inch baking dish. Combine water and picante sauce or taco sauce; pour over manicotti shells. Cover with vented plastic wrap. Microcook on high for 10 minutes, giving dish a half turn once. using tongs, turn shells over. Microcook, covered, on medium for 17-19 minutes, or until pasta is tender, giving dish half turn once. Combine sour cream, onions and olives. Spoon down center of casserole. Top with cheese. Cook on high 2-3 minutes until cheese melts.

Patti Tremaine (Mrs. Chuck)

ENCHILADA CASSEROLE

1½ pounds ground beef
½ cup chopped onion
1 15½-ounce can refried beans
½ teaspoon salt
¼ teaspoon pepper
1 cup cooking oil
12 canned or frozen tortillas
2 tomatoes, peeled and chopped (¾ cup)
4 tablespoons butter or margarine

¼ cup all-purpose flour
½ teaspoon salt
¼ teaspoon paprika
2 cups milk
1 10-ounce can enchilada sauce
1½ cups (6 ounces) shredded natural cheddar cheese
¾ cup sliced ripe olives
4 drops bottled hot pepper sauce

In skillet, cook beef and onion till meat is brown and onion tender; drain. Stir in beans, first ½ teaspoon salt and the pepper. In another skillet, heat oil. quickly dip tortillas in hot oil just till softened. Place ⅓ cup meat mixture on each tortilla. Top each with chopped tomato; roll tightly. Place, seam side down, in 13x9x2-inch baking dish. Melt butter or margarine; stir in flour and seasonings. Add milk and enchilada sauce. Cook and stir till boiling; boil 1 minute. Stir in remaining ingredients. Pour over tortillas. Bake in 350° oven for 30 minutes. Makes 6 servings.

APPLESAUCE BEEF LOAF

1 slightly beaten egg
1 cup soft bread crumbs (1¼ slices)
½ cup applesauce
2 tablespoons finely chopped onion
1 teaspoon dried celery flakes

1 teaspoon Dijon-style mustard
½ teaspoon salt
Dash pepper
1 pound ground beef

½ cup applesauce
1 tablespoon brown sugar

1 tablespoon vinegar
1 teaspoon Dijon-style mustard

Combine first 8 ingredients; add beef and mix well. Shape into round loaf in 9x9x2-inch baking pan. With a spoon, make a depression in top of loaf. Combine remaining ingredients; pour into depression in meat loaf. Bake in 350° oven for 1 hour. Makes 4-5 servings.

EASY LASAGNA

1 large jar Ragu spaghetti sauce   2 pounds ground beef

First brown about 2 pounds ground beef with onions (to your taste). Use dehydrated—it's easier. Drain all fat off. Add the sauce to the meat. Set aside. Boil in a large pot, about 12 lasagna noodles. Add 1 tablespoon oil to the salted boiling water. Boil 20 minutes. Drain noodles and run cold water oven them. Slice 1 hunk of mozzarella cheese with cheese cutter. Mix 1 pint ricotta cheese with 2 eggs. In large loaf pan, spread a little sauce over bottom to keep from sticking. Add 1 layer of noodles, spread with ricotta, top with sliced cheese, then sauce, then sprinkle with parmesan. Now repeat layers, noodles, ricotta, cheese, sauce, parmesan until you have 4 layers. Save enough sauce to cover top of noodles. Cover with foil and bake 1 hour at 350°. Let stand a few minutes before cutting—holds together better.

Fran Hartsfield (Mrs. Hank)

CRAFTY CRESCENT LASAGNE

Meat Filling:
½ pound sausage
½ pound ground beef
¾ cup chopped onion
½ clove garlic, minced
1 tablespoon parsley flakes

½ teaspoon leaf basil
½ teaspoon leaf oregano
½ teaspoon salt
Dash pepper
1 can (6 ounces) tomato paste

Cheese Filling:
1 cup creamed cottage cheese
¼ cup grated parmesan cheese

1 egg

Crust:
2 cans Pillsbury Refrigerated Quick
   Crescent Dinner Rolls
2 slices (7x4) mozzarella cheese

1 tablespoon milk
1 tablespoon sesame seed

Meat Filling: In large skillet, brown meat; drain. Add onion, garlic, parsley, seasonings, and tomato paste. Simmer, uncovered, for 5 minutes. (Meat mixture may be made ahead and refrigerated.)

Cheese Filling: Combine all ingredients.

Crust: Unroll crescent dough and separate into 8 rectangles. Place rectangles of dough together on ungreased cookie sheet, overlapping edges slightly to form a 13x15-inch rectangle. Press edges and perforations to seal.

Spread half of meat filling lengthwise down center half of dough to within 1 inch of each 13-inch end. Top meat filling with cheese filling; spoon remaining meat filling over top, forming 3 layers. Place cheese slices over meat filling. Fold 13-inch ends of dough over filling 1 inch. Pull long sides of dough rectangle over filling, being careful to overlap edges only ¼ inch. Pinch overlapped edges to seal. Brush with milk; sprinkle with sesame seed. Bake at 375° for 20 to 25 minutes, or until deep golden brown. Pretty to serve on a heated serving tray, buffet style. Slice in diagonal slices about 1½ inches wide. Serves 4-6.

Helen Funderburk (Mrs. Hanley)

This is a nice for a luncheon with just a salad and dessert.

NORWEGIAN SPAGHETTI

1½ pounds ground meat
1 onion, chopped
1 green pepper, chopped
3 small cans tomato sauce
1 small can water

1 can whole kernel corn, drained
1-2 tablespoons Worcestershire sauce
1 tablespoon salt
1 package spaghetti, cooked
Cheddar cheese

Brown meat. When almost done, add onion and green pepper. Cook 8 minutes more. Add everything else, except spaghetti and cheese, and bring to a boil. Reduce heat to low and cook 15 minutes. Add spaghetti and pour in casserole. Cover top with cheese and cook 40 minutes in 300° oven. Be sure to keep covered tightly. Freezes well.

PARTY EGGPLANT PARMIGIANO

¾ cup soft bread crumbs (1 slice bread)
⅓ cup milk
1 teaspoon seasoned salt
½ teaspoon seasoned pepper
1 pound ground beef
½ pound ground veal
¼ cup cooking oil

1 medium eggplant
¼ cup all-purpose flour
1 15-ounce can tomato sauce with
   mushrooms
¼ teaspoon dried oregano, crushed
½ cup grated Parmesan cheese

Combine crumbs, milk, salt and pepper. Add beef and veal; mix well. Shape into 8 patties. Brown on both sides in small amount of the oil. Pare eggplant; cut into eight ½-inch slices. Brush with remaining oil; coat with flour. Brown in same skillet. Place in 13x9x2-inch baking pan; top each with meat patty. Mix tomato sauce, ¼ cup water, and the oregano; pour over all. Top with cheese. Bake in 350° oven for 20 to 25 minutes. Makes 8 servings.

BLEU CHEESE BURGERS

Season hamburger meat with salt and pepper. Make 2 thin patties per person. Between these put 3 tablespoons bleu cheese and seal edges. Wrap a piece of raw bacon around the edge. Cook over a charcoal fire. Delicious with English muffin or with Worcestershire sauce.

BROILED HAMBURGERS

1 pound hamburger
½ cup chili sauce
1 teaspoon horseradish
1 teaspoon dry mustard
2 teaspoons diced onion

1 teaspoon Worcestershire sauce
1 egg
1 teaspoon chili powder
Salt and pepper

Mix all ingredients. Spread about ¼ inch thick on lower half of bun. Broil about 10 minutes. Toast top half of bun.

Peggy Turnquist (Mrs. Paul)

CORNED BEEF ROLL

1 12-ounce can corned beef, broken up
1 8-ounce can potatoes, drained & diced
1 slightly beaten egg
¼ cup milk
2 tablespoons chopped onion

2 cups packaged biscuit mix
⅔ cup milk
½ cup sour cream
½ cup mayonnaise or salad dressing
1 tablespoon prepared mustard

Combine corned beef, potatoes, egg, the ¼ cup milk, and the chopped onion. Combine biscuit mix and the ⅔ cup milk; knead 5-10 strokes on lightly floured surface. Roll out to a 12-inch square. Spread corned beef mixture on dough to within ½ inch of edges. Starting at one side, roll up jellyroll fashion, sealing edges together. Bake 25 minutes. Serves 6.

CREAMED DRIED BEEF IN TOAST CUPS

6 bacon slices, fried, drained & crumbled
2 tablespoons butter or margarine
2 4-ounce packages dried beef
2 tablespoons flour

1½ cups milk
3 hard-boiled eggs, quartered
2 tomatoes, quartered
Pepper

Melt 2 tablespoons oleo in pan and saute dried beef. Sprinkle flour over beef and add milk. Stir and fold in tomatoes and eggs. Serve in toast cups with bacon sprinkled on top. This serves 6.

It is great for company breakfast, or for before the game brunches. It can be kept warm during serving on an electric hot tray.

ROAST LEG OF LAMB

1 5-pound whole leg of lamb or sirloin
   leg of lamb
Olive oil

3 cloves of peeled garlic
½ teaspoon rosemary
Fresh ground pepper & salt

Wipe the meat with a damp cloth. Coat meat completely with olive oil. Make cuts in fat about ½-inch deep and ½-inch long. Place 1 sliver of garlic in each cut and fill cuts with rosemary. Dust the leg of lamb with freshly ground pepper. Roast it in an open pan, fat side up, on a rack at 325° for 3 hours or to an internal temperature of 180° on a meat thermometer for well-done. If you like your meat rare, reduce cooking time accordingly. Salt meat at end of cooking. Let it stand before carving. Serve with mint sauce.

Mint Sauce for Roast Lamb:
¼ cup dried, crushed mint leaves
¼ cup vinegar

¼ cup sugar
½ cup water

Simmer until well blended; serve hot.

PORK

BARBECUED RIBS

1 cup soy sauce
1 cup brown sugar
½ tablespoon cinnamon

1 clove garlic, pressed
¼ cup bourbon
1 rack spareribs

Marinate ribs in the above ingredients for 24 hours. Grill over charcoal.

BARBECUED SPARERIBS L'ORANGE

3 pounds spareribs, cut into serving-size
pieces
6 tablespoons Worcestershire sauce
3 tablespoons finely chopped onion

½ cup orange marmalade or frozen
orange juice concentrate
1½ teaspoons salt

Brush half the Worcestershire sauce over both sides of the ribs. Bake on broiler
pan at 400° for 40 minutes, turning occasionally. Pour off drippings and reduce
heat to 350°. Combine remaining ingredients into sauce, mixing well. Brush over
ribs and bake 20-30 minutes, basting occasionally. Serves 4.

BARBECUE SAUCE

2 tablespoons butter
1 chopped onion
1 clove garlic, minced
¾ cup water
1 cup catsup
2 tablespoons vinegar

2 tablespoons lemon juice
2 tablespoons Worcestershire sauce
2 tablespoons brown sugar
1 teaspoon dry mustard
1 teaspoon salt
¼ teaspoon pepper

Melt butter. Add onion and garlic. Cook until tender. Add other ingredients and
simmer for 20 minutes. Delicious served over pork that has cooked slowly in
oven or on grill and then pulled into bite-size pieces.

Jeanne Swanner Robertson (Mrs. Jerry)

ORANGE PORK CHOPS

6 ½-inch thick pork chops
6 tablespoons oleo
1 6-ounce can orange juice concentrate
2 tablespoons brown sugar

1½ teaspoons ground ginger
½ teaspoon ground allspice
¼ teaspoon hot pepper sauce
2 oranges, sliced ½-inch thick

Brown chops in butter. Pour off fat. Combine next 5 ingredients. Pour over chops. Cover and simmer 45 minutes, basting occasionally. Put orange slices over pork chops for the last 5 minutes of cooking time. Serves 6.

SPANISH PORK CHOPS I

4 thick pork chops
2 teaspoons Kitchen Bouquet
1 can (6 ounces) tomato paste
2 cups water
2 teaspoons sugar
2 teaspoons salt

1 teaspoon paprika
½ teaspoon ground ginger
1 cup diced onion
½ cup diced green pepper
1 cup uncooked rice

Brush meat with Kitchen Bouquet. Grease skillet with piece of pork fat. Brown meat lightly on both sides over moderate heat. Combine remaining ingredients except rice and pour over pork. Cover and cook slowly until tender, about 45 minutes. Pour rice around meat in pan mixing with sauce. Cover and cook until rice is just tender, about 25 minutes. Makes 4 servings.

SPANISH PORK CHOPS II

Brown chops, salt and pepper. Then put a scoop of rice (cooked) on each, after that a slice of onion and green pepper on each. Salt and pepper again and add a little onion, salt and Worcestershire. Over this pour one large can of tomatoes and let simmer for 30-45 minutes.

PORK A LA MANZANA

Pierce 3 to 4-pound boned and rolled pork loin roast with fork. Combine 1¾ cups dry white wine, 1 small onion, sliced, and ½ teaspoon ground cinnamon. Pour over roast in plastic bag; tie. Marinate overnight in refrigerator; turn occasionally. Remove meat; pat dry. Reserve 1 cup marinade and onions. Season the meat with 1 clove garlic, minced, 1 teaspoon salt, and ¼ teaspoon pepper. Sprinkle oven roasting bag with 1 tablespoon flour. Place meat, onions, and reserved marinade in bag; punch holes in bag according to package directions. Roast in 325° oven 2½ to 3 hours. Pour meat juices into pan; boil till reduced to 1½ cups. Combine 3 tablespoons flour, ½ cup water, and ½ teaspoon Kitchen Bouquet; add to juices. Cook and stir till bubbly. Season with salt and pepper. Core and slice 2 cooking apples; cook in 2 tablespoons butter or margarine till soft. Garnish pork with apples. Pass gravy. Makes 8-10 servings.

PORK STEAKS, SPANISH STYLE

6 pork shoulder steaks (or chops) ¾ inch
2 tablespoons shortening
2 16-ounce cans tomatoes (stewed)

1 cup regular long grain rice
2 tablespoons butter, softened

About 1 hour and 15 minutes before serving: sprinkle meat with salt and pepper. In large skillet over medium heat, melt shortening. Add steak and brown well; drain. Preheat oven to 350°. In greased 13-inch pan, combine tomatoes and their liquid, rice and butter or margarine and 1 teaspoon salt. Arrange pork in an overlapping row on top of rice and in center of baking dish. Cover dish tightly with foil and bake one hour or until meat is tender. For a party meal, use pork chops.

PORK CHOPS AND SPAGHETTI

6 pork chops	½ teaspoon pepper
12 ounces spaghetti	8 or more mushrooms, washed, dried,
3 cloves garlic	sliced
2 cups tomatoes, peeled and chopped	¼-½ cup red wine
1 6-ounce can tomato paste	Oregano to taste
1 teaspoon salt	

Fry pork chops in butter or oil with garlic until golden. Remove chops, drain excess oil and sauté mushrooms. Add to mushrooms the tomatoes, tomato paste, salt, pepper and oregano and wine. Mix well, and return chops to sauce. Remove garlic, and simmer covered for 45 minutes. Cook the spaghetti until tender, and drain. When chops are done, remove them from the sauce and stir in the spaghetti. Place spaghetti on platter, sprinkle with Parmesan cheese and top with the chops. Serves 6.

STUFFED PORK CHOPS

Have pork chops cut about 1½ inches,	1 teaspoon dry sage
cut slits for pockets	½ teaspoon salt
2 cups lightly toasted bread	Dash of pepper
½ cup chopped celery	2 tablespoons melted butter
¼ cup chopped onion	½ cup hot water
2 teaspoons chopped parsley	

Mix the above ingredients and stuff in the pockets of the chops. Fasten with toothpicks. Sprinkle the chops with salt, pepper, and garlic powder (optional) to taste. Place in a pan and cook in the oven at 350° for about 2 hours or until tender. Serves 4.

Dr. Harry M. Philpott

PLUM DELICIOUS PORK CHOPS

4-6 pork chops	½ teaspoon grated lemon rind
1 large size baby food jar of plums with	1 teaspoon lemon juice
tapioca	½ cup red wine
Pinch of cinnamon and cloves	

Dredge pork chop in seasoned flour and brown in butter. Put pork chops in a shallow baking dish. Combine rest of ingredients and pour over chops. Bake at 325° for 1 hour. Baste chops once.

FRENCH-CUT RIB PORK LOIN ROASTS WITH GRAVY

4 teaspoons garlic salt
4 teaspoons paprika
Pepper
2 6-8-rib pork loin roasts (each 5-6 pounds), cut French style*

½ cup all-purpose flour
2 teaspoons salt
Apple slices for garnish

About 4½ hours before serving:
Preheat oven to 325°. On waxed paper, combine garlic salt, paprika and ½ teaspoon pepper; rub mixture into surface of roasts. Place roasts, fat-side up, on rack in open roasting pan; insert meat thermometers into center of each roast, being careful not to touch bone. (Or, use one thermometer and check center of second roast during final cooking.) Roast about 2½ to 3 hours until thermometers reach 170°. Remove roasts to platter. Prepare gravy: remove rack from pan. Into 4-cup measure or large bowl, pour pan drippings (set pan aside); let stand a few seconds until fat separates from meat juice. Skim 6 tablespoons fat from drippings into 2-quart saucepan; skim off and discard any remaining fat. Add ½ cup water to roasting pan; stir until brown bits are loosened; add to meat juice in cup and add enough water to make 3 cups. Into fat in saucepan, over medium heat, stir flour, salt and ¼ teaspoon pepper until blended. Gradually stir in meat-juice mixture and cook, stirring constantly, until gravy is thickened. Pour gravy into gravy boat to serve over roasts. If you like, garnish roasts with apple slices. Makes 12 servings. *Ask your meatman to expose about 1 inch of rib bone by cutting out meat between ribs.

VILLA MONTANA BAKED HAM
(from Villa Montana, Morelia, Mexico)

Pre-cooked, boneless ham
Whole cloves
1½ cups brown sugar
2 cups pineapple juice

1 tablespoon mustard
2 cups diced pineapple
Ginger ale

Stud ham with cloves. Mix next 4 ingredients in blender and pour over ham. Bake 1 hour at 350°. Reduce to 300° and cook 2 hours. As juice in pan cooks down, add ginger ale. Baste ham every 15 minutes, adding ginger ale as needed.   Ruth Brittin (Mrs. Norman)

GINGERED HAM

ham steak 1½ to 2 inches thick
½ cup ginger ale
½ cup orange juice
¼ cup brown sugar
1 tablespoon salad oil

1½ teaspoons vinegar (wine)
1 teaspoon dry mustard
¼ teaspoon ground ginger
⅛ teaspoon ground cloves

Pour over ham and refrigerate overnight or 2 hours at room temperature. Broil.

Angie Dollar (Mrs. Mason)

HAM SAUCE

3 tablespoons currant jelly
2 tablespoons catsup

1 tablespoon vinegar
1 tablespoon butter

Melt jelly, add other ingredients, simmer until well-blended. Serve hot.

Martha Applebee (Mrs. Frank)

CREOLE COLD MUSTARD SAUCE FOR MEATS

This is an old recipe that combines two basic dressings: a creme-fraiche or sour cream dressing and an old horseradish dressing. The old recipes call for grated horseradish, but the prepared store-bought horseradish, if drained thoroughly, can be used. The modern store-bought sour cream is every bit as good as the creme-fraiche in this recipe, but will not keep as long in a refrigerator.

The Creme-Fraiche Dressing:
3 tablespoons fresh lemon juice
¼ to ½ cup olive oil
1 tablespoon Dijon mustard
Salt and pepper to taste

½ to ¾ or 1 cup creme-fraiche—made by using 1 cup whipping cream with 2 tablespoons buttermilk. Leave in refrigerator 1 to 3 days stirring often until consistency of thick sour cream.

Will keep 3 to 6 weeks in refrigerator—will not curdle when added to hot foods or boiled.

The Horseradish Sauce:
2 full tablespoons horseradish
1 tablespoon wine vinegar—at least—more for tartness
1 tablespoon white wine in which 1 tablespoon Coleman's dry mustard has been softened—all lumps out

½ cup of homemade (preferred) or good commercial mayonnaise

If too tart, sugar (about ½ teaspoon) can be added. If not tart enough, add more lemon juice, wine, or wine vinegar. Recipe can be altered—adding or subtracting—to suit your taste. Now combine the 2 above dressings—the creme-fraiche and the horseradish sauce—and you have the old-fashioned creole mustard sauce. Parsley, minced garlic, chopped green onions or grated onion, can be added. Will improve flavor, but if added, sauce cannot be kept for very long in refrigerator. Also, if chopped dill pickles, olives and onions are added, will make good tartar sauce for fish.

Alva Current-Garcia (Mrs. Eugene)

Alva brought this recipe to Auburn from her native Lake Charles, LA.

SAUSAGE ALSACE-LORRAINE

1 pound smoked link sausage
2 cans sauerkraut
5 onions, quartered
12 small new potatoes, unpeeled, cut in half

5 apples, cored and quartered
1 tablespoon whole caraway seeds
1 tablespoon whole celery seeds

Cut sausage in ½-inch slices. Put sausage in a large covered pot. Pile apples, onions, potatoes, sauerkraut, caraway and celery seeds on top. Add ½ can of beer (cook can drink the rest). Bring to a boil, immediately turn down and simmer 30 minutes or until potatoes are done. Serve in the pot on a platter with an assortment of dark and light breads and mustard. To dress up, pour a cup of champagne over it at the table. Serve while it is still steaming and bubbling. Drink rest of champagne with the meal.

Gail Gilchrist (Mrs. Dick)

Dick, the Chaplain to students at St. Dunstan's Episcopal Church, enjoyed this dish while he lived in France.

SAUSAGE AND APPLE FRY

2 pounds small link sausage
6 red cooking apples, cored and sliced

Bacon drippings

Parboil sausage and sauté in frying pan. Drain. Put in small amount of bacon drippings and sauté on both sides apple slices which have been sprinkled with brown sugar. Serves 8.

Wonderful for brunches.

RED BEANS, SAUSAGE AND RICE

4 onions (large)
5 stalks celery
1 green pepper (or 2 if you like it)
2 cloves minced garlic
Olive oil (1 small bottle)
2-3 pounds smoked link sausage
1 large can tomatoes and 1 small can
1 bunch fresh chopped parsley
1 large can black olives, sliced

3 cans red kidney beans
1 can tomato paste (small)
1 can tomato sauce (small)
1 tablespoon salt
1 tablespoon pepper
3 bay leaves
1 tablespoon thyme, basil, oregano and sugar
1 box Uncle Ben's rice

Cook onion, garlic, celery and green pepper in olive oil (add Wesson oil if you need a little more). Cook until tender and add sausage and cook 5 minutes. Add all other ingredients (except rice), simmer for 1 hour. Cook rice in separate pan according to package directions. Put one scoop of rice in soup bowl and pour red beans and sausage mixture over top (like gumbo is served). Serves 10.

SAUSAGE AND BLACK-EYED PEAS

1 pound dried black-eyed peas
½ pound bacon, cut in small pieces
A dash or two of garlic salt
1 tablespoon sugar

1 teaspoon salt
5 cups boiling water
1½ pounds smoked sausage links, cut
  bite-size

Wash peas and put in a large Dutch oven or baking dish. Add bacon pieces, garlic, sugar and salt. Add boiling water. Cover and bake 1½ hours at 350°. Remove from oven and add sausage pieces, also more salt and water if needed. Cover and bake 45 minutes longer.

A true Southern dish for New Year's day. Serve with corn relish and Sour Cream Cornbread.

CHICKEN AND POULTRY

STUFFED BREAST OF CHICKEN RICHMOND

4 boned and skinned chicken breasts
1 package frozen spinach, thawed and
   well-drained
1 tablespoon butter
1 tablespoon finely chopped onion
6 slices uncooked bacon, finely chopped

6 large mushrooms, finely chopped
2 cloves garlic, crushed
2 tablespoons tomato puree
Salt, pepper, flour, melted butter

Melt butter in skillet. Add onions and sauté lightly, then bacon, then mushrooms. Stir in spinach, garlic and tomato puree and season to taste. Mix thoroughly and cool. Place some stuffing mixture in center of each chicken breast; fold ends in and roll. Roll each in flour and place breasts seam side down in buttered baking pan. Drizzle with melted butter and bake at 450° for 15-20 minutes. Serve with Chaud-Froid sauce. Leftover stuffing may be used to stuff large mushrooms. Sprinkle with Swiss cheese and butter and broil until browned. Serves 4.

Chaud-Froid Sauce:
2 tablespoons butter
3 tablespoons flour
1 cup well-seasoned chicken stock

1/2 cup heavy cream
Black olives and pimentos

Melt butter in heavy bottom saucepan and stir in flour. Cook over moderate heat, stirring constantly with wooden spoon, but do not let flour brown. Slowly stir in hot chicken stock and cook until smooth and thickened. Stir in the cream and heat through. Pour sauce over cooked chicken breasts on warmed platter, garnish with olives and pimentos, and serve at once.

This was served at Holy Trinity Episcopal Churchwomen's Christmas Luncheon.

CHICKEN BREASTS EN PAPILLOTE

4 whole chicken breasts, halved, boned,
   and skinned
½ cup flour
1 teaspoon salt
½ teaspoon pepper
½ teaspoon curry
3 tablespoons butter

2 tablespoons sherry
⅓ cup orange marmalade
3 tablespoons brown sugar
3 tablespoons vinegar
1 11-ounce can mandarin oranges,
   drained
8 large squares heavy foil

Dredge chicken in mixture of flour, salt, pepper and curry powder. Sauté in butter about 3 minutes on each side. Combine sherry, marmalade, sugar and

189

vinegar. Place on each square of foil. Cover each with sauce and oranges. Fold up so each is leak-proof. Place on cookie sheet and bake at 350° for 15 minutes or until puffed. Slit top with knife to serve.

Donna Burchfield (Mrs. Ron)

CHICKEN ARBOR

2 tablespoons all-purpose flour
¼ teaspoon dried basil, crumbled
¼ teaspoon dried tarragon, crumbled
¼ teaspoon paprika
Salt and freshly ground white pepper
8 chicken pieces
1 tablespoon oil
1 tablespoon butter

2 small garlic cloves, minced
½ cup dry white wine
1 cup red grapes, halved and seeded
½ cup chicken broth
1 teaspoon fresh lemon juice
1 tablespoon finely chopped fresh
    parsley (garnish)

Mix flour, basil, tarragon, paprika, salt and pepper in large bowl. Add chicken and toss gently to coat. Heat oil with butter in heavy large skillet over medium-high heat. Stir in garlic. Add chicken and sauté on both sides until golden brown. Pour in wine. Cover and cook just until chicken is done, about 5 minutes. Add grapes, broth and lemon juice and continue cooking until heated through. Transfer chicken and grapes to heated serving platter using slotted spoon. Continue cooking sauce until reduced by half. Pour sauce over chicken. Top with parsley and serve. Serves 4.
Serve with sautéed mushrooms and pan-roasted potatoes.

CHICKEN JAMAICA

6 pineapple slices
6 boned half chicken breasts
1 chicken bouillon cube
⅓ cup boiling water
1 teaspoon dry instant coffee

1 10½-ounce can cream of chicken
    soup
¼ teaspoon salt
¼ pound sharp cheddar, shredded

Put pineapple slices in casserole; top each with chicken breast. Dissolve bouillon in water. Combine with coffee, soup and salt. Pour over chicken. Bake 375° for 40 minutes. Sprinkle with cheese. Return to oven until cheese melts. Serves 6.

MEXICAN CHICKEN

1 chicken, cut for frying, or 6 breasts
¼ teaspoon cayenne
Salt
¼ cup cooking oil
½ cup raisins
⅓ cup blanched almonds

½ cup pineapple
¼ teaspoon cinnamon
1½ cups orange juice
2 tablespoons flour
¼ cup water

Season chicken with salt and cayenne. Brown in oil. Add almonds, raisins, pineapple, cinnamon, and orange juice. Simmer one hour. Remove chicken. Make paste of flour and water. Add to skillet, stirring until thickened. Garnish with avocado wedges or orange slices. Serve on rice.

COMPANY CHICKEN

3 tablespoons oil
4 tablespoons flour
1 teaspoon salt
Pepper to taste
3 cups chicken stock
⅓ cup dry milk

½ pound sliced mushrooms
¼ cup diced green pepper
¼ cup pimento, chopped
2 cups cooked chicken
4 tablespoons sherry
1 tablespoon chopped parsley

Heat oil in skillet. Add flour and cook for a few minutes. Add stock, stirring until smooth. Season and stir in milk. Cook one minute. Remove from heat. Sauté mushrooms and add this and rest of ingredients. Heat and sprinkle with parsley.

CHICKEN CALIFORNIA

6 chicken breast halves or legs and thighs
Flour
3 tablespoons butter
2 tablespoons oil
¾ cup orange juice
⅓ cup dry white wine
⅓ cup sliced fresh mushrooms
2 tablespoons minced parsley

1 teaspoon grated orange peel
Pinch rosemary
3 tablespoons raspberry or tarragon
  vinegar
2 oranges, peeled, sectioned and
  seeded
2 avocados, peeled, pitted and sliced

Dust chicken with flour and shake off excess. Heat butter with oil in heavy skillet and add chicken, sautéing on both sides until well-browned. Add orange juice, wine, mushrooms, parsley, orange peel and rosemary and bring to simmer. Let simmer 5 minutes. Transfer chicken to heated platter. Add vinegar to skillet and continue simmering, scraping up browned bits until sauce is reduced by ⅓. Pour sauce over chicken, garnish with avocado and orange slices and serve with spood bread, spinach salad, dry white wine and a chocolate dessert for an elegant meal. Serves 6.

CHICKEN KIEV

Herb Butter:
1 cup butter or regular margarine,
  softened
2 tablespoons chopped parsley
1½ teaspoons dried tarragon

1 clove garlic, crushed
¾ teaspoon salt
⅛ teaspoon pepper

6 boned whole chicken breasts
¾ cup unsifted all-purpose flour
3 eggs, well-beaten

1½ cups packaged dry bread crumbs
Salad oil for deep-frying

Thoroughly mix butter, herbs, salt and pepper. On foil, shape into a 6-inch square. Freeze until firm. Meanwhile, skin, wash and dry chicken. Cut whole breast into halves. Place chicken smooth side down on waxed paper; cover with a second sheet. Pound chicken to about ¼-inch thickness, being careful not to break the meat. Cut frozen butter into 12 pats. Place a pat of herb butter in the center of each flattened piece of chicken. Fold ends over, making sure that no butter is showing. Fasten with toothpicks. Roll each piece in flour. Dip the floured chicken in beaten egg then roll in bread crumbs. Shape each one with palms of the hands into a triangle. Refrigerate, covered, 1 hour. Heat about 3 inches of oil to 360°. Fry until browned (5 minutes). Keep warm in 200° oven 15 minutes (no more). These may be cooked ahead and frozen. Cool, wrap in foil and freeze. To serve, unwrap packets. *Do not defrost.* Bake, uncovered, 35 minutes in 350° oven.

Dartie Flynt (Mrs. Wayne)

Make extra herb butter to serve over rice. This is a great dish for dinner parties because it can be prepared ahead of time.

EASY MUSHROOM CHICKEN

1 fryer, cut up	1 can cream of mushroom soup
2 tablespoons butter	¼ cup toasted slivered almonds

Put butter in 12x8x2 oblong baking dish and put in oven until butter melts. Place chicken skin side down in melted butter. Bake 20 minutes at 400°; turn chicken; bake another 20 minutes. Remove from oven. Turn chicken again. Stir soup until smooth and pour over top of chicken. Sprinkle with almonds and bake another 20 minutes. Serve with rice, a fresh fruit salad and hot rolls.

This is a quick and easy meal to prepare for unexpected company or to take a sick friend.

CHICKEN IN SHERRY

4 chicken breasts	¾ cup sherry
1 clove garlic	1 teaspoon salt
1 tablespoon lemon juice	Paprika
2 tablespoons olive oil	

Combine ingredients (except chicken and paprika). Pour over chicken in a bowl. Marinate 24 hours. Remove from marinade and place in baking dish. Sprinkle with paprika. Bake (uncovered) at 375° for 50 minutes. Heat sauce and stir into it 1 tablespoon soft butter and 1 tablespoon flour (mixed). Serve sauce separately.

Olivia H. Harrison (Mrs. Joseph)

THE MAYOR'S CHICKEN IN PASTRY PUFF

6 chicken thighs
2 tablespoons butter
1 chicken bouillon cube
½ cup hot water
3 tablespoons flour
¼ teaspoon salt
¼ teaspoon paprika
Dash pepper

1 cup light cream
1 6-ounce can sliced mushrooms, drained
¼ cup white wine
6 brown-and-serve sausages
1 10-ounce package frozen patty shells, thawed

In skillet, brown chicken on both sides in butter. Dissolve bouillon cube in hot water. Add to chicken. Cover, simmer until tender. Remove chicken from broth. Cool and remove bones carefully. Measure broth from skillet, add water to equal 1 cup liquid, and return to skillet. Combine flour, salt, paprika and pepper. Stir in cream and add cream mixture to broth. Cook quickly, stirring constantly, until mixture thickens and bubbles. Stir in mushrooms and wine. Place sausage in bone cavity of each thigh. On lightly floured surface roll each patty shell to 6-inch square. Place thigh in center of each patty and top with 2 tablespoons mushroom sauce. Fold pastry over and seal seam. Place seam side down. Brush with cream. Bake at 400° oven for 30 minutes. Heat remaining sauce. Pour over chicken puffs and serve.

Mayor Jan Dempsey (Mrs. Richard)

CHICKEN ELEGANTÉ

12 chicken breast halves
¾ cup oil
1 stick oleo
1 onion, thinly sliced

2 cans consommé
¾ cup tomato juice
4 tablespoons flour
½ cup sherry

Skin and salt chicken breasts. Brown in oil and butter. Put breast side down in baking dish. Sauté onion in pan, and add tomato juice and consommé. Blend in flour and simmer 10 minutes. Stir in sherry and pour over chicken. Cover with foil and bake 3 hours at 300°. Freezes well. Serves 12.

"MY" CHICKEN

Arrange chicken thighs and legs in large rectangular baking dish. (I use my lasagna pan.) Allow 2 pieces per person, plus some extra. Sprinkle liberally over them:

Garlic salt
Jane's Crazy Mixed-Up Salt
Minced onion, toasted

Parsley, shredded
Paprika

Cover with white wine. Cover entire pan with Broil-Foil tucked in all around.

Bake in 325° oven for approximately 2 hours. It will keep well, with low oven, as long as it is air-tight, if not ready to serve for awhile.

Marjorie Tyre Sykes (Mrs. Maltby)

So easy!

CHICKEN PICCATA

Use boned chicken breasts. Pound with a meat mallet to tenderize and flatten. Season with garlic salt and black pepper and coat in seasoned bread crumbs. In a large skillet, melt 1 stick butter with 1 large lemon squeezed in it. Brown (sauté) chicken on each side until done. This tastes like real piccata. It is delicious alone or with hollandaise sauce.

Merrilyn Henry (Mrs. Robert)

BISHOP'S CHICKEN

8 halves chicken breast	2 teaspoons paprika
2 cups sour cream	2 cloves garlic (pressed)
¼ cup lemon juice	4 teaspoons pepper
4 teaspoons Worcestershire sauce	1¾ to 2 cups bread crumbs
2 teaspoons celery salt	½ cup oleo
½ cup Crisco	

Make a marinade of all ingredients except fats and crumbs. Pour over chicken and cover well. Refrigerate several hours or overnight. Dip in crumbs and put in a roasting pan. Melt ½ cup Crisco with ½ cup oleo and drizzle over chicken. Cook at 350° uncovered for 1 hour, or until brown and crusty.

CHICKEN BENNEVIER

4 chicken breasts (skinned and boned)	4 tablespoons sesame seeds (toasted)
Salt	4 tablespoons margarine
Paprika	6 tablespoons dry vermouth
8 tablespoons sliced almonds	

Sprinkle chicken breasts with salt and paprika. Roll in sesame seeds. Place in center of 12x12-inch sheet of foil and fold up sides. Sprinkle each breast with 2 tablespoons almonds, 1½ tablespoons vermouth and top with 1 tablespoon pat of margarine. Close foil and seal. Place on grill and cook, about 4 inches from heat, for 1 hour or until done. This may also be cooked in oven. Place salted and rolled in seeds chicken breasts in baking dish. Sprinkle almonds over top. Place pats of margarine on each and then pour the vermouth over all. Cover with foil and bake at 325° for 1 hour. Remove foil and bake 30 minutes longer. Serves 4.

Wesley C. Ellis

This is an original recipe by Wesley that was a finalist in the Alabama Poultry cook-off.

CHICKEN IN WHITE WINE SAUCE

1 3½-pound fryer, cut in pieces
1 cup basic seasoned flour (see below)
½ cup butter
½ cup bacon drippings
1 jar small onions (about 8 ounces)

3 tablespoons all-purpose flour
1½ cups chicken stock
2½ cups Chablis or other dry wine
Salt and pepper to taste

Dredge the chicken pieces with seasoned flour. Sauté the chicken on all sides in the butter and bacon drippings. Remove the chicken and sauté onions about 10 minutes. Remove onions and pour off all but 2 tablespoons of pan drippings. Stir in flour to make a smooth paste, then brown lightly. Add the stock slowly, stirring constantly. Then stir in the wine slowly. Season with salt and pepper. This sauce should be thickened somewhat, not soupy. Place chicken and onions in a casserole dish. Pour sauce over it and bake at 350° for 50-60 minutes. Baste occasionally. Serves 6-8. Freezes well. The Basic Seasoned Flour will make about 3 recipes.

Basic Seasoned Flour:
2 cups all-purpose flour
1½ teaspoons salt
1 tablespoon pepper, preferably ground
fresh
1 tablespoon dry English mustard

½ teaspoon basil
½ tablespoon paprika
½ teaspoon thyme
½ teaspoon parsley flakes

Sift first 5 ingredients together. Stir in herbs and store in airtight container for use as needed. This makes about 2¼ cups seasoned flour. Store in refrigerator.

Caroline Lipscomb

ITALIAN CHICKEN

6 chicken breast halves
Salt, pepper
Garlic powder
Curry powder
Flour
¼ cup butter

½ pound fresh mushrooms, sliced
¼ cup amaretto
1 tablespoon lemon juice
Grated rind from 1 lemon
1½ cups chicken stock
1 tablespoon cornstarch

Remove the skin and debone chicken. Cut into 1-inch cubes. Sprinkle with seasonings. Dredge in flour. Brown in butter. Add mushrooms, amaretto, lemon juice and rind. Simmer for 5 minutes. Mix chicken stock and cornstarch. Add and stir until bubbles and thickens. Season to taste and serve with fettucini.

CHICKEN RODGER

Debone chicken breasts. Marinate 10 minutes in lemon pepper and salt. Melt ¼ to ½ stick butter. Add: paprika, chopped shallots, crushed garlic. Melt and fry for about 5 minutes, low heat, turn off. Dredge chicken meat in butter sauce. Do not cook. Arrange coated chicken in baking dish. Do not put extra butter over. Cover and bake in low oven for about 10 minutes, till barely cooked (meat is still pink). Pour rest of butter/onion/garlic over chicken. Put peach slices over chicken, sprinkle a small amount of nutmeg over. Cook a few minutes—roast. Mix: ½ cup sour cream, ¼ cup mayonnaise, 2 teaspoons chives. Put cream mixture over peaches and chicken. Sprinkle Parmesan cheese over. Roast for about 5 minutes. Serve hot.

Rodger Wood

CHICKEN, INDIAN STYLE

Chicken:
12 pieces of chicken (any pieces you like)
2 cloves of crushed garlic
2 tablespoons lemon juice
¼ cup vegetable oil
3 sliced onions
2 chopped green chilies

1-inch piece fresh ginger root, chopped finely
1 teaspoon turmeric
2 tablespoons ground almonds
1 cup chicken stock

Rice:
2 tablespoons butter or margarine
1 medium onion, chopped
1½ teaspoons sugar
½ cup water

2 cups long-grain rice, soaked in cold water for 30 minutes
1 tablespoon cardamon seeds
1 teaspoon salt

Garnish:
2 tablespoons butter
2 large bananas, peeled and sliced in half, lengthwise, then halved

3 tablespoons chopped unsalted cashew nuts, roasted
1 tablespoon chopped coriander leaves

Combine the garlic, salt and lemon juice together and rub all over the chicken pieces. Set aside for one hour. Heat the oil in a large frying pan. Add the onions and fry until they are golden brown. Stir in the chilies, ginger and turmeric and fry for 1 minute. Add the chicken pieces and fry until they are evenly browned. Stir in the ground almonds and fry for 1 minute. Pour in the stock and stir to mix. Reduce the heat to low, cover the pan and simmer for 50 minutes, or until the chicken is cooked through. Meanwhile, cook the rice. Melt the butter in a saucepan. Add the onion and fry until it is soft. Stir in the sugar and cook until it is brown and caramelized. Stir in the water and bring to a boil, stirring constantly. Add the rice, cardamon seeds and salt and stir to mix. Add just enough water to cover the rice by about ½ inch. Cook slowly over low heat until rice is done (15-20 minutes). Meanwhile, prepare the garnish. Melt butter in a small pan and fry bananas for about 3 minutes. Put rice on a serving platter and arrange chicken pieces over rice. Pour the cooking juices from the pan over chicken. Sprinkle the cashew nuts over top and sprinkle coriander leaves over top. Arrange banana slices around chicken and serve at once.

CHICKEN CURRY

9 large chicken breasts
1 cup finely chopped onion
1 stick butter
4 tablespoons flour
3 tablespoons curry powder
1 teaspoon salt
2 tablespoons sugar

1 teaspoon cinnamon
½ teaspoon ginger
3½ cups hot chicken stock
1 cup chopped tart apple
1 cup seedless raisins
1 cup half and half

Cook chicken breasts in water to cover until just tender. Reserve broth. Debone chicken. In a large skillet, sauté 1 cup finely chopped onion in 1 stick of butter until golden brown. Use a wooden spoon and add 4 tablespoons flour, 3 tablespons curry powder, 1 teaspoon salt, 2 tablespoons sugar and 1 teaspoon cinnamon, ½ teaspoon ginger. Then add slowly, stirring constantly, 3½ cups hot chicken stock. When this has thickened, remove from heat and add 1 cup chopped tart apples and 1 cup seedless raisins and chicken cut in bite-size pieces. Keep in refrigerator overnight, or for several hours, or until raisins have plumped. Add 1 cup of half and half just before serving. Heat thoroughly. Serve over white rice.

Side Dishes:
1 cup Major Grey's chutney
1 cup chopped roasted peanuts—dry roasted
1 cup toasted or frozen, drained coconut

1 cup sweet pickles, chopped fine
1 cup chopped onion, green are best
1 cup chopped crisp bacon
1 cup grated, boiled eggs

Place these side dishes in small bowls arranged around the chicken curry. This is an attractive dinner as well as delicious. Serve with baked fruit (pears, peaches, apricots, cherries, pineapple), drain and bake with butter, brown sugar and 1 teaspoon curry powder.

Nancy Beardsworth (Mrs. C.J.)

SWEET AND SOUR CHICKEN

4-6 chicken breasts (skinned and boned)
Salt and pepper to taste
1 teaspoon ground ginger

2 or 3 egg whites, beaten lightly
2 tablespoons cornstarch
Sufficient oil for deep frying

Sauce:
¼ cup oil
2-inch piece of ginger root, peeled and chopped
1 large green pepper, chopped or cut in strips
1 cup water chestnuts, sliced
5 spring onions
1 can bean sprouts

1 8-ounce can pineapple (reserve juice)
4 tablespoons wine vinegar
1½ tablespoons soy sauce
2 tablespoons tomato paste
2 tablespoons brown sugar
1 tablespoon cornstarch

Cut the chicken into bite-size pieces and rub the flesh with salt; pepper and ground ginger. Put the pieces into a *shallow dish*. Beat the egg whites and cornstarch together, then pour the mixture over the chicken, coat thoroughly. Set aside about 15 minutes. Deep fry chicken 3 or 4 minutes, a few pieces at a time. Drain on paper towel. Heat ¼ cup oil in a very large frying pan. Add ginger and stir-fry for 30 seconds. Remove ginger. Add the vegetables and pineapple chunks and stir-fry for 3 minutes. Combine pineapple juice that was drained off pineapple and the remaining ingredients, except cornstarch. Pour into vegetables and cook one minute. Stir in cornstarch and cook, stirring constantly until the sauce thickens. Add chicken. Serve at once on a bed of rice.

CHICKEN SPAGHETTI

1 large hen	2 tablespoons Worcestershire sauce
1 stick oleo	1 can cream of mushroom soup
1 large onion	1 can tomato soup
2 green peppers	1 pound Velveeta cheese
1 cup celery, chopped	Lawrey's seasoning salt
1 small jar pimentoes	Salt, pepper

Boil hen with 1 bay leaf until done. Sauté in 1 stick oleo, chopped onion, green pepper, celery. Cool hen. In broth, cook one 16-ounce package thin spaghetti. Add sautéed mixture, pimentoes, Worcestershire sauce, soups, diced hen, seasonings and 1 pound Velveeta cheese. Simmer 15 minutes. Freezes nicely.

Betsy Perry (Mrs. Kermit)

CHICKEN AND DUMPLINGS

1 4-pound chicken	2 cups flour
7 cups water	Shortening, size of small egg
1½ teaspoons salt	1 teaspoon salt
2 hard boiled eggs	Enough milk to make dough
¼ teaspoon pepper	

Boil chicken in water 1 hour with 1½ teaspoons salt. Remove chicken, skin and debone. Put flour in mixing bowl with teaspoon of salt. Cut shortening in. Add cold milk a little at a time until a soft ball can be formed out of dough. Roll out on floured waxed paper until fairly thin (not as thin as pie crust), slice into long strips with a knife. Cut across again, making 2 or 3-inch size pieces. Drop 2 or 3 at a time into boiling broth (sometimes I add a little milk to my broth). Cook uncovered for 20 minutes. Add sliced eggs, chicken pieces and pepper. Cover and let set a few minutes (or until ready to serve).

Faye Baggett (Mrs. W.C.)

AMERICAN CHICKEN CHOW MEIN

4 tablespoons salad oil
2 cups thinly sliced Chinese cabbage
3 cups thinly sliced celery
1 #303 can bean sprouts, drained
1 4-ounce can water chestnuts, sliced, drained
2 teaspoons sugar

2 cups chicken stock
2½ tablespoons cornstarch
¼ cup soy sauce
¼ cup cold water
2 cups cooked chicken, shredded

Heat oil. Add celery, cabbage, bean sprouts, water chestnuts, and sugar. Stir constantly for about 2 minutes. Add chicken stock. Bring to boil. Blend cornstarch, cold water, and soy sauce. Add to vegetable mixture and stir until thickened. Add chicken and beat thoroughly. Serve over chow mein noodles.

CHICKEN AND CASHEW NUTS

1 3-pound broiler-fryer chicken
1 3¾-ounce bag cashew nuts
1 bell pepper, diced
2 teaspoons ground ginger root
5 tablespoons soy sauce
4 tablespoons cornstarch

2 tablespoons sugar
2 tablespoons rice wine or dry sherry
½ cup water
¼ teaspoon salt
1 clove garlic, crushed
Oil

Cut chicken into bite-size pieces. Combine 2 tablespoons soy sauce and ginger, and marinate chicken for 15 to 30 minutes. Mix cornstarch with the marinated chicken and fry pieces separately until golden brown over medium high heat (about 3 minutes), then bell pepper and cashew nuts for 1 minute each. Drain well. (Recipe can be prepared to this point in advance.) Heat 1 tablespoon oil in pan. Add garlic and fry 30 seconds. Discard garlic. Add chicken and cashew nuts and pour the mixture of water, 3 tablespoons soy sauce, sugar, salt and rice wine into the pan. Cook over medium high heat for 5 minutes, stirring constantly. Add bell pepper and cook 2 minutes more. Serve hot.

Sheba Hiers (Mrs. Charles)

This dish was served when Japanese Architect Kikutake was the Hiers' dinner guest.

CHINESE DRUMSTICKS

8 drumsticks
4 slices fresh ginger root
2 green onions, cut into 3 pieces each
¼ cup soy sauce

1 tablespoon sherry
1 tablespoon sugar
2½ tablespoons salad oil
1 cup water

Wash drumsticks. Heat oil in wok. Add ginger root and onions and cook until you can smell the ginger root. Add drumsticks and stir-fry for 5 minutes. Add sherry, soy sauce, sugar, and last, the cup of water. Cook over medium heat until the liquid is almost gone. Turn drumsticks occasionally while cooking. Serve hot with parsley sprigs. Can be done ahead and warmed in a 350° over for 5 minutes.

CHICKEN LIVERS IN WHITE WINE

¾ to 1 pound chicken livers
Flour
Salt, pepper

½ cup white wine
¼ cup water
¼ cup margarine

Remove all visible fat from livers. Cut large livers in 2 pieces. Drain. Roll in flour that has been generously seasoned with salt and pepper. Heat margarine until bubbly. Add livers and brown completely on both sides. When all are browned, return all to the pan and add the wine and water. Reduce heat to simmer and cover tightly. Cook 5 minutes. Serve with rice or noodles.

CHICKEN VERONIQUE

3 pounds chicken
Flour, salt and pepper
½ stick butter
2 tablespoons oil
1 cup chicken stock

1 teaspoon cornstarch
Seedless green grapes
½ cup white wine
Half and half

Cut chicken into serving pieces, salt, pepper and coat with flour. Heat oil and butter in heavy frying pan and brown chicken on all sides. Place chicken in a casserole dish. Add wine and chicken stock to pan juices and reduce slightly. Scrape pan well and strain into small saucepan. Mix cornstarch with 1 table-spoon water and add to stock mixture and stir until it boils. Pour over chicken pieces, cover with foil and bake at 350° for 40 minutes. Just before serving add grapes, stir in cream, heat for 5 minutes and serve.

ARROZ CON POLLO
(Panama—main dish)

1 chicken, cut in pieces
1 tablespoon salt
2 cloves garlic, minced
½ teaspoon pepper
½ teaspoon oregano powder
2 ounces salt pork
¼ pound ham, cut in pieces
½ cup butter

1 green pepper, cut in pieces
1 medium onion, chopped
2 medium tomatoes, cut in pieces
1½ pounds rice
1 tablespoon capers
½ cup olives, chopped
3 cups water
1 cup peas, cooked

Cover chicken pieces with mixture of salt, garlic, pepper, and oregano. Make sofrito sauce by cooking salt pork, ham, butter, green pepper, onion, garlic and tomatoes. Sauté chicken in sauce for 30 minutes. Add rice, capers, and olives.

Mix well. Add water and salt to taste. Bring to a boil, when it starts drying, lower heat. Add butter if needed. Cover and cook until rice grain is soft. Garnish with peas. Yield: 6-8 servings. Part of water may be substituted with cooking wine.

Devon Luther (Mrs. William A.)

Colonel and Mrs. Luther brought this recipe back from Panama where they were stationed for 6 years. They serve this at buffet dinners with rolls and a salad.

ENCHILADAS

2 whole chicken breasts
¼ cup chicken stock
6 ounces cream cheese
2 cups heavy cream
10-ounce can Rotel tomatoes
12 tortillas

Parmesan cheese
5 tablespoons corriander
1 egg
1½ teaspoons salt
¼ teaspoon pepper
1 small onion

Simmer chicken 20 minutes. Bone, shred in small pieces. Beat cream cheese with ½ cup of cream, 3 tablespoons at a time. Add onion and chicken. Blend tomatoes and ¼ cup stock. Add 1½ cups cream, eggs, salt and pepper, and corriander. Blend 10 seconds in blender.

Dip tortillas in tomato sauce and fry 1 minute on each side; fill with chicken and roll up; put in pan seam side down. Pour leftover tomato sauce over and top with Parmesan cheese. Bake 350° for 15 minutes.

CHICKEN ENCHILADAS WITH SOUR CREAM

Oil
12 or more tortillas
1 cup cream
1 cup very rich chicken stock
½ cup chopped onion
2 tablespoons butter
2 cups cooked chicken, chopped

1 small can green chili peppers, chopped
1½ cups sour cream
Salt
1½ cups Monterrey Jack cheese, grated

Heat oil; cook tortillas a *few seconds* on each side. Dip in cream and chicken stock which have been combined and heated. Sauté onion in butter, add chicken, chopped chilies and 1 cup sour cream. Salt to taste. Spread tortillas with chicken mixture. Roll and place seam side down in 9x13x2 dish. Pour in liquid; spread ½ cup sour cream over folded enchiladas. Sprinkle with cheese. Bake 350° about 25 minutes.

Patti Tremaine (Mrs. Chuck)

CHICKEN ENCHILADA CASSEROLE

2 tablespoons butter
1 large onion, chopped
1 3-pound chicken, stewed & boned
1 can cream of chicken soup

1 can cream of mushroom soup
1 4-ounce can chopped green chilies
1 dozen corn tortillas
Grated cheddar cheese

Brown onion in butter. Combine with chicken, soups and chilies. In a large casserole dish, put a small amount of the chicken mixture, then put a layer of tortillas, layer of chicken mixture, layer of cheese; repeat 3 layers once. Heat in 350° oven until cheese is melted (usually about 30-40 minutes). This is better prepared a day ahead and heated just before serving. Serves 6-8.

Janet Rogers (Mrs. Jack)

MEXICAN CHICKEN CASSEROLE

1 3½-pound broiler-fryer
2 tablespoons butter or margarine
1 medium onion, chopped
1 green pepper, chopped
1 teaspoon garlic salt
1 10¾-ounce can cream of mushroom
soup, undiluted

½ cup plus 2 tablespoons tomatoes
and green chiles
1½ dozen frozen corn tortillas, thawed
2 cups (8 ounces) shredded Cheddar
cheese

Boil chicken in enough water to cover. Cover and simmer 1 hour or until tender. Remove chicken, reserving ½ cup broth. Remove chicken from bone, and cut into bite-size pieces. Set aside. Melt butter in a skillet; add onion, green pepper, and garlic salt. Sauté until tender. Combine onion mixture, soup, reserved chicken broth, and tomatoes and green chiles in a bowl; stir well. Tear tortillas into bite-size pieces; place half of tortilla pieces in a greased 13x9x2-inch baking dish. Top with half of soup mixture, then add half of diced chicken. Sprinkle with half of cheese. Repeat layers. Bake at 350° for 30 minutes or until bubbly. Yield: 6-8 servings.

CHEESY MEXICAN CHICKEN PIE

1 broiler-fryer
1 10-ounce can enchilada sauce
1 10¾-ounce can cream of mushroom
soup, undiluted
1 large onion, chopped
½ teaspoon garlic salt

Dash of pepper
1 8½-ounce package regular size corn
chips
1 cup (4 ounces) shredded Cheddar
cheese
1 cup chicken broth

Place chicken in a Dutch oven with water to cover. Bring to a boil; cover and simmer 1 hour or until tender. Remove chicken, reserving broth; cool. Remove chicken from bone, and cut into bite-size pieces. Combine chicken, enchilada sauce, soup, onion, garlic salt, and pepper. Place half of corn chips in a greased 12x7x2-inch baking dish. Top with chicken mixture, then with remaining corn chips. Sprinkle with cheese; pour chicken broth over casserole. Bake at 350° for 30 minutes. Yield: 6-8 servings.

SWISS CHICKEN

Debone four chicken breasts. Brown in butter. Sauté ½ pound mushroom caps. Arrange chicken and mushrooms in baking dish. Make a medium white sauce.

Add ¼ cup sherry and ⅓ cup grated Swiss cheese to sauce. Pour sauce over chicken and mushrooms. Sprinkle with ¼ cup Swiss cheese. Bake at 300° for 25 minutes.

CHICKEN TETRAZZINI

1 pound spaghetti
1 bay leaf
Chicken broth
1 chicken, diced
1 quart milk
½ pound American cheese
½ pound cheddar cheese

⅔ cup flour
¼ pound oleo
1 can mushrooms
1 onion, diced
1 green pepper, diced
Buttered bread crumbs

Cook spaghetti in salted chicken broth with bay leaf. Cook milk, cheese, flour and oleo until thick. Add mushrooms, onion and green pepper to cooked milk mixture. Add milk mixture to cooked (drained) spaghetti and diced chicken. Place in greased casserole dish; top with buttered bread crumbs. Bake 350° 30 minutes.

Patti Tremaine (Mrs. Chuck)

WINE AND WILD RICE CASSEROLE

1 6-ounce package long grain and wild
   rice mix
½ cup onion, chopped
½ cup celery, chopped
2 tablespoons butter
1 can cream of mushroom soup

½ cup sour cream
⅓ cup dry white wine
½ teaspoon curry powder
2 cups cubed cooked chicken or
   turkey
¼ cup snipped parsley

Prepare rice mix according to package directions. Meanwhile, in saucepan cook onion and celery in butter until tender but not brown. Blend in soup, sour cream, wine and curry. Stir in chicken and cooked rice; turn into 12x7½x2 baking dish. Bake uncovered at 350° 35-40 minutes. Stir before serving. Garnish with parsley. Yield: 4-6 servings.

Patti Tremaine (Mrs. Chuck)

CHICKEN CASSEROLE

3 cups rice, Uncle Ben's Quick Long
   Grain
2 cans cream of chicken soup
3⅔ cups chicken broth
1 chicken, cooked and boned

1 package green peas, defrosted
1 small jar pimentos
1 cup mushroom pieces, drained
1 teaspoon soy sauce
½ teaspoon salt

Mix chicken mixture not more than 1 hour ahead of baking time. Can be frozen

at this point, or baked now for 30 minutes at 350°, after topping is added. Topping:
Melt 6 tablespoons butter. Add 2 cups Pepperidge Farm stuffing and ½ package blanched, slivered almonds. Toss together until well mixed. If you plan to freeze casserole, add topping when preparing to bake. At this time add a cup of liquid (such as chicken broth, bouillon cube or cream of chicken soup) before putting topping on. Serves 12 easily.

Peggy Turnquist (Mrs. Paul)

CHICKEN PARMESAN

6-8 boned chicken breasts

Dip pieces into 2 beaten eggs. Roll in ½ Progresso Italian Bread Crumbs, and ½ Parmesan cheese. Brown in 1 stick butter. (Can freeze at this point.) Place in casserole, and pour 1 regular jar Ragu spaghetti sauce over. Cover top with mozarella cheese. Bake at 350° for 45 minutes.

Jackie Norman (Mrs. Dan)

CHICKEN AND RICE CASSEROLE

2 cups minute rice, uncooked
1 can cream of chicken soup
1 can cream of celery soup

½ package dry onion soup
1 chicken, cut up

Mix together and put into cake pan. Lay raw chicken over the rice mixture and cover with remaining ½ package of dry onion soup. Cover with foil and seal edges well. Bake 3 hours at 300°.

CHICKEN WITH SAUSAGE AND MUSHROOMS

1 chicken, boiled and cut in large pieces
1 pound sausage, cooked and drained
1 small box Uncle Ben's Long Grain and
  Wild Rice, cooked

1 can (10¾ ounces) mushroom soup
1 can (6 ounces) mushrooms, sliced
  (do not drain)

Mix all ingredients in shallow 2-3-quart casserole and bake at 350° for 30 minutes. Serves 6-8.

CHICKEN CASSEROLE

1 chicken, cooked and chopped
1 cup celery
3 eggs, hard-boiled and chopped
2 tablespoons onions
½ cup mayonnaise
Dash Worcestershire sauce

¼ cup slivered almonds
½ cup cracker crumbs
1 can cream of chicken or mushroom
  soup
1 tablespoon lemon juice
Salt and pepper

Combine above and put in casserole dish and cover. Bake at 325° until hot.

Donna Beardsworth (Mrs. Jim)

CHICKEN SPECTACULAR

3 cups cooked chicken (diced), 1 box Uncle Ben's White and Wild Rice (fixed according to directions). Mix 1 can cream of celery soup, 1 chopped onion, 1 med. jar pimentos chopped, 2 cans French Style green beans, drained, 1 cup mayonnaise, 1 small or med. can water chestnuts (chopped). Combine with chicken and prepared rice. Bake at 350° covered, until bubbly.

Jean Winters (Mrs. William)

ESTHER'S CHICKEN CASSEROLE

6 chicken breasts, skinned and cooked
1 stack Ritz crackers to line casserole
  (save a few to sprinkle over top)

Melt 1 stick oleo and pour over crust. Mix:

1 can cream of chicken soup
1 can cream of mushroom soup

1 carton sour cream
1 can water chestnuts, sliced

Mix soups and sour cream, after lining casserole (9x13) and spreading oleo over it. Place chicken over crackers, then, half the soup mixture, layer the water chestnuts and pour the rest over. Bake 350° for 30 minutes. Good!

Faye Baggett (Mrs. W.C.)

CHICKEN CHEESE NOODLE RING

1 package short noodles, cooked in
  boiling water, drained well
Beat together:
3 eggs yolks
1 cup grated American cheese
½ pint half and half

1 tablespoon Worcestershire sauce
4 tablespoons ketchup
4 tablespoons onion

Add to the noodles and fold in beaten egg whites. Poor in well-buttered ring mold, place mold in pan of hot water and cook 30 minutes in a 350° oven. Fill with creamed chicken in center.

Grace Jones (Mrs. Allen)

CHICKEN 'N STUFFING SCALLOP

1 8-ounce package herbed stuffing
  (Pepperidge Farm)
3 cups chicken, cooked and cubed
½ cup butter or margarine

½ cup flour
¼ teaspoon salt
4 cups chicken broth
6 eggs, slightly beaten

Prepare stuffing according to package directions. Spread in greased 13x9-inch pan. Top with the chicken. In a large saucepan melt butter; blend in flour and seasonings. Add cool broth and stir until thickened. Stir a small amount of hot mixture into eggs; return to hot mixture in pan. Pour over chicken. Bake at 325-350° for 45 minutes, or until knife inserted in center comes out clean. Let stand 5 minutes to set. Cut in squares and serve with sauce. Serves 12.

Pimento-Mushroom Sauce:

Mix, heat and stir:

1 can cream of mushroom soup
¼ cup milk

1 cup sour cream
¼ cup chopped pimento

Mary Christenberry (Mrs. Dan)

This casserole was served at the State P.E.O. Convention when it was held in Auburn. It was a big hit!

CHICKEN PIE SOUFFLÉ

4 pound stewing hen
½ cup chicken fat
½ cup flour
1 teaspoon dry mustard
2 cups bread crumbs

1 quart chicken stock
4 eggs
Salt and pepper

Stew 4-pound hen in salted water. Bone chicken and cut into cubes. Make a gravy with chicken fat, flour and dry mustard. Cool, Then beat eggs and pour them in the gravy. Blend well. To assemble casserole: put in layer of bread crumbs, layer of chicken and layer of gravy. Repeat ending with gravy. Bake 350° for 45 minutes.

Mrs. Wilbur DeVall

This is a favorite with the Forestry Department.

CHICKEN LAYER CASSEROLE

3 cups cooked rice
3 packages frozen broccoli—2 spears and
1 chopped—cooked just till tender,
drained

1 chicken, cooked and taken off the
bone

Sauce:
3 tablespoons chopped onion
Butter or margarine
1 can cream of chicken soup

½ soup can of milk
1 pound Velveeta cheese

Place the cooked rice in prepared 13x9x2-inch casserole, top with broccoli. Sauté onion in butter in skillet. Add the soup, milk and Velveeta cheese. I also add a small can of chopped mushrooms. Stir until the sauce is smooth. Add the chicken and heat through. Pour on top of other ingredients in casserole dish.

Grate fresh cheddar cheese on top and bake in 350° oven 25-30 minutes. This freezes well. Serves 6-8.

Linda Voitle (Mrs. Robert)

EASY CHICKEN DIVAN

8 chicken breast halves, cooked
2 packages cooked broccoli
½ teaspoon curry powder
1 tablespoon lemon juice

1 cup mayonnaise (not Miracle Whip)
2 cans cream of chicken soup
2 cups cooked rice

Combine soup, mayonnaise, lemon juice and curry powder. Put rice in bottom of 1x13 greased pan. Arrange broccoli over rice. Cut chicken into strips and arrange on top of broccoli. Pour sauce over chicken and broccoli. Top with ½ cup cheddar cheese, grated and ½ cup buttered bread crumbs. Bake at 350° for 25 minutes.

Judy Godsil (Mrs. Ray)

CHICKEN CONTINENTAL

Chicken breasts (3 pounds)
1⅓ cups Minute rice
1 can condensed cream of chicken soup
  (10½-ounces)
⅓ cup seasoned flour (with salt and
  pepper added)
¾ cup shortening for frying (use ½
  shortening and ¼ margarine)

2½ tablespoons grated onion
1 teaspoon salt
Dash pepper
1 tablespoon chopped parsley
½ teaspoon celery flakes or chopped
  fresh celery
1⅓ cups water

Roll chicken in seasoned flour, brown in margarine and shortening. Remove chicken. Stir soup, seasonings and water into drippings. Cook and stir to a boil. Spread rice into 1½-quart shallow casserole. Pour all but ⅓ cup soup over rice. Stir to moisten. Top with chicken and remainder of soup. Bake covered at 350° for 1 hour or 1¼ hours. Makes 4 or 5 servings. This casserole can be made ahead of time and baked just before the meal.

Thelma Thomas (Mrs. Ben F., Jr.)

COQ AU VIN I

1 chicken, cut up
6 slices bacon
2 tablespoons margarine
4 small onions
1 cup canned or fresh mushrooms
4 medium potatoes, quartered
1 clove garlic

2 tablespoons flour
1 teaspoon salt
⅛ teaspoon pepper
¼ teaspoon thyme
2 cups burgundy
1 cup chicken stock
Parsley

Sauté bacon until crisp. Remove and drain bacon. Add margarine to bacon drippings and brown chicken on all sides. Place in baking dish. Add onions, mushrooms, potatoes and garlic to grease and cook slowly for 10 minutes. Add these to baking dish. Add bacon which has been crumbled. Stir flour and thyme into pan drippings. Gradually add stock and burgundy. Bring to a boil, then pour over chicken and vegetables. Cover. Place in refrigerator overnight. Cook 1 hour and 50 minutes covered at 400°. Top with parsley.

COQ AU VIN II

½ cup flour
1½ teaspoons salt
¼ teaspoon pepper
1 3-3½-pound fryer, cut into serving
  pieces
6 slices bacon
6 small onions
8 ounces mushrooms, sliced
½ teaspoon thyme

1 bay leaf
Parsley
4 carrots, scraped and halved
1 teaspoon instant chicken broth or 2
  chicken bouillon cubes
1 cup hot water
1 cup burgundy or red cooking wine
1 clove garlic, pressed

Mix flour, 1 teaspoon salt and pepper and coat chicken by shaking in mixture in paper bag. Fry bacon in large skillet until crisp, remove bacon and brown chicken in bacon fat over medium heat. Remove chicken and sauté onions and mushrooms until tender (about 5 minutes). Drain fat. Tie herbs in cheesecloth bag. Crumble bacon and stir bacon, herbs, and remaining ingredients into skillet. Add vegetables and chicken. Cover and simmer 1 hour. Spoon off fat. Serve in soup bowls with salad and crusty French bread.

   I usually substitute a jar of small boiled onions for the fresh.

DAWSON STEW

2 fryers, cut-up
2 cans tomato paste
6 cans water, add to paste
3 medium onions, sliced

1½ sticks butter or margarine
Crushed red pepper to taste
Salt and pepper to taste

Salt and pepper washed, cut up chicken. Sear chicken pieces in ½ inch of bacon drippings about 5 minutes. Pour out grease and layer chicken, onions, and sauce (paste and water) with seasonings. Add butter or margarine and cook slowly about 1 hour. Serve with rice and corn bread.

                                                    Sue Dye (Mrs. Pat)

This is Coach Dye's favorite!

BRUNSWICK STEW

1 whole chicken, cut up
1 onion, quartered
2 ribs celery, diced
1 teaspoon salt
¼ teaspoon pepper
16½-ounce can white shoepeg corn
10 ounces frozen small butter beans
1 pound canned tomatoes

2 small potatoes, cubed
⅓ cup catsup
2-3 tablespoons vinegar
1 tablespoon brown sugar
1 teaspoon Worcestershire sauce
½ teaspoon Tabasco
¼ teaspoon marjoram
2-3 tablespoons butter

Place chicken in Dutch oven and add enough water to cover well. Add onion, celery, salt and pepper. Boil until chicken comes off bones easily. Remove chicken to cool and add corn, butter beans, tomatoes, potatoes, catsup and vinegar; cook 2 hours or until tender. Remove chicken from bones and add to vegetables along with Worcestershire sauce, Tabasco, marjoram and butter.

Betsy Judkins (Mrs. Joe)
Betsy's on Ross

The AU Poultry Science has an annual summer picnic. The menu is as follows:

Barbecued Chicken*

Potato Salad   Deviled Eggs or Pickled Eggs

French Bread

Watermelon

*The "right" barbecue sauce is a matter of grave discussion. Several of their favorites are listed below:

OUTDOOR LEMONY BARBECUED CHICKEN

2 broiler-fryer chickens, quartered
1¼ cups catsup
1 can (6 ounces) frozen lemonade,
    thawed, undiluted
¾ cup water

¼ cup Worcestershire sauce
¼ cup mustard
¼ cup corn oil
2 tablespoons instant minced onion
1 teaspoon flavor enhancer

Marinate chicken in Zesty Italian Dressing for several hours before cooking for a nice flavor.

Doris Gardner (Mrs. H.A., Jr.)

Mix a ratio of ⅔ vinegar to ⅓ cooking oil. Baste the chicken during cooking and salt the chicken to taste near the end of cooking time.

Dr. Claude Moore

The Moore's used this barbecue sauce for an Alfresco barbecue supper announcing the engagement of their daughter, Marianne.

"PROF." GOODMAN'S BARBECUE SAUCE

½ gallon vinegar
½ gallon oil
1 pint water
2 tablespoons liquid smoke

3 cloves garlic, whole
Salt and pepper
3 tablespoons Worcestershire sauce

Mix all ingredients and heat. Keep on grill to keep warm. Place chickens on grill skin side up, baste with sauce, sprinkle with salt. Lay foil on top of chicken to hold in heat, remove every 20 minutes, turn chicken, baste with sauce and sprinkle with salt. When done, remove foil and continue cooking until skin is brown and crispy. Use the following finishing sauce after the foil is removed.

Finishing Sauce:
1 pound margarine
1 quart vinegar
Salt and pepper

2 tablespoons Worcestershire
3 cloves garlic, whole
1 pint catsup

Mix together and simmer for about 10-15 minutes to blend flavors. Keep on grill to keep warm.

This is the most traditional barbecue sauce used by the Poultry Department. It was used for years, until Professor John Goodman retired. The Department agrees that it is the best. It is enough for 40 chicken halves.

JAKE FORTNER'S BARBECUE SAUCE
(for 10 chickens)

5 cups catsup
1 pound oleo
10 tablespoons lemon juice
10 tablespoons vinegar
5 tablespoons sugar

3 cloves garlic
Hot pepper to taste
Salt to taste
Black pepper to taste

Bring sauce to just below simmer. Use with chicken halves barbecued over charcoal and green hickory. Serves 20.

Emmalu Foy (Mrs. James E.)

This is the sauce for the chicken barbecue Jim prepared each summer for student leaders at their home. It was served with homegrown vegetables—corn on the cob, green beans, tomato slices—and freezer ice cream.

BARBECUE SAUCE
(for 8 chicken breasts on grill)

½ cup melted margarine
½ cup catsup
½ cup lemon juice
1½ cup salad oil
4 tablespoons brown sugar
2 tablespoons prepared mustard
2 teaspoons salt

2 teaspoons paprika
½ teaspoon pepper
1 tablespoon Worcestershire sauce
½ teaspoon Tabasco
4 teaspoons grated onion
4 garlic cloves

Simmer all ingredients about 30 minutes, stirring several times. Cover until ready to use. This recipe may be made the day before and refrigerated. Brush on chicken while cooking on charcoal grill .

Dell Chester (Mrs. Rollie)

BARBECUE CHICKEN
(Slaterville Springs Fire Department, Slaterville Springs, New York)

Cook chicken slowly on outside grill and baste with the following sauce:

¼ pint oil
½ pint vinegar
3 teaspoons salt

¼ teaspoon pepper
1½ teaspoons poultry seasoning
1 egg

Ethel Vaughan (Mrs. Tom)

This small volunteer fire department had a barbecue one Sunday out of each month to raise money. This was a favorite and nice change from the tomato base sauce.

BARBECUED CHICKEN, STAN STYLE

Sauce for basting chicken (or ribs) on grill:
1 quart bone stock (made as for soup)
¾ tablespoon dry mustard
¾ tablespoon salt
½ tablespoon garlic powder
¼ tablespoon ground bay leaf
½ tablespoon chili powder

¾ tablespoon paprika
½ tablespoon hot pepper sauce
1 cup Worcestershire sauce
½ cup vinegar
½ cup oil
¾ tablespoon monosodium glutamate

Dry Seasoning:
3 tablespoons salt
1½ tablespoons black pepper
1 tablespoon monosodium glutamate
1 tablespoon garlic powder

1 tablespoon ground bay leaves
½ tablespoon paprika
1 tablespoon dry mustard

Mix all ingredients for sauce and let stand overnight. Sprinkle chicken halves or quarters with dry seasoning and allow to marinate several hours in refrigerator. Grill chicken over low charcoal fire. May be covered with brown wrapping paper to hold heat and flavor in. Baste chicken often with the sauce. Recipe will be adequate for 12 chickens. Extra sauce may be frozen for use later.

Barbara Wilson (Mrs. Stan)

This recipe is a favorite for the Wilsons' large picnics on special holidays like July 4th or Labor Day, which coincides with Stan's birthday quite often. Informal picnics are a favorite way of the Wilsons for entertaining large groups.

BILL'S BAROQUE (BROKE) CHICKEN
(cook at the end of the month)

Chicken halves (with skin)   Cavender's seasoning

Sauce:
Lemon juice, 1 part   Karo syrup, 4 parts
Worcestershire sauce, 1 part   Catsup, 4 parts

Mix sauce ingredients together and stir until blended evenly. Place chicken halves low over *hot* charcoal fire. Baste and turn frequently for first 5 minutes to harden and build up sauce coating. Take care not to burn coating at this stage. After initial 5 minutes of high heat, close lid of grill (allow ½-inch opening to maintain fire) to slow cooking. Continue to periodically turn and baste. Sauce coating should gradually take on a rich brown color. When chicken is almost done, baste thoroughly and coat generously with Cavender's. Continue to cook until this final basting becomes firm. Remove from fire and serve hot.

STUFFED ROAST DUCKLING

¼ cup chopped salt pork   ¼ cup fresh parsley
1 onion, chopped   ⅓ cup sugar
4 or 5 tart apples, chopped   ¾ cup fine bread crumbs
½ cup raisins   Salt and pepper
½ cup celery

Mix these ingredients and stuff the duck. Bake at 325°, uncovered, 30 minutes to a pound. Prick often, pouring off fat each time. After duck is brown, mix drippings with 1 cup of hot orange juice and baste.

MARYLAND TURKEY
(War Eagle Cafeteria)

2 cups flour   Salt
2 eggs   2 cups milk
Black pepper   2 teaspoons baking powder

Beat egg whites until stiff. Fold into batter of milk, egg yolks, flour, salt and pepper. Dip slices of baked hen or turkey into batter and fry in deep fat, 375-400°. Serves 10.

Inez Tucker (Mrs. Howard)

Thousands of Auburn alumni, faculty and students have enjoyed luncheon and banquet servings of this most-famous of War Eagle Cafeteria dishes—all under the impeccable supervision of Mrs. Tucker, ably assisted over the years by Charlie Will Brunson!

CURRIED TURKEY

3 cups cooked turkey, diced large
6 tablespoons margarine or oil
1 medium onion, minced
2 tablespoons green pepper, diced
4 tablespoons flour
1½ cups turkey or chicken broth
1¼ cups sliced mushrooms, lightly
 sautéed, or 6-ounce can

1 large tart apple, cored and diced
5-ounce can water chestnuts, drained
 and sliced thin
3 tablespoons chopped pimento
1 tablespoon parsley, minced
Salt and pepper
1½ teaspoons curry powder, or to
 taste

Heat the fat in a large casserole and sauté the onion and green pepper until soft. Stir in the flour, cook a moment, and blend in the turkey or chicken broth and the mushrooms. (Add the liquid if using canned mushrooms.) Simmer the mixture 15-20 minutes. In a large bowl mix the turkey, apple, water chestnuts, pimento, parsley and salt and pepper. Stir the curry powder into the sauce, as much as you like, and check the seasoning. Stir in the turkey mixture, heat slowly, and simmer 10-15 minutes over the lowest possible heat. Serves 6-8. It is easily doubled or quadrupled.

Curry improves with time. Make this in the morning or the day before, bring to room temperature, and merely reheat at serving time.

Serve with plenty of fresh hot rice and an assortment of accompaniments: chutney, fresh and/or roasted coconut, chopped salted peanuts, candied ginger, chopped hard-boiled eggs, raisins, and chopped green pepper.

Martha's favorite way to serve this dinner is from a tiered lazy-susan for the accompaniments, wooden bowls for the rice and curry, and wooden plates for the guests. An Indian table cover and bronze pieces for accent lend to the flavor of the evening.

Martha W. Edwards (Mrs. Jim)

JAN'S SECRET SMOKED TURKEY

Soak whole turkey in Morton's Sugar Cure—1 pound/2 gallons water—2 hours. Add other condiments of preference. Smoke (Cajun Smoker, Brinkman, or equal) 12 hours. Flavor with hickory/sassafras. After smoking, cool, then place in plastic bag in refrigerator for 12-24 hours. (Smoke flavor absorbs into meat.) Slice thin for enjoyment of full flavor.

Dr. Jan Bartels

GAME

DOVES WITH ORANGE GLAZE

6 to 12 doves, cleaned (whole)
Juice of 3 lemons
¾ cup Worcestershire sauce
1 teaspoon salt

Dash of pepper
½ slice bacon per dove
1 12-ounce can frozen orange juice,
 thawed and undiluted

Place doves in large bowl; pour lemon juice over each bird (bottled concentrate lemon juice works real well), then Worcestershire sauce, salt and pepper and marinate several hours or overnight. Turn doves to marinate on all sides. Remove from marinade. Wrap each dove in bacon and secure with toothpick (you can wrap with bacon before using marinade). Place in a shallow roasting dish and pour concentrated orange juice over birds. Bake at 350° for 1 hour, turning and basting at least every 20 minutes. Delicious served with grits or over rice.

Sara Russell (Mrs. W.M.)

This recipe can be used for quail.

QUAIL PIE
(An original recipe)

14 quail

Boil quail with onion and celery until done—30 minutes. Debone quail. Use I chopped celery and 1 cup onions chopped and sauté 3 wine sap apples, peeled and slivered, in real butter (2 tablespoons). Make cream sauce, using chicken broth, add a little, then cream. Add 1 large can mushrooms. Season with salt and white pepper. Pour in unbaked pie shell. Pour ½ cup white sherry over filling before baking. Top with pie crust. Bake at 400° in oven for 10 minutes. Then 350° until crust is brown. I use a 2-quart pyrex dish for this.

Virginia Goodwin (Mrs. J.W.)

Auburn is indebted to the Goodwins for their generous gift which supported construction of the Goodwin Music Building.

214

VENISON IN BURGUNDY

2 pounds venison, cubed
½ cup bacon drippings
1 can beef broth
1¾ cups burgundy wine
2 medium onions

1 large can mushrooms, drained
4 tablespoons flour
Salt, pepper, thyme and marjoram to taste
Kitchen Bouquet for flavor and color

Sauté sliced onions in bacon drippings until golden brown. Remove onions and save for later. Brown venison. Stir in flour. Add wine, beef broth, and seasonings. Cover and simmer very gently for 3-4 hours. Then add the fried onions and mushrooms and cook a bit longer. Stir frequently to keep from sticking. Serve over hot buttered noodles or rice. Serves 6 people.

Shirley Bartels (Mrs. Jan)

VENISON ROAST TREAT

1 4-6 pound venison roast
1½ cups catsup
1½ cups coke

1 teaspoon salt
½ teaspoon pepper
¾ cup water

Salt and pepper roast and place in 350° oven for 30 minutes; then mix coke and catsup together and pour a little over the roast with part of the water poured around the roast and cook as you would a pot roast only basting frequently. The gravy is delicious and goes well with rice—most unusual "yummy" flavor. Always keep a little water in the roasting pan as venison has very little moisture and the gravy will dry out. If the roast is larger, use more catsup and coca cola. I make a tent of aluminum foil and place over this.

Sara Russell (Mrs. W.M.)

Folks who vow they don't like game will love this dish!

VENISON STROGANOFF

1 pound ground venison
1 3-ounce can mushrooms, chopped
½ cup onion
1 clove garlic, minced
2 tablespoons butter

3 tablespoons flour
3 tablespoons tomato paste
1 cup beef stock or beef broth
1 cup sour cream
Noodles

Brown venison and onion and garlic, then add mushrooms. Next add butter and blend in flour. Stir in the tomato paste and beef broth and let simmer until thick and bubbly. Remove from heat and stir in sour cream. Serve over hot buttered noodles.

Angie Dollar (Mrs. Mason)

VENISON CABBAGE ROLLS

1 egg
1 teaspoon salt
Dash of pepper
1 teaspoon Worcestershire sauce
¼ cup chopped onion

⅔ cup milk
1 pound ground venison
1 pound *hot* sausage
¾ cup cooked rice

About 10 large cabbage leaves
1 10¾-ounce can condensed tomato
  soup

1 tablespoon brown sugar
1 tablespoon lemon juice

Combine egg, salt, pepper, Worcestershire sauce, onion and milk in a bowl. Next add venison and hot sausage and mix thoroughly; and last, fold in cooked rice. (Have rice cooked, but still a good, firm texture.) Immerse cabbage leaves in boiling water for about 3 minutes or just until limp. Remove and drain. The heavy vain may be split a little way. Place about ½ cup to ¾ cup meat mixture on each leaf; fold in sides and roll ends over meat. Placed folded side down into baking dish (12x7½). Blend together soup, brown sugar, and lemon juice. Pour over cabbage rolls. Bake at 350° for about 1 hour. Baste twice with sauce. Serves 10.

Angie Dollar (Mrs. Mason)

SEAFOOD

COD PROVENCAL

2 pounds cod fillets
Salt and pepper
Flour
2 tablespoons grated Parmesan cheese
Grated nutmeg
1 small onion, chopped
1 clove garlic, chopped

½ cup oil
6 anchovy fillets, soaked in a little milk
  and mashed
1 teaspoon parsley, chopped
½ cup dry white wine
3 cups hot milk
1 tablespoon butter

Clean and skin cod and cut in large pieces. Sprinkle with salt and pepper and roll in flour. Arrange in 1 layer in an ovenproof dish and sprinkle with the Parmesan cheese mixed with a pinch of nutmeg. In a pan, sauté the onion and garlic lightly in oil, then add the anchovy fillets, parsley and white wine. Reduce on low heat, then pour in the hot milk, stirring thoroughly, and add the butter in small pieces. Pour over the fish, bring to a boil, cover, and cook in a slow oven (250°) for 2 hours. After cooking, the cooking juices should be almost completely absorbed. Serve with piping hot polenta or mashed potato.

FILLETS OF SOLE MEUNIERE

2 soles (1 to 1¼ pounds each) or 1½
  pound sole fillets, fresh or frozen
Flour
Salt and pepper

½ cup butter
Juice of 2 lemons
Parsley, chopped
Lemon slices

Remove and discard the heads from the soles, and skin them. Wash and drain. Make an incision along the center bone of each sole and detach the 4 fillets carefully with a knife. Roll the fillets lightly in flour seasoned with salt and pepper, and cook slowly in a pan in 4 tablespoons of the butter until they are golden on all sides. Arrange them on a warm serving platter, sprinkle with the lemon juice, and the chopped parsley to taste. Melt the remaining butter in the pan, cook until lightly golden, then pour evenly over the sole. Serve immediately, garnished with lemon slices.

FLOUNDER PARMESAN

1 pound frozen or fresh fillets
1 cup sour cream
¼ cup grated Parmesan cheese
2 to 3 tablespoons lemon juice
1 tablespoon grated onion

½ teaspoon salt
Dash of liquid hot pepper sauce
Paprika
Chopped parsley
Maybe a few capers

Thaw fillets and cut to serving size. Place on aluminum foil in baking dish or pan. Combine remaining ingredients except paprika. Spread sour cream mixture over fish, sprinkle with paprika. Bake in moderate oven, 350°, for 25 to 30 minutes, until fish flakes easily when tested with fork. Garnish with more parsley. Serves 6. I like to use plenty (even more) of sour cream and lemon juice so fish will be moist. Since living alone, I have butcher cut fillet (1 pound package) in half and that makes 2 meals for my cook and me. Freeze ½ to cook for second meal. Using foil in pan makes cleaning pan easier—just throw away—and then wash pan—less fish odor. The entire pound package will serve 4 or 5 people if you use the product from Canada—but "Taste of Sea" has fewer ounces and smaller servings—but good—won't feed but 4 people with only 1 helping.

Caroline Draughon (Mrs. Ralph)

Mrs. Draughon, the beloved first lady of Auburn, entertains beautifully.

FISH CASSEROLE

3 pounds fish fillets
½ cup flour
½ stick butter
2 or 3 raw potatoes, thinly sliced and
   peeled

½ cup cream
1 teaspoon paprika
Salt and pepper

Score the fish fillets every 2 inches, then rub with salt and pepper. Roll fish in flour and paprika. In a well-greased casserole pan, line the bottom with sliced potatoes. (You should not see the bottom of the casserole.) Place fish on top of potatoes. Dot with butter, pour on the cream and bake in 350° oven for 35 minutes, or until light brown. Serve hot.

BAKED FISH

4 pounds or large whole fish (snapper, halibut, mackerel, etc., whole or filleted)
1 clove garlic
1 tablespoon olive oil
½ cup white wine
4 tomatoes

2 onions
8 new potatoes
½ cup green onions, chopped
½ cup green pepper, chopped
½ cup celery, chopped
½ cup parsley, chopped
1 can tomato paste

Select a shallow casserole; oil bottom with olive oil. Put fish down skin side up. Cut 4 slits diagonally; put slivered garlic in slits. Slice new potatoes (with skins) thinly. Arrange tomato slices, sliced onions and potatoes alternately around fish. Put chopped celery, green pepper and green onions over top of fish. Mix tomato paste with white wine and pour over all. Top with parsley and dot with butter. Cook in oven 350° for 30-45 minutes covered with metal foil. Serve in same dish. Good with salad and rolls.

BAKED STUFFED WHOLE FISH

Stuffing:
1 egg, beaten
¼ teaspoon thyme
½ teaspoon dill seed
2 tablespoons chopped parsley
¼ teaspoon salt
Dash pepper
2 tablespoons butter or margarine

½ cup butter or margarine
3 tablespoons onion, finely chopped
3 cups white bread crumbs (day-old bread, grated)
1 (3-to 5-pound) whole fish, dressed and split
Salt and pepper

Preheat oven to 500°. Make stuffing: combine egg, thyme, dill seed, parsley, salt and pepper in a large bowl; mix well. In hot butter, sauté onion until it is golden, about 5 minutes. Combine all stuffing ingredients with 2 tablespoons hot water. Toss lightly with a fork. Season inside of fish and place in a shallow baking dish. Stuff and close with toothpicks. Brush top with melted butter then bake uncovered 10 minutes. Reduce heat to 400°; bake 10 minutes per pound, or until fish flakes easily with fork.

STUFFED SALMON SLICES

2 slices fresh salmon, or other similar fish such as halibut, ¾-inch thick and about 10 ounces each
1 slice onion, chopped
1 tablespoon parsley, chopped
Butter or margarine

1 generous handful of bread, soaked in milk and squeezed dry
1 cup mushrooms, finely sliced
Salt
Pepper
1 cup light cream

Fry the onion and parsley lightly in 2½ tablespoons butter or margarine on low heat. Mix in a bowl with the bread, mushrooms, and salt and pepper to taste. Butter generously an ovenproof dish, put in one salmon slice, and spread the mushroom mixture over it. Cover with the second salmon slice, pour over the cream, previously heated. Dot with butter, and sprinkle with salt and pepper. Cook in a moderate (350°) oven for about ½ hour, basting occasionally with the cooking juices. Transfer to a warm serving platter, sprinkle with chopped parsley and serve with boiled potatoes.

SALMON CROQUETTES

Mix 2 cups salmon, 1 cup bread crumbs, 1 tablespoon parsley, dash of paprika, dash of pepper, 1 cup white sauce, and 1 teaspoon lemon juice until well blended. Chill mixture and shape into balls. Beat 2 eggs with 4 tablespoons milk. Roll in bread crumbs, dip in egg mixture and roll again in bread crumbs. Fry in deep fat, 375°, until golden brown. Drain on absorbent paper. Serve hot. Makes 14 to 16 small croquettes.

FISH FILLETS IN WINE SAUCE

1 pound fish fillet (rock cod, butter fish
  or sea bass)
2 green onions, cut into 1-inch pieces
3 tablespoons cornstarch mixed with ½
  cup water
2 egg whites, beaten
¾ cup peanut oil

1 cup chicken stock
3 tablespoons sherry
1 teaspoon salt
1 tablespoon sugar
Thickening: 1½ teaspoons cornstarch
  mixed with 2 tablespoons water
2 green onions, cut into 1-inch pieces

Cut fillets into 2x3-inch pieces. Cut onions, set aside. Prepare cornstarch and water in one bowl; egg whites in another. Dip fish into egg whites then into cornstarch/water mixture. Heat oil in wok until warm and immerse fish in oil for 2 minutes. In a saucepan heat chicken stock, sherry, salt and sugar. Remove fish from oil and cook fish in sauce for 2 minutes. Add the thickening and 1 tablespoon hot oil from wok to cooking sauce. Add green onion. Heat thoroughly and serve immediately.

COD WITH OLIVES

Soak 1½ pounds fresh cod in cold water for ½ hour. Dry it, and place in an ovenproof dish with 2½ tablespoons melted butter. Sprinkle the fish with breadcrumbs, place over it 2 tomatoes, sliced; 4 tablespoons pitted green olives, finely chopped; 1 tablespoon capers; and salt and pepper to taste. Add ¼ cup oil, and bake in a moderate oven (350°) for about 30 minutes. This dish can also be cooked on top of stove.

TROUT MARQUERY

1 2½-pound trout
1 tablespoon oil
1 cup water
2 sticks oleo or butter
3 egg yolks

Juice of 1 lemon
Salt and pepper
12 shrimp
1 small can mushrooms, stems and
  pieces

Skin and fillet trout and place folded fillets in a pan with oil and water. Cook in 400° oven for 15 minutes. Make Hollandaise sauce by beating egg yolks and lemon juice in a double boiler. Put over hot water and gradually add melted butter, stirring constantly until thickened. Add seasonings, shrimp and mushrooms to sauce and pour over fish and serve. This serves 2.

    This recipe was brought back from New Orleans when Auburn played in the Sugar Bowl.

POLYNESIAN TUNA

1 (9 ounce) can pineapple tidbits
1 tablespoon butter or margarine
1 cup green pepper, cut in strips
1 chicken bouillon cube
¾ cup boiling water
2 tablespoons cornstarch

¼ cup cold water
2 tablespoons soy sauce
2 tablespoons cider vinegar
2 tablespoons sugar
¼ teaspoon pepper
1 (7 ounce) can solid pack tuna

Drain pineapple and reserve the syrup. Melt margarine or butter in saucepan over low heat; add pineapple and cook for about 3 minutes until lightly browned. Measure ½ cup of the pineapple juice and add to pineapple with the green pepper. Cover and simmer for 10 minutes. Dissolve bouillon cube in boiling water and add to pineapple mixture. Stir in cornstarch mixed with cold water until smooth. Add soy sauce, vinegar, sugar and pepper. Cook, stirring constantly, until thickened and clear. Drain tuna; break into chunks; fold gently into pineapple mixture. Heat and serve over crisp chow mein noodles. Serves 4.

Bonnie Henderson (Mrs. Jim)

COQUILLE ST. JACQUES

1 tablespoon chopped onion
1 tablespoon oleo
½ cup white wine
1 pound scallops

1 cup mornay sauce
Grated Parmesan cheese
Salt and pepper

Sauté onion in oleo. Add wine and scallops and cook 5 minutes. Remove scallops and cook liquid until reduced to 2 tablespoons. Add ¾ cup mornay sauce, parsley and scallops. Put into scallop shells or casserole, top with remaining sauce and sprinkle with cheese. Brown shells under broiler or heat casserole at 375° until bubbly.

Mornay Sauce:
2 tablespoons oleo
2 tablespoons flour
½ teaspoon dry mustard
Salt

Dash cayenne pepper
1 cup milk
½ teaspoon Worcestershire sauce
½ cup grated parmesan cheese

Blend first five ingredients. Slowly add milk, stirring to make white sauce. Add other ingredients.

SARAH'S DEVILED CRAB

1 pound crab meat
4 tablespoons butter or oleo
2 tablespoons flour
2 teaspoons lemon juice
1 teaspoon prepared mustard
½ teaspoon bottled horseradish

1 teaspoon salt
1 teacup milk
2 hard-cooked eggs, minced
½ cup bread crumbs
1 teaspoon pepper sauce or tabasco
1 small wine glass sherry

Make cream sauce of butter, flour and milk. Add wine, seasonings, crab and eggs. Put in casserole. Sprinkle with bread crumbs if you wish. I hardly ever do. Warm in 325° oven until bubbly—about 20 minutes. Serves 6-8.

Sarah McRory (Mrs. George)
Tallahassee, Florida

This is *the best* crab recipe!

OYSTER PIE

1 pint oysters
1 stick butter or margarine
1 cup rich milk (½ cup milk and ½ cup half and half)

2 eggs, beaten
20 to 25 saltine crackers

Melt butter. Crumble crackers in a bowl (medium size pieces). Add melted butter to crackers and stir to mix crackers and butter. Add eggs to milk. Grease pyrex dish 8x8 inches square or similar size glass dish. Spread almost half of crackers in bottom of glass dish. Add a layer of oysters to cover crackers. Add plenty of black pepper to this layer of crackers and oysters. Now add almost all of the crackers saving enough to cover the top of final oyster layer. Next add rest of oysters—more black pepper (no salt). Finally, crush remaining crackers until they are crumbs. Sprinkle on top of oysters. Now pour milk over oysters and crackers. Bake 45 minutes to 1 hour at 350°—make sure that you *do not overcook*—final product should look custard-like—it will also puff up and be brown on top when it is done. Crackers will absorb the milk.

Gwen Ferris Reid

This is a traditional Thanksgiving dish of Gwen's family.

OYSTERS EN BROCHETTE

2 sticks butter
4-5 tablespoons lemon juice
2 teaspoons tabasco

2 teaspoons salt
1½ tablespoons Worcestershire sauce

Melt butter and make sauce of the above ingredients.

8 dozen oysters
24 pieces bacon—cut in 1½-inch pieces
24 mushroom caps
½ cup parsley

24 cherry tomatoes
Salt and pepper
Flour

Cook bacon partially—skewer ingredients beginning and ending with bacon. Sprinkle with salt, pepper and flour. Shake off excess. Put skewers in shallow pan and brush sauce on both sides. Place on center rack of broiler and cook 5 minutes on each side, basting as turning. Serve on toasted French bread. Sprinkle with parsley.

HADDOCK-SHRIMP BAKE

2 pounds fresh or frozen haddock or sole fillets
1 can cream of shrimp soup
¼ cup butter or margarine, melted
½ teaspoon onion, grated
½ teaspoon Worcestershire sauce

¼ teaspoon garlic salt
1¾ cups rich round crackers, preferably oyster crackers
Parsley (garnish)
Lemon slices (garnish)

Place fresh or slightly thawed fillets in greased 13x9-inch baking dish; spread with soup. Bake in 375° oven 20 minutes. Combine butter and seasonings; mix with cracker crumbs. Sprinkle over fish. Bake 10 minutes longer. Before serving, garnish with parsley and lemon slices, if desired. Serves 6 to 8.

Hank Hartsfield

Fran Hartsfield says the Haddock-Shrimp Bake is delicious and is one of Hank's own creations. Even busy astronauts can find time to fix this one.

SEAFOOD CASSEROLE

1 pound shrimp, boiled, cleaned and deveined
1 6½-ounce can crabmeat (or equivalent fresh)
1 cup mayonnaise
1 cup soft bread crumbs
¾ cup milk

3 hard-cooked eggs, chopped
⅓ cup chopped onion
¼ cup sliced green olives
¾ teaspoon salt
Dash pepper
½ cup soft bread crumbs for topping

Mix all above ingredients just before baking. Top with ½ cup bread crumbs. Bake at 350° for 20 to 25 minutes.

Barbara Wilson (Mrs. Stan)

This dish is a favorite for our New Year's Day Football Buffet. The men and those women who wish may watch games to their heart's content, while those who prefer engage in conversation.

SEAFOOD CASSEROLE

3 cups seafood (I use shrimp and crabmeat)
3 cups cooked rice
1 cup chopped celery

1 cup chopped onions (I use scallions)
1 cup chopped bell pepper
1½ cups mayonnaise
3 tablespoons Worcestershire sauce

Sauté vegetables lightly, then mix with cooked rice, mayonnaise, and seafood. Top with bread crumbs—dot with butter. I increase rice for a luncheon. Serves 14.

Sara Russell (Mrs. Pete)

SEAFOOD NEWBURG

4 tablespoons butter

4 tablespoons flour

Make roux. Cook 2 minutes. Do not brown.
½ teaspoon salt
¼ teaspoon nutmeg

½ teaspoon paprika
1½ cups whipping cream

Blend into above mixture. Stir and bring to a boil. Reduce heat and simmer 5 minutes. Add a little to yolks (4 egg yolks, slightly beaten), return yolks to hot sauce. Blend in and cook over low heat 1 pound crab meat, or cooked shrimp, or combination, until mixture is thickened. Do *not* boil. Stir in ¼ cup sherry. Serve over wild rice.

Ursula Higgins
Greenhouse Restaurant

ROULADE DE SAUMON
(Salmon Roll)

Cooked fresh salmon (10 ounces), or
   Red Sockeye canned salmon
4 eggs, separated
2 tablespoons melted butter
3 tablespoons flour
Salt and pepper to taste

*2 teaspoons chopped chives
*1 teaspoon chopped fresh fennel
*½ teaspoon chopped fresh marjoram
2 tablespoons heavy cream
2 teaspoons white wine vinegar

Preheat oven to 350°. Grease a jelly roll pan and line the pan with lightly-greased wax paper. (Allow paper to stand up on edges.) Put salmon in food processor or blender and puree, then set aside. Beat egg yolks until they are pale and thick. Gradually mix in the melted butter, next stir in the flour, a little at a time. Mix until these ingredients are completely combined. Stir in salmon, herbs and seasonings and the vinegar and cream until mixture is smooth. Beat the egg whites until stiff. Carefully fold the egg whites into the salmon mixture. Pour this mixture into the pan and smooth the top. Put into the oven and bake for 15 minutes, or until mixture is just firm to the touch and a pale golden brown. Remove from the oven. Turn the mixture out onto a large piece of waxed paper, then remove the paper from cooked mixture. (I turn mine out on a damp dish cloth.) Roll up the mixture like a jelly roll. Transfer to a serving plate and serve with sour cream. Serve warm.

*If using dried spices, use ½ as much.

SHRIMP SAUCE FOR BAKED POTATOES

2 4½-ounce cans shrimp
2 tablespoons butter
2 egg yolks, beaten
½ cup whipping cream

½ teaspoon salt
½ cup sour cream
⅛ teaspoon ginger
2 teaspoons parsley

Drain shrimp and reserve liquid. Heat ¼ cup liquid with the butter. Add eggs and cream. Cook until thick. Remove from heat and add other ingredients. Cook 5 minutes. Add shrimp. It gets thin if overcooked or if you make too far ahead.

Bobbie Umbach (Mrs. Arnold)

Bobbie is a wonderful cook. She is the daughter-in-law of "Swede" Umbach, wrestling coach emeritus.

SUCCULENT SHRIMP

5 pounds raw, unshelled shrimp, headless (I use the #50-60 per pound size frozen shrimp, which I thaw in cold water.)
2 packages Good Seasons Italian Dressing Mix and ingredients needed to mix it (see back of package)

Juice of 2 lemons
1 stick butter, melted
1 ounce ground black pepper (Don't be afraid to use this much pepper.)

Place the washed shrimp in an ovenproof casserole. Make the Italian dressing and combine it with the lemon juice, butter, and pepper. Pour this mixture over the shrimp. Cover dish and cook for 50-60 minutes in 350° oven. Serve the shrimp with plenty of sauce and hunks of unbuttered hot French bread. Everyone shells their own shrimp and dips bread into the succulent sauce. Be sure to provide plenty of napkins. Serves 8. The fresher the shrimp and pepper, the better.

Margaret N. Wright (Mrs. Emil)

This was served at a wonderful, informal summer supper party.

SHRIMP CREOLE

3 tablespoons oil
2 large onions
1 tablespoon flour
4 pounds shrimp, peeled, washed and salted
2 green peppers, chopped
1 can tomato paste, 6-ounce size

1 can tomatoes, 1-pound size
1 cup each parsley and shallots, minced
3 cloves garlic, minced
1 bay leaf
¼ teaspoon cayenne pepper
2 cups water

Heat oil, add onions and cook on low flame until they are light brown. Stir flour in well and add shrimp and peppers, cook a few minutes, stirring all the time. Add tomato paste, tomatoes, and garlic, stirring them in to cook until tomatoes turn a deep red (about 10 minutes). Add water (enough to cover shrimp), parsley, shallots, bay leaf and cayenne. Salt and pepper. Cover and simmer about 30 minutes.

SHRIMP STROGANOFF

3 tablespoons butter
½ cup chopped onion
1 small clove garlic, minced
¼ cup flour
1 teaspoon salt
½ teaspoon dillweed

1 10½-ounce can beef broth
1 2-ounce can sliced mushrooms, with liquid
3 cups shrimp, cooked
1 cup yogurt, at room temperature

Melt butter in a large electric skillet. Add onion and garlic and cook until tender.

Stir in flour, salt and dillweed. Gradually stir in beef broth and mushrooms with liquid. Cook, stirring constantly, until thickened. Add shrimp and cook slowly until hot through. Just before serving, stir in yogurt and heat to serving temperature. Do not boil. Serve over hot rice. Makes an excellent buffet dish when served from a chafing dish. Shrimp mixture may be transferred to blazer pan just before adding yogurt.

Dean Hayes (Mrs. Kirby)

This recipe came to me via Mrs. Joe Thomas, Florence, AL; adapted from Southern Living *Fondue and Buffet Cookbook.*

SHRIMP CURRY

3 tablespoons butter
1 cup chopped onion
1 cup chopped celery
1 cup chopped green pepper
1 cup chopped apple
1 clove garlic, crushed
4 teaspoons (or more) curry powder
¼ cup all-purpose flour
¼ teaspoon ground ginger
¼ teaspoon ground cardamon
¼ teaspoon pepper

2 cans (10¾ size) condensed chicken
    broth, undiluted
2 tablespoons lime juice
2 teaspoons grated lime peel
2 pounds raw shrimp, shelled and
    deveined (18-20 per pound)
1 tablespoon salt
1 small onion, sliced
½ lemon, sliced
5 whole black peppers

In a large skillet, sauté onion, apple, garlic, celery, green pepper, and curry powder in hot butter about 5 minutes. Remove from heat and stir in flour, ginger, cardamon, and pepper. Gradually stir in broth, lime juice and peel. Bring mixture to a boil, stirring constantly. Reduce heat and simmer uncovered for 20 minutes, stirring occasionally.

Meanwhile, cook shrimp: Rinse shrimp under cold running water. In large saucepan combine 1 quart water, 1 tablespoon salt, onion, lemon and black peppers. Bring to a boil. Add shrimp and return to boil. Reduce heat and simmer uncovered 5 to 10 minutes until tender when tested with a fork. Drain shrimp and add to the curry sauce. Heat gently just to boiling.

Serve with rice and individual bowls of chutney, chopped tomato, chopped green pepper, chopped peanuts, chopped egg yolks, chopped egg whites, and coconut.

Serves 6-8.

Terry Steckler (Mrs. Joseph)

SHRIMP IN SOUR CREAM

1½ pounds shrimp
1 cup sour cream
¼ cup sherry
½ cup melted butter or oleo
6 scallions, chopped

Small bottle of mushrooms
2 tablespoons flour
1 teaspoon salt
Pepper to taste

Peel shrimp and sauté shrimp and scallions in butter until shrimp are pink. Add mushrooms and cook 5 minutes longer and blend in flour, salt and pepper. Add sour cream gradually and cook until thick, stirring constantly. Remove from heat and add sherry. Serve over rice. Should serve at least 8 people. Can also be served in patty shells.

Sara Russell (Mrs. W.M.)

LOBSTER AND SHRIMP

1½ green peppers, quartered
3 medium tomatoes
2 packages (6 ounces) wild and plain rice
½ pound fresh mushrooms, sliced
¼ pound butter, divided
¾ pound lobster, cooked and shelled

1 pound shrimp, cooked and cleaned
1 15½-ounce can pearl onions
¾ cup dry sherry
1 teaspoon lemon juice
Worcestershire sauce
Salt and white pepper to taste

Partially cook green pepper in boiling water. Remove and cut quarters in half. Reserve. Scald tomatoes in boiling water for 60 seconds, drain, remove skin, cut in half. Squeeze out, discard tomato juice and cut each half into 4 pieces. Reserve. Cook rice according to package instructions. Sauté mushrooms quickly in small piece of butter and reserve. Cut lobster in bite-size pieces. Melt remaining butter over medium heat and sauté lobster, shrimp and onions. Add sherry, lemon juice and seasonings. Add green pepper, tomato and mushrooms and cook over low heat, stirring until heated through. Arrange seafood and vegetables on heated serving dish with rice.

SHRIMP HARPIN

2½ pounds large raw shrimp, shelled, deveined
1 tablespoon fresh, or bottled lemon juice
3 tablespoons salad oil
¾ cup raw regular or processed rice, or 1 cup packaged precooked rice
2 tablespoons butter or margarine
¼ cup minced green pepper
¼ cup minced onion

1 teaspoon salt
⅛ teaspoon mace
Dash cayenne pepper
1 10½-ounce can condensed tomato soup, undiluted
1 cup whipping cream
½ cup sherry
¾ cup slivered blanched almonds

Early in the day:
Cook shrimp in boiling salted water for 5 minutes; drain. Place in 2-quart casserole; sprinkle with lemon juice and salad oil. Meanwhile, cook rice as label directs; drain. Refrigerate all.

About 1 hour and 10 minutes before serving:
Start heating oven to 350°. Set aside about 8 shrimp for garnish. Put butter in skillet, sauté green pepper and onion for 5 minutes. Add, with rice, salt, pepper, mace, cayenne pepper, soup, cream, sherry, and ½ cup almonds, to shrimp in casserole. Toss well. Bake, uncovered 35 minutes. Then top with 8 reserved

shrimp and ¼ cup almonds. Bake 20 minutes longer or till mixture is bubbly and shrimp are slightly browned. Makes 6 to 8 servings.

Shrimp Harpin, Buffet Style:

Make 3 times above recipe, using 5-quart casserole and topping with about 1 dozen shrimp and ¼ cup almonds. Bake as directed, increasing second baking to 35 minutes. (With 2½-quart casseroles, divide same mixture between them; top each with about 8 shrimp and ¼ cup almonds; bake as directed.) Makes 18 to 24 servings.

This is a favorite recipe for large buffet dinners. Serve with ham and biscuits, a green vegetable, and an avocado mold for easy serving and eating.

SCAMPI

About 24 raw jumbo shrimp in shells	2 teaspoons lemon juice
7 tablespoons butter or margarine	¼ teaspoon salt
1 teaspoon garlic, finely chopped	½ cup dry white wine
3 tablespoons parsley, chopped	½ teaspoon prepared mustard

This recipe requires the shrimp to remain in the shell from cleaning to serving. Split the shrimp down the back with a sharp knife only as far as the tails and remove the veins (when cooked they will fan out to butterfly shape). Shortly before serving time, melt fat in a skillet, then add all the other ingredients except shrimp; cook about 3 minutes. Stand shrimp in pan or heatproof baking dish and brush with sauce from skillet, reserving enough sauce to pour over shrimp when served. Broil shrimp about 5 minutes. Serve as an entree with rice and a green salad, pouring strained hot sauce over shrimp, or as an hors d'oeuvre. This amount will serve four persons. If you'd rather, scampi may be made with shelled whole shrimp using 2 pounds medium raw shrimp, same sauce ingredients as above. Shell and clean shrimp. Melt butter in heavy skillet, cook shrimp in this for about 5 minutes, then remove the shrimp to a hot dish. Add the rest of the ingredients to the juice in the skillet and cook 3 minutes. Again, serve shrimp with strained sauce over it as an entree with rice and a green salad or as an hors d'oeuvre. This quantity will be plenty for four or five people.

SHRIMP-CRABMEAT IN PATTY SHELLS

1 6-ounce package frozen crabmeat (or fresh)	1 #2 cans mushrooms, drained
	Tabasco to taste
2 pounds cooked shrimp	½ cup sherry, added just before serving
1 can undiluted mushroom soup	

MIx all ingredients and put in chafing dish or casserole and heat. Serve in patty shells. Scallops may also be added.

SHRIMP REMOULADE

Sauce:

2 cups catsup	3 cloves garlic
1 cup olive oil	1 green onion
3 ounces tomato paste	1 stem of parsley
1 cup mayonnaise	1 bell pepper, seeded
1 large dill pickle	

Put through food grinder or process coarsley. Then:

1 tablespoons Dijon mustard	4 green olives
1 egg white	1 teaspoon melted butter
1 tablespoon horseradish	Pinch of sugar
1 tablespoon A-1 Sauce	1 teaspoon salt
1 teaspoon Tabasco	½ teaspoon black pepper

Mix all together well. Mix with cooked, peeled and deveined shrimp. Keeps well. Serve on lettuce-lined plate with wedge of lemon.

The Greenhouse Restaurant
Opelika, AL

SHRIMP-NOODLE CASSEROLE

Shell and devein 3 pounds shrimp and cook in boiling salted water until just done. Cook 8 ounces green spinach noodles in boiling water for 10 minutes. Drain and mix with a little butter so it won't stick. Butter casserole dish and spread noodles evenly. Cover with cooked shrimp and over this spread a sauce made with 1 cup Hellman's mayonnaise, 1 8-ounce carton sour cream, 1 can cream of celery soup, 1 teaspoon prepared mustard and 6 tablespoons dry white wine mixed together. Bake in 350° oven till bubbly. Serves 10 to 12.

Betty Wittel (Mrs. Dave)

Betty served this at a Chi Omega house corporation luncheon.

SHRIMP AND GREEN NOODLE CASSEROLE

1 package green noodles	1 can cream of mushroom soup
1 bunch green onions, chopped fine	2 tablespoons prepared mustard
3 pounds shrimp, cooked and cleaned	2 eggs, beaten
1 cup mayonnaise	1 cup sharp cheese, grated
1 cup sour cream	½ cup melted butter

Cook noodles and drain. While still hot, toss with green onions. Place in a buttered casserole dish; top with the shrimp. Make the following sauce: combine mayonnaise, sour cream, soup, mustard and eggs. Cover the shrimp layer with this sauce. Then combine cheese and melted butter. Pour over the layer of sauce and bake at 350° for 30 minutes. Serve with a good salad and bread. Serves 8-10.

Rose Ann Denson (Mrs. John)

OYSTER AND WILD RICE CASSEROLE

4 cups uncooked wild rice (I use Uncle Ben's half and half cooked with half the seasoning)
Sauce:
1 box fresh mushrooms
1½ sticks butter
1 cup combined minced onion, celery, green pepper
6 tablespoons flour

1 or 2 pints oysters, drained
1 cup grated Parmesan cheese

1 pint heavy cream
2 cans mushroom soup
2 tablespoons curry
Salt and pepper to taste

Cook rice. Make sauce by washing, slicing and sautéeing mushrooms in 2 tablespoons butter. Drain. Add 2 more tablespoons butter and sauté other vegetables. Drain. In saucepan melt stick of butter. Blend in flour. Stir in soup, cream, curry, salt and pepper. Add sautéed vegetables. In 3-quart casserole, layer rice, half of sauce, and oysters. Repeat again and top with cheese. Bake ½ hour at 375°. Serves 12 generously. This recipe is another one that is excellent to serve at large buffet dinners.

SAVORY TUNA ROLL

Pastry:
1 cup all-purpose flour
½ teaspoon salt
⅓ cup shortening

½ cup shredded cheddar cheese
3 to 4 tablespoons cold milk

Sift flour with salt into mixing bowl. Cut in shortening and cheese until particles are size of small peas. Sprinkle milk over mixture while stirring with fork until dough holds together. Wrap in waxed paper; refrigerate while making the following filling:

1 tablespoon margarine
1 tablespoon chopped onion
1 tablespoon flour
¼ cup milk
¼ teaspoon salt
Dash powdered marjoram

Dash powdered thyme
Dash pepper
6½-ounce can tuna, drained
2 tablespoons minced parsley
1 egg, slightly beaten

Melt margarine in saucepan; sauté onion until tender. Blend in flour, add milk, salt, marjoram, thyme and pepper. Bring to a boil, stirring constantly. Remove from heat. Stir in tuna, parsley and egg. Set aside. Roll out pastry on floured surface to a 12x7-inch rectangle. Spread filling lengthwise down center. Moisten edges. Pinch edges of long sides together over filling; seal ends. Place seam side down on ungreased cookie sheet. Brush with milk. Prick to allow steam to escape. Bake at 400° for 35-45 minutes, until golden brown. Serves 6. A delicious, inexpensive luncheon dish.

Betty Horton (Mrs. George)

Betty served this at her sewing group luncheon.

TUNA AND NOODLES AU GRATIN

3 tablespoons butter	1 teaspoon salt
2 tablespoons flour	¼ teaspoon pepper
1½ cups milk	

Make white sauce of above and add ½ pound grated American cheese. Stir until cheese is melted. Add 1 4-ounce can sliced mushrooms, 2 cans tuna, 1 package fine noodles, boiled in salted water. In greased baking dish, place mushrooms, tuna and noodles in the dish in the order named with part of the cheese sauce over each layer. Garnish with button mushrooms. Cook in 350° oven for about 45 minutes.

HORSERADISH SAUCE FOR FISH

2 tablespoons butter, melted in saucepan

Add: 2½ tablespoons flour and cook until foams. Remove from heat and add: 1 cup scaled milk and 1 cup fish stock. Cook over moderate heat, stirring until thickened. Simmer 10 minutes more. Remove from heat. Stir in 3 tablespoons prepared horseradish, drained. Season to taste with salt and pepper. Serve with fish.

Martha Applebee (Mrs. Frank)

PAELLA
(a Spanish Potpourri)

3 tablespoons olive oil	½ teaspoon saffron threads
8 chicken thighs	1½ cups peeled, coarsely chopped
Salt	tomatoes
Pepper	3 cups uncondensed chicken broth
½ pound chorizo sausage or hot Italian sausage, sliced ¼-inch thick	½ cup dry white wine or vermouth
	1 pound shrimp, peeled and uncooked
1 cup chopped onion	1 package frozen peas, partially
1 clove garlic, minced	thawed
1¼ cup long grain white rice, uncooked	1 dozen clams in shells, well scrubbed or 1 24-ounce can clams in shells
	2 tablespoons sliced pimentos

In a large skillet, heat oil and brown chicken well on all sides over medium high heat. With a slotted spoon, transfer chicken to a 10x15-inch baking pan or 5-quart casserole and sprinkle lightly with salt and pepper. In same skillet slowly brown sliced sausage; add it to chicken. Pour off all but 2 tablespoons drippings from skillet; add onion, garlic and rice, and cook, stirring, until golden. Soak saffron in 1 tablespoon boiling water and stir into rice. Turn rice mixture into the baking pan and stir in tomatoes. Prepare ahead to here, if you like, and refrigerate, covered. Preheat oven to 350°. Add broth and wine to rice mixture and bring to a simmer on top of the stove. Cover pan and bake for about 20 minutes. Stir in shrimp and peas, cover and bake 20 minutes more until shrimp are done. (Meanwhile, if you're using fresh clams, steam them in ¼ cup water until shells open. Discard any that don't open.) Season paella with salt and pepper, if needed. Arrange clams and pimentos on top. Serves 6 to 8.

SAMFORD TOWER

DESSERTS

. . . music at the close,
As the last taste of sweets, is sweetest last,
Writ in remembrance more than things long past.
Richard II (II-i-12/14)

SAMFORD HALL

The building whose stately Victorian facade and clock tower form the central pictorial image of Auburn. Built in 1888; named for William James Samford, whose public service included terms in the state legislature, in Congress, and election as Alabama's 31st Governor (1900).

COOKIES

ALMOND CRISPIES

1 cup butter (no substitutes)
¾ cup confectioners sugar
1 teaspoon vanilla extract
½ teaspoon almond extract

2 cups all-purpose flour
¼ teaspoon salt
Granulated sugar

Cream butter and sugar in large mixing bowl until light and fluffy. Beat in extracts. Combine flour and salt. Add gradually to creamed mixture. Beat until well combined. Chill dough 45 to 60 minutes. Preheat oven to 350°F. Shape dough into 1-inch balls. Roll in granulated sugar and place about 2 inches apart on ungreased cookie sheets. Stamp with ceramic cookie stamp or glass dipped in granulated sugar, or flatten with tines of fork. Bake 12 to 15 minutes. Remove to wire racks to cool. Yields 3 dozen.
Excellent cookie for teas or parties, or for family.

Grace Jones (Mrs. Allen)

BANANA BAR COOKIES

1 cup sifted flour
¼ cup dry milk
1 cup sugar
1 egg
¼ teaspoon baking powder

½ teaspoon salt
⅓ cup soft shortening
½ cup nuts
½ cup bananas

Cream sugar and shortening. Add egg. Sift all dry ingredients together. Add ½ to cream mixture, add bananas and then rest of dry ingredients. Stir in nuts. Bake at 350° for 35 minutes in 9x9 inch baking pan.

Gaynell Parks (Mrs. Paul F.)

THE BEST BROWNIES
(Very Chewy)

2 eggs
1¼ cups sugar
½ teaspoon vanilla
¼ teaspoon baking powder
¾ cup parched pecans

2 squares chocolate
⅓ cup Wesson oil
½ teaspoon salt
½ cup flour

Combine beaten eggs, Wesson oil and sugar. Melt chocolate in double boiler. Combine with egg mixture. Stir in flour, baking powder, salt, vanilla and blend.

Stir in nuts. Pour into waxed paper lined square cake pan. Bake for 30 minutes at 350°. Cut into squares. Turn out onto cake rack and peel off waxed paper while brownies are still warm.

BROWNIES

1 stick margarine
1 cup sugar
2 eggs
3 or 4 tablespoons cocoa
1 teaspoon vanilla

½ cup sifted all-purpose flour
½ cup chopped nuts
½ teaspoon salt
½ teaspoon baking powder

Cream butter, sugar and vanilla, beat in eggs. Add chocolate (cocoa) and all other ingredients. Bake in greased pan at 325° for 25 minutes.

CHOCOLATE PEPPERMINT BROWNIES I

4 squares unsweetened chocolate
1 cup butter or margarine
4 eggs
2 cups sugar

½ teaspoon vanilla
1 cup all-purpose flour
2 pinches salt
1 cup salted nuts

Melt chocolate and butter; add eggs which have been beaten with sugar. Stir in remaining ingredients. Bake in a well-greased, long, shallow pan (12x18 cookie sheet with rim). Cool. Spread with frosting.

Frosting:
1 pound confectioners sugar
½ cup butter or margarine
4 tablespoons milk

2 teaspoons peppermint extract
A few drops of green food coloring
   makes it pretty

Mix frosting ingredients and beat until smooth. Spread on cold, uncut brownies. I then freeze brownies until frosting is quite firm. This prevents the glaze from mixing with the frosting.

Glaze:
4 squares unsweetened chocolate
4 tablespoons butter or margarine

⅔ cup confectioners sugar

Melt chocolate and butter; add sugar. Beat until smooth. Cool slightly and spread over frozen frosting. These are best served cold or frozen. Because these are very rich, I cut them in 1-inch squares while still frozen.

Dartie Flynt (Mrs. Wayne)

Each year the History Department holds an authors' reception honoring the history faculty and alumni who have published books. Dartie served these brownies at these receptions.

CHOCOLATE PEPPERMINT BROWNIES II

Brownies:
2 square unsweetened chocolate
½ cup butter
2 eggs
1 cup sugar

¼ teaspoon peppermint extract
½ cup flour
Pinch salt
½ cup chopped nuts

Frosting:
1 cup confectioners sugar
2 tablespoons butter
1 tablespoon evaporated milk

½ teaspoon peppermint extract
A drop or two of green food coloring

Glaze:
2 squares unsweetened chocolate

2 tablespoons butter

Melt chocolate and butter. Add eggs which have been beaten with sugar. Stir in remaining brownie ingredients and bake in a buttered 8 or 9-inch square cake pan at 350° for 15 minutes. They will not look done, but remove at this time. Cool. Mix frosting ingredients, spread on cookies and chill. Melt butter and chocolate for glaze. Spread over frosting. Store in the refrigerator in warm weather. This recipe doubles easily.

Wanda Dobie (Mrs. Jim)

BUTTER PECAN TURTLE SQUARES

Crust:
2 cups flour
1 cup brown sugar

½ cup real butter

Preheat oven to 350°. Mix crust and press firmly into 13x9 pan. Sprinkle 1 cup chopped pecans on it.

Carmel layer:
1 cup real butter

⅔ cup brown sugar

Combine, cook, stirring until surface boils no more than 1 minute. Pour it over pecans. Bake 18 to 22 minutes. The entire layer will be bubbly. Sprinkle 1 cup chocolate chips on top and swirl as it melts. Cool and cut.

Bobbie Umbach (Mrs. Arnold)

CHOCOLATE CARAMEL LAYER SQUARES

1 14-ounce bag Kraft caramels
⅔ cup evaporated milk, divided
1 18½-ounce package German chocolate
  cake mix

¾ cup butter, softened
1 cup chopped nuts
1 6-ounce package semi-sweet
  chocolate morsels

Combine caramels and ⅓ cup evaporated milk in double boiler, cook stirring constantly until caramels are melted. Remove from heat. Combine cake mix, remaining ⅓ cup milk, and butter, mixing with electric mixer until dough holds together. Stir in nuts. Press ½ cake mixture into greased 13x9x2 baking pan. Bake at 350° for 6 minutes. Sprinkle chocolate morsels over crust. Pour caramel mixture over chocolate morsels, spreading evenly. Crumble remaining cake mixture over caramel mixture. Return pan to oven and bake 15-18 minutes; cool. Chill 30 minutes and cut into small bars. Yield: about 5 dozen.

                                                                Elizabeth Glynn

CARAMEL SQUARES

1 stick oleo	1 pound brown sugar
2 eggs	2 cups flour
1 teaspoon baking powder	1 cup pecans
1 teaspoon vanilla	

Cream margarine, add sugar and eggs. Add dry ingredients, vanilla and nuts in order. Bake in greased 9x13 pan, 35 to 40 minutes. Start in oven 400 °F and reduce to 325°F after 15 minutes. Test with toothpick. Makes 2 dozen.

CHESS SQUARES

1 box Duncan Hines Yellow Deluxe II cake mix	1 stick margarine (melted)
1 egg	

Mix and press into 9x15 greased pan. (This is bottom layer)

Topping:
3 eggs	1 8 ounce cream cheese (softened)
1 box powdered sugar	

Mix together and pour on top. Bake 350° 35-45 minutes. Do not overbake! Cool and cut into squares.

                                                        Sarah Orgel (Mrs. Frank)

CATHEDRAL WINDOW COOKIES

12-ounce package chocolate chips	½ cup chopped pecans or walnuts
½ stick butter or margarine	10½ ounce package colored miniature
2 eggs, well beaten	marshmallows

Slowly melt together chocolate chips and butter. Remove from heat and add eggs. Mix thoroughly. Add nuts and cool. Add miniature marshmallows, stir well to coat. Sprinkle powdered sugar on 3 pieces of waxed paper. Spoon chocolate mixture onto powdered sugar and form into 3 rolls. Sprinkle more powdered sugar on top. Refrigerate until firm, several hours or overnight. Slice to serve.

CHURCH WINDOW COOKIES

Melt 1 stick margarine or butter with one 12-ounce package chocolate bits. Cool slightly.

Add:
10½-ounce package small colored   1 teaspoon vanilla
  marshmallows
1 cup nut meats, cut large

Mix all together. Divide mixture into thirds. Sprinkle flaked coconut on waxed paper, put mixture on top and make into a roll 1½ inches in diameter. Refrigerate overnight. Slice ¼ inch thick.

I prefer to make these without the coconut. They are pretty, but must be served soon after removing from refrigerator and slicing.

Helen Funderburk (Mrs. Hanly)

CHOCOLATE CHIP-OATMEAL COOKIES

2 sticks margarine   1 teaspoon soda
1 cup brown sugar   1½ cups flour
½ cup granulated sugar   2 cups oatmeal
1 teaspoon vanilla   1 (12-ounce) package chocolate chips
2 eggs   (Imitation chocolate works fine)
1 teaspoon salt

Blend margarine, sugars, and vanilla. Add eggs and beat well. Add soda, salt, flour and oatmeal and mix well. Fold in chocolate chips. Drop by ½ teaspoonful on greased baking sheets. Bake 10-12 minutes at 350°. Makes about 200 small cookies (about 1½ inches diameter).

Carolyn Lipscomb (Mrs. Lan)

CONGO BARS

1 box light brown sugar   2 teaspoons vanilla
4 eggs   2 cups pecans, broken
2½ cups self-rising flour

Beat eggs and sugar. Cook over hot water until sugar is melted. Remove from heat. Add nuts, flour, and vanilla. Beat until well mixed. Bake in greased pan for 35 to 45 minutes at 325°.

Ruth L. Brittin (Mrs. Norman)

DANISH APPLE BARS

2½ cups flour
1 teaspoon salt
1 cup shortening
1 egg yolk
Enough milk to make ⅔ cup egg yolk
5-10 apples
Crushed corn flakes
1 cup sugar

1 teaspoon cinnamon
Dash nutmeg
1 egg white
1 cup powdered sugar
1 tablespoon water
Vanilla

Mix first 5 ingredients as for pie crust. Roll ½ of dough to fit 10½x15½-inch cookie sheet. Sprinkle with 2 handfuls of crushed corn flakes. Peel and slice apples and place over dough. Sprinkle with sugar, cinnamon and nutmeg. Roll rest of dough and place on top. Pinch edges together. Beat egg whites stiff and brush over crust. Bake at 350°F for 45 minutes. While warm, frost with powdered sugar, water and vanilla. This freezes well.

DATE CRISPIES

1 7-ounce package pitted dates
1 cup sugar
1 stick margarine
3 tablespoons water

4 cups rice crispies
1 cup chopped pecans
1 teaspoon vanilla

Combine first 4 ingredients in heavy saucepan. Cook over low heat about 7 minutes or until dates look mushy. Remove from heat and add vanilla, rice crispies and nuts. Spread on greased cookie sheet. Cool. Shape in balls and roll in powdered sugar. Wonderful at morning coffees.

DATE REFRIGERATOR COOKIES

1 box light brown sugar
3 cups all-purpose flour
2 eggs
½ teaspoon soda
1 cup chopped dates (1 box)

1 teaspoon baking powder
1 stick butter or margarine
Pinch salt
1 cup chopped nuts

Cream butter and sugar. Add eggs, then dry ingredients. Roll in waxed paper and place in refrigerator over night. Slice and bake on greased cookie sheet in 350° oven about 10 minutes or until light brown.

These are delicious cookies. They are a favorite every time I serve them. I ate these as a child and still love them.

Grace Jones (Mrs. Allen)

AUNT GERTIE'S FRUIT CAKE COOKIES

1½ cups light brown sugar
4 eggs
3½ cups flour
1 teaspoon each cloves, cinnamon,
 nutmeg, allspice
3 teaspoons soda
3 tablespoons milk

1 stick oleo
¾ cup whiskey or wine
1½ pounds candied cherries
1½ pounds candied pineapple
1 package white raisins
1 package dark seedless raisins
6 cups chopped nuts

Use about ¾ cup flour to sprinkle over fruit and nuts. Mix batter as for any cake; cream sugar, oleo, eggs—adding flour and liquid alternately. Add fruit and mix well with hands. Put into petite four cases and cook at 325° for 10 to 12 minutes.
 Gaines Blackwell loves these cookies!

GINGERBREAD COOKIES

1 cup shortening
1 cup sugar
¾ cup buttermilk
1 cup honey
6 cups flour
2 teaspoons baking soda

2 teaspoons salt
1 teaspoon baking powder
3 teaspoons ginger
2 teaspoons cinnamon
1 teaspoon allspice

Mix all ingredients except flour. Mix well. Add flour a little bit at a time. Roll out on floured board. No need to chill. Cut with cookie cutters. Bake 8 to 10 minutes on greased cookie sheet at 350°. If you make this in food processor, do half a recipe at a time.

ICE BOX COOKIES

2 sticks oleo
2 cups brown sugar, well packed
1½ cups chopped pecans
3½ cups flour

½ teaspoon salt
1 teaspoon soda
3 eggs

Sift dry ingredients together and add nuts. Cream butter and sugar and add eggs, then flour and nuts. Mix well. Roll into long round rolls and wrap in waxed paper to stand overnight in the refrigerator or until ready to bake. This can be kept a week or longer. Slice thinly and bake on slightly greased pans until light brown. Bake at 375° about 6 minutes. Take up with spatula and cool on wire rack. These are delicious crispy butterscotch-flavored cookies.

LEMON SQUARES

1 cup flour
1 stick margarine
¼ cup sugar
2 eggs

2 tablespoons lemon juice
1 cup sugar
2 tablespoons flour
½ teaspoon baking powder

Mix flour, sugar and margarine; press firmly in greased 9x9-inch pan. Bake 15 minutes at 350°. Beat eggs with fork, mix in remaining ingredients and pour over first mixture. Bake 25 minutes at 350°. When cool, sprinkle with confectioners sugar.

OLD FASHIONED COOKIES

2 pounds butter (not oleo)   9 cups plain flour
1 box confectioners sugar   ¼ cup vanilla

Mix, roll out (about ¼-inch thick), cut with tea cake cutter and bake at 375° until *very light* brown (about 10 minutes). This recipe makes so many, I usually half it. They will freeze.

Josephine Teague (Mrs. Wayne)

ORANGE-COCONUT BALLS

1 6-ounce can frozen orange juice,   1 stick butter, softened
  thawed   1 box powdered sugar
1 12-ounce box vanilla wafers, finely 1 cup pecans, chopped
  crushed   1 3½-ounce can Angel Flake coconut

Mix the first 5 ingredients and roll into 1-inch balls and *then* roll in the coconut. *Do not mix the coconut!* Place in covered container and let set in refrigerator over night, before serving. If dough becomes too sticky to handle, chill for a few minutes. Yields 5 dozen.

A delicious cookie for any occasion. Nice gift. They also pack and transport well.

Hazel Cooper (Mrs. Ben F.)

PEANUT BUTTER COOKIES

2 cups sifted flour   ½ cup brown sugar, firmly packed
3 teaspoons baking powder   1½ cups granulated sugar
½ teaspoon salt   2 eggs, unbeaten
½ cup butter or other shortening   3 tablespoons milk
½ cup peanut butter

Sift flour and measure. Add baking powder and salt and sift again. Cream butter thoroughly. Add peanut butter and cream together until smooth. Add sugars gradually, creaming well. Add eggs, beating thoroughly. Add flour mixture, alternating with milk. Chill. Shape into tiny balls and mash criss-crossed with floured fork. Bake in 400° oven for 7-8 minutes. Makes 6 dozen.

POTATO CHIP COOKIES

1 pound butter
1 cup sugar
3 cups sifted flour

1½ cups crushed potato chips
2 teaspoons vanilla
Confectioners sugar

Mix together butter, sugar and flour until smooth. Add potato chips and vanilla. Drop by teaspoons on cookie sheet. Bake at 325° until light brown; about 20 minutes. Cool and sprinkle with sifted powdered sugar.

Rose Ann Denson (Mrs. John)

These are good to take to a tailgate picnic.

PRALINE STRIPS

24 graham crackers
1 cup butter

1 cup brown sugar
1 cup pecans, chopped

Put crackers in ungreased pan. In saucepan, blend together butter, sugar. Heat to boiling point. Reduce heat and simmer 2 minutes. Add pecans. Spread over crackers and bake at 400° for 5 minutes. Cut in strips while warm. Yields 3 dozen.

RICE KRISPIES MARSHMALLOW SQUARES

⅓ cup butter
½ pound marshmallows (about 2½ dozen)

½ teaspoon vanilla (if desired)
1 package Kellogg's Rice Krispies (5½ ounces)

Melt butter and marshmallows in double boiler. Add vanilla; beat thoroughly to blend. Put Rice Krispies in large buttered bowl and pour on marshmallow mixture, stirring briskly. Press into shallow buttered pan. Cut into squares when cool. Yields 16 2½-inch squares (10x10-inch pan).

Nut meats and coconut may be added. Two ounces of melted unsweetened chocolate or 4 ounces of melted semi-sweet chocolate may be added to the marshmallow mixture just before pouring over Rice Krispies.

SUGAR COOKIES I

2½ cups sifted flour
1 teaspoon baking soda
1 teaspoon cream of tartar
¼ teaspoon salt

1 cup butter or margarine
1 teaspoon vanilla
2 cups sugar
3 egg yolks

Sift first four ingredients together. Cream butter and vanilla until soft. Add sugar gradually until fluffy. Add egg yolks one at a time, beating well after each. Add dry ingredients and beat until blended. Form dough into balls and roll in sugar.

Dip bottom of glass in butter, then sugar, and flatten each ball. Bake at 350° for about ten minutes or until lightly browned. Makes about 3 dozen.

Jimmie Lyn Bounds

SUGAR COOKIES II

1 cup oleo
2 cups sugar
2 eggs
1 teaspoon vanilla
4 cups flour (about)

3 teaspoons baking powder
¼ teaspoon soda
1 teaspoon salt
2 teaspoons nutmeg
¼ cup buttermilk or soured milk

I always put my baking powder, soda, salt and nutmeg in about 1 or 2 cups flour, then add rest of flour. To sour sweet milk, put 2 or 3 teaspoons lemon juice in it and it will sour in a few minutes. The secret of these cookies is not to add too much extra flour. After cutting out shapes, put on tin and sprinkle a bit of sugar on each cookie. These cookies are crisp and delicious. It might take a short time to get on to rolling out. I use pastry cloth and cover for rolling pin. Bake at 375° for about 15 minutes.

Theo Mosley (Mrs. Kelly)

TOLL HOUSE COOKIES

2¼ cups *unsifted* flour
1 measuring teaspoon baking soda
1 measuring teaspoon salt
1 cup butter, softened
¾ cup sugar
¾ cup firmly packed brown sugar

1 measuring teaspoon vanilla extract
2 eggs
1 12-ounce package (2 cups) Nestle
   Semi-Sweet Real Chocolate Morsels
1 cup chopped nuts (optional)

Preheat oven to 375°. In small bowl, combine flour, baking soda and salt; set aside. In large bowl, combine butter, sugar, brown sugar and vanilla extract; beat until creamy. Beat in eggs. Gradually add flour mixture; mix well. Stir in Nestle Semi-Sweet Real Chocolate Morsels and nuts. Drop by rounded measuring teaspoonfuls onto ungreased cookie sheets. Bake at 375° 8-10 minutes. Makes 100 2-inch cookies.
Toll House Pan Cookie
Spread the Toll House Cookie dough into greased 15x10x1-inch baking pan. Bake at 375° for 20 minutes. Cool; cut into 35 2-inch squares.

DATE CRISPS

3 eggs, well beaten
1 cup sugar
1 cup flour, sifted with 1 teaspoon baking
   powder

1 teaspoon vanilla
1 cup chopped dates
1 cup chopped pecans

Mix in order ingredients are listed. Bake in broad shallow pan, well-greased, for about 30 minutes in 350° oven. Cut in squares while still warm.

Marietta Kettunen

MRS. STRAUSS—HER FAMILY'S RECIPE FOR TEA CAKES

4 hard boiled egg yolks (use yolks only)
2 sticks butter
1 lemon (rind and juice)
1 cup sugar
1½ raw eggs (use raw egg yolk in mixture and save raw whites for topping)

4 cups flour
1 tablespoon vanilla
Pecan halves

Cream butter and sugar, add grated yolks of hard-boiled eggs, and raw egg yolk. Add lemon juice, rind and vanilla. Add flour gradually. Roll thin—about ⅛-inch. Cut with cookie cutters and brush with slightly beaten egg white. Sprinkle lightly with sugar and center a pecan half on each cookie. Bake at 400° until brown at edges.

Alva Current-Garcia (Mrs. Gene)

This recipe has been used in our hometown well over a hundred years and has been printed in three separate cookbooks. In each of the separate cookbooks, the recipe is given by someone who had a connection with Lake Charles, Louisiana, where the recipe has been well known for all those years. It is worth giving here because these particular tea cakes remain fresh and crisp even in damp or muggy weather, (the use of the hard-boiled egg yolks makes this possible), and because they are very, very good!

EASY TEA CAKES

3 cups plain flour
2 teaspoons cream of tartar
1 teaspoon soda
½ teaspoon salt

1 cup sugar
1 cup shortening (Crisco is best)
2 eggs
1 teaspoon vanilla

Cut shortening into dry ingredients until the consistency of meal. Add well-beaten eggs and vanilla. Mix well. Roll into small balls and flatten with damp fingers. Bake at 400° until brown at edges, about 8 to 10 minutes.

These are delicious when iced with melted semi-sweet chocolate chips.

SAND TARTS

2 sticks oleo
4 tablespoons sugar
2 cups plain flour
2 teaspoons vanilla

2 cups finely chopped pecans (don't skimp)
Pinch of salt

Melt oleo and then mix in other ingredients. Roll into small oval shapes. Bake on ungreased cookie sheet at 350° for 15 minutes. Cool slightly and roll in powdered sugar. Makes about 6 dozen.

Carolyn Lipscomb (Mrs. Lan)

SCOTCHEROOS

1 cup peanut butter
1 cup Karo syrup (light)

1 cup sugar

Cook over medium heat until mixture bubbles. Stir constantly. Add 5 cups Rice Krispies and mix. Pat mixture into greased 9x13 pan. Melt together 1 package chocolate chips and 1 package butterscotch chips. Pour over Rice Krispie mixture.

Judy Godsil (Mrs. Ray)

SCOTCH SHORTBREAD
(from Nell Forrest, Carnwath, Aberdeen, Scotland)

1 cup sugar
1 pound butter (not oleo)

About 7 cups flour (depending upon how much the butter will take up)

Mix the above. Pat into pie plate or rectangular pan to depth of ¼ inch to ½ inch. Prick entire surface with fork. Bake 250° for one hour, until pale brown. If baked in pie pan, cut into wedges to serve. One-half the recipe fits into a 9x13-inch pan. If baked in rectangular pan, cut into small rectangular pieces. Very rich. I usually make ½ of the recipe:

½ cup sugar
½ pound butter, softened, but not oily

1 pound flour, approximately 4 cups

Measure 3½ cups flour into bowl. Cream sugar and butter, add flour. Use the 3½ cups first. Add the remainder of the flour, if the mixture will take it. This mixture can be patted into 2 pie plates or roll onto cookie sheet. Prick with fork. Bake at 250° for 1 hour.

Thelma Thomas (Mrs. Ben)

TOFFEE BARS

½ cup brown sugar
½ cup white sugar
1 cup shortening
2 teaspoons vanilla
½ teaspoon salt

2 eggs
1 cup sifted flour
1 cup rolled oats, quick-cooking
Nuts and coconut

In bowl, put all sugar, shortening, vanilla, salt and eggs and beat until well mixed. Add flour and rolled oats. Mix well, Pour into greased pan, 11x7x1½-inches, and bake at 350°F for 30 minutes. While hot, put your favorite chocolate frosting and nuts on bars. When cool, cut in squares or finger shapes.

IMPERIAL COOKIES

¼ cup confectioner's sugar
1 stick oleo
1¼ cups sifted all-purpose flour

½ teaspoon vanilla
½ cup chopped nuts

Mix oleo and sugar. Add flour and vanilla. Stir in nuts. Shape into small balls and flatten with a fork. Bake at 400° for 8 minutes. Coat with confectioner's sugar. Makes 3 dozen small cookies.

Angie Dollar (Mrs. Mason)

CAKES

I will make an end of my dinner;
There's pippins and cheese to come.

Merry Wives of Windsor (I-ii-11-12)

NANA'S APPLE CAKE

Cream 1 cup butter and 2 cups sugar. Add 3 eggs, one at a time. Add 1 teaspoon soda dissolved in ½ cup water, 1½ cups flour, sifted, 3 peeled and grated apples, 2 tablespoons cocoa, ¾ teaspoon salt, ½ teaspoon cinnamon, ½ teaspoon allspice, ½ teaspoon nutmeg and 2 cups chopped pecans, which have been mixed with 1 cup flour. Bake in greased and floured tube pan about 1¼ hours at 325°.

Carla Candler (Mrs. Bill)

FRESH APPLE CAKE

3 cups plain flour
2 cups sugar
1 teaspoon soda

1 teaspoon cinnamon
½ teaspoon salt

Make a nest in center of dry ingredients. Add 2 well-beaten eggs, 1 cup oil, 2 teaspoons vanilla, 1 cup nuts, 3 cups peeled, diced apples. Bake 1 hour, 15 minutes at 350° in ungreased tube pan. Before cake is done, mix and cook three minutes:

1 cup brown sugar
1 stick butter or margarine

¼ cup milk

Pour this over cake while cake is still hot. Let sit in pan at least 2 hours.

APPLE CAKE MORITZ

7 medium-size apples (about 2½
  pounds)
1 large orange
⅓ cup sugar
6 tablespoons butter or margarine

⅓ cup sugar
3 eggs, separated
1½ cups soft bread crumbs (3 slices)
¾ cup light cream

249

Wash, pare and core apples; slice into thin wedges. Grate 1 teaspoon orange rind; reserve. Squeeze ¼ cup orange juice. Combine apples, sugar and orange juice in a large saucepan; cook, stirring occasionally, until apples are tender, about 10 minutes. Turn into an 8-inch square shallow baking dish (2-quart size). Beat butter or margarine, sugar and orange rind in medium-size bowl with electric mixer until fluffy. Add egg yolks, one at a time, beating well after each addition. Continue beating about 1 minute longer until mixture is fluffy. Stir in bread crumbs. Beat egg whites until stiff peaks form; fold into yolk mixture. Spread over apples in baking pan to cover completely. Carefully pour cream over top. Do not mix in. Bake in moderate oven (350°) for 1 hour, or until top is golden brown and apples are bubbly. Serve warm with whipped cream, if you wish. Makes 8 servings.

Cream poured over dessert, seeps through the cake layer to meld with the apples during baking.

BLACK MAGIC CAKE

1¾ cups flour	1 teaspoon salt
2 eggs	1 cup strong black coffee
2 cups sugar	1 cup buttermilk
¾ cups cocoa	½ cup vegetable oil
2 teaspoons baking soda	1 teaspoon vanilla
1 teaspoon baking powder	

Preheat oven to 350°. Grease and flour bundt pan, combine dry ingredients, add eggs, coffee, milk, oil and vanilla. Beat at medium speed 2 minutes. Batter will be thin. Bake 30 to 40 minutes. Serve each slice with dollop of carmel fluff: in chilled bowl, beat 2 cups chilled whipping cream, ¾ cup brown sugar and 1 teaspoon vanilla until stiff. Can sprinkle with shaved chocolate for additional decoration.

Linda Voitle (Mrs. Bob)

BOTERKOEK
(Buttercake from the Netherlands)

2 cups flour	Dash salt
1 cup sugar	1 small egg, beaten
1 cup butter (do not use margarine)	

Mix all ingredients, using half the beaten egg. Press dough into a greased 8-inch pie pan. Spread remaining egg on top. Bake for 30 minutes at 350°. Cut into small wedges or squares.

Jean Bullock (Mrs. William)

BROWNIE-FUDGE CAKE

4 ounces bitter chocolate
½ pound butter
4 eggs
2 cups sugar

1 cup flour
1 teaspoon vanilla
1 cup chopped nuts

Melt chocolate and butter. Let cool. In large bowl beat eggs, add sugar and slowly add cooled chocolate mixture. Add flour, vanilla and fold in nuts. Pour in greased pan (8x12) and bake at 300° for 50 minutes. These are very good as brownies or you may add icing for a richer cake:

Icing:
1 can condensed milk
2 packages chocolate chips (semi-sweet)

1 tablespoon butter

Melt in top of double boiler until blended. Add butter and spread on top of cake.

Hattie Yeager (Mrs. Joseph)

CHEESE CAKE

1 pound cream cheese
½ pound cottage cheese (put through strainer)
8 ounces sour cream

1 cup sugar
3 eggs
1 teaspoon vanilla

Use graham cracker crust for bottom of spring form pan. Have ingredients at room temperature. Blend in blender. Then beat at high speed for 10 minutes. Pour over graham cracker crust. Bake at 450° for 10 minutes. Lower to 300° for about 50-60 minutes. Cool in oven with door ajar 3 inches for 1 hour.

We enjoy the cake topped with cherry pie filling.

Ethel Carrington (Mrs. Thomas)

BITE-SIZE-CHEESE CAKES

2-8 ounces Cream Cheese
3 egg yolks (keep whites)

¾ cup sugar

Mix, beat until fluffy. Beat egg whites and fold into mixture. Use mini-muffin tins. Butter generously. Put approximately ½ teaspoon graham cracker crumbs in each cup. Shake to lightly cover bottom and sides. Fill tins with cheese mixture. Bake 350° for 20 minutes. Cool five minutes. Top with blueberry or cherry pie filling.

Betsy Perry (Mrs. Kermit)

WONDERFUL CHEESE CAKE

3 pounds cream cheese at room
   temperature
¾ cup sugar
½ teaspoon salt
6 eggs

2 tablespoons lemon juice
1¼ teaspoons vanilla extract
Crushed graham cracker crumbs

Preheat oven to 400°. Put cream cheese, salt, and sugar into large bowl. Mix at medium speed. Add rest of ingredients and mix until smooth batter. Grease 10-inch pan with 3-inch sides. Dust with cracker crumbs and mash down to make a crust. Pour in mixture and bake 400° for 30-35 minutes. Let cool a few hours. Turn out on plate then turn right side up. Cut with a wet knife.

    This is a very large cheesecake and very rich. I often use it as the only dessert for a large buffet supper and have a bowl of hulled strawberries beside it. This was brought back from the Greenbriar Hotel where the Chi Omega's held their convention for many years.

FROZEN CHOCOLATE CHEESECAKE

Crust:
1½ cups chocolate wafer crumbs

⅓ cup melted oleo

Cake:
8 ounces cream cheese, softened
¼ cup sugar
1 teaspoon vanilla
1 6-ounce package chocolate chips,
   melted

2 egg yolks beaten
2 egg whites, beaten until stiff with ¼
   cup sugar
1 cup whipping cream, whipped
¾ cup chopped nuts

For crust, combine crumbs and butter; press into bottom of 9 or 10-inch spring form pan. For cake, combine cream cheese, sugar, vanilla and melted chocolate. Fold egg yolks, whites and whipping cream into chocolate mixture. Add nuts. Pour into crust and freeze. Remove from freezer a few minutes before serving.

                    Donna C. Burchfield (Mrs. Ron)

CHOCOLATE CAKE

Cream:
2 cups sugar
1 cup shortening or 2 sticks margarine

2 whole eggs

Sift:
2½ cups flour
2 teaspoons soda

½ cup cocoa
¼ teaspoon salt

Add alternately with:
1 cup buttermilk

1 teaspoon vanilla

Beat until smooth. Add ¾ to 1 cup boiling water and fold in. Bake at 300° for 1 hour.

Icing:
1 stick butter
6 tablespoons cocoa

6 tablespoons milk

Stir, cook one minute before adding 1 box of powered sugar, sifted. One teaspoon vanilla should be added after the powdered sugar. Beat.

Jennifer Baggett

CHOCOLATE SNACK CAKE

1⅔ cups all-purpose flour
1 cup brown sugar (packed)
¼ cup cocoa
1 teaspoon baking soda
½ teaspoon salt

1 cup water
⅓ cup vegetable oil
1 teaspoon vinegar
½ teaspoon vanilla

Heat oven to 350°. Mix flour, brown sugar, cocoa, baking soda and salt in with fork. Stir in water, oil, vinegar and vanilla completely. Bake in ungreased 8x8x2-inch pan until wooden pick inserted in center comes out clean, 35 to 40 minutes. Dust with powdered sugar if desired.
   Applesauce Snack Cake: Omit cocoa and vanilla. Stir 1½ teaspoons allspice into the flour mixture. Reduce water to ½ cup and stir in ½ cup applesauce.
   Chocolate Chip Snack Cake: Omit cocoa and vanilla. Stir ⅓ cup chopped walnuts into the flour mixture. Sprinkle ⅓ cup mini chocolate chips over batter in pan.
   Double Chocolate Snack Cake: Sprinkle ½ cup semisweet chocolate chips over batter in pan.
   Maple Nut Snack Cake: Omit cocoa and vanilla. Stir ½ cup chopped pecans into the flour mixture. Stir in ½ teaspoon maple extract with the water.

CHOCOLATE CAKE

Devils Food Cake Mix:

Make according to directions, but substitute buttermilk for liquid called for. Bake in 2 layers. When cool, split layers.

Icing:
12 ounces sour cream
12 ounces cool whip

1 cup granulated sugar (or slightly less)

Stir and frost between layers. Refrigerate.

Peggy Holloway (Mrs. Clarke)

This recipe came from a friend in Athens, Georgia when we stayed at their house during a football weekend. It's an easy cake to prepare ahead of time and take to a potluck dinner. I took it to a Sunday School party recently at the Merritt's cabin at Lake Martin.

CHOCOLATE CHIP CAKE

1 package yellow cake mix
1 package instant vanilla pudding mix
4 eggs
1 bar grated German Sweet Chocolate
   (save ½ cup grated chocolate for top)

1 cup cooking oil
1 cup milk
6-ounce package chocolate chips
1 tablespoon powdered sugar

Mix cake and pudding mix well. Add eggs, milk and oil. Beat 4 minutes. Add chips and fold in grated chocolate. Pour in greased and floured bundt pan. Bake at 350° for 45-60 minutes. Mix reserved grated chocolate with powdered sugar and sprinkle on cake while hot.

CHOCOLATE ICE-BOX CAKE

1 10¾-ounce pound cake
2 8-ounce packages German Sweet
   Chocolate
4 tablespoons sugar
4 tablespoons water

6 egg yolks, beaten light*
6 egg whites, beaten stiff*
1½ teaspoons vanilla
1 cup cream, whipped
½ cup nuts, chopped fine

Divide cake lengthwise into 3 equal pieces. Line loafbread pan with waxed paper. Place one piece of cake in bottom of pan. Melt chocolate in double boiler, add sugar, water and egg yolks. Cook until smooth, stirring constantly. Cool. Add vanilla and fold in beaten egg whites. Pour ⅓ of chocolate mixture over cake in pan; add second piece of cake and pour ⅓ of remaining chocolate mixture over second piece. Add third piece of cake and top that with remaining chocolate mixture. Chill in refrigerator for 12 hours or overnight, so chocolate will set. To serve: slice crosswise, add whipped cream for topping and sprinkle with nuts. Serves 8 to 10. This is a favorite recipe of my mother's.
*I have reduced 6 eggs to 4 successfully.

Martha Applebee (Mrs. Frank)

Former Art Head Frank Applebee acquired Auburn's valuable State Department Collection after WW II: paintings by Ben Shahn, Edward Hopper, Georgia O'Keefe, among others.

CHOCOLATE POUR CAKE

Mix in large bowl:
   2 cups flour
   2 cups sugar

½ teaspoon salt

Mix in small sauce pan:

1 cup water	½ cup Crisco or oil
3 tablespoons cocoa	1 stick butter

Bring to a boil and pour over first mixture. Add:

2 eggs	1 teaspoon soda
½ cup buttermilk	1 teaspoon vanilla

Mix well and pour on jelly roll pan. Bake 350° for 20 minutes.

Icing:

6 tablespoons milk	1 stick butter
3 tablespoons cocoa	Pinch salt

Start icing 5 minutes before cake is done. Bring to rapid boil and add 1 pound box powdered sugar and ½ cup nuts. Pour on cake as soon as it comes from oven.

Donna Beardsworth (Mrs. Jim)
"Big Orange" Fan

FRANCES WOODALL'S COCONUT CAKE

1 cup Crisco	2½ teaspoons baking powder
2 cups sugar	¾ teaspoon salt
4 eggs	1 cup milk
3 cups sifted cake flour	½ teaspoon almond extract

Cream Crisco and sugar. Add eggs one at a time, beating thoroughly after each addition. Sift together flour, baking powder, and salt. Add alternately with milk. Add almond extract and mix well. Bake at 350° in 3 9-inch round cake pans until done (about 20-25 minutes.) Frost with generous amounts of seven-minute frosting between layers and on sides and top of cake. Sprinkle sides and top with finely grated fresh coconut.

DATE CAKE

1 cup butter or margarine	2 cups boiling water
2 cups sugar	4 cups flour
3 eggs	2 teaspoons baking powder
1 package chopped dates	1 cup chopped nuts
2 teaspoons soda	

Sprinkle soda over dates. Cover with boiling water and stir until dark brown. Cream butter and sugar. Add eggs, beat. Add cooled date mixture. Add dry ingredients and nuts. Bake in a greased, floured tube pan at 325° for 40 minutes. Frost with butter-cream frosting and sprinkle with nuts.

FIG CAKE

2 cups plain flour
3 eggs
2 cups sugar
1 cup oil
1 cup buttermilk
1 teaspoon baking soda
1 cup chopped fresh or dried figs

1 teaspoon cinnamon
1 teaspoon cloves
1 teaspoon salt
1 teaspoon nutmeg
2 teaspoons vanilla
1 cup chopped pecans

Beat eggs. Add sugar to eggs and beat until fluffy. Add oil. Stir baking soda into buttermilk. Add flour and buttermilk alternately. Add all remaining ingredients. Pour into a greased tube pan and bake at 350° for one hour. (You may need to cook a little longer, 10 more minutes.)

Fig Cake Sauce:
1 cup sugar
½ cup buttermilk
2 teaspoons vanilla

1 tablespoon light corn syrup
1 stick margarine
½ teaspoon soda

Mix all ingredients in a pan and boil 3 minutes. Pour over fig cake while cake is still warm.

LIEPE'S FRUIT CAKE

1 pound butter
1 pound sugar
1 pound flour
1 pound nuts
1½ pounds raisins (white)

¼ pound citron
1 whole nutmeg, grated
½ cup whiskey
10 eggs

Cream butter and sugar. Add beaten egg yolks. Add whiskey and nutmeg. Add half the flour and mix other half with fruit. Fold in beaten egg whites and stir in nuts and fruit. Bake 2-3 hours at 275°-300°. Put in cold oven.
This is like a poundcake with fruit. It is delicious!

HONEY-GLAZED PECAN CAKE

1 tablespoon vinegar
About 1 cup milk
1 cup salad oil
1½ cups sugar
3 eggs
1 teaspoon vanilla
2 cups plain flour
1 tablespoon baking powder

½ teaspoon soda
1 teaspoon cinnamon
¼ teaspoon ground cloves
½ cup chopped pecans
¼ cup honey
1 tablespoon lemon juice
1 tablespoon water

Combine vinegar and enough milk to make 1 cup liquid (vinegar will sour milk).

Stir well and set aside. Combine oil, sugar, eggs and beat 1 minute at medium speed. Combine flour, baking powder, soda, cinnamon and cloves; add to creamed mixture alternately with sour milk, beat 1 minute. Stir in pecans. Pour into greased and floured 10-inch bundt pan. Bake at 350°F for 40 minutes. Let stand 10 minutes; remove from pan, and prick holes in cake. Combine honey, lemon juice and water and drizzle over cake.

DANISH PUDDING CAKE

Mix together just as you would any cake that requires the butter and sugar to be creamed, reserving a little of the flour to dredge the dates and nuts.

1 cup butter	3 cups flour
1¾ cups sugar	1 cup chopped nuts
Dash salt	1 cup chopped dates
Grated rind of 1 orange	1 teaspoon orange juice
3 whole eggs	
1½ teaspoons soda dissolved in 1 cup buttermilk	

Bake in a greased tube pan or loaf pan for 1 hour in a 350° oven. While cake is still warm from the oven, punch about 15 to 20 holes in top and pour over cake:

1 cup orange juice	Grated rind of orange
1 cup sugar	

Blend well, but do not cook. Let stand until cake absorbs juice before serving.

GINGERBREAD

1 cup molasses	2 eggs
1 cup sugar	½ teaspoon salt
½ cup Wesson oil	2 cups sifted flour
1½ teaspoons cloves	½ teaspoon ginger
1 teaspoon vanilla	½ teaspoon cinnamon
2 teaspoons soda	1 cup boiling water

Mix molasses, sugar and oil. Sift flour with spices. Add eggs and beat, then add flour mixture. Mix soda with boiling water and when dissolved, add to mixture immediately. Bake in 350° oven in 13x9x2-inch pan for 40 minutes. Serve with vanilla sauce: mix 2 eggs, 1 cup sugar, little cornstarch with 2 cups milk. Cook until thickened. Add 1 teaspoon vanilla flavoring.

This is an old recipe that is delicious and moist. The stronger, thicker the molasses, the better the gingerbread.

Grace Jones (Mrs. Allen)

LEMON CAKE

1 package Lemon Supreme (Duncan Hines) cake mix
1 package lemon jello
¾ cup cooking oil

¾ cup water
4 whole eggs
1 teaspoon lemon flavoring
Dash of salt

Mix cake mix and jello. Add oil and water. Beat eggs one at a time. Add lemon flavoring and salt. Cook in floured, greased tube pan. Preheat oven to 300°. Cook 1 hour. Take out of pan while hot. Pour juice of 2 lemons and ½ box confectioners sugar mixed over top of cake.

LEMONADE CAKE

1 box cake mix—yellow or white
4 eggs
½ cup cooking oil
1 box lemon jello—4 ounces

¾ cup hot water
1 can frozen lemonade—6 ounces
2 cups powdered sugar

Thaw lemonade and completely dissolve sugar in it. Set aside. Dissolve jello in hot water. Set aside to cool. Beat eggs and oil together; add cake mix and fold in jello. Pour into greased tube pan with waxed paper lining the bottom. Bake at 300° for about 1 hour and 10 minutes. Remove from oven and spoon lemonade and sugar mixture over cake immediately. Let cake cool before removing from pan. Let set in a cool place overnight before serving (not refrigerator).

Hazel Cooper (Mrs. Ben F.)

A family favorite, which my "chocoholics" request!

LIME CAKE

1⅓ cups sugar
⅔ teaspoon salt
1 teaspoon baking powder
½ teaspoon baking soda
2 cups all-purpose flour
1 3-ounce package lime-flavored gelatin
1⅓ cups cooking oil
¾ cups orange juice

1 teaspoon lemon extract
½ teaspoon vanilla extract
5 eggs
⅓ cup lime juice (fresh, preferably)
⅓ cup powdered sugar
Lime sherbet (garnish), or
Whipped cream and lime slices (garnish)

Preheat oven to 350°. Place sugar in mixing bowl and sift salt, baking powder, baking soda, and flour into sugar. Add gelatin. Slightly beat eggs and add. Mix. Add orange juice, oil, vanilla, and lemon extract. Beat mixture until well-blended. Pour batter into bundt pan, tube pan or 9x13x2-inch pan and bake 25 to 30 minutes until tests done. Remove cake from oven and let stand in pan about 15 minutes. Prick cake all over with fork and drizzle well with mixture of lime juice and powdered sugar. If bundt or tube pan is used, remove from pan before adding lime juice mixture. Serve in slices or squares from 9x13x2 pan. Top with lime sherbet or whipped cream and lime slices.

Jack Blackburn

LYNCHBURG MUFFIN CAKES

Cake batter:
1⅓ cups sugar
1½ cups flour
½ teaspoon salt
3 eggs

1½ teaspoons baking powder
½ cup water
1 teaspoon vanilla

Beat eggs with sugar until light and fluffy. Sift together flour, salt and baking powder. Add to egg and sugar mixture alternately with water and vanilla. Grease miniature muffin pans. Fill ¾ full. Bake at 350°. Remove from pan while hot and dip in glaze. Dry on rack over waxed paper.

Glaze:
Juice of 2 oranges
Juice of 2 lemons
Grated rind of 1 lemon and 1 orange

1¼ pound confectioners sugar
Pinch salt

Combine and stir to dissolve sugar.
This recipe won a prize in a cooking contest.

CREAM CHEESE POUND CAKE

1 stick butter
2 sticks margarine
1 8-ounce package cream cheese
6 eggs

3 cups sugar
3 cups sifted cake flour
1 teaspoon vanilla

Cream butter, margarine and cream cheese well. Gradually add remaining ingredients, mixed well. Pour in large greased tube pan and bake at 325° for 1 hour and 20 minutes. Touch cake to test doneness. Let cool 15 minutes, turn out. Bundt cake pan will not hold all of batter.
This is very good texture and tastes like cheese cake. Also good to serve pie filling fruits on it and whipped cream.

BOURBON PECAN POUND CAKE

3 cups pecans, finely chopped
1 cup bourbon
3½ cups all-purpose flour, sifted
1½ teaspoons baking powder
½ teaspoon salt
½ teaspoon nutmeg

½ teaspoon cinnamon
¼ teaspoon ground cloves
8 eggs
2 cups butter, softened
2 cups sugar
1 teaspoon vanilla

Coffee Glaze:

2 tablespoons milk	¼ teaspoon vanilla
1 teaspoon instant coffee	1¼ cups confectioners sugar
2 tablespoons butter	½ pint cream, whipped

Grease and flour 10-inch tube pan. In small bowl, combine 2 cups pecans and ½ cup bourbon; mix well; let soak. Sift together flour, baking powder, salt, spices. With electric mixer, beat eggs until thick and light; in another bowl, beat butter and sugar until light; beat in vanilla. Add eggs; beat until mixture is thick and fluffy. Beat in flour mixture until combined; stir in bourbon/pecan mixture. Pour batter into pan, with batter slightly higher at side and against tube. Place 12-inch square of brown paper over pan. Bake 70 minutes at 350°; remove paper after 30 minutes. Cool on cake rack for 15 minutes; remove from pan and cool completely on rack. Soak 18-inch square of cheesecloth in ½ cup bourbon; wrap cake in cloth and foil and store several days in airtight container. Before serving, glaze with coffee glaze. To make glaze, heat milk with coffee and butter, stirring until coffee dissolves. Remove from heat; stir into sugar and beat until smooth. Add vanilla; let cool for about 5 minutes. Cover top of cake completely and let glaze run over side. Sprinkle with 1 cup pecans; serve in thin slices with a teaspoon of whipped cream.

This recipe won a prize with the *Auburn Bulletin* contest.

Julie Donnan

GERMAN CHOCOLATE POUND CAKE

2 cups sugar	1 cup buttermilk
1 cup shortening	3 cups sifted all-purpose flour
4 eggs	½ teaspoon soda
2 teaspoons vanilla	1 teaspoon salt
2 teaspoons butter flavoring	1 package German's Sweet Chocolate

Cream sugar and shortening. Add eggs, flavors, and buttermilk. Sift flour, soda and salt. Add to creamed mixture. Mix well and add German's Chocolate that has been softened. Bake in 9-inch stem pan, greased and dusted with flour. When done, place cake under tight-fitting cake cover while still hot and leave covered until cold. May be iced or glazed with chocolate.

Jimmie Lyn Bounds

BANANA SPLIT CAKE

3 sticks butter or margarine, softened	1 9-ounce container frozen whipped topping, thawed
2 cups graham cracker crumbs	1 4-ounce bottle maraschino cherries, drained
2 cups powdered sugar	
2 eggs	Chopped nuts (optional)
4 to 6 bananas	
1 15¼-ounce can crushed pineapple, drained	

Melt 1 stick butter or margarine in a saucepan. Combine with cracker crumbs and press into 13x9x2 pan. Beat remaining butter with powdered sugar and eggs for 15 minutes. (Stop mixer off and on if it tends to overheat.) Pour mixture over cracker crumbs. Slice bananas over this. Top with pineapple and whipped topping. Dot with cherries and sprinkle with nuts. Refrigerate.

Fran Hartsfield (Mrs. Hank)

Do let it "age" for a day in the refrigerator; it's much better the second day.

PHILADELPHIA VELVET CAKE

Crust:
1½ cups crushed chocolate wafers   ⅓ cup melted butter

Mix and press into a 13x9x2-inch pan. Bake 10 minutes at 325°.

Filling:
4 eggs, separated
1 cup sugar
2 8-ounce cartons heavy cream for whipping
2 8-ounce packages cream cheese, softened

1 teaspoon vanilla
12 ounces semi-sweet chocolate morsels, melted

Beat egg whites until stiff with ½ cup sugar, adding gradually. Whip cream. Beat cream cheese, egg yolks, remaining sugar and vanilla until smooth and creamy. Fold in chocolate, then whipped cream and then egg whites. Spread over crumb crust. Freeze. If desired, sprinkle with finely chopped pecans or walnuts.

Fran Hartsfield (Mrs. Hank)

Fran prefers hers refrigerator cold, not frozen. She halves the recipe and uses an 8x8x2 pan.

BROWN SUGAR POUND CAKE

1 box light brown sugar
1 cup white sugar
½ pound butter or margarine
½ cup Crisco
5 eggs

3 cups plain flour
1 teaspoon baking powder
1 cup sweet milk
1 teaspoon vanilla
1 cup nuts

Bake 325° for 1½ hours in tube pan.

Bourbon Sauce:
1½ cups sugar
1 small can Pet milk

1 stick butter
1 beaten egg

Cream butter and sugar. Add milk, then egg. Cook in double boiler until thick.

Remove from heat and add 1 or 2 ounces of bourbon. Serve warm over cake. Will keep in refrigerator and can be warmed up.

Grace Kane

MARGIE'S MILLION-DOLLAR POUND CAKE

1 pound butter or oleo
3 cups sugar
4 cups flour
¾ cups milk
6 eggs

2 teaspoons vanilla, or 1 teaspoon vanilla and 1 teaspoon almond flavoring, or 1 teaspoon vanilla and 1 teaspoon lemon extract

Cream butter, add sugar and cream again. Add eggs one at a time. Beat after each. Sift flour three times; then measure. Add flour and milk alternately, beginning and ending with flour. Add vanilla. Bake 1 hour 40 minutes in large tube pan that has been greased and floured. Preheat oven to 325°.

Margie Kemp (Mrs. Ed)

OLD-FASHIONED POUND CAKE

2 sticks butter
1 stick Parkay oleo
1 package (8 ounces) cream cheese
3 cups sugar
6 eggs

3 cups Swansdown cake flour
1 teaspoon vanilla
½ teaspoon almond extract
2 tablespoons brandy or bourbon

Sift flour three times and set aside. Cream butter, oleo and cream cheese. Add sugar. Fold in eggs, flour and flavoring. Mix on low speed for about four minutes. Cook in a greased bundt cake pan at 325° for about an hour.

Jonnie Dee Little (Mrs. Ted)

SOUR CREAM POUND CAKE I

½ pound butter
3 cups sugar, sifted
5 eggs
3 cups sifted cake flour

1 cup sour cream
¼ teaspoon soda
Vanilla or other flavoring to taste

Blend butter and sugar. Add eggs one at a time, beating well after each addition. Sift flour three times. Add to egg mixture alternately with sour cream, mixing on medium speed with electric mixer. Add soda and flavoring. Pour into well-greased pan and bake at 325° for 1¼ hours. Yields 18 servings.

Gaynell Parks (Mrs. Paul)

Really delicious!

SOUR CREAM POUND CAKE II

2 sticks oleo
6 eggs
3 cups sugar
3 cups flour

¼ teaspoon soda
⅓ teaspoon mace
1 cup sour cream

Cream oleo and sugar (add sugar gradually). Add eggs, beating one minute after each egg. Sift flour, soda and mace together. Add flour mixture and sour cream alternately. Bake at 300° for 1½ to 2 hours in a greased and floured tube pan. May ice with mixture of 1 cup powdered sugar and 1 teaspoon lemon juice combined and spooned over cake.

Helene Alexander (Mrs. Milton)

(A superb pound cake!)

MISSISSIPPI MUD CAKE

2 cups sugar
1 cup shortening
4 eggs
1½ cups plain flour
⅓ cup cocoa

3 teaspoons vanilla
⅓ teaspoon salt
1 cup chopped pecans
1 small package small marshmallows

Cream sugar and shortening; add eggs and beat well. Sift flour and cocoa together and add to creamed mixture. Add vanilla and nuts. Pour into a greased and floured 9x13x2-inch pan. Bake for 35 minutes in 300° oven. Place marshmallows evenly over cake and return to oven for 5 minutes. Make frosting and spread evenly over melted marshmallows.

Frosting:
2 sticks butter or margarine
1 teaspoon vanilla
1 box sifted confectioners sugar

½ cup cocoa
½ cup evaporated milk
1 cup chopped pecans

Combine margarine and milk and place over low heat until margarine melts. Sift cocoa and sugar together and stir into warmed mixture and continue stirring until smooth. Add vanilla and nuts. Spread on cake.

ORANGE CREAM CAKE—LAYERED

1 can sweetened condensed milk
½ cup frozen orange juice, concentrate, thawed

1 cup whipping cream, whipped

Combine sweetened condensed milk and juice concentrate; mix well, fold in whipped cream. Split angel food cake crosswise into 3 layers. Spread one-third orange mixture on bottom layer, top with second cake; repeat layering, ending with orange mixture. Freeze 3 hours. Garnish as desired. Refrigerate leftovers. Makes 12-15 servings.

PINEAPPLE CAKE I

2 eggs
1 teaspoon vanilla
1 20-ounce can crushed pineapple, undrained
2 cups sugar

2 cups flour
2 teaspoons baking soda
½ teaspoon salt
½ cup chopped pecans

In a large bowl, beat eggs lightly. Add vanilla, pineapple and sugar and mix lightly by hand. Combine dry ingredients. Add dry ingredients and nuts. Mix by hand just until all ingredients are combined. Pour into oiled and floured 9x13 cake pan and bake in 350° oven 40-50 minutes, or until center springs back when touched. Cake will be tough if overbeaten. Cool and ice.

Cream Cheese Icing:
1 package (8 ounces) cream cheese
¼ pound softened butter

1 teaspoon vanilla
2 cups powdered sugar

Cream cheese and butter well. Add vanilla and sugar and beat well. Spread over cooled cake. This cake, iced or uniced, freezes very well.

Anna Louise McKown (Mrs. Delos)

(This is an easy and favorite recipe from my sister in Kansas City, Arkansas.)

PINEAPPLE CAKE II

1 box Duncan Hines Yellow Cake Mix
1 4-ounce package vanilla instant pudding
1 cup water (pineapple juice may be used)

1 large can crushed pineapple, drained
½ cup Crisco oil
4 eggs

Preheat oven to 350°. Generously grease and flour bundt pan. Blend all ingredients in a large bowl, beat at medium speed for 2 minutes, fold in pineapple (reserve 2-3 tablespoons). Bake at 350° for 45-55 minutes. Cake is done when toothpick inserted in center comes out clean. Cool in pan for 25 minutes.

Glaze:
1 cup powdered sugar
1 tablespoon pineapple juice

2-3 tablespoons pineapple

Blend and drizzle over cake.

Laucita D. Swinson (Mrs. Frank)

COCOA COLA CAKE

Cake:
2 cups unsifted flour
2 cups sugar
2 sticks oleo
2 tablespoons cocoa
1 cup cola
½ cup buttermilk

1 teaspoon soda
2 eggs
1 teaspoon vanilla
¼ teaspoon salt
1½ cups miniature marshmallows

Sift flour and sugar in bowl. Heat oleo, cocoa and coke to boiling point; pour over flour mixture. Add buttermilk, soda, eggs, vanilla, salt and marshmallows. Batter will be thin and marshmallows will float on top. Pour batter into oiled and floured 13x9x2 pan. Bake 350° 30-35 minutes. Ice cake while hot.

Icing:
½ cup butter
2 tablespoons cocoa
6 tablespoons cola

1 box confectioners sugar
1 cup chopped nuts (optional)
1 teaspoon vanilla

Combine first 3 ingredients; heat to boiling. Pour over sugar; add remaining ingredients. Spread on warm cake.

Patti Tremaine (Mrs. Chuck)

PISTACHIO POUND CAKE

1 box Duncan Hines Deluxe white cake
mix
1 box pistachio instant pudding mix
3 whole eggs

1 cup cooking oil
1 cup gingerale
½ cup black walnuts, cut fine

Blend dry pudding mix and dry cake mix. Add rest of ingredients except nuts and mix well, beating for 4 minutes. Pour into greased and floured tube pan and bake at 350°F for 50-60 minutes or until it tests done. Add walnuts to batter by hand just before putting into cake pan. Cake is light green.

Frosting:
1 large package Dream Whip
(2 envelopes)

1¼ cups cold milk

Beat until soft peaks form. Gradually add 1 box pistachio instant pudding mix and beat 2 minutes longer. Ice cake and keep refrigerated. Cake is good without frosting.

PLUM CAKE

2 cups sugar
¾ cup cooking oil
3 eggs
1 teaspoon nutmeg
1 teaspoon cinnamon

2 cups self-rising flour
2 small (or 1 large) jars baby food
plums
1 teaspoon vanilla
1 cup chopped nuts

Mix sugar and oil. Add eggs, one at a time and beat after each. Add plums. Mix. Add flour and spices. Add vanilla. Lastly, add nuts that have been dredged in flour. Bake in preheated oven 300° for 1¼ to 1½ hours. Use greased tube pan.

RUSSIAN TEA LOAF

1 angel food cake
1½ cups milk, warmed
5 egg yolks
1 cup sugar

1 tablespoon Knox gelatin soaked in
⅓ cup cold water
1 pint whipping cream
1 teaspoon vanilla

Soak gelatin. In double boiler make custard of eggs, sugar and milk. Add gelatin and put in refrigerator until it begins to congeal. Fold in 1 pint of cream, whipped, and 1 teaspoon vanilla. Cool again until sauce begins to congeal. Split cake through center. Put sauce ½ inch thick on bottom layer and fill tube pan hole. Put top layer on and ice top and sides with remaining custard. Refrigerate until congealed.

An old Tallahassee, Florida recipe.

SOUR CREAM CHEESE CAKE

3 cups sour cream
2 (8-ounce) packages Philadelphia cream
  cheese
1 cup sugar
3 eggs, well-beaten

¼ teaspoon salt
2 teaspoons vanilla extract
½ teaspoon almond extract
Graham cracker crust

Set out all ingredients so they are room temperature before starting. Combine sugar, cream cheese. Add eggs and salt and extracts. Blend in sour cream. Sprinkle graham cracker crumbs on top. Bake in spring form pan at 375° for 35 minutes. Chill (the longer the better).

Graham Cracker Crust:
1¾ cups graham crumbs
¼ cup nuts

½ teaspoon cinnamon
½ cup butter

Mix all ingredients. Reserve 3 tablespoons for topping.

RUM CAKE

½ cup chopped pecans
1 18½-ounce package yellow cake mix
1 3¾-ounce package vanilla instant
  pudding and pie filling mix
½ cup light rum

½ cup water
½ cup salad oil
4 eggs
Hot Rum Glaze

Grease and flour a 10-inch tube pan or bundt pan; sprinkle chopped pecans over bottom. Combine cake mix, pudding mix, rum, water, salad oil, and eggs; beat exactly 2 minutes at medium speed of an electric mixer. Pour batter into tube pan; bake at 325° for 50 to 60 minutes. Pour Hot Rum Glaze over hot cake. (The glaze will cause cake to settle.) Allow cake to cool in pan 30 minutes before turning out. Yield: 1 10-inch cake.

Hot Rum Glaze:
1 cup sugar
½ cup butter or margarine
¼ cup light rum
¼ cup water

SHERRY CAKE

4 eggs, separated
1 cup sugar
½ cup sherry
1½ envelopes plain gelatin

⅓ cup milk
1 pint heavy cream, whipped
1 angel food cake, crust cut off and
pulled into 1-inch pieces

Beat egg yolks with ½ cup sugar and sherry. Cook in double boiler until thickened. Soften gelatin in milk and dissolve in hot custard. Beat egg whites, fold in whipped cream and add ½ cup sugar. Fold in custard. Grease large tube pan with oil. Alternate layers of cake and custard ending with cake. Chill overnight. To serve, unmold and slice. Serves 12 or more. This can be frozen.
   Wonderful to make ahead for buffet dinners.

STRAWBERRY CAKE

Package white or yellow cake mix
2 tablespoons flour
¾ cup oil
4 eggs

½ cup water
1 3-ounce package strawberry jello
½ box frozen strawberries

Mix cake mix, jello and flour, eggs and water and beat 2 minutes. Add strawberries and juice to batter and beat one minute. Add oil and beat one minute. Bake in 350° oven 35-40 minutes in well-greased and floured cake pan or 45-50 minutes in well-greased bundt pan.

Icing:
½ cup oleo
1 box powdered sugar

½ box strawberries
½ teaspoon vanilla

Mix together.

Laucita D. Swinson (Mrs. Frank)

WHIPPING CREAM CAKE

2 sticks oleo
6 eggs
½ teaspoon salt
3 cups sugar

3 cups flour
1 8-ounce carton whipping cream
1 teaspoon vanilla

Cream butter and sugar. Add eggs and cream. Add dry ingredients. Pour in greased tube pan (grease bottom only). Start in cold oven and cook at 300° for 1½ hours.

WINE CAKE

1 box yellow cake mix
1 3-ounce package instant vanilla
　　pudding
4 eggs

¾ cup sherry
¾ cup oil
1 teaspoon nutmeg

Beat all ingredients together for 5 minutes. Pour into greased and floured bundt pan. Bake 45 minutes at 350°. Let stand 5 minutes in pan. Turn out on rack to cool.

ICING

CARAMEL FUDGE FROSTING

1 pound light brown sugar
2 cups water
4 tablespoons butter

Dash of salt
1 teaspoon vanilla

Bring brown sugar and water to a boil, boil until a small amount forms a soft ball when dropped into cold water. Remove from heat and add butter, salt and vanilla. Beat until mixture is thick enough to spread.

Elizabeth K. Allison (Mrs. Fred)

The Fred Allison Physics Laboratory reminds us of the late Dean Allison's place in Auburn's history; Mrs. Allison is one of the town's most beloved citizens.

CARAMEL ICING

Mix 3 cups sugar with ¾ cup milk and bring to boiling point. Brown ½ cup sugar in 2 tablespoons hot water and add to boiling syrup. Remove from stove and add 1 stick of butter, ½ teaspoon vanilla and ¼ teaspoon salt. Beat until creamy and ice cake. (Try 2 cups sugar and ½ cup milk if frosting a sheet cake.)

Helene Alexander (Mrs. Milton)

GOOD ANGEL FOOD ICING

1 egg white
1 cup sugar
1 tablespoon light corn syrup

¼ cup water
1 teaspoon vanilla

Beat egg white in small bowl of mixer at high speed for 2 minutes. Boil sugar, corn syrup, and water to hard ball stage, or until it forms a thread when poured from a spoon. Pour hot syrup slowly into beaten egg whites while beating at high speed. Continue to beat until mixture will hold peak when beater is raised. Add vanilla and mix. Spread on cake. Add cocoa or unsweetened chocolate for chocolate flavor.

DECORATOR ICING

1 box confectioners sugar
3 egg whites

½ teaspoon cream of tartar
1 teaspoon vanilla

Add unbeaten egg whites to sifted sugar and cream of tartar and vanilla. Beat until mixture holds its shape. Keep covered to prevent drying. Add food coloring and use to decorate cookies or cakes.

BUTTERCREAM DECORATING ICING

½ cup butter
½ cup solid vegetable shortening
1 teaspoon vanilla
⅛ teaspoon salt

1 pound (about 4 cups) confectioners sugar
3 tablespoons cool milk, or cream

Cream butter and shortening together with an electric mixer. Add vanilla and salt. Beat in sugar, 1 cup at a time, blending well after each addition. Scrape sides and bottom of bowl often with a spatula. Add milk and beat at high speed until light and fluffy. Keep icing covered with lid or damp cloth and store in refrigerator when not in use. Yield: 3 cups.

This icing is good to use with decorating bags and tubes, or just for frosting a cake. However, if a thinner consistency is desired when using only as a frosting, thin with 2 tablespoons of milk. This icing can be stored for a week in an air-tight container in the refrigerator, then whipped up again before using. It is a good idea to chill icing for ½ hour before using for decorating.

PIES

HERSHEY BAR PIE

6 small chocolate almond Hershey bars
16 large marshmallows
½ cup milk

1 cup whipping cream
1 prepared 9-inch pie shell

Melt chocolate bars, marshmallows and milk in top of double boiler. Cool thoroughly. Beat whipping cream until stiff. Fold into chocolate mixture. Pour into prepared crust. Refrigerate until serving time.

Hattie Yeager (Mrs. Joseph)

QUICK CHOCOLATE CREAM PIE

1 package (4 ounces) sweet chocolate
⅓ cup milk
2 tablespoons sugar
1 package (3 ounces) cream cheese,
  softened

3½ cups or 1 container (8 ounces)
  nondairy whipped topping, thawed
1 baked 8-inch graham cracker crust

Heat chocolate and 2 tablespoons milk in saucepan over low heat—or put in microwave on high power for 30 seconds in large glass bowls. (Chocolate just needs to melt.) Beat sugar into cream cheese; add remaining milk and chocolate mixture and beat until smooth. Fold chocolate mixture into whipped topping, blending until smooth. Spoon into crust. Freeze until firm (about 4 hours). Garnish with chocolate curls, if desired. Keep in freezer or refrigerator after initial freezing.

DIVINE CHOCOLATE PIE

Crust:
2 cups crushed vanilla wafers

⅓ cup butter

Filling:
1 large package Nestle's Semi-Sweet
  Chocolate Bits
1 whole egg
2 egg yolks

1 teaspoon rum
1 pint whipping cream
2 egg whites

Beat one egg and 2 yolks. Add to melted chocolate. Add rum. Whip ½ pint cream. Beat egg whites until stiff. Fold both into chocolate mixture. Pour and freeze for several hours. Top with ½ pint cream, whipped.

CHOCOLATE DELIGHT

Crust:
1 cup plain flour
2 tablespoons powdered sugar

1 stick melted oleo
½ cup chopped pecans

Mix crust ingredients together and press into a 13x9 pyrex dish and bake at 350° for 20 minutes. Let crust cool.

Filling:
1 8-ounce package cream cheese, softened
1 cup powdered sugar

1 cup cool whip

Mix the filling ingredients and spread over cooled crust.
Next, mix and spread over filling:

2½ cups cold milk

2 small (or 1 large) instant chocolate pudding

Garnish with whipped cream or cool whip and shaved chocolate or chopped pecans.

GERMAN CHOCOLATE PIE

1 4-ounce package German Sweet Chocolate
¼ cup butter
1 14½-ounce can evaporated milk
1¼ cups sugar
3 tablespoons cornstarch
⅛ teaspoon salt

2 eggs
1 teaspoon vanilla
1 unbaked 10-inch pie shell
1⅓ cups grated coconut
½ cup chopped pecans

Melt chocolate and butter in double boiler, stirring until blended. Remove from heat and blend in milk. Mix sugar, salt and cornstarch thoroughly. Beat in eggs and vanilla, then chocolate mixture. Mix nuts and coconut and sprinkle over filling. Bake at 375° about 45 minutes until top is puffed and browned.

GERMAN CHOCOLATE PIE

3 eggs
1 stick butter
½ bar German chocolate
1 cup sugar

½ cup plain flour
1 teaspoon vanilla
1 cup chopped nuts

Melt butter and chocolate. Cool. Beat eggs until thick and lemony. Add sugar and flour. Mix. Add vanilla, nuts and chocolate mixture. Mix well and pour into ungreased 9-inch glass pie pan. Bake at 325° for only 30 minutes. Inserted knife will be clean only around the edges (not in center). Serve warm with whipped cream. Serves 8.

Katherine Swanner Mussell (Mrs. Walter E., Jr.)

CHOCOLATE CHIP PIE I

1 package chocolate chips (regular size bag)
4 tablespoons milk
3 tablespoons sugar
4 egg yolks

1 teaspoon vanilla
4 egg whites
1 carton cream, whipped

Melt chocolate bits, milk and sugar in top of a double boiler. Add slightly beaten egg yolks and vanilla. Beat well. Cool. Beat egg whites until stiff and fold into chocolate mixture. Fill baked pie crust and chill several hours. Top with whipped cream and garnish with shaved chocolate curls.

CHOCOLATE CHIP PIE II

1 cup chocolate chips
1 cup English walnuts
2 eggs, beaten
1 cup sugar

1 stick butter, melted and cooled
½ cup flour
1 teaspoon vanilla
1 unbaked pie shell

Mix sugar and flour, add eggs and butter. Add walnuts, chocolate chips and vanilla. Pour into an unbaked pie shell and bake 30 minutes at 350°. Test with a toothpick. Should be chewey but not runny. Pecans can be substituted for the walnuts.

Jean Bullock (Mrs. William)

CRANBERRY CHEESE PIE

9-inch graham cracker crust:
1¼ cups graham cracker crumbs
3 tablespoons sugar

6 tablespoons butter

Combine crumbs and sugar in medium-sized bowl. Stir in melted butter until thoroughly blended. Press mixture firmly to sides and bottom of 9-inch pie dish. Bake in 350° oven for 8 minutes. Cool.

Filling:
12 ounces cream cheese
2 eggs
½ cup sugar

½ teaspoon vanilla
1 pint sour cream
Cranberry topping

Let cream cheese soften at room temperature. Beat until smooth. Add eggs and beat well. Gradually mix in sugar and vanilla. Beat until light and fluffy. Fold in sour cream. Pour into cooled graham cracker crust. Bake at 375° for 30 to 35 minutes or until center is firm. Cool. Just before serving, spoon cranberry topping over pie.

Cranberry topping:
1 tablespoon cornstarch   1 pound can whole cranberry sauce
3 tablespoons sugar
½ teaspoon grated orange rind or ½
    teaspoon vanilla

Stir cornstarch, sugar, grated orange rind or vanilla and whole cranberry sauce together in saucepan. Cook slowly, stirring constantly, until mixture thickens (about 5 minutes). Cool. Spoon over cheese pie just before serving.

This has long been a favorite company dessert and can be varied merely by changing the topping. (Substitute a can of crushed pineapple for the cranberry sauce.)

Martha W. Edwards (Mrs. Jim)

MILDRED'S PIE

Sprinkle one small package of chocolate chips in a pie crust. Melt 1 stick of oleo, add 1 cup sugar, 1 cup flour, 1 teaspoon vanilla and 2 eggs. Pour this mixture over chocolate chips and bake at 350° for 45 minutes.

Gaynelle Parks (Mrs. Paul F.)

DEEP DISH PEACH PIE

Pare and slice 6 or 8 ripe peaches in baking dish. Sprinkle 1 teaspoon almond extract over peaches. Add ¾ cup sugar mixed with 2 tablespoons Minute tapioca. Dot with 2 tablespoons butter. Cover with prepared crust. Cut slices in top of crust. Bake at 425° for about 25 minutes until crust is golden brown. (I usually use a bought, frozen deep-dish pastry shell. Just thaw until it will lie flat; cut in strips and put on top of cobbler.)

Crust:
Sift 1 cup flour, ½ teaspoon salt and 2 teaspoons sugar. Cut in ⅓ cup Crisco and mix with 3 tablespoons sweet milk. Roll out thin. Place on top of peach mixture. Other fruits may be substituted for the peaches. I've used, in addition to peaches, blueberries, blackberries, and blueberries and peaches mixed. Delicious and easy!

The ¾ cup sugar may be decreased according to taste, especially if using frozen peaches that already have some sugar added.

Nancy Gardner (Mrs. Dan)

FUDGE PIE

½ stick butter
1½ cups sugar
3 tablespoons cocoa

1 teaspoon vanilla
2 eggs
½ cup evaporated milk

Melt margarine in heavy sauce pan. Add sugar and cocoa. Stir well and add eggs. Stir mixture; do not beat. Add milk and vanilla. Pour into a 9-inch unbaked pie shell. Bake at 400° for 10 minutes. Then reduce to 350° and bake for 20 to 25 minutes or until crust is brown.

DOTTIE'S CHOCOLATE PIE

3 cups sugar
7 tablespoons cocoa
1 teaspoon salt

½ cup butter, melted
1 (13 ounces) can Pet milk
5 eggs

Sift together sugar and cocoa, add salt, melted butter and eggs. Add milk, mix well. Pour equally into 2 Johnson's Redicrust graham cracker shells. Bake 325° for 45 minutes to 1 hour until firm. Chill and serve with Cool Whip.

Jackie Norman (Mrs. Dan)

Jackie says this is the best she's ever eaten and that it makes 2 pies.

SWEETIE PIE

1 8-ounce package cream cheese
1 cup sugar
1 large package Dream Whip

3 or 4 ripe bananas, sliced
1 can peach pie filling
2 baked pie shells

Cream first 2 ingredients well. Mix Dream Whip by package directions and mix with creamed mixture. Line baked shells with bananas and pour peach filling over this. Pour cream cheese mixture over top of this. Chill for several hours before serving.

MANDARIN ANGEL PIE

3 egg whites
¼ teaspoon cream of tartar
1 cup sugar
1 3⅝ or 4-ounce package lemon
   pudding mix (not instant)
½ cup sugar

¼ cup water
3 egg yolks
1 11-ounce can mandarin orange
   sections
1 tablespoon lemon juice
½ cup whipping cream, whipped

Beat egg whites and cream of tartar to stiff peaks. Spread on bottom and sides of well-greased 9-inch pie plate. Bake at 275° for 1 hour. Turn off heat; let dry in oven (door closed) 2 hours. Combine pudding mix, the ½ cup sugar, and water;

blend in egg yolks. Drain orange sections, reserving syrup. Add lemon juice and enough water to syrup to make 1¾ cups; stir into pudding mixture. Cook and stir over medium heat till boiling. Cool completely. Fold in whipped cream and ¾ cup orange sections. Spoon into meringue shell. Chill several hours or overnight. Top with additional whipped cream and orange sections.

Jean Cox (Mrs. Grady)

This is Grady's favorite dessert!

HEAVENLY PIE

1 can sweetened condensed milk
¼ cup lemon juice
1 small can crushed pineapple, well drained
¾ cup chopped nuts

½ cup coconut
1 package Dream Whip
Graham cracker crust

Mix milk with lemon juice. Add pineapple, nuts and coconut. Prepare Dream Whip according to package directions. Fold into mixture. Pour into pie crust and chill for several hours before serving.

PEACH PIE

1 stick oleo
¾ cup sugar
4 fresh peaches, diced

2½ heaping tablespoons flour
3 egg yolks

Cream oleo and sugar; add other ingredients. Pour into unbaked pie shell. Bake in preheated oven 400° 10 minutes; reduce temperature to 350° and bake 20 to 30 minutes longer or till golden brown. Top with meringue or let it cool and use favorite cool whip topping. Ann serves this flavorful and easy to make dessert on most any occasion.

Ann Henry (Mrs. John F.)

PUMPKIN PIE (NO-BAKE)

1 envelope unflavored gelatin
½ teaspoon ground nutmeg and ground ginger
½ teaspoon salt
2 eggs, well beaten
1 16-ounce can pumpkin, or 2 cups fresh

1 teaspoon cinnamon
1 14-ounce can sweetened condensed milk (not evaporated)
1 graham cracker crust

In saucepan, combine gelatin and spices; stir in sweetened condensed milk and eggs. Mix well. Let stand one minute. Over low heat, cook and stir constantly until gelatin dissolves and mixture thickens—about 10 minutes. Remove from heat and stir in pumpkin—be sure to mix well. Pour into graham cracker pie crust. Garnish with whipped cream.

LIMELIGHT PIE

Sift together:
¾ cup sifted all-purpose flour   2 tablespoons sugar
¼ teaspoon salt

Cut in ¼ cup shortening. Drip ½ square melted chocolate over mixture, tossing lightly with fork (or 2 tablespoons cocoa). Sprinkle 1 to 2 tablespoons cold water, tossing lightly until dough holds together in ball. Roll into a 10-inch circle and fit into 8-inch pie pan. Fold edge to form standing rim. Flute. Prick crust with fork. Bake in hot oven (400°) for 10-12minutes.

Combine:
1 15-ounce can sweetened condensed   ¼ teaspoon salt
    milk
¼ cup lime juice

Stir until thickened. Blend in 1 cup crushed, drained pineapple and 2 or 3 drops green coloring. Mix well. Pour into cooled baked pie shell. Chill 2 or 3 hours. Top with whipped cream sprinkled with 1 tablespoon grated chocolate.

Emmalu Foy (Mrs. James S.)

(Mrs. Ina Crane, famous for excellence of her food service at University of Alabama, gave this recipe to Jim after he enjoyed it at a banquet there. Mrs. Inez Tucker, famous for excellence of her food service at Auburn University, served it at Jim's retirement banquet, along with her memorable Maryland Turkey!)

STRAWBERRY PIE

3 egg whites, beaten until stiff   1 teaspoon vanilla flavor
23 Ritz crackers, crushed   ½ cup chopped pecans
1 cup sugar

To beaten egg whites, add sugar, blending well. Fold in crackers, nuts and vanilla. In pie pan sprayed with Pam, spread mixture to make crust with sides. Bake 350° for 30 minutes. Cool thoroughly.

Filling:
Mix 1 carton, 8-ounces, Cool Whip and 1 package frozen, thawed strawberries. Add to cooled pie crust. Garnish with more strawberries if desired. Refrigerate at least 2 hours before serving. Serves 6-8.

Inez Saia (Mrs. Claude)

FRESH STRAWBERRY PIE

1½ cups sugar   1 3-ounce package strawberry gelatin
1½ cups water   1 quart fresh strawberries, mashed
2 tablespoons cornstarch   1 9-inch baked pie shell
¼ teaspoon salt   1 pint whipped cream

Combine sugar, water, cornstarch and salt and cook on low heat until thick and clear. Add gelatin and stir until well dissolved. Chill mixture until it begins to jell. Add berries and pour mixture into baked shell. Cover with Saran Wrap tightly and refrigerate. Top with whipped cream when ready to serve.

When using frozen sweetened berries, omit ½ cup water and 1 cup of the sugar.

STRAWBERRY PIE

1 cup sugar
3 tablespoons cornstarch

1 can 7-up
Red food coloring

Mix and cook until mixture thickens. Cool while baking crust. Add food coloring to make rich red. Pour in 1 quart fresh strawberries. Top with whipped cream.

STRAWBERRY REFRIGERATOR PIE

2 cups sliced strawberries
⅔ cup sugar
1 tablespoon lemon juice
⅛ teaspoon salt
2 teaspoons plain gelatin

½ cup water
1 cup heavy cream, whipped
1 teaspoon vanilla
1 baked pie shell

Combine strawberries, sugar, lemon juice, and salt. Soften gelatin in water 5 minutes, then dissolve over hot water. Fold gelatin, whipped cream and vanilla into strawberry mixture. Pour into pie shell and chill until firm.

KEY LIME CHIFFON PIE

1 baked pie crust
4 eggs
1 cup sugar
1 tablespoon gelatin soaked in ½ cup cold water

1 carton whipping cream
½ cup lime juice
1 lime rind grated fine
½ teaspoon salt

Beat egg yolks. Add ½ cup sugar, lime juice, and salt. Cook in double boiler until the mixture coats a spoon. Remove from heat and add gelatin and rind. Stir well until mixture begins to thicken. Beat egg whites with remaining ½ cup sugar. Fold into custard. Pour into pie crust and chill. Spread with whipped cream just before serving.

LEMON SPONGE PIE
From Mary H. Simister

1 cup sugar
1 tablespoon butter

1 heaping tablespoon flour
¼ teaspoon salt

Cream the above. Beat yolks of 2 eggs, add 1 cup milk. Add to sugar mixture plus juice and rind of 1 lemon. Beat 2 egg whites with dash of salt until stiff. Fold in whites. Bake 400° for 30 minutes or until knife in center comes out clean, as in a baked custard. If I have plenty of lemons and eggs, I use this recipe:

2 tablespoons butter	1 cup milk
1 cup sugar	1 teaspoon grated lemon rind
4 eggs, separated	⅓ cup lemon juice
2 tablespoons flour	¼ teaspoon salt

Mix as in other recipe. Bake 425° for 1 hour. Oven temperature depends on oven! Pie should be delicately brown on top and "set" as a custard.

Thelma Thomas (Mrs. Ben)

CHEESE CAKE PIE

1 cup graham cracker crumbs	⅓ cup sugar
¼ cup sugar	½ cup evaporated milk
¼ cup butter	1 teaspoon vanilla
1 8-ounce cream cheese	1 can crushed pineapple
2 eggs	

Mix crumbs, sugar and butter. Press in bottom and sides of pie dish. Cream the cream cheese until soft. Add eggs and sugar. Beat until smooth. Add milk and vanilla. Pour into crumb crust and bake at 300° for 45 minutes. When cool top with drained pineapple.

BEST EVER APPLE COBBLER

½ cup (1 stick) butter	½ cup shortening
2 cups sugar	⅓ cup milk
2 cups water	2 cups apples, finely chopped
1½ cups sifted Martha White self-rising flour	1 teaspoon cinnamon

Heat oven to 350°. Melt butter in a 13x9x2 baking pan. In a saucepan, heat sugar and water until sugar melts. Meanwhile, cut shortening into flour until particles are like fine crumbs. Add milk and stir with fork only until dough leaves the side of the bowl. Turn out on floured board, knead until smooth. Roll dough into a large rectangle about ¼-inch thick. Sprinkle cinnamon over apples, then sprinkle apples evenly over dough. Roll up dough like a jelly roll. Dampen the edge with a little water to seal. Slice dough into about ½-inch thick slices. Place in pan of melted butter. Pour sugar syrup carefully around rolls. (This looks like too much liquid, but the crust will absorb it.) Bake 55-60 minutes.

Variation: This cobbler may be made with other fresh, frozen or canned fruits, such as blackberries, blueberries, cherries or peaches. If packed in liquid, drain and substitute for part of the sugar syrup. *Always* use 2 cups of liquid.

An all time favorite, this swirled cobbler is moist and juicy yet flaky on top.

Patti Tremaine (Mrs. Chuck)

FINGER LICKING SWEET POTATO PIE

1½ to 1¾ cups mashed cooked sweet
  potatoes
2 cups sugar
3 eggs

1 stick butter, melted
1 small can evaporated milk
1 teaspoon vanilla
2 pie shells (not deep dish)

Blend potatoes and sugar with mixer; add eggs, 1 at a time. Beat after each egg. Add butter, milk and vanilla. Pour in pie shells. Bake at 350° for 40-45 minutes.

Patti Tremaine (Mrs. Chuck)

RALEIGH HOUSE BUTTERMILK PIE

1 stick butter
2 cups sugar
3 eggs
2 rounded tablespoons flour

1 cup buttermilk
Dash nutmeg
1 teaspoon vanilla
1 unbaked 9-inch pie shell

Have butter at room temperature and cream with sugar. Add eggs and flour. Mix well. Stir in buttermilk, nutmeg and vanilla. Pour into pie shell and bake at 350° for 35 minutes. Reduce heat to 300° and bake for 25 minutes. Freezes well.

MAKES-ITS-OWN-CRUST EGG CUSTARD

3 eggs
1 can (13 ounces) evaporated milk
1 cup sugar

3 tablespoons all-purpose flour
3 tablespoons melted margarine
Nutmeg to taste

Grease and flour a 9-inch glass pie plate. Be sure all areas are well covered. Combine all ingredients in a blender container; blend 30 seconds. Pour into pie plate and bake at 350° for 40 to 45 minutes or until knife inserted in center comes out clean. Pie will rise but will settle as it cools and form a light crust.

QUICK CUSTARD PIE

4 slightly beaten eggs
½ cup sugar
¼ teaspoon salt

1 teaspoon vanilla
2½ cups milk, scalded
1 9-inch unbaked pastry shell

Thoroughly mix eggs, sugar, salt, and vanilla. Slowly stir in hot milk. At once pour into unbaked shell. Dash top with nutmeg. Bake in very hot oven (475°) for 5 minutes. Reduce temperature to 425° and bake 10 minutes or until knife inserted comes out clean. Cool on rack.

CHESS PIE I

1½ cups sugar
4 eggs
1 tablespoon cornmeal

1 teaspoon vanilla
Pinch of salt
1 stick melted oleo

Mix all ingredients together and pour into pie shell. Bake 35 minutes in 350° oven.

CHESS PIE II

1 stick butter
1½ cups sugar
2 tablespoons flour

3 tablespoons buttermilk
3 eggs, beaten
1 teaspoon vanilla

To melted margarine, add sugar, flour and buttermilk. Mix well. Add eggs and vanilla, mix well. Pour into unbaked pie shell. Bake at 300° until set and golden brown, about 1 hour. Pie will look like coconut on top.

LAVINIA TAYLOR'S BLACKBOTTOM PIE

3 eggs, separated
1½ cups milk
1½ cups sugar
1 tablespoon cornstarch
1 tablespoon gelatin

1½ squares bitter chocolate
Dash of nutmeg; vanilla
1 cup heavy cream, whipped
Grated bitter chocolate
Pie crust of ginger snaps

Cook egg yolks, milk, sugar and cornstarch until mixture coats a spoon. Add gelatin dissolved in 3 tablespoons water. Take out one-third of custard and mix with melted chocolate. Flavor with vanilla and spread on pie pan that has been lined with rolled ginger snaps and butter. Cool remaining mixture; fold in whipped whites and nutmeg. Pour over chocolate layer. Cool and top with whipped cream and grated bitter chocolate. Keep in refrigerator until ready to serve.

Emmalu Foy (Mrs. James E.)

Lavinia (Jim's sister) and Mother Foy were both superb cooks. This is a blackbottom pie given me years ago by Lavinia.

FRENCH SILK

Meringue:
    Beat 2 egg whites, ⅛ teaspoon salt, ⅛ teaspoon cream of tartar. Add ½ cup sugar gradually. Beat very stiff. Add ½ cup of nuts and ½ teaspoon vanilla. Grease pie pan with butter. Cook 300° for 55 minutes.

Filling:

1 square unsweetened chocolate
1 stick butter
⅔ cup sugar

2 eggs
1 teaspoon vanilla

Melt chocolate. Let cool. Cream butter; add sugar gradually. Add eggs one at a time, beating 5 minutes each. Add chocolate and vanilla. Top with whipped cream.

David E. Johnson

MINI PECAN PIES

1 3-ounce package cream cheese
½ cup margarine or butter, softened
1 cup all-purpose flour
1 beaten egg
¾ cup packed brown sugar

1 tablespoon butter or margarine, softened
1½ teaspoons vanilla
Dash salt
¾ cup broken pecans

Blend cheese and ½ cup butter. Stir in flour. Chill 1 hour. Shape dough into 24 1-inch balls. Place in ungreased 1¾-inch muffin pans—press dough over bottom and up sides of pans. In small bowl, beat together egg, brown sugar, the 1 tablespoon butter, vanilla and salt just until smooth. Divide pecans among pastry shells. Spoon ½ tablespoon egg mixture over pecans in pastry. Bake 325° for 25-30 minutes. Cool. Makes 2 dozen.

Merrilyn Henry (Mrs. Robert)

FROSTY ORANGE PIE

1 cup uncooked oats (quick or old-fashioned)
¾ cup flaked coconut, divided
⅓ cup firmly packed brown sugar

⅓ cup melted margarine
1 quart vanilla ice cream, softened
¼ cup frozen orange juice concentrate, thawed

Place oats in a shallow baking pan and toast at 350° about 10 minutes. Combine toasted oats, ½ cup coconut, brown sugar, and margarine; mix until crumbly. Press firmly onto bottom and sides of a 9-inch pie plate. Chill. Spread half of ice cream in pie shell. Drizzle with 2 tablespoons orange juice concentrate. Repeat layers. Toast remaining coconut, sprinkle on pie. Freeze.

Betty Horton (Mrs. George)

KENTUCKY DERBY PIE

1 9-inch unbaked pie shell
¼ cup melted oleo
1 cup sugar
1 cup light corn syrup

4 eggs, beaten
2 tablespoons bourbon
½ cup chocolate morsels
1 cup chopped pecans

Combine eggs, sugar and syrup. Pour in melted oleo. Add bourbon, chocolate chips and pecans. Pour into pie shell and bake 325° for 60 minutes or until firm. Serve warm with whipped cream.

A favorite for dessert bridge, especially if men are present.

Johnnie McGraw (Mrs. Leon)

JAPANESE FRUIT PIE

1½ sticks butter melted (use pure butter)   3 eggs, beaten
1½ cups sugar   1½ tablespoons vinegar

Mix first 4 items together. Add:

¾ cup pecans, chopped   ¾ cup raisins
¾ cup coconut

Mix well. Pour into unbaked pie shell. Bake at 300° to 325° about 50 minutes, or until brown.

Helen Funderburk (Mrs. Hanly)

TARTS

CHERRY TARTLETS

1 8-ounce package cream cheese
1 egg
½ cup sugar

1 teaspoon vanilla
vanilla wafers
cherry pie filling

Beat cream cheese until fluffy. Add egg, sugar and vanilla. In bottom of small cupcake liner put one vanilla wafer. Top with a spoonful of cream cheese mixture. Repeat until all the mixture is used. Bake at 325° for 14 minutes or until very light. Do not bake too long. Spoon on prepared cherry pie filling and chill.

Betsy Judkins (Mrs. Joe)

GLAZED STRAWBERRY TARTS

1 pint strawberries
1 cup red currant jelly

2 tablespoons sugar

Combine sugar and jelly in saucepan; boil until thickened. Fill cooled miniature pastry shells with fresh cleaned strawberries and pour cooked glaze over them.

REESE CUP COOKIE TARTS

1 roll refrigerated sugar or peanut butter
   cookies

1 box bite-sized Reese's peanut butter
   cups

Preheat oven according to cookie package directions. Slice roll into 9 sections and quarter each section. Grease miniature muffin tin and press section of dough as for tart shell into each muffin cup. Cook according to directions until slightly brown. Remove from oven and immediately push one small Reese cup into center of hot cookie. Cool thoroughly before removing from tin. These are an excellent finger dessert and freeze well. It makes 36 tarts.

MARGIE AND BETH'S PECAN TARTS

1 cup flour
1 3-ounce package cream cheese

1 stick oleo

Mix cheese and butter. Add flour and chill one hour. Make into 24 balls and pat out in small muffin pans.

Filling:
¾ cup brown sugar
1 teaspoon vanilla
¾ cup broken pecans

1 large egg
¼ teaspoon salt

Bake at 350° for 30 minutes. Let cool in pan.

Helene Alexander (Mrs. Milton)

LEMON CURD TART FILLING

2 cups sugar
½ cup fresh lemon juice

2 sticks oleo
4 eggs, well beaten

Combine sugar and lemon juice in the top of a double boiler. Add oleo. Heat over gently boiling water, stirring until oleo melts. Stir in eggs as quickly as possible. Continue stirring constantly until mixture thickens enough to pile slightly, about 15 minutes. This recipe will fill at least 5 dozen small (1½ to 2-inches) tart shells. Keep refrigerated.

Frances Woodall (Mrs. Jim)

These are the best lemon tarts I've ever tasted!

KIWI SOUR CREAM TART

Crust:
1 stick butter, softened
⅓ cup ground almonds

¼ cup sugar
1 cup unsifted all-purpose flour

Prepare crust by mixing butter, sugar and almonds until creamy. Add flour just to blend. Press mixture into bottom and up sides of a 9-inch tart pan; chill. Bake in 325° preheated oven about 20 minutes or until golden; cool.

Filling:
3 eggs beaten
¾ cup sugar
¼ cup butter or margarine
⅓ cup lemon juice

1 cup (maybe a little more) sour cream
3 to 4 kiwi (fruit), peeled and sliced
Melted apple jelly as needed

In saucepan mix eggs, butter, sugar and lemon juice. Cook and stir over medium heat until mixture thickens, about 5 minutes. Pour into baked crust. Spread (after cooling lemon mixture) a layer of sour cream over lemon mixture and arrange sliced kiwi over the top of sour cream. Brush with melted apple jelly to glaze. Refrigerate until ready to serve.

RAISIN TART

Pie Shell:
2 cups flour
⅔ cup shortening

1 teaspoon salt
6 tablespoon water

Mold into oiled muffin pan.

Filling:

1 stick margarine	1 cup raisins
1 cup sugar	1 teaspoon vanilla or lemon extract
2 eggs	Pinch of salt

Bake for 30 minutes as 325°.

Sheba Hiers (Mrs. Charles)

Sheba served this at an elegant dinner for members of the Art Department and other friends. This is so good!

People look forward to being entertained by the Hiers. Not only is the food always delicious, but the creative presentation is a visual delight!

DESSERTS

BISCUIT TORTINI

3 eggs
¾ cup sugar
Dash salt
¼ cup whole blanched almonds

Almond extract
1½ cups heavy cream
¾ teaspoon vanilla extract
12 maraschino or candied cherries

Separate eggs. Turn each white into a small bowl of electric mixer as it is separated. Refrigerate yolks. Let whites warm to room temperature—1 hour. Mix ¼ cup water with the sugar in 1-quart saucepan; stir over low heat to dissolve. Boil, uncovered, without stirring, to 236°F on candy thermometer. (Syrup spins 2-inch thread when dropped from spoon.) Beat egg whites with salt just until stiff peaks form when beater is slowly raised. Pour hot syrup in thin stream over whites; beat constantly until very stiff peaks form when beater is raised. Refrigerate, covered, 30 minutes. Preheat oven to 350°F. Place almonds in shallow baking pan; bake just until lightly toasted—8-10 minutes. Chop almonds finely. Turn into small bowl. Stir in 1½ teaspoons almond extract. Set aside. In medium bowl, beat cream with ¼ teaspoon almond extract and the vanilla extract until quite stiff. With a rubber scraper, gently fold into egg white mixture until well combined. Spoon into 12 paper-lined, 2½-inch size muffin pan cups. Sprinkle with almond mixture; top with cherry. Cover with foil; freeze until firm—several hours or overnight. Makes 12.

Carol Rogow (Mrs. Bob)

BOCCONE DOLCE

Meringue layers:
Beat until stiff:
4 egg whites
Pinch of salt

¼ teaspoon cream of tartar

Gradually beat in 1 cup sugar and 1 teaspoon vanilla until glossy. Line cookie sheets with waxed paper. Spread the meringue into 3 8-inch circles. Bake at 250° for 20-25 minutes until slightly colored but still pliable. Peel off waxed paper and put on cake racks.

Filling:
6 ounces semi-sweet chocolate chips and
  3 tablespoons water (melted).
3 cups cream, whipped. Add ¼ cup
  sugar and whip until very stiff.

1 pint sliced fresh strawberries.

To assemble. Place maringue layer on serving plate. Drizzle over ⅓ of the

286

chocolate. Carefully spread on ⅓ of the whipped cream. Top with ⅓ of the strawberries. Repeat for the other 2 layers. May refrigerate up to 2 hours before serving.

Carla Candler (Mrs. Bill)

DOLCE TORINESE

½ pound semisweet chocolate, cut in small pieces
¼ cup rum
½ pound soft unsalted butter
2 tablespoons sugar
2 eggs, separated

1½ cups (5 ounces) grated blanched almonds
Pinch salt
12 butter biscuits (like Social tea), cut into 1x1½-inch pieces
Confectioners sugar

Lightly grease bottom and sides of 1½-quart loaf pan with vegetable oil and invert over paper towels to drain. In heavy saucepan melt chocolate over low heat, stirring constantly. Stir in rum and remove pan from heat. Cool to room temperature. Cream butter until light and fluffy. Beat in sugar, then egg yolks one at a time. Stir in grated almonds and cooled chocolate. In separate bowl with rotary beater, beat egg whites with salt until they cling to beater in soft peaks. Fold into chocolate mixture. Fold in cut-up biscuits, discarding crumbs. Spoon into pan. Smooth top, cover with plastic wrap, and refrigerate at least 4 hours, or until loaf is very firm. Unmold an hour before serving time by dipping pan quickly in hot water and running spatula around pan sides. Return to refrigerator until serving time. Cut loaf into thin slices and serve with whipped cream if desired.

This is great for Easter made in a rabbit mold.

CHOCOLATE FONDUE

6 bars Swiss Chocolate (3 light, 3 dark)
1 cup cream

Honey (½ cup)
2 ounces Cream de cacao or Brandy

Melt chocolate, add honey and cream; stir until melted. Add liqueur. Serve with fruits (strawberries, bananas)/or pound cake cut in small cubes.

Betsy Perry (Mrs. Kermit)

EASY CHOCOLATE ROLL

½ stick butter
1 cup chopped pecans
1⅓ cups flaked coconut
1 can sweetened condensed milk (15½ ounces)
3 eggs

1 teaspoon vanilla
1 cup sugar
⅓ cup cocoa
⅔ cup all-purpose flour
¼ teaspoon baking soda
⅓ cup water

Line a 15x10-inch jelly roll pan with foil. Melt butter in pan, sprinkle nuts and coconut evenly in pan; drizzle with condensed milk. In mixer bowl, beat eggs at high speed 2 minutes until fluffy. Gradually add sugar; continue beating 2 minutes. No need to sift flour; spoon into cup—level. Add remaining ingredients; blend 1 minute at low speed. Pour evenly into pan. Bake at 375° for 20-30 minutes until cake springs back in center. Sprinkle cake with powdered sugar (in the pan). Cover with light towel. Place cookie sheet over towel; invert. Remove pan and foil. Start with 10-inch side, roll up jelly roll style. Be careful not to roll the towel in the cake.

CHOCOLATE FILLED ROLLED CAKE

1 cup cake flour	1 teaspoon salt
4 eggs, separated	1 cup sugar
1 teaspoon baking powder	1 teaspoon vanilla

Sift flour, baking powder and salt three times. Beat egg yolks until thick, gradually adding ½ cup of the sugar and vanilla and beat until thick and light in color and fluffy. Beat egg whites in separte bowl with remaining ½ cup of sugar added gradually until stiff. Fold yolk mixture into whites and add dry ingredients gradually mixing carefully, but thoroughly. Spread in a shallow baking pan (12x18-inches) lined on bottom with greased, thin, plain paper. Bake in moderate oven (350° to 375°) for 12 to 15 minutes. Loosen sides and turn out on a towel sprinkled generously with powdered sugar. Immediately remove paper and trim off the crisp crusts. Quickly roll up cake, wrap in the towel and set on a rack to cool. Unroll cooled cake; spread with chocolate filling and re-roll. Wrap filled roll in waxed paper and chill in refrigerator for at least one hour before serving.

Chocolate filling for cake roll:

1 tablespoon gelatin	Dash of salt
¼ cup cold water	½ cup whipping cream
1 square (1 ounce) unsweetened	½ cup milk
chocolate	½ teaspoon vanilla
1 tablespoon water	
⅓ cup sugar	

Soften gelatin in cold water. Melt chocolate over hot water. Add 1 tablespoon water and blend in well. Then add sugar and salt. Using a whisk, gradually stir in milk and cook until smooth and thick—stirring constantly. Stir in softened gelatin until dissolved. Remove from heat and add vanilla and chill until thin custard consistency. Whip the cream until stiff and fold into chilled chocolate mixture. Spread on baked roll and proceed as directed above.

This is an elegant dessert. Garnish with sweetened whipped cream.

CHOCOLATE ROULADE

6 ounces block semisweet chocolate	3-4 tablespoons instant coffee or water
6 eggs	½ pint whipping cream
8 rounded tablespoons sugar	

Set oven at 350°. Line jelly roll pan or cookie sheet with sides with waxed paper and rub paper with Wesson oil. Separate eggs. Beat yolks with sugar until thick and mousse-like. Melt chocolate in water over low heat. Cool. Whip egg whites until they hold peak, (not until real dry). Add chocolate to egg yolk mixture. Then cut and fold in whites. Turn into prepared pan. Bake 10-12 minutes. Have ready a light cloth wrung out in cold water. Take out roulade and cool slightly. Cover with cloth and leave in cool place a number of hours or over night in the refrigerator. Loosen waxed paper with spatula and turn cake out onto another piece of waxed paper sprinkled with confectioners sugar. Peel off waxed paper. Spread with whipped cream. Roll up into jelly roll using ends of waxed paper to make roll. Wrap in foil and refrigerate. Slice into 12 slices.
Easy, delicious and impressive!

CHOCOLATE LEAVES

Melt 1 8-ounce package of chocolate chips in double boiler. Put ivy leaves on sheet of waxed paper. Spread chocolate on back side of each leaf with a spoon. Put in freezer for ½ to 1 hour. Peel away green leaf. Use as garnish on chocolate or citrus desserts.

FRIED APPLE TURNOVERS

3 medium cooking apples, peeled and
  chopped
1 tablespoon water
⅔ cup sugar

1 tablespoon all-purpose flour
⅛ teaspoon each ground cinnamon
  and nutmeg
Hot vegetable oil

Combine apples and water in a saucepan. Cover and cook over low heat 10-15 minutes. Drain off any liquid that accumulates. Combine sugar, flour and spices, stir well. Add to apples and cook over medium heat 10 minutes or until thickened. Roll pastry to ⅛-inch thick. Cut out 8 5-inch circles. Spoon about 2½ tablespoons filling on each pastry circle. Moisten edges of circles, fold pastry in half, making sure edges are even. Using a fork dipped in flour, press edges together to seal. Heat 1-inch oil to 375°. Fry until golden, turn once. Drain on paper towels. Makes 8 turnovers.

Pastry:
2 cups all-purpose flour
½ cup milk

1 teaspoon salt
½ cup vegetable oil

Combine flour and salt. Combine milk and oil, stirring well. Pour milk mixture and stir just until blended. Shape dough into a ball. Yield: pastry for 8 turnovers.

Donna Beardsworth (Mrs. Jim)

APPLE YUM

1 box jiffy cake mix—yellow
1 can apple pie filling

1 stick melted butter
Cool whip

Put pie filling in bottom of pan. Sprinkle with cinnamon and sugar to taste (2 tablespoons, mixed). Spread dry cake mix on top pie filling and pour melted butter over top. Bake at 350° until crust is browned.

CHERRY CRUNCH

Combine and set aside:
1 cup finely ground pretzels   ½ cup granulated sugar
1 stick butter or oleo, melted

Prepare as per package instructions 2 packages Dream Whip; add ½ cup powdered sugar and 3 ounces softened cream cheese. Press half of pretzel mixture into bottom of 9x9x2-inch pan. Spread half of Dream Whip on pretzel layer. Spread one can cherry pie filling on Dream Whip layer. Spread remaining Dream Whip on cherries. Sprinkle rest of pretzel mixture on top and press lightly. Chill *at least* 2 hours. Serves 9.

Peggy Turnquist (Mrs. Paul)

EASY APPLE TORTE

1 egg   ½ cup flour
¾ cup sugar   ¼ teaspoon almond or vanilla flavoring
¾ cup apples, diced   ¼ cup pecans, chopped
1 teaspoon baking powder   Pinch salt

Beat egg lightly, add sugar and apples. Stir in remaining ingredients. Pour into greased pie pan. Bake at 325° for 25 minutes. Serve with whipped cream or ice cream.

FRESH PEACH CRISP

½ cup margarine   1½ cups toasted bread cubes
1 cup sugar   2 cups corn flakes
2 eggs   4 cups peeled, sliced peaches
½ teaspoon nutmeg   1 tablespoon lemon juice
½ teaspoon vanilla

Combine margarine and ½ cup sugar. Beat well. Add eggs and beat. Stir in nutmeg, vanilla, bread cubes and corn flakes. Spread half of this mixture in a 1½-quart buttered, shallow baking dish. Arrange peaches over this. Sprinkle with lemon juice and ½ cup sugar. Put remaining mix on top. Bake at 375° for 20 minutes.

QUICK FRUIT COBBLER

¾ cup flour   ½ cup butter
2 tablespoons baking powder   2 cups fruit (sliced peaches or pears,
2 cups milk   or blueberries or blackberries)
2 cups sugar

Mix dry ingredients and 1 cup sugar. Stir in milk. Melt butter in 8x8x2 pan. Pour in batter but don't stir. Mix remaining cup of sugar with fruit and spoon carefully over batter. Bake 350° for 1 hour.

CREOLE BREAD PUDDING

6 slices bread, cubed
3½ cups milk, divided
4 eggs, separated
½ cup sugar, divided
1 tablespoon vanilla extract

Pinch of salt
¼ cup butter or margarine, melted
½ cup raisins
Rum sauce (recipe follows)

Combine bread cubes and 1 cup milk; set aside. Beat egg yolks, 6 tablespoons sugar and remaining 2½ cups milk. Stir in vanilla, salt, butter and raisins. Pour mixture over bread and mix well. Pour into shallow 2-quart baking dish. Place dish in a pan of hot water. Bake at 300° about 50 minutes or until knife inserted in center comes out clean. Beat egg whites until stiff; gradually beat in remaining 2 tablespoons sugar. Spread meringue over pudding; bake at 350° about 10 minutes or until golden. Serve with rum sauce. Yield: 6 to 8 servings.

Rum Sauce:
½ cup sugar
¼ cup water

2 tablespoons butter or margarine
1 tablespoon rum

Combine sugar, water and butter in a small saucepan; bring to a boil and boil 1 minute. Remove from heat; stir in rum. Serve warm. Yield: about ½ cup.

Clarie Debardeleben (Mrs. Charles)

CREPES—BASIC RECIPE

1 cup milk
1 cup water
½ teaspoon salt

2 cups flour
4 eggs
4 tablespoons melted oleo, butter or oil

Put milk, water, salt into blender. Add the flour and butter. Blend for one minute. Scrape down the sides and blend 5 more seconds. Put in refrigerator, covered, for an hour or two. Batter will be thin, like a light cream. If too thick, add a little water. Use a small crepe pan or skillet. Brush pan with oil and heat. Pour small amount of batter into pan and roll the pan around until the pan is covered with batter. Pour back the batter that does not adhere to the pan. Cook for only about 1 minute. Edges will come away from the pan. Pick up crepe—using a flat knife to help and turn over with your hands. Cook for only a half of a minute. These crepes can be refrigerated to use later or frozen.

CREPES AU MOCHA

1 cup flour
1½ tablespoons sugar
Pinch salt
1½ tablespoons cocoa

1½ tablespoons instant coffee
2 eggs, beaten
1⅓ cups milk
2 tablespoons melted butter

Sift flour, sugar, salt, cocoa, coffee. Add eggs. Stir in milk and melted butter until smooth. Strain as necessary. Let batter set 2 hours or more. Batter will be as thin as cream. For each crepe, melt a bit of butter in 6 to 8-inch skillet and cook crepes. Makes about 24.

Rum Cream Filling:
2 cups whipping cream
¼ cup sugar

¼ cup light rum

Whip cream, add sugar, fold in rum. Fill each crepe and roll. You may do ahead and refrigerate.

Hot Fudge Topping:
1 cup butter (real)
4½ cups powdered sugar

1⅓ cups evaporated milk
4 1-ounce squares chocolate

Melt butter in double boiler. Add sugar and milk, stir to dissolve. Add chocolate and melt. Continue to cook over hot water for 30 minutes WITHOUT STIR-RING. Remove from heat, stir until creamy. May be refrigerated and reheated. Makes 5 cups.

You can make the crepes ahead and freeze between waxed paper. I fill the crepes several hours before serving and add fudge sauce when serving. One crepe is enough. They are just enough dessert. They are light and not too rich or filling.

Bobbie Umbach (Mrs. Arnold)

BANANA SPLIT DESSERT

Melt 1 stick butter or margarine. Mix with 2 cups graham cracker crumbs and pat on bottom of 13x9-inch pyrex dish. Mix in a bowl: 2 eggs, 2 sticks margarine, softened, 2 cups powdered sugar. Beat 15 minutes until it looks like whipped cream. Spread over crumbs. Slice 3 or 4 bananas over this. Spread on 16-ounce can crushed pineapple, drained. Spread on large container of Cool Whip. Sprinkle on 2 cups pecans. Decorate with cherries. Let set in refrigerator.

It is delicious and disappears fast!

Joanne Patton (Mrs. Ed)

COLD LEMON SOUFFLE

2 envelopes unflavored gelatin
½ cup cold water
2 teaspoons grated lemon rind
1 cup lemon juice
Fresh whole strawberries (optional)

Slivered almonds (optional)
8 eggs
1 teaspoon salt
2 cups sugar
2 cups heavy cream

Day before, or early in the day, fold a 30-inch piece of foil in half lengthwise; tie around outside of 1½ quart souffle dish as collar. Sprinkle gelatin over cold water to soften. Grate lemon rind; then extract juice. Separate egg yolks from whites. In top of double boiler, combine egg yolks, lemon juice, salt and 1 cup sugar. Cook over boiling water, stirring constantly until slightly thickened and custardy. Then stir in gelatin and lemon rind; turn into a 3-quart bowl, cool. Beat egg whites until they hold a shape, then gradually beat in 1 cup sugar, continuing to beat until mixture holds a peak. Whip cream until stiff. Now on top of lemon mixture pile stiffly beaten egg whites and cream, gently fold mixtures together. Pour into souffle dish; refrigerate until firm (at least 3 hours). May serve with fresh strawberries and toasted, slivered almonds.

Libby Brown (Mrs. Jerry)

LEMON ICE BOX PUDDING

2 egg yolks
1 cup sugar

Juice of 2 lemons
1 lemon rind, grated

Cook together in double boiler until thick. Add 2 egg whites, beaten stiff to mixture when cool. Add 1 tall can evaporated milk which has been chilled and beaten. Crush vanilla wafers; line ice tray with part of these. Pour in mixture and cover top with remaining crumbs. Freeze in tray. Cut and serve with or without whipped cream.

ICE BOX DESSERT

3 cups pie cherries
2 cups sugar
⅛ teaspoon salt
½ cup flour
½ pound vanilla wafers (rolled)
½ cup butter

1 cup powdered sugar
1 egg, beaten
2 cups cooked rice
1 cup whipping cream, whipped
1 cup chopped pecans

Cook the cherries with sugar, salt and flour as for a cherry pie until thickened. Cool. Line a flat baking dish with the wafers that have been rolled to which the butter, powdered sugar and beaten egg have been added. Add rice on top of crust mixture, then the cooled cherry mixture. Add whipped cream and nuts. Let stand 3 to 4 hours or overnight in refrigerator before serving.

JENNY'S DESSERT

1 egg white
2 tablespoons sugar
1 tablespoon instant coffee
½ pint whipping cream

¼ cup sugar
½ teaspoon vanilla
¼ teaspoon almond extract

Beat egg white. Add sugar and coffee. Whip cream. Add sugar and flavoring. Fold in egg white mixture (and toasted slivered almonds, if desired). Sprinkle toasted slivered almonds on top and freeze.

Gaynell Parks (Mrs. Paul F.)

This is Gaynell's favorite luncheon dessert.

KAHLUA TORTE

1 angel food cake
½ gallon vanilla ice cream
⅓ cup kahlua

1 cup whipping cream
½ cup toasted almonds

Slice cake to make four layers. Soften ice cream and add all of the kahlua except for 1 tablespoon. Mix thoroughly. Spoon ice cream on first layer and sprinkle with almonds. Repeat for other layers. Whip cream. Add 1 tablespoon Kahlua and ice the cake with this mixture. Sprinkle last of almonds and freeze several hours.

LEMON FREEZE

1 cup graham cracker crumbs
¼ cup lemon juice
1½ teaspoons grated lemon rind
⅛ teaspoon salt

½ cup sugar
3 eggs, separated
1 can (6 ounces) evaporated milk, chilled

Line refrigerator tray with ½ cup of the crumbs. Blend lemon juice, rind, salt and sugar into well-beaten egg yolks. Stir over low heat until mixture thickens. Cool. Beat egg whites until stiff peaks form. Whip chilled milk. Fold egg whites and whipped milk into lemon mixture. Turn into crumb-lined tray. Top with remaining crumbs and freeze.

Hattie Yeager (Mrs. Joseph)

LEMON TORTE

3 pakages of plain lady fingers—or do
    your own, or substitute thin strips of
    sponge cake (lady fingers look best)
6 eggs, separated
1½ cups sugar

¾ cup lemon juice
1½ teaspoons gelatin
½ cup water
1 tablespoon grated lemon peel
Pinch of salt

Dissolve gelatin in ½ cup water. Combine ½ cup sugar, lemon juice and egg yolks in top of double boiler. Cook until thick. Add dissolved gelatin. Beat whites until stiff, add remainder of sugar, slowly beating until mixture forms soft peaks. Fold whites into yolk mixture (after it has cooked). Line pan (spring pan) with lady fingers. Pour in lemon mixture (½)—add layer of lady fingers—add remaining lemon-yolk mixture. Let it set in refrigerator up to 24 hours before serving or freezing. To serve, add whipped cream to top of lemon tort crown as it is removed from spring pan.

Marleah Hobbs (Mrs. Ed)

CHOCOLATE MOUSSE

4 egg yolks
4 eggs
¼ teaspoon salt
12 ounces semisweet chocolate, melted

2 teaspoons vanilla, or 2 tablespoons brandy, or Grand Marnier Liqueur
½ pint whipping cream
2 tablespoons powdered sugar

Beat egg yolks, eggs and salt until light. Beat in cooled chocolate, sugar and flavoring. Add cream and continue beating until mixture is smooth and thick. Turn into serving dish or individual dishes and chill thoroughly. For those who do not count calories, top with whipped cream, ice cream, or dairy cream topping. Serves 8.

Dr. Harry Philpott

NANNIE'S CHOCOLATE MOUSSE

2 giant milk chocolate bars (8 ounces, each)
2 blocks (2 ounces) unsweetened chocolate
2 tablespoons water
2 tablespoons rum or brandy
2 egg yolks

¼ cup butter
1½ cups heavy cream
2 packages split ladyfingers (use angel food cake, if you can't find ladyfingers)
4 egg whites

Break chocolates into pieces; combine milk chocolate and unsweetened chocolate with water and rum or brandy in top of a double boiler. (Use your microwave if you have one.) Chocolate needs to melt and stay smooth—do not overcook. I use my hand mixer to smooth out the chocolate at this point. Remove from heat; blend in egg yolks. Add butter a little at a time, stirring until blended. Whip cream; carefully fold into chocolate mixture. Chill one hour or until mixture begins to set. Meanwhile, line bottom and sides of an 8 or 9-inch spring form pan with ladyfingers. Beat egg whites until stiff but not dry. Carefully fold into chocolate mixture. Pour into lined mold and chill 8 hours or overnight. Garnish with chopped almonds if desired. Makes 14 servings.

FROZEN PUMPKIN MOUSSE

4 egg yolks
¼ teaspoon salt
1½ cups sugar
1 can (1 pound) pumpkin
Finely cut crystallized ginger or powdered
  ginger

1 teaspoon cinnamon
¼ teaspoon ground cloves
½ teaspoon mace
¼ teaspoon nutmeg
½ cup cognac or bourbon
Heavy cream

Beat egg yolks and salt until thick. Dissolve sugar in ½ cup water in saucepan, bring to boil and boil rapidly until syrup spins a thread—about 230°F on candy thermometer. Rapidly beat syrup into egg yolk mixture and continue beating until it begins to cool. This is best done in an electric mixer at high speed. When slightly cooled, combine with pumpkin, ¼ cup ginger (or 1 teaspoon dry ginger), other spices and cognac. Taste for spice. Whip 2 cups cream and fold into mixture. Pour into 2-quart mold or 2 smaller molds; cover and freeze 6 to 8 hours. To unmold, place in refrigerator 20 to 30 minutes, then dip in hot water. Turn out on serving dish. Put back in freezer several minutes, then decorate with whipped cream and ginger. Makes 8 to 10 servings.

COEUR A LA CREME I

8 ounces cream cheese, at room
  temperature
1½ tablespoons whipping cream
1 cup confectioners sugar

Raspberry sauce

1½ tablespoons lemon juice
½ teaspoon vanilla
1 cup whipping cream, whipped

Cream the cheese in an electric mixer until light and fluffy. Beat in the cream and sugar and continue beating until very smooth. Beat in lemon juice and vanilla. The mixture must be very smooth. Gently fold in the whipped cream. Line 6 individual coeur a la creme molds or 1 large coeur a la cream mold with damp cheesecloth. Spoon into mold. Fold cheesecloth over so that the cheese mixture and the molds are wrapped. Place on a plate and chill in the refrigerator for several hours. To serve, unwrap molds, turn them over and unmold onto small plates. Discard cheesecloth. Pass the raspberry sauce in a clear, glass pitcher. To prepare and serve without coeur a la creme molds, cheesecloth is not needed. Spoon the mixture into individual dessert goblets or a glass serving bowl. Chill several hours and serve with raspberry sauce. Make sauce by warming raspberry preserves.

COEUR A LA CREME II

8 ounces cream cheese, room
  temperature
⅔ cup confectioners' sugar
1 teaspoon vanilla
1¼ cups heavy cream

1 egg white (or 2 whites and 1 cup
  cream)
2 cups strawberry sauce
1 basket strawberries
confectioners' sugar

Sauce:
2 cups strawberries, sliced   1 cup currant jelly
¼ cup Kirsch or cassis or orange liqueur

Beat cheese with 2 tablespoons cream until light and fluffy. Beat in sugar and vanilla—whip cream, then whip egg whites separately. Stir ladleful of whites into the cheese. Fold in remaining whites and cream. Rinse 4 layers of cheesecloth in cold water. Wring dry. Line perforated mold or colander with cloth. Fill mold with cheese mixture. Fold extra cheesecloth over top surface of dessert. Chill overnight on a plate allowing excess liquid to drain out. To make sauce, melt jam over low heat. Remove pan, stir in liqueur. Mix with berries and chill. To serve, fold back cloth from top. Invert and unmold on serving plate. Remove cheesecloth. Sprinkle top with sugar. Garnish around edge of mold with strawberries. Pour some of sauce on plate around dessert and pass additional sauce.

This is the perfect Valentine dessert. It is usually made in a special perforated heartshaped mold, but a colander will do.

RASPBERRY SAUCE FOR COEUR A LA CREME

4 10-ounce packages frozen raspberries   1 tablespoon rum
Sugar to taste (about 2 tablespoons)

Defrost berries in their plastic pouch. Drain the berries well. Force through a fine sieve or strainer into a bowl. Discard the seeds. Stir in the sugar. This sauce must remain somewhat tart to be at its best, so taste as you add the sugar. Stir in the rum. Pour into a clear glass pitcher and refrigerate until serving time.

ORANGE BAVARIAN CREAM

1 envelope unflavored gelatin (1   Pinch salt
   tablespoon)   ½ cup boiling water
½ cup cold water   2 cups orange pulp
3 tablespoons lemon juice   1 cup heavy cream, whipped
½ to ⅔ cup granulated sugar

Sprinkle gelatin on cold water, let soften 5 minutes. Add with lemon juice, sugar (amount depends on sweetness of fruit), and salt to boiling water. Stir until gelatin is dissolved. Chill until a small amount mounds when dropped from a spoon. Then stir in fruit. Fold in whipped cream and chill until set. Makes 6-8 servings.

ORANGE CHARLOTTE DESSERT

3 tablespoons, or 3 envelopes, of gelatin   2 cups orange juice and orange
⅔ cup cold water   pulp—no white parts, just orange
⅔ cup boiling water   meat
2 cups sugar   6 egg whites
6 tablespoons lemon juice (more if not   6 tablespoons wine—sherry preferred
   acid enough)   1 pint of whipped cream
½ teaspoon salt

Soak gelatin in cold water, dissolve in boiling water. Add sugar, lemon juice, orange juice and pulp. Chill in pan of ice water. When white and thick, whip until frothy. Then add whites of egg beaten stiff, and then fold in whipped cream. Line mold with orange sections and fill with mixture and chill. (Be sure to taste for proper amount of lemon juice!) Allow at least 6 hours to set. Will serve 20 persons.

Alva Current-Garcia (Mrs. Eugene)

In our family we always had two charlottes for our Christmas Day dessert—one, the traditional Charlotte Russe from my mother's family recipes and this Orange Charlotte from my father's family. The Orange Charlotte is a lighter dessert, easily made, and almost always successful.

ORANGE TORTE

1 Duncan Hines Orange Supreme cake mix

1 4-ounce package vanilla instant pudding

Follow directions on package for pound cake. Bake in tube pan. Cool well in refrigerator. Split into 3 layers.

Filling:
1 can Eagle Brand condensed milk
1 6-ounce can orange juice, thawed

7 tablespoons lemon juice

Spread layers with filling. Refrigerate overnight or for several hours. Just before serving, pile Cool Whip on top of cake. Sprinkle with chopped nuts.

Dean Hays (Mrs. Kirby)

POT DE CREME

2 cups heavy cream
¼ cup sugar
Pinch salt

10 egg yolks
4 ounces sweet chocolate
1 tablespoon vanilla

Put cream, sugar and salt in top of double boiler. Over hot water, bring this mixture to scalding. Remove from heat and cool. Melt chocolate over hot water. Beat egg yolks until light and foamy. When cream mixture is cool, pour over egg mixture slowly, beating constantly. Add melted chocolate, return to boiler pan and stir constantly over low heat until mixture coats back of wooden spoon. Add vanilla. Strain and place in 10 pot de creme cups or demitasse cups and chill until it has a solid consistency.

A delicious rich dessert for seated dinner parties.

PEACHY CHEESECAKE 'N CREAM

Crust:
2 cups quick oats
⅔ cups brown sugar

½ cup butter, melted

Mix well and press into ungreased 9-inch spring pan. Bake 350° for 10 minutes. Cool.

Filling:
11 ounces cream cheese, softened
¾ cups creamed cottage cheese
¾ cups sugar
3 eggs
1 teaspoon vanilla flavor

Combine cream cheese and cottage cheese at high speed of mixer for 7 minutes. Gradually add sugar, beating constantly. Add eggs, one at a time, beating well after each. Mix in vanilla. Pour into crust and bake at 350° for 35 to 40 minutes, or until firm.

Glaze:
1 cup orange juice
2 teaspoons cornstarch
¼ cup sugar
1 large can sliced peaches, drained
Nutmeg

Combine orange juice and cornstarch and sugar in saucepan. Bring to a boil and cook until mixture is thick and clear. Cool to room temperature. Arrange peaches on cheesecake around outer edge working to center. Pour cooled glaze over peaches. Sprinkle lightly with nutmeg. Chill several hours or overnight before serving, covered with Saran wrap.

Inez Saia (Mrs. Claude)

STRAWBERRY WHIP

1 envelope unflavored gelatin
¼ cup cold water
½ cup hot water
½ cup sugar
2 tablespoons lemon juice
¼ cup orange juice
¼ teaspoon salt
1 pint strawberries
1 egg white, stiffly beaten

Soften gelatin in cold water; dissolve in hot water. Stir in sugar, lemon juice, orange juice and salt. Chill until partially set. Beat until frothy. Crush 1½ cups strawberries; add to gelatin mixture. Fold in egg white. Place in oiled mold. Chill until firm. Unmold. Garnish with remaining strawberries. Yield: 6-8 servings.

Devon Luther (Mrs. William A.)

TRIFLE

3 eggs
½ cup sugar
2 cups milk
1 teaspoon almond extract
1 sponge cake or 4 packages ladyfingers
¾ to 1 cup dry sherry
1 quart fresh or 1 pound, 13 ounces
   canned fruit
1 cup whipped cream
Toasted slivered almonds

Make custard—Beat eggs; combine with sugar, dash salt in top of double boiler. Stir in milk. Cook stirring constantly until mixture thickens. Chill. Break cake in bite-size pieces. Arrange half on bottom of serving dish. Sprinkle cake with half of the sherry. Arrange half the fruit, then half the custard. Then repeat. Top with whipped cream and almonds. Chill.

WATERGATE COVERUP

1 cup flour (generous)   1 stick margarine (soft)
1 teaspoon sugar

Mix as pie crust. Pat in 9x13 pan. Bake at 350° for 15 minutes. Let cool.

8 ounces cream cheese (soft)   1 cup powdered sugar

Cream together. Fold in 1 cup cool whip. Spread on top of crust.

2 small packages pistachio instant   3 cups cold milk
    pudding

Let stand 20-30 minutes. Spread on top of cheese mixture. Add the rest of cool whip (8-ounce size). Sprinkle top with walnuts and let stand for 3-6 hours in refrigerator.

Linda Voitle (Mrs. Bob)

WHITE GRAPES AND SOUR CREAM

6 cups (2½ pounds) stemmed, seedless   1½ cups sour cream
    white grapes   ¾ cup light brown sugar

Wash grapes and dry thoroughly. Chill for several hours. Sweeten the sour cream to taste (about ½ cup sugar). Toss grapes and cream together. Serve with remaining brown sugar sprinkled over the top. Serves 8.

ICE CREAMS

APRICOT ICE CREAM DESSERT

⅔ cup chopped toasted almonds
6 tablespoons melted butter
2 cups vanilla wafer crumbs

2 teaspoons almond extract
½ gallon vanilla ice cream (soft)
2 12-ounce jars apricot preserves

Combine butter, crumbs, almonds and extract—mix well. Save ½ cup for top. Line 9x13 pan with foil. In layers (half of ingredients for each layer) put crumbs, ice cream and preserves, in that order, in pan. Repeat for second layer. Top with reserved crumbs. Freeze. Serves 12.

Mary Christiansen (Mrs. Dan)

CASSIS ICE CREAM

1 quart (4 cups) half and half
1¼ cups (or 1 10-ounce jar) seedless
   blackberry jam or preserves

¾ cup creme de cassis
½ cup sugar
2¼ teaspoons vanilla

Combine all ingredients in a bowl until blended. Freeze in ice cream maker. Mixture will be soft. Freeze until ready to serve. Garnish each serving with a sprinkling of chopped walnuts. Very elegant!

Donna C. Burchfield (Mrs. Ron)

COCONUT ICE CREAM

3 eggs
Grated rind of one lemon
1 pint milk
1 cup shredded coconut, fresh or canned

1½ cups sugar
Juice of one lemon
1 quart cream

Beat together the eggs, grated lemon rind and milk. Place in a double boiler and heat, stirring constantly, until mixture begins to thicken, approximately two minutes. Add coconut and set aside to cool. When cool add sugar, lemon juice and cream. Mix thoroughly and freeze until firm.

EASY ICE CREAM

1 cup sugar
4 eggs
¼ teaspoon salt

1 tablespoon vanilla
½ pint whipping cream

301

Blend together the above and then put into ice cream freezer can and add 2 cans Eagle Brand milk and 1½ quarts whole milk. Freeze in either electric freezer or hand freezer.

Carol Savage (Mrs. Morris)

MILKY WAY ICE CREAM

8 1½-ounce Milky Way bars	1½ cups sugar
3 cups milk	2 teaspoons vanilla
6 eggs, well beaten	2 13-ounce cans evaporated milk

Melt candy bars in 2 cups milk in top of double boiler, then cool. Mix eggs and sugar in large bowl and beat well. Add evaporated milk and vanilla. Add Milky Way mixture and mix well. Pour into a one-gallon freezer container and add 1 cup milk. Mix well and freeze.

Betty B. Horton (Mrs. George)

All the neighbors love to be invited to the Horton's for this delicious ice cream.

OREO ICE CREAM

1 stack oreos	½ gallon good vanilla ice cream

Crush cookies coarsely between waxed paper with rolling pin. Stir into softened ice cream. Keep in freezer.

Mary Littleton

This is delicious as is, or served in parfait glasses with chocolate sauce.

PEPPERMINT ICE CREAM

6 eggs	1 (13-ounce) can evaporated milk
1⅔ cups sugar	1 tablespoon peppermint extract
Dash of salt	10-15 round peppermint candies,
3 cups milk, scalded	crushed
	½ to 1 pint whipping cream

Combine eggs, sugar, and salt; heat until light and fluffy. Gradually add ½ cup scalded milk to egg mixture, stirring constantly. Gradually stir egg mixture into remaining scalded milk. Pour custard into freezer can of a 1-gallon hand-turned or electric freezer. Stir in evaporated milk, peppermint extract and candy. Add enough whipping cream to fill freezer container to within 4 inches from top; stir in red food coloring, if desired. Freeze according to manufacturer's directions. Let ripen about 1 hour. Yield: 1 gallon.

Hattie Yeager (Mrs. Joseph)

HOMEMADE PEACH ICE CREAM

8 very ripe peaches, peeled and mashed
1 cup sugar
4 eggs
3 cups sugar

2 quarts milk
1 quart whipping cream
1½ tablespoons vanilla

Stir one cup of sugar into mashed peaches. (I use my food processor to mash peaches and add sugar while mashing.) Set peaches aside. Beat eggs in a large bowl, add sugar and mix well. Heat 1 quart of milk to scalding point and add to egg mixture, beating constantly. Pour into the freezer container and blend in the other quart of milk. Beat whipping cream, not too stiff, and fold into mixture in the container with the peaches and vanilla. Freeze in a large electric freezer. If using a 1-gallon freezer, half this recipe.

This ice cream stays wonderfully creamy in the freezer if you have leftovers.

DELICIOUS PEACH ICE CREAM

4 very ripe peaches
½ cup sugar
2 eggs
1½ cups sugar

1 quart milk
1 pint whipping cream
2 teaspoons vanilla

Peel and cut up peaches. Place in blender with ½ cup sugar and chop for about 30 seconds. Set peaches aside. Beat eggs in a large bowl; add 1½ cups sugar and mix well. Heat 1 pint milk to scalding point and add to egg mixture, beating constantly. Pour into ice cream freezer and stir in the other pint milk. Beat the whipping cream, not too stiff, and fold into the container with the peaches and vanilla. Freeze in electric ice cream freezer. Makes 1 gallon.

Caroline Lipscomb

(Remains incredibly creamy in freezer.)

CRANBERRY SHERBET

1 envelope unflavored gelatin
⅓ cup fresh lemon juice
1 pint cranberry juice
1 cup sugar

½ teaspoon grated lemon rind
¼ teaspoon salt
2 egg whites

Dissolve gelatin in ¼ cup cold water. Heat cranberry juice and sugar enough to dissolve gelatin. Add lemon rind and lemon juice. Freeze until mushy. Add salt to egg whites and beat until stiff. Fold into frozen cranberry mixture and freeze until firm. Serves 8-10.

If you want to freeze this recipe in an ice cream freezer, leave out egg whites and gelatin.

PUMPKIN ICE CREAM WITH RUM-RAISIN SAUCE

2 cups sugar
3 tablespoons all-purpose flour
1 teaspoon salt
2½ cups milk
3 eggs
1 29-ounce can pumpkin
1 tablespoon cinnamon

1 teaspoon nutmeg
½ teaspoon ginger
2 cups half and half
About 20 pounds cracked ice
2 to 3 pounds rock salt (about 3 cups)
Rum-raisin sauce

Early in day or up to 1 month before serving:
In 4-quart heavy saucepan, combine sugar, flour and salt. In medium bowl with wire whisk or fork, beat milk and eggs until well blended; stir into sugar mixture until smooth. Cook over low heat, stirring constantly, until mixture thickens and coats a spoon, about 20 to 25 minutes. Stir in pumpkin, cinnamon, nutmeg and ginger until well mixed. Cover surface with waxed paper and refrigerate to cool, about 2 hours. Pour half and half and cooled pumpkin mixture into 4- to 6-quart ice cream freezer can. Place dasher in can; cover and put into freezer bucket; attach motor or hand crank. (If using 5- or 6-quart can, add 2 cups water to bucket.) Fill bucket half full with ice; sprinkle with about ¼ cup rock salt. Add about an inch of ice and about ¼ cup rock salt; repeat thin layers of ice and salt until about an inch below can lid. Freeze according to manufacturer's directions, adding more ice and salt as needed. It will take about 30 to 35 minutes to freeze. After freezing, ice cream will be soft. Remove motor, wipe lid clean and remove dasher. With spoon, pack down ice cream, cover open of can with waxed paper, plastic wrap or foil. Replace lid and put cork in hole in center of lid; add more ice and salt to cover can lid. Let stand to harden ice cream about 2 to 3 hours, adding more ice and salt as needed. (Or place ice cream in a home freezer to harden, about 2 to 3 hours.) Serve ice cream with Rum-Raisin sauce. Makes about 3 quarts or 18 servings.

Home Freezer Method:
    Prepare and cool pumpkin mixture as directed above. Stir half and half into pumpkin mixture; pour mixture into 13x9-inch baking pan; cover and freeze until partially frozen, about 3 hours. Spoon mixture into chilled, large bowl; with mixer at medium speed, beat mixture until smooth but still frozen; return to pan; cover and freeze until firm, about 4 hours.
Rum Raisin Sauce:
In 2-quart saucepan over medium heat, heat 2 cups water and 1 cup raisins to boiling; reduce heat to low; cover and simmer 10 minutes or until raisins are tender. Meanwhile, in small bowl, combine ¾ cup sugar, 2 tablespoons cornstarch, 1 tablespoon grated orange peel, ¼ teaspoon salt and ½ cup water; gradually stir into hot raisin mixture; cook, stirring constantly, until sauce is thickened. Stir in ½ cup dark rum and 2 tablespoons butter or margarine and cook until butter or margarine is melted. Refrigerate sauce in covered jar up to 1 month.

VANILLA ICE CREAM

4 eggs
2 cups sugar
1 can Eagle Brand milk

1 package vanilla junket mix
4 teaspoons pure vanilla extract
½ gallon homogenized milk

Mix all ingredients and freeze in an ice cream freezer.

Carol Rogow (Mrs. Bob)

PRALINE ICE CREAM DESSERT

1 cup dark brown sugar
¼ cup melted butter
½ cup toasted slivered almonds

2½ cups crushed rice chex
1 cup angel flake coconut
½ gallon ice cream

Cover bottom of 13x9 pan with half of mixture. Soften the ice cream a little and cover mixture. Put the other half of mixture on top of ice cream and chill in freezer. When ready to serve, remove from freezer, cut and serve.

Joanne Patton (Mrs. Ed)

FRANCES WOODALL'S PECAN ICE CREAM BOMBE

1 tablespoon oleo
38 pecan halves
¼ teaspoon salt

1 quart softened coffee ice cream
1 quart softened chocolate ice cream
1 recipe butterscotch sauce

In shallow baking pan, melt oleo. Add salt and pecans. toss lightly and toast in pre-heated 300° oven 10-15 minutes. Set aside to cool. Chill a 7-cup mold or stainless steel mixing bowl in freezer. Spread coffee ice cream as evenly as possible with back of spoon on bottom and sides of mold to form a shell lining about 1-inch thick. Place mold in freezer to harden ice cream. Remove mold from freezer and spoon chocolate ice cream into center to fill mold. Place mold in freezer until chocolate ice cream hardens. Unmold by dipping mold into warm water and turn out bombe onto a chilled plate. Garnish with toasted nuts to conform to the shape of the bombe. Drizzle ¼ cup butterscotch sauce over top of bombe. Serve rest of sauce in separate dish. This recipe serves 10-12.

Butterscotch Sauce:
¼ cup oleo
¾ cup light brown sugar

1 tablespoon light corn syrup
¼ cup whipping cream

Melt oleo in a small pan. Add sugar and corn syrup. Bring mixture to a boil and cook until sugar is dissolved. Gradually add cream, stirring constantly, and bring to a boil. Cool before drizzling over bombe. If you like a lot of sauce, double the recipe.
One of Taylor Littleton's favorite desserts.

ICE CREAM PIE

Graham cracker crust

Vanilla ice cream

Meringue:
2 egg whites   ½ teaspoon vanilla
4 tablespoons sugar   Pinch of salt

Beat whites until stiff but not dry. Beat in sugar gradually and continue beating until well blended. Add flavoring. Fill graham cracker crust with ice cream and then cover with meringue. Place, covered in plastic wrap, in freezer and freeze until firm.

Sauce:
1 can condensed milk   ¼ cup water (or less)
2 squares semi-sweet chocolate

Heat sauce in top of double boiler and stir until smooth and hot. Pour hot sauce over frozen wedges of pie. Serves 8.

Cora Lipscomb Swanner (Mrs. James C., Jr.)

DESSERT SAUCES

TOM'S MOTHER'S CHOCOLATE SYRUP

1 tablespoon margarine   2 tablespoons white Karo
1 square unsweetened chocolate   ½ teaspoon vanilla
⅓ cup boiling water   ⅛ teaspoon salt
1 cup sugar

Melt butter and chocolate. Add boiling water. Add sugar and syrup. Bring to boil and simmer 5 minutes. Add vanilla and salt. Pour into pint jar and cover.

Ethel Vaughan (Mrs. Tom)

FUDGE SAUCE FOR HOT FUDGE SUNDAE

1 cup sugar   3 tablespoons butter or margarine
1 cup milk   Dash salt
2 tablespoons flour   1 teaspoon vanilla
3 tablespoons cocoa

Melt butter and wisk in dry ingredients. On medium heat, slowly add milk while stirring constantly. Cook until thick.

This sauce is perfect for making hot fudge sundaes or cake topped with ice cream, then fudge sauce. Top with whipped cream and add a cherry. Your kids will love you for this dessert!

HOT BITTERSWEET CHOCOLATE SAUCE

¼ cup oleo   ¾ cup sugar
1½ squares unsweetened chocolate, cut   ¼ cup cream or milk
  into small bits   ⅛ teaspoon salt
¼ cup cocoa   1 teaspoon vanilla

Melt butter and chocolate in saucepan, stirring over low heat until smooth. Stir in cocoa, sugar, cream and salt. Bring slowly to boil. Do not stir. Remove from heat and blend in vanilla. Serve warm. Makes 1½ cups.

CANDY

CHOCOLATE COATED COCONUT BALLS

2 boxes confectioners sugar
1 can sweetened condensed milk
1 stick butter
1 can flaked coconut

Pinch salt
¼ cup chopped pecans
2 packages chocolate chips
1 block paraffin (¼ pound)

Melt butter slowly and add milk. Stir in sugar and salt. Add coconut and pecans. Chill until it can be easily handled. Roll into balls. Place in refrigerator or freezer until firm. Melt chocolate and paraffin together in top of double boiler. Remove from heat and dip each candy ball in chocolate (with toothpick) quickly and place on waxed paper. Use another toothpick to push ball from inserted toothpick. Take a small number of balls from refrigerator at a time to prevent them from getting soft.

Donna Beardsworth (Mrs. Jim)

Donna gives this candy at Christmas-time. We all look forward to gifts from her kitchen.

PECAN ROLL

2 cups chopped pecans
1 cup Eagle Brand milk

1 box vanilla wafers, crushed fine

Mix all ingredients together and roll in waxed paper. Put in refrigerator and then slice in cookie size.

PEANUT BUTTER FUDGE

½ cup butter or margarine
1 pound light brown sugar
1 pound confectioners sugar

½ cup milk
¾ cup smooth or crunchy peanut
   butter
1 teaspoon vanilla extract

In medium saucepan, melt butter, stir in brown sugar and milk. Bring to a boil; boil and stir 2 minutes. Remove from heat; stir in peanut butter and vanilla. Mix confectioners sugar; beat until smooth. Spread into buttered 9-inch square baking pan. Chill until firm. Cut into squares.

CHOCOLATE CANDY

1 package (8 ounces) unsweetened
   chocolate
1 package (4 ounces) sweet cooking
   chocolate

1 can (14 ounces) sweetened
   condensed milk
Chopped pecans or walnuts or flaked
   coconut

Melt chocolates together over hot water. Add condensed milk and mix until smooth and blended. Cool a few minutes, then shape in balls, using about 1 teaspoonful mixture for each. Roll in nuts. Store in airtight container. Makes 6 dozen.

BRANDY ROLLS

½ cup unsulfured molasses
½ cup butter, softened
1¼ cups all-purpose flour
¼ teaspoon salt

⅔ cup sugar
1 tablespoon ground ginger
3 tablespoons brandy

In saucepan, bring molasses to boil. Add butter and stir until melted. Mix next 4 ingredients together and gradually add to molasses mixture. Add brandy and stir until well mixed. Drop by level measuring teaspoonfuls 3 inches apart onto greased cookie sheet, baking only 6 to 8 at a time. Bake in preheated 300°F oven 10 minutes. Cool 1 minute, then remove with wide spatula and roll at once around handle of wooden spoon. Press where cookie overlaps. (If removed from pan too soon, wafer will shrink; if not soon enough, wafer will be too brittle to roll. If too brittle, put back in oven a few minutes to soften again.) Repeat until all of mixture is used, lightly greasing cookie sheet each time. Makes about 3½ dozen. Store in airtight container. Can be frozen. Not good shippers—cookies break easily.

PEANUT BUTTER LOG

½ cup peanut butter
2½ tablespoons nonfat dry milk (3½
   instant)—more as needed

½ cup raisins
2 tablespoons honey (optional)

Blend peanut butter (and honey), then work in as much powdered milk as you need to make the mixture easy to handle and fairly stiff. Pick up the mixture and knead in the raisins, distributing them evenly. Roll into a 1-inch thick and 10-inch long log. Chill and slice or pull apart.

    This mixture can be molded into any shape and even pressed into cookie molds to make an exciting snack for small children (and big ones too).

PARTY MINTS

½ stick margarine
2½ tablespoons whipping cream
6 drops oil of peppermint

4 drops coloring
1 pound box powdered sugar

Melt margarine and add whipping cream, peppermint, and coloring. Empty box of powdered sugar in bowl. Add other ingredients. Set in bowl of warm water and mix well. Mold.

ENGLISH TOFFEE
(Shhh—secret recipe)

1 cup water
2 cups white sugar
¾ pound butter

1 pound chopped pecans
2 pounds milk chocolate (giant Hershey bars)

Soften chocolate in double boiler. Do not stir. Boil water, sugar and butter on medium heat until it reaches 280°. Add ½ pound chopped nuts at 280° and stir constantly until it reaches 310°. Pour real thin on marble slab (ungreased) and spread with spatula. Spread half of chocolate on one side; immediately sprinkle ¼ pound pecans and lightly pat. Run spatula under slab of candy and turn over. Spread this side with remaining chocolate and pecans. Put in cool room, preferably overnight. When cool, loosen from marble and break into desired size pieces. (Cook on medium entire time.) Chop pecans and soften chocolate before beginning. This recipe is easy and fool proof.

PEANUT BUTTER-DIPPED COCOA BONBONS

2 packages (3 ounces each) cream cheese
1 tablespoon milk
4 cups confectioners sugar
⅓ cup cocoa
1 teaspoon vanilla

1 cup finely chopped nuts (optional)
1 package (12 ounces) peanut butter flavored chips (2 cups)
2 tablespoons vegetable shortening

Beat cream cheese and milk in small mixer bowl; blend in confectioners sugar, cocoa and vanilla. Stir in nuts. Chill until firm enough to handle, about 1 hour. Shape into ½-inch balls; place on waxed paper-lined tray. Chill, uncovered, 3 to 4 hours or overnight. Centers should feel dry to touch. Stir peanut butter chips and shortening in top of double boiler over hot, not boiling, water until melted. Using a fork or clean hat pin, dip each center into peanut butter mixture. Gently tap fork on side of pan to remove excess peanut butter mixture. Slide bonbon from fork upside down onto waxed paper, swirling "thread" of peanut butter from fork across top for a decorative touch. Chill. Store in a cool place. Makes about 3½ dozen.

ANNIE GOLDEN'S KISSES

3 egg whites

1 cup sugar

Beat in electric mixer 30 minutes. Fold in 1 teaspoon vanilla, 2 cups chopped nuts. Place on cookie sheet in ½ teaspoon lots. Bake in 250° oven until kisses can be lifted from cookie sheet.

MAMA'S PEANUT BRITTLE

Pinch of salt   ½ cup boiling water
1½ cups sugar   ½ cup Karo syrup (white)

¼ cubic inch paraffin   1½ teaspoons soda
2 cups raw peanuts

Cook first 4 ingredients until you can spin a thread. Put in nuts and cook until syrup turns tan (low heat—about 10 minutes). Take off burner, add soda and pour at once on greased cookie sheet. Cool and break into pieces. Store in airtight container.

Joanne McLaughlin (Mrs. Wayne)

CRACKER JACKS

2 sticks oleo   ½ teaspoon salt
2 cups brown sugar   7 quarts unsalted popped corn
½ cup white Karo syrup   1 teaspoon soda

Stir oleo, sugar, karo and salt together and boil 5 minutes. Add 1 teaspoon soda and stir in as you remove from stove. Pour mixture over popcorn and place in oven (200°) for 1 hour. Stir every 15 minutes while baking. Use turkey roaster or large pan.

PRALINES, NEW ORLEANS

1½ cups firmly packed brown sugar   3 tablespoons butter
1½ cups white sugar   ½ teaspoon vanilla extract
1 cup evaporated milk   2 cups pecan halves

Combine sugars and milk. Place over low heat and stir until dissolved. Bring to boil; lower heat and cook to 234°F. Remove from heat; add butter, vanilla; cook 200°F without stirring. Add pecans. Beat until creamy and candy holds shape. Drop by large spoonfuls on buttered surface or waxed paper. Yields 12-18 pralines.

PRALINES

1½ cups sugar   ¾ stick real butter
¾ cup brown sugar   1½ cups pecans
½ cup milk

Combine all ingredients. Bring to soft ball (240°). Remove from heat. Beat until mixture thickens. Spoon out on buttered waxed paper.

I got this recipe from Mr. Cook of the New Orleans School of Cooking, 835 Conti, in the French Quarter. It never fails.

Ethel Vaughan (Mrs. Tom)

INDEX

Abbie's Squash Soufflé, 153
Alabama Spoon Bread, 127
Almond Crispies, 235
Always Perfect Eye of Round, Rib Eye or Bottom Round, 29
American Cheese Appetizer, 45
American Chicken Chow Mein, 199
Anchovy or Smoked Oyster Puffs, 44
Annie Golden's Kisses, 309
Ann's Cheese Ball, 17
Antipasto, 39
Apple and Sausage Quiche, 103
Apple-Cabbage Slaw, 81
Apple Cake Moritz, 249
Apple Sandwich, 69
Applesauce Beef Loaf, 178
Apple Yum, 289
Apricot Ice Cream Dessert, 301
Apricot Ring Mold, 82
Arroz Con Pollo, 200
Artichoke Dip, 20
Artichokes and Peas, 132
Artichoke Squares, 40
Asparagus Deviled Eggs, 97
Asparagus Rolls, 66
Asparagus Salad, 74
Asparagus Vinaigrette, 76
Aunt Gertie's Fruit Cake Cookies, 241
Aunt Margaret's Cheese Soup, 52
Avocado Bacon Salad, 76
Avocado Cocktail Dip, 22
Avocado Crabmeat Quiche, 103
Avocado Mold, 74
Avocado Soup, 51
Avocado-Tomato Aspic, 74

Bacon-Pepper Sandwich, 66
Baked Apricots, 131
Baked Butternut Squash, 154
Baked Fish, 218
Baked Fruit, 131
Baked Potatoes in Crumb Coats, 148
Baked Stuffed Whole Fish, 219
Banana Bar Cookies, 235
Banana Split Cake, 260
Banana Split Dessert, 292
Barbara's Gazpacho, 54
Barbecue Chicken, 211
Barbecued Baked Beans, 134
Barbecued Chicken, Stan Style, 211

Barbecued Ribs, 182
Barbecued Sausage Balls, 30
Barbecued Spare Ribs, 29
Barbecued Spareribs L'Orange, 182
Barbecue Sauce, 182
Barbecue Sauce, 210
Basic Bread, 112
Basic French (Plain) Omelet, 312
Batter Rolls, 115
Bean Bundles, 132

Beef, 165-181

Beef and Bean Enchiladas, 174
Beef Burgundy, 171
Beef Roulades in Red Wine, 167
Beef Turnovers, 166
Beef with Mushrooms, 170
Beet Salad (Congealed), 75
Bell Ringer Punch, 4
Best Brownies, The, 235
Best Ever Apple Cobbler, 278
Bette's Mystery Soup, 52

Beverages, 1-10

Bill's Baroque (Broke) Chicken, 212
Biscuit Tortini, 286
Bishop's Chicken, 194
Bite-Size-Cheese Cakes, 251
Black Magic Cake, 250
Blond Sangria, 10
Blueberry Muffins, 125
Blueberry Salad, 82
Blue Cheese Burgers, 180
Blue Cheese Mold with Apples, 34
Blue Cheese or Roquefort Dressing, 93
Boccone Dolce, 286
Boterkoek, 250
Bouillabaise, 60
Bourbon Pecan Pound Cake, 259
Bowknots, 116
Brandy Rolls, 308
Brandywine Punch, 8
Brazilian Salad, 91

Breads, 109-127

Bread Sticks, 121
Brie in Puff Pastry, 13
Broccoli and Cauliflower Casserole, 136
Broccoli-Cheese Soup, 51
Broccoli Gruyere, 135
Broccoli Soup, 51

Broiled Hamburgers, 180
Broiled Tomatoes, 156
Broun Hall Mushrooms, 144
Brownie-Fudge Cake, 251
Brownies, 236
Brown Sugar Pound Cake, 261
Brunswick Stew, 209
Brussels Sprouts and Mushrooms, 137
Brussels Sprouts in Sweet and Sour Sauce, 137
Brussels Sprouts with Tarragon-Mustard Sauce, 137
Buttercream Decorating Icing, 269
Butter Crescents, 115
Butter Pecan Turtle Squares, 237

Cakes, 249-268

California Casserole, 172
Camel Rider Sandwiches, 70
Camembert Melt, 13
Candied Apple Salad, 86

Candy, 307-310

Caramel Fudge Frosting, 268
Caramel Icing, 268
Caramel Squares, 238
Carolyn Lipscomb's Hot Shrimp Sandwiches, 72
Carrot-Cucumber Relish, 160
Carrot Pennies, 138
Carrot Vichyssoise, 57
Cassis Ice Cream, 301
Catfish Gumbo, 61
Cathedral Window Cookies, 238
Cauliflower Salad, 76
Cepes Sautés Paysanne, 143
Chafing Dish Oysters, 35
Champagne Punch, 9
Chasen Chili, 173
Cheddar Cheese Soup, 52
Cheese and Apple Spread, 26
Cheese Ball, 18
Cheese Balls, 14
Cheese Boxes, 43
Cheese Cake, 251
Cheese Cake Pie, 278
Cheese Chilies, 14
Cheese Christmas Trees, 14
Cheese Crepes for Brunch, 101
Cheese Grits, 101
Cheese-Olive Spread, 23
Cheese Pepper Bread, 120
Cheese Pine Cone, 16
Cheese Puffs, 14
Cheese Soufflé, 102

Cheese Strata, 101
Cheese Straws, 13
Cheese Tartlets, 47
Cheese Triangles, 45
Cheesy Mexican Chicken Pie, 202
Cherry Crunch, 290
Cherry Tartlets, 283
Chess Pie, 280
Chess Squares, 238
Chicken and Cashew Nuts, 199
Chicken and Dumplings, 198

Chicken and Poultry, 189-213

Chicken and Rice Casserole, 204
Chicken Arbor, 190
Chicken Bennevier, 194
Chicken Breasts in Papillote, 189
Chicken California, 191
Chicken Carrot Salad, 91
Chicken Casserole, 203
Chicken Casserole, 204
Chicken Cheese Noodle Ring, 205
Chicken Continental, 207
Chicken Curry, 197
Chicken Dip, 38
Chicken Eleganté, 193
Chicken Enchilada Casserole, 201
Chicken Enchiladas with Sour Cream, 201
Chicken, Indian Style, 196
Chicken in Sherry, 192
Chicken in White Wine Sauce, 195
Chicken Jamaica, 190
Chicken Kiev, 191
Chicken Layer Casserole, 206
Chicken Livers in White Wine, 200
Chicken 'n Stuffing Scallop, 205
Chicken Parmesan, 204
Chicken Piccata, 194
Chicken Pie Soufflé, 206
Chicken Rodger, 195
Chicken Salad Pie, 90
Chicken Spaghetti, 198
Chicken Spectacular, 205
Chicken Tetrazzini, 203
Chicken Veronique, 200
Chicken Wings, 30
Chicken with Sausage and Mushrooms, 204
Chile-Cheese Appetizer, 41
Chilled Squash Soup, 55
Chinese Chicken Salad, 89

Chinese Drumsticks, 199
Chinese Vegetables, 157
Chocolate Cake, 252
Chocolate Cake, 253
Chocolate Candy, 308
Chocolate Caramel Layer Squares, 237
Chocolate Chip Cake, 254
Chocolate Chip-Oatmeal Cookies, 239
Chocolate Chip Pie, 272
Chocolate Coated Coconut Balls, 307
Chocolate Delight, 271
Chocolate Filled Rolled Cake, 288
Chocolate Fondue, 287
Chocolate Ice-Box Cake, 254
Chocolate Leaves, 289
Chocolate Mousse, 295
Chocolate Peppermint Brownies, 236
Chocolate Peppermint Brownies, 237
Chocolate Pour Cake, 254
Chocolate Roulade, 288
Chocolate Snack Cake, 253
Christmas Aroma Punch, 8
Church Window Cookies, 239
Chutney Pie, 18
Clam-Vegetable Soup, 58
Cocktail Quiche, 46
Cocktail Sandwich Spread, 67
Cocktail Spinach Squares, 41
Cocoa Cola Cake, 265
Coconut Ice Cream, 301
Cod Provencal, 217
Cod with Olives, 220
Coeur a la Creme, 296
Coeur a la Creme with Caviar, 31
Coffee Cake, 123
Cold Lemon Soufflé, 293
Cold Vegetable Salad, 77, 78
Company Beans, 133
Company Chicken, 191
Congo Bars, 239

Cookies, 235-247

Coq au Vin, 207
Coq au Vin, 208
Coquille St. Jaques, 221
Corn Chowder, 53
Corned Beef Roll, 181
Corn Pudding, 140
Crab Canapés, 46
Crab Dip, 27
Crab Meat Dip, 27

Crabmeat Quiche, 47
Crabmeat Salad or Hors D'Oeuvre Ring, 89
Crabmeat Soup, 61
Cracker Jacks, 310
Crafty Crescent Lasagne, 179
Cranberry Cheese Pie, 272
Cranberry Mold, 83
Cranberry Salad, 83
Cranberry Sherbert, 303
Cranberry Wine Salad, 84
Cream Cheese 'n Bacon Appetizers, 69
Cream Cheese Pound Cake, 259
Creamed Dried Beef in Toast Cups, 181
Creamed Mushrooms, 144
Creamy Broccoli Casserole, 136
Creole Bread Pudding, 291
Creole Cold Mustard Sauce for Meats, 186
Creole Courtbouillon, 60
Crepes au Mocha, 292
Crepes—Basic Recipe, 291
Crisp Vegetable Medley, 158
Crunchy Cocktail Meatballs, 38
Cucumber Sandwiches, 66
Curried Rice, 151
Curried Rice and Beef Shish Kabobs, 165
Curried Shrimp Salad, 89
Curried Turkey, 213
Curry Almond Spread, 23
Curry Beef in Pastry, 175
Curry Dip, 27

Daiquiri Slush, 9
Danish Apple Bars, 240
Danish Pudding Cake, 257
Date Cake, 255
Date Crispies, 240
Date Crisps, 244
Date Refrigerator Cookies, 240
Dawson Stew, 208
Decorator Icing, 269
Deep Dish Peach Pie, 273
Deepfreeze Daiquiri, 9
Deep Fried Eggplant, 143
Delicious Peach Ice Cream, 303

Desserts, 233-310

Dessert Sauces, 306

Deviled Brussels Sprouts, 138
Deviled Ham and Eggs for Brunch, 97
Deviled Ham Cornucopias, 68

Diane's Spinach Dip, 21
Different and Delicious Eggplant
    Spread, 21
Dill Bread, 119
Dill Dip in Bread Bowl, 25
Dilled Okra Pickles, 160
Dip for Fresh Fruit, 25
Dip for Raw Vegetables, 24
Divine Chocolate Pie, 270
Dolce Torinese, 287
Donna's Favorite Guacamole, 22
Dottie's Chocolate Pie, 274
Doves with Orange Glaze, 214

Easter Egg Salad, 85
Easy Apple Torte, 290
Easy Chafing Dish Hot Dogs, 38
Easy Cheese Cubes, 43
Easy Chicken Divan, 207
Easy Chocolate Roll, 287
Easy Crescent Danish Rolls, 125
Easy Ice Cream, 301
Easy Lasagna, 178
Easy Mushroom Chicken, 192
Easy Tea Cakes, 245
Eggplant Cakes, 141
Eggplant Casserole, 142
Egg Puff, 97

Eggs, Cheese, Pasta, 95-107

Eggs Portugal, 98
Enchilada Casserole, 178
Enchiladas, 201
English Toffee, 309

Entrees, 163-232

Esther's Chicken Casserole, 205

Fairbanks Chowder, 64
Faux Wine Punch, 3
Faye's Maple Syrup, 126
Fettucini Alfredo, 106
Fiesta Corn Muffins, 122
Fig Cake, 256
Fillets of Sole Meuniere, 217
Finger Licking Sweet Potato Pie,
    279
Fish Casserole, 218
Fisherman's Wharf Avocado
    Salad, 92
Fish Fillets in Wine Sauce, 220
Fish Salad, 88
Flounder Parmesan, 217
Frances Woodall's Coconut
    Cake, 255
Frances Woodall's Pecan Ice
    Cream Bombe, 305
Franklin's Favorite Chili, 173

French Bread, 114
French-Cut Rib Pork Loin Roasts
    with Gravy, 185
French-Fry Bake, 147
French Onion Soup, 56
French Pancakes, 126
French Silk, 280
Fresh Apple Cake, 249
Fresh Peach Crisp, 290
Fresh Strawberry Pie, 276
Fried Apple Turnovers, 289
Fried Mushrooms, 143
Fried Okra, 144
Fritto Di Mozzarella, 13
Frosty Melon Mold, 84
Frosty Orange Pie, 281
Frozen Cheese Squares, 43
Frozen Chocolate Cheesecake,
    252
Frozen Cranberry Salad, 84
Frozen Fruit Salad, 87
Frozen Pumpkin Mousse, 296

**Fruits and Vegetables,
129-161**

Fudge Pie, 274
Fudge Sauce for Hot Fudge
    Sundae, 306

Game, 214-216

Garden Medley, 145
Garlic Cheese Grits, 101
Gazebo I's Petite Quiche, 46
Gazpacho, 53
George's Favorite Spinach, 151
German Beer Cheese, 18
German Chocolate Pound Cake,
    260
German Chocolate Pie, 271
Gingerbread, 257
Gingerbread Cookies, 241
Gingered Ham, 185
Glazed Carrots, 139
Glazed Strawberry Tarts, 283
Good Angel Food Icing, 268
Grapefruit-Avocado Mold, 84
Grape Juice Punch, 4
Great Dinner Rolls, 117
Greek Lemon Soup, 55
Green and Gold Casserole, 157
Green Beans in Red Wine, 133
Green Beans in Sour Cream,
    133
Green Christmas Cheese Ball, 16
Greenhouse Chicken Salad, 90
Greek Spinach Pie, 104
Ground Beef Casserole, 176
Guacamole Dip, 21

Guacamole Paste, 22

Haddock-Shrimp Bake, 222
Ham and Cheese Sandwiches,
    French Toasted, 71
Ham Sauce, 186
Hawaiian Banana Nut Bread,
    124
Hearty Supper Casserole, 176
Heavenly Pie, 275
Herbed Tomato Slices, 77
Helen Nanos' Greek Artichoke
    Hearts, 39
Hershey Bar Pie, 270
Holiday Appetizer Pie, 18
Homemade Boursin Cheese, 15
Home-Made Orange Brandy, 10
Homemade Peach Ice Cream,
    303
Hominy Bake for Cookouts, 140
Honey-Glazed Pecan Cake, 256

Hors D'Oeuvres, 11-47

Horseradish Sauce for Fish, 231
Hot Artichoke Dip, 20
Hot Bittersweet Chocolate
    Sauce, 306
Hot Buttered Rum, 6
Hot Chicken Sandwich, 70
Hot Cheese Dip, 22
Hot Chipped Beef-Pecan Dip, 26
Hot Cider, 6
Hot Cocoa Mix, 6
Hot Crab Dip, 29
Hot Crab Meat Dip, 28
Hot Fruit, 131
Hot Percolator Punch, 6
Hot Seafood Dip, 35
Hot Spiced Percolator Punch, 7
Hot Spinach Balls, 40
Hot Spinach Dip, 37
Hot Spinach Squares, 152
Hush Puppies, 122

Ice Box Cookies, 241
Ice Box Dessert, 293
Ice Cream Pie, 305

Ice Creams, 301-306

Ice Green Tomato Pickles, 160

Icing, 268-269

Imperial Cookies, 247
Instant Parmesan Appetizer, 41
Instant Spiced Tea Mix, 6
Instructor's Salary Sandwich, 71
Italian Bean and Sausage Soup,
    59
Italian Chicken, 195

Italian-Style Vegetable-Sausage Soup, 58
Italian Vegetable Sstew, 156

Jake Fortner's Barbecue Sauce, 210
Jan's Secret Smoked Turkey, 213
Japanese Fruit Pie, 282
Jenks Knight's Hot Broccoli Dip, 36
Jenks Knight's Spinach Dip, 21
Jenny's Dessert, 294
Jezebel Sauce, 23

Kabobs Ursula, 165
Kahlua Torte, 294
Katherine Cater's Favorite Spoon Bread, 126
Kentucky Derby Pie, 281
Key Lime Chiffon Pie, 277
Kiwi Sour Cream Tart, 284

Lace-Edged Corn Cakes, 123
Lan's Favorite Carrot-Shrimp Salad, 88
Lavinia Taylor's Blackbottom Pie, 280
Layered Potato Salad, 79
Lemonade Cake, 258
Lemon Cake, 258
Lemon Curd Tart Filling, 284
Lemon Freeze, 294
Lemon Ice Box Pudding, 293
Lemon Sponge Pie, 277
Lemon Squares, 241
Lemon Torte, 294
Lemon Veal and Mushrooms, 168
Libba's Tomato Sandwich, 69
Liepe's Fruit Cake, 256
Lime Cake, 258
Limelight Pie, 276
Lipscomb's Drug Store Fruit Punch, 3
Lobster and Shrimp, 227
Lucy Burwell's Orange Nut Bread, 120
Lynchburg Muffin Cakes, 259

Macaroni-Crabmeat Salad, 88
Make Ahead Bloody Mary, 10
Makes-Its-Own-Crust Egg Custard, 279
Mama's Peanut Brittle, 310
Mandarin Angel Pie, 274
Marinated Barbecued Chicken Wings, 30
Marinated Broccoli, 136

Marinated Mushrooms, 39
Marinated Potato Salad, 80
Marinated Slaw, 81
Marinated Squash, 153
Marinated Vegetable Platter, 157
Margie and Beth's Pecan Tarts, 283
Margie's Million-Dollar Pound Cake, 262
Mary George Lamar's Carrot-Cucumber Relish, 160
Maryland Turkey, 212
Mary's Pumpkin Bread, 119
Mary Timberlake's Fruit in Melon Baskets, 86
Mary Woody's Toasted Pecans, 40
May Bowle, 9
Mayor's Chicken in Pastry Puff, The, 193
Mexican Casserole, 174
Mexican Chicken, 190
Mexican Chicken Casserole, 202
Mexican Manicotti, 177
Mexican Stuffed Zucchini, 158
Mildred Pitts' Buttermilk Aspic, 75
Mildred's Pie, 273
Milky Way Ice Cream, 302
Mini Pecan Pies, 281
Mint Tea, 5
Mississippi Mud Cake, 263
Molded Gazpacho, 75
Molly's Egg Salad and Caviar Mold, 34
Moussaka, 141
Mrs. Strauss—Her Family's Recipe for Tea Cakes, 245
Mulligatawny, 55
Mushroom Eagle's Nest, 35
Mushroom Frittata, 98
Mushroom Lovers' Chicken Salad, 91
Mushroom Sandwiches, 67
"My" Chicken, 193
Mystery Salad, 76

Nana's Apple Cake, 249
Nannie's Chocolate Mousse, 295
Never-Fail Biscuits, 121
New England Squash Pie, 154
Norwegian Spaghetti, 180
Nutmeg Coffee Cake, 124

Old Fashioned Cookies, 242
Old Fashioned Pound Cake, 262
Olive Cheese Bread, 119
One-Step Tropical Coffee Cake, 124

Onion Canapés, 45
Onion Pie, 145
Onion-Potato Soup, 57
Orange Bavarian Cream, 297
Orange Charlotte Dessert, 297
Orange-Coconut Balls, 242
Orange Cream Cake—Layered, 263
Orange Fruit Dip, 26
Orange Glazed Carrots, 139
Orange Julius, 4
Orange Pork Chops, 182
Orange Torte, 298
Oreo Ice Cream, 302
Outdoor Lemony Barbecued Chicken, 209
Oyster and Wild Rice Casserole, 230
Oyster Pie, 222
Oysters en Brochette, 222

Pacific Chowder, 62
Paella, 231
Paella Salad, 87
Parker House Rolls, 117
Parmesan Bread Sticks, 121
Parmesan Casserole Bread, 117
Parmesan Potato Sticks, 40
Party Eggplant Paarmigiano, 180
Party Mints, 308
Party Pimento Potatoes, 147
Party Seafood Dip, 35
Party Tea, 5
Pasta Primavera, 106
Pastel Paradise, 86
Paté, 20
Patty's Corn Casserole, 140
Peaches and Cream Omelet, 100
Peach Pickle Salad Mold, 85
Peach Pie, 275
Peachy Cheesecake 'n Cream, 298
Peanut Butter Cookies, 242
Peanut Butter-Dipped Cocoa Bonbons, 309
Peanut Butter Fudge, 307
Peanut Butter Log, 308
Peanut Carrot Sandwich, 67
Peanut Soup, 56
Pecan Roll, 307
Pecan Sticky Buns, 118
Peppered Eggs and Salmon, 99
Pepper Jelly, 43
Pepper Jelly, 42, 43
Peppermint Ice Cream, 302
Pepper-Nut Sandwich Spread, 67

Philadelphia Velvet Cake, 261
Philly Cheese Ring, 16

Pies, 270-282

Pimento-Cheese Soufflé, 102
Pineapple Cake, 264
Pineapple-Pepper-Nut Cheese
  Ball, 16
Pink Champagne Punch, 10
Pistachio Pound Cake, 265
Pizza-wiches, 72
Plum Cake, 265
Plum Delicious Pork Chops, 184
Polynesian Beef, 169
Polynesian Tuna, 220
Poppy Seed Dressing, 93
Porcupine Meatballs, 175

Pork, 182-188

Pork a la Manzana, 183
Pork Chops and Spaghetti, 184
Pork in Curry Sauce, 37
Pork Steaks, Spanish Style, 183
Portugese Bean Soup, 59
Portwine Cranberry Mold, 83
Potato Casserole, 146
Potato Casserole, 147
Potato Casserole, 148
Potato Chip Cookies, 243
Potatoes and Cheese Risolle, 146
Potato Pie, 146
Potato Salad, 79
Potato Salad Dressing, 93
Pot de Creme, 298
Praline Ice Cream Dessert, 305
Pralines, 310
Pralines, New Orleans, 310
Praline Strips, 243
"Prof." Goodman's Barbecue
  Sauce, 210
Protein Dip, 25
Puffy Toasted Saltines, 15
Pumpkin Bread, 118
Pumpkin Ice Cream with
  Rum-Raisin Sauce, 304
Pumpkin Pie (No Bake), 275
Punch, 5
Pureed Parsnips with Madeira,
  144

Quail Pie, 214
Quick & Easy French Bread, 114
Quick Chocolate Cream Pie, 270
Quick Custard Pie, 279
Quick Fruit Cobbler, 290
Quick Hot Mushroom Dip, 36
Quick Vichyssoise, 57

Radish Sandwich, 67

Raleigh House Buttermilk Pie,
  279
Raisin Tart, 284
Ramaki, 39
Raspberry Sauce for Couer a la
  Creme, 297
Red Beans, Sausage and Rice,
  187
Red Christmas Cheese Ball, 15
Reese Cup Cookie Tarts, 283
Refried Beans, 134
Refrigerator Bran Muffins, 122
Refrigerator Rolls, 116
Ricagne, 177
Rice Krispies Marshmallow
  Squares, 243
Rice Oriental, 150
Rice Romanoff, 150
Rice Salad, 80
Rich Basic Sweet Dough, 118
Rich Dinner Rolls, 116
Roast Beef Spread, 27
Roast Leg of Lamb, 181
Roast Marinade, 169
Roquefort-Caviar Cheese Ball,
  17
Roulade de Saumon, 224
Rum Cake, 266
Russian Green Beans, 133
Russian Tea Loaf, 266

Salad Merrilyn, 78

Salads, 73-93

Salmon Croquettes, 219
Salmon Loaf, 70
Salmon or Tuna Mousse, 33
Sand Tarts, 245

Sandwiches, 65-72

Sarah's Deviled Crab, 221
Sauces or Dips for Raw
  Vegetables, 24
Sauerbraten, 168
Sausage Alsace-Lorainne, 187
Sausage and Apple Fry, 187
Sausage and Black-Eyed Peas,
  188
Sausage and Egg Casserole, 98
Sausage-Coffee Cake, 125
Sausage Swirls, 44
Sautéed Scallop Hors
  D'Oeuvres, 20
Savory Stuffed Round Steak,
  170
Savory Tuna Roll, 230
Scampi, 228
Scotcheroos, 246

Scotch Shortbread, 246
Scrambled Egg Casserole, 99

Seafood, 217-232

Seafood Casserole, 223
Seafood Gumbo, 61
Seafood Gumbo, 61, 62
Seafood Stew, 63
Sherried Fruit Casserole, 131
Sherry Cake, 267
Sherry Party Mold, 34
Sherry Peach Salad, 86
Sherry Punch, 10
Shish Kabob, 165
Shrimp and Green Noodle
  Casserole, 229
Shrimp-Crabmeat in Patty Shells,
  228
Shrimp Creole, 225
Shrimp Curry, 226
Shrimp Dip, 28
Shrimp Harpin, 227
Shrimp in Sour Cream, 226
Shrimp Mold, 33
Shrimp Mousse, 33
Shrimp-Muenster Roll, 42
Shrimp Noodle Casserole, 229
Shrimp Remoulade, 229
Shrimp Sauce for Baked
  Potatoes, 224
Shrimp Spread, 28
Shrimp Stroganoff, 225
Simple Corn Soufflé or Pudding,
  141
Simply Elegant Steak and Rice,
  169
Skillet Cabbage, 140
Smoked Mullet Paté, 27
Smoked Oyster Roll, 19
Smokey Salmon Ball, 19
Souffléed Broccoli Roulade, 135
Soufflé of Cauliflower, 139

Soups, 49-64

Sour Cream Cheese Cake, 266
Sour Cream Corn Bread, 123
Sour Cream Cucumbers, 77
Sour Cream Enchiladas, 176
Sour Cream Hamburger Bake,
  175
Sour Cream Potato Salad, 79
Sour Cream Pound Cake, 262,
  263
Spanish Pork Chops, 183
Spanish Seafood Salad, 92
Sparkling Iced Tea, 5
Spinach and Artichoke
  Casserole, 151

Spinach Mimosa, 152
Spinach Mold, 32
Spinach Salad, 82
Spinach-Stuffed Squash, 152
Spinach-Stuffed Tomatoes, 153
Spinach with Sour Cream, 152
Squash and Vidalia Onions, 154
Squash Casserole, 154
Squash Pickles, 159
Squash Poulet Potage, 155
Squash Soup, 55
Steak and Kidney Pie, 167
Steak and Oyster Roulade, 167
Strawberry Cake, 267
Strawberry Daquiri, 9
Strawberry Pie, 276, 277
Strawberry Refrigerator Pie, 277
Strawberry Whip, 299
Stuffed Breast of Chicken
    Richmond, 189
Stuffed Cherry Tomatoes, 31
Stuffed Eggplant, 142
Stuffed Garden Eggplant, 142
Stuffed Ham Buns, 72
Stuffed Mushroom Caps, 31
Stuffed Mushrooms, 30
Stuffed Onions, 145
Stuffed Peppers, 172
Stuffed Pork Chops, 184
Stuffed Roast Duckling, 212
Stuffed Salmon Slices, 219
Stuffed Sweet Potatoes, 149
Stuffed Zucchini, 172
Succulent Shrimp, 225
Sunday Night Soup, 60
Sunshine Punch, 4
Sugar Cookies, 243, 244
Super Ham Sandwich, 71
Swedish Slaw, 81
Sweet and Sour Chicken, 197
Sweet and Sour Meatballs, 38
Sweetie Pie, 274
Sweet Potato Casserole, 148
Sweet Potato Special, 149
Swiss Cheese, Leek and Ham
    Pie, 104
Swiss Cheese Sauce, 135

Swiss Cheese Soup, 52
Swiss Chicken, 202
Swiss-Crab Appetizer, 45
Swiss Quiche with Crabmeat
    Sauce, 103
Swiss Style Green Beans, 138

Tabbuli, 80
Taco Dip, 23
Tallahassee Baked Beans, 134

Tarts, 283-285

Tazewell's Seafood Geechee
    Gumbo, 63
Tea Room Salad, 85
"The Best" Tomato Marinade, 92
Tiger Tingle Punch, 4
Tiny Party Pizzas, 44
Toast Cups for Chafing Dish, 36
Toffee Bars, 264
Toll House Cookies, 244
Tomato and Squash Casserole,
    155
Tomato Bouillon, 54
Tomato Casserole, 155
Tomato Cheese Tart, 104
Tomato Dressing, 93
Tomatoes Langdon, 156
Tomato Gazpacho with Avocado,
    54
Tom's Mother's Chocolate Syrup,
    306
Toomer's Corner Lemonade, 3
Trifle, 299
Trout Marquery, 220
Tuna and Noodles au Gratin,
    231
Tuna Paté, 19
Tuna Salad, 92
Tuna (Tastes Like Shrimp) Mold,
    32
Turnips and Round Steak, 170
Twenty-Four Hour Salad with
    Fruit, 87

Ukranian Goulash, 171

Vanilla Ice Cream, 305
Vegetable Bouquet, 158
Vegetable Mold, 32
Vegetable Medley Salad, 77
Vegetable Sandwiches, 68
Veloute Sauce, 136
Venison Cabbage Rolls, 216
Venison in Burgundy, 215
Venison Roast Treat, 215
Vension Stroganoff, 215
Very Good Sweet Potatoes, 149
Vichyssoise, 57
Vidalia Onion Dip, 25
Vidalia Onion Quiche, 105
Villa Montana Baked Ham, 185
Vineyard Spread, 17

Wa-a-ar Eagle!, 8
Wassail Bowl, 7
Watercress Sandwiches, 68
Watergate Coverup, 300
Watermelon Rind Preserves, 161
Whipped Cream Tea
    Sandwiches, 68
Whipping Cream Cake, 267
Whiskey Punch, 8
Whiskey Sour Punch, 8
White Bread, 113
White Grapes and Sour Cream,
    300
Whole Wheat Bread, 113
Williamsburg Wassail, 7
Wine and Wild Rice Casserole,
    203
Wine Cake, 268
Wine Rice, 150
Winter Broiled Tomatoes, 156
Wonderful Cheese Cake, 252

Yummy Biscuits, 115
Yummy Yams, 149

Zucchimi and Tomatoes, 159
Zucchini Custard Molds, 159
Zucchini Lasagne, 106
Zucchini Quiche, 105
Zucchini Soup, 58
Zucchini Tea Bread, 120

RUTLEDGE HILL PRESS
513 Third Avenue South
Nashville, TN 37210

Please send _____ copies of Auburn Entertains at $14.70 per copy
($12.95 plus $1.75 postage and handling).

Name _____

Street _____

City _____ State _____ Zip _____

Enclosed is check or money order for $ _____ .
Make checks payable to Rutledge Hill Press

(cut along this line)

RUTLEDGE HILL PRESS
513 Third Avenue South
Nashville, TN 37210

Please send _____ copies of Auburn Entertains at $14.70 per copy
($12.95 plus $1.75 postage and handling).

Name _____

Street _____

City _____ State _____ Zip _____

Enclosed is check or money order for $ _____ .
Make checks payable to Rutledge Hill Press

(cut along this line)

RUTLEDGE HILL PRESS
513 Third Avenue South
Nashville, TN 37210

Please send _____ copies of Auburn Entertains at $14.70 per copy
($12.95 plus $1.75 postage and handling).

Name _____

Street _____

City _____ State _____ Zip _____

Enclosed is check or money order for $ _____ .
Make checks payable to Rutledge Hill Press